Flann O'Brien
A portrait of the artist as a
young post-modernist

Flann O'Brien
A portrait of the artist as a young post-modernist

KEITH HOPPER

SECOND EDITION
with a foreword by J. Hillis Miller

CORK UNIVERSITY PRESS

First edition published in 1995 by
Cork University Press
Youngline Industrial Estate
Pouladuff Road, Togher
Cork, Ireland

Second edition 2009

British Library Cataloguing in Publication Data

Hopper, Keith
Flann O'Brien : a portrait of the artist as a young
post-modernist. – Rev. ed.
1. O'Brien, Flann, 1911–1966 – Criticism and interpretation
2. Experimental fiction, English – History and criticism
3. Postmodernism (Literature) – Ireland 4. Ireland – In
literature
I. Title
828.9'1209

ISBN-13: 9781859184479

Typeset by Tower Books, Ballincollig, Co. Cork
Printed by Gutenberg Press, Malta

www.corkuniversitypress.com

This book is dedicated to my wife,
Niamh Moriarty,
who continues to sustain me.

Once it's happened, you're never
The same again, fearing to gulp in
Draughts of air lest its invisible
Compound might contain traces,
Like De Selby's motes of darkness . . .

From Bernard O'Donoghue,
'Grief Suspended', *Gunpowder*, 1995

Contents

A portrait of the critic as a young post-modernist

The highest praise I can give a critical book is that it makes me want to read or re-read the works discussed. Keith Hopper's book on Flann O'Brien does that. He makes reading Flann O'Brien sound like an exciting and productive thing to do. I identify four things Hopper's book conspicuously accomplishes. Lists, by the way, are identified by Hopper as a post-modern device. Does that make this foreword a post-modern text? Heaven forfend!

First and foremost, Hopper's book is a lovingly detailed and circumstantial reading of O'Brien's work, especially of *The Third Policeman*, which Hopper views as O'Brien's masterpiece. This reading takes place under the aegis of what Hopper calls 'decoding'. *The Third Policeman*, like O'Brien's other work, is full of somewhat mysterious, anomalous, and not altogether perspicuous textual details. The first-time reader, or even the third-time reader, who 'doesn't get it', accustomed as she or he may be to realist or modernist fiction, is puzzled and perhaps even annoyed by these details. What are they doing there? Why is it that they so obviously don't fit other details? Why doesn't the whole thing 'make sense' in a monological way? Just what story is O'Brien trying to tell, perhaps incompetently, out of sheer ineptness? Did O'Brien just forget at one time what he had written at another? What are all those footnotes doing there? Novels are not supposed to have footnotes. Keith Hopper's book is primarily concerned to decode all these strange features of *The Third Policeman*, to explain to the reader just what they mean and just why they are 'queer' in the way they are queer. 'Queer', as Hopper shows, is a key word in O'Brien, including even its function as a code word for 'homosexual', though it doesn't always mean just that in O'Brien. It won't do to be too solemn about *The Third Policeman*, however. Like its great exemplar, *Tristram*

Shandy, *The Third Policeman* is a comic masterpiece, if that sort of thing makes you laugh. It certainly makes *me* laugh.

Hopper's 'decoding' of O'Brien's *The Third Policeman* takes place by way of the identification in it of the chief features of post-modernist fiction, as they have been pinpointed not only inductively by Hopper through reading O'Brien, but also by reference to work by other critics, such as Patricia Waugh, Susan Stewart and Brian McHale. The second valuable thing Hopper's book does is to give the reader a compendious knowledge of what leading critics have said about post-modernist fiction.

The third thing this book has done for me is to persuade me of something about which I have now and then had my doubts, that is, that there really is such a thing as post-modernist fiction (with distinctive features distinguishing it from realist and modernist fiction). Hopper also shows in detail how having a clear grasp of what those features are makes it possible to 'make sense' of all the strangenesses of *The Third Policeman*. A post-modernist novel like *The Third Policeman* is, Hopper shows, a 'metafiction'. Its chief goal is to put in question traditional assumptions about the way story-telling can accurately correspond to 'reality'. Instead of that, a 'metafiction' uses all sorts of linguistic devices to suggest that any fictional representation is an arbitrary, linguistic construct, a projection, not a reflection. The implication is that 'real life', personal, social and political, is also governed by such unfounded projections. These linguistic devices or 'frame-breaking strategies' include the use of a self-conscious narrator who habitually reflects on the way fictions work. A second device is the use of metalepsis, that is, in Gerard Genette's definition, 'the transition from one narrative level to another'. The footnotes in *The Third Policeman*, hilarious parodies of academic interpretations of texts, are a prime example of metalepsis. A third device is what Hopper, following Bakhtin, calls 'the dialogic imagination', that is, an exploitation of intertextuality to capitalise on the way narration, from the micrological to the largest levels, can be 'polyphonic', not monological. Such a fiction therefore resists any single, coherent interpretation. (One might say, paradoxically, however, that an explanation by way of post-modernist features makes coherent sense, even a kind of monological sense.) The foregrounding of clichés by literalising them or using them in unfamiliar contexts is a dialogical device. Other formal features of post-modern fiction include the Chinese-box structure of stories within stories within stories, a use of charts, graphs, tables and maps (at least virtual maps, in O'Brien's case), the use of different typefaces, and a diffuse and pervasive irony, both overt and covert, that is generated by the use of such dialogic devices. Is this foreword by any chance at all ironic? Heaven forfend. How, in any case, would you tell for sure?

The fourth thing this book has done for me is to place O'Brien's work historically as corresponding to a specific moment in post-colonial Ireland. *The Third Policeman* and *The Dalkey Archive* are post-modernist fictions, all right, but they have a specificity of form and theme that embeds them in their time. This is the time after freedom from Britain, when the Catholic Church reigned supreme in Ireland and when state and church censorship of publications was still in place, but when this hegemony was beginning to weaken. Hopper elegantly summarises O'Brien's historical moment: 'Flann O'Brien is writing at the cusp of a new, emergent society where gender roles are slowly coming under scrutiny. The "sacred society" – the patriarchal, Catholic hegemony of post-colonial Ireland – is beginning to creak at its joints, and a more cosmopolitan consciousness is beginning to emerge from the colonial legacy of Victorian prudery.'

A brief foreword can do little to indicate the page-by-page richness, cogency, patient perspicuity and specificity of this admirable book. (No irony there!) I can only say, in conclusion, 'Read it for yourself and see. Also read O'Brien again in the light of its illuminations.'

J. Hillis Miller
University of California, Irvine, 2007

Preface to the second edition

The commentators, it is to be feared, have not succeeded in extracting from that vast store-house of his writings any consistent, cohesive or comprehensive corpus of spiritual beliefs and praxis.

Flann O'Brien, *The Third Policeman*, p. 144

In a brief entry in *The Cambridge Companion to Modern Irish Culture* in 2005, the authors suggest that of all modern Irish prose writers 'only Brian O'Nolan, better known as Flann O'Brien or Myles na Gopaleen, [. . .] has managed to combine Joycean exuberance, Gaelic culture and modernist innovation in an Irish context' (see Riggs and Vance, p. 260). This is a fairly good summary of that eclectic mix in Flann O'Brien's writings which makes his work so enjoyable to read but so difficult to analyse. To foreground any one aspect of the work is to risk disregarding (or at least downplaying) other elements, while a complete critical synthesis is virtually impossible to achieve. Thus O'Brien is the trickiest (and, some would say, the tricksiest) of writers to write about, and no single monograph – by definition 'a separate treatise on a single subject or aspect of it' (*OED*) – can ever fully cope with these competing critical demands. Nonetheless, it seems important to try.

When this book was first published in 1995, my decision to place O'Brien in the context of literary post-modernism met with broad general approval, although it did ruffle a few traditionalist feathers too. In truth, I had no great fidelity to post-modernism as a philosophical concept, but it did seem to lend itself particularly well to thinking about the intricacies of O'Brien's metafictional novels. Most of all, it was a sincere attempt to reconfigure O'Brien as a writer of genuine international importance, and to detach him from the sticky organicism of more traditional liberal humanist or biographical criticism.

Biographers have a job to do, and good luck to them. I deliberately avoided that treacherous terrain because of a personal antipathy to the genre, and a critical intuition that O'Brien's work deserved a more rigorous, textually-based approach. Flann O'Brien means more to me than just an arbitrary collection of chronological dates: like Sligo Rovers, *Wanderly Wagon* and The Undertones, he was a part of my growing up. Certainly, amongst Myles na Gopaleen's 'Plain People of Ireland', O'Brien completes the Holy Trinity of Irish fiction: alongside Joyce the Father and Beckett the Son, he remains the Holy Ghost in the Machine. Yet within the groves of academia, this exalted status was far from secure. In Irish critical circles, O'Brien was frequently depicted as a kind of 'poor man's Joyce', a talented prodigy who ultimately squandered his genius through drink and hack journalism (even if his journalistic alter ego, Myles na Gopaleen, was often considered his greatest creation). At the same time, O'Brien was becoming something of a cult figure in universities throughout Western and Central Europe, where a legion of post-structuralist critics were finding all kinds of wonderful things in his work (even if some of these findings were rather decontextualised and ahistorical).

As an Irish critic, I felt obliged to attempt some form of tribal retrieval which would replant O'Brien in a native context (post-colonial, Catholic Ireland), but one which would also employ some of the interpretative strategies of modern literary theory (formalism, deconstruction, feminism, queer theory, Marxism and reader response). Such a synthesis, I felt, would enable me to get to grips with that strange brand of dark and violent comedy which is characteristic of his best novel, *The Third Policeman*. Indeed, as John Updike has noted, *The Third Policeman*, 'for all its shape-shifting comedy, has a heft of despair to it, an honest nihilism' (*The New Yorker*, February 2008, p. 150), and in this novel, at least, O'Brien seems even bleaker than Beckett and funnier than Joyce.

It is, of course, notoriously difficult to talk about comedy in a serious fashion; either you can tell a joke or you can't, and there's nothing duller than somebody blandly explaining the punchline. It becomes doubly problematic when the comedy in question is a Menippean satire, i.e. a mocking of intellectual pedantry. I had hoped to avoid that particular minefield by celebrating O'Brien as well as critiquing him, which is why the first edition of this book began with a fairytale (by my then six-year-old daughter) and ended with a short story (a de Selbian-length mock footnote), in homage to O'Brien.

In between, my argument is driven by a theoretically engaged and textually detailed attempt to place O'Brien's work within the context of post-modernism. By 1940, I argue, O'Brien was confronted with two towering traditions: the jaded legacy of Yeats's Celtic Twilight and the problematic complexities of Joyce's modernism. With *The Third Policeman* O'Brien forges a powerful synthesis between these two traditions, and the paraliterary path he chooses marks the historical transition from modernism to post-modernism. This is why I stress the hyphen in 'post-modernism', signifying a type of reactionary literature which came after the great modernist experiment. Quite simply, Flann O'Brien has produced a meta-literature which is post-realist, post-colonial and post-Joycean, and which bears striking resemblances to writers such as Beckett, Borges and Nabokov, i.e. it is quintessentially *post*-modernist. Regardless of how one defines it as a concept, though, post-modernism remains a provocative and playful way of drawing attention to a subversive writer who in the past has been either ignored or misconstrued. And, for the most part, I think this analysis has been proved correct; in any case, towards the end of the first decade of the twenty-first century, *The Third Policeman* is now considered to be one of the earliest – and most exciting – examples of post-modernist fiction.

For the purposes of this second edition, I have corrected a few minor errors, and deleted some redundancies and repetitions. In terms of new material, I have incorporated some recent O'Brien scholarship but only as it relates to my original thesis, and I have substantially extended and updated the bibliography (including some earlier criticism which I missed the first time around). Insofar as possible I have taken on board some of the comments made about the first edition of this book by my friends, colleagues and students, and I have thoroughly revised some key concepts and topics. On the whole, though, and for better or for worse, the central thesis remains unchanged: tinkering with it too much would have unravelled it completely, and I would have ended up with an entirely different book. I have also resisted the temptation – suggested by some fellow students of O'Brien – to add an extra chapter at the end developing the links between O'Brien and Beckett, which is work for another day. There is room, perhaps, for a sequel of sorts – *A Portrait of the Artist as a Young Post-colonialist* certainly springs to mind – but that's a book for someone else to write. For my own part, to quote Mylesian scripture, 'I have no ecclesiastical ambitions; I am merely a spoiled Proust'.

Keith Hopper
Oxford, 2009

Acknowledgements

I wish to express my abiding gratitude to the following people: Prof. Tom Kilroy for suggesting this project in the first place; Dr Riana O'Dwyer, my MA supervisor at the National University of Ireland, Galway, for her criticism and patience; the late Prof. Pat Sheeran for his generosity and kindness; Dr Anne Keane for her critical and theoretical advice; Prof. Kevin Barry for his encouragement and assistance; Martin Finan and all the crew of *The Buzz* magazine for their logistical support. I am grateful to the Magritte estate for granting permission to reproduce 'Reproduction Prohibited' (1937), and to Bernard O'Donoghue for kindly allowing me to use an extract from his poem 'Grief Suspended' (1995). I would also like to take this opportunity to thank family, friends, and colleagues who helped me out along the way: Sara Wilbourne, Caroline Somers, Maria O'Donovan and Mike Collins; Brendan O'Connor, Rose Heffernan, the late Bernie Walsh, Ann O'Dea, Noreen Collins and Vinny Browne; Prof. George Watson, Prof. Neil Murphy, Dr Ondřej Pilný, Prof. Joan Dean, Dr Dan O'Hara, Dr Seosamh Mac Muirí, Prof. Nollaig Mac Congáil, Prof. Jim Spates and the late Tracy Spates; Jennika Baines, Giordano Vintaloro, Graham Lampard, John Wyse Jackson and the late Noel Reilly; Robert Ballagh, Kevin Atherton, James Connolly, and Ian Harris for their help with the cover; Jack Adams, Steven Short, Damien Devaney, and Mikel Murfi; Prof. Rüdiger Imhof, Prof. Werner Huber, and Prof. J. Hillis Miller; Eileen Moriarty and the late Jack Moriarty, Sheila McLynn and the late Padraig McLynn, Suzanne and Joe McGee, Dalton Hopper, Annette Hopper and the late Donald Hopper, and Katie Moriarty-Hopper.

Abbreviations

AS2B   *At Swim-Two-Birds* (1939; London: Penguin, 1980)

PM   *The Poor Mouth* (*An Béal Bocht*, 1941, trans. Patrick C. Power, 1973; London: Grafton, 1986)

HL   *The Hard Life* (1961; London: Grafton, 1986)

DA   *The Dalkey Archive* (1964; London: Picador, 1976)

3P   *The Third Policeman* (1967; London: Grafton, 1986)

Noman   The nameless narrator of *The Third Policeman*

Beyond the Celtic Twilight zone: metafiction, post-modernism and formalism

It must all be considered as if spoken by a character in a novel.

Roland Barthes, *Roland Barthes*, 1977[1]

The Object

Katie, my daughter, tells a powerful bedtime story. Here's one of hers:

> *Once upon a time there was a little girl. In the attic of her grand-mother's house there was an old wooden trunk full of clothes, which the little girl used for dressing up. One day she opened the trunk and found a roll of woven cloth, which she had never seen before. This fabric was as delicate as a web and so beautiful that she knew straight away it must be magic. She rummaged around some more until she found some scissors, and a needle and thread. And she cut and she sewed and she cut and she sewed until she had made herself a beautiful dress. And she wore and she wore, and she wore and she wore the dress, until it was all worn out. Then she took her scissors and her needle and thread, and she cut and she sewed until she had made herself a beautiful waistcoat. She wore and wore the waistcoat until it was all worn out. So she cut and she sewed and she cut and she sewed . . .*

This fractal pattern repeated itself through an entire wardrobe of hats, scarves, gloves and ribbons. The material diminished and the clothes kept getting smaller in size. I interrupted to remind her of the ritual elements of storytelling: every story must have an opening, a middle and (most of all) an end; and that fairytale protocol usually required only three variations on a situation, before its reversal and the final catharsis. Be patient, she chastened, it's my story. It's bad manners to interrupt a person making a story, and anyways, the end was coming:

> *After making all these clothes, and having worn them all out,*
> *there was only a little bit of the magic material left, not even*
> *enough to make a button. But she cut and she sewed anyways*
> *until all of the magic material was gone. She opened her hands,*
> *slowly, to find out what she had made ... and found she had*
> *made a beautiful story. (And the little girl lived happily ever after.)*

All literature is either shamanistic or ritualistic.[2] Most novels
are ritualistic in that they follow a prescribed order of procedures
and conventions which are handed down by history. In the novelistic tradition the dominant ritual practice is *realism*, which in
itself is a problematic and contentious category. In his 1921 essay
'On Realism in Art', Roman Jakobson offers three possible meanings for this term:

1 Realism may refer to the aspiration and intent of the author,
  i.e. a work is understood to be realistic if it is conceived by its
  author as a display of verisimilitude, as true to life . . .
2 A work may be called realistic if I, the person judging it, perceive it as true to life . . .
3 One which comprehends the sum total of the features characteristic of one specific artistic current of the nineteenth century.[3]

From a formalist perspective not only is the definition of realism
unstable but the entire concept is dubious, or as Jakobson comments: 'verisimilitude in a verbal expression or in a literary
description makes no sense whatsoever. Can the question be raised
about a higher degree of verisimilitude of this or that poetic trope?'[4]
As an artistic ideal, realism is an utterly unrealistic venture. No
matter how true to life a novel may seem, it can only ever be a *representation* of reality, even if it strives (by necessity, through
integrity) to be something more.

Paradoxically, this staging of representation does manage to
enter the real world we inhabit. It becomes an object – removed
from the author's intention – which worms its way into our lives
and becomes an actual component of the social reality which
surrounds us. On a simple level a text can become a material thing,
a book that is held in the hand, just as you, the reader, hold this
book. However, this simple relationship between life and literature
also suggests something far more complex, or as Boris
Tomashevsky wrote in 1923: 'It is sometimes difficult to decide
whether literature recreates phenomena from life or whether in

fact the opposite is the case: that the phenomena of life are the result of the penetration of literary clichés into reality.'[5]

This posits an interesting riddle: for example, would romantic love exist if poets did not conceive of it? In a similar vein, the novelist Erica Jong claimed she first learned that she could have an orgasm from reading D.H. Lawrence. And I learned from reading Lawrence and Jong some of the ways in which the literary canon has shaped, and continues to shape, people's lives – a kind of intertextual poetics in process. (Another anecdote: When I went to (an all-male) school we studied *Blackcock's Feather* (1932) by Maurice Walsh. We could equally have studied *Pride and Prejudice* (1813) but we didn't, the convent girls did. *Blackcock's Feather* taught us about patriotism and power; how to fight off the competition; how to be a man and how to win a wife. Meanwhile, the girls listened to Jane Austen declare that 'It is a truth universally acknowledged, that a single man in possession of a good fortune, must be in want of a wife'. These novels might speak softly – and at times even ironically – but they still carry big ideological sticks.)

Criticism, it has been said, is the intellectual's revenge upon the imagination of art. It is parasitical, anxious and laden with jargon. It adopts a superior moral tone because deep down it feels inferior to the object it studies. But it doesn't always have to be like that. Good storytelling is a celebration of life's carnival, and good criticism should be a celebration of storytelling. Through criticism we can discover cultural ideology, and the way that literature's slice-of-life slices into our own lives. The shape of literature comes from, and in turn consolidates, the ideological conventions of the dominant culture. Critical study of the conventions of literature is also a study of the ways in which our lives are moulded by convention. Literary criticism is rather like fractal geometry,[6] 'a way of describing, calculating and thinking about shapes that are irregular and fragmented, jagged and broken-up . . . [It] implies an organising structure that lies hidden among the hideous complication of such shapes'.[7]

Occasionally, and throughout the relatively short history of the novel, certain works emerge which deliberately, and quite playfully, question the ideology of ritual convention. Such works, I believe, are shamanistic. In any tribe, a shaman is a medicine man: a healer of the relationship between mind and body, between matter and spirit, between people and their environment, between culture and nature:

The outstanding quality of the shaman, regardless of culture, is the inclination towards engagement, or creative activity. Knowledge and understanding are not enough, nor does passive acceptance hold any appeal. The shaman plunges into life with mind and senses, playing the role of co-creator. There is a type of soul content to admire the shape and place of a fallen tree. The shaman is more like a sculptor who views the tree and is seized by the desire to transform it into some semblance of an internal image. [. . .] There is respect and admiration for the tree as it is, as well as the impulse to join with the tree and produce something new.[8]

Within the context of the novel this shamanism is usually called *metafiction*, and this is the object of this present work. Providing an adequate definition of metafiction is a surprisingly difficult exercise. As a loose critical term it is tossed around carelessly by a legion of modern critics, yet remains undefined by most of the standard dictionaries of literary terms. One exception is Jeremy Hawthorn's definition in *A Concise Glossary of Contemporary Literary Theory*:

Literally, fiction about fiction [. . .]. It is generally used to indicate fiction including any self-referential element [. . .]. Metafiction typically involves games in which levels of narrative reality (and the reader's perceptions of them) are confused, or in which traditional realist conventions governing the separation of mimetic and diegetic elements are flouted and thwarted.[9]

This last feature characterises the way in which metafictions typically disrupt the artificiality of traditional narrative modes by forcing a distinction between the *mimetic* (the illusion that the author is *not* the speaker) and the *diegetic* (the illusion that the author *is* the speaker). Often, the degree of consciousness allowed to a metafictional protagonist is in a constant state of flux or narrative flicker, and this existential condition becomes a metaphor for ontological determinism – the idea of being trapped in someone else's order.

Metafiction involves a 'laying bare' of the literary process; the metafictionalist is primarily concerned with literary convention *itself* as a thematic issue. The metafictionalist deconstructs the magic of fiction by unveiling the magician's props, and in the process creates an imaginative, self-conscious discourse which attempts to free itself from traditional obligations to fossilised mimetic or diegetic constructions. This method of unveiling mocks the assumptions of the accepted narrative contract between author, text and reader, and calls into question that 'willing suspension of disbelief' which classical, realist fiction is contingent upon. As Rüdiger Imhof describes it: 'The dominant textual strategies of metafiction are those which make the reader aware that a novel is nothing but an artefact made up of words, or – to adopt one of Beckett's dicta – that telling stories is telling lies.'[10]

The subversive impulse behind this aesthetic deconstruction is partly motivated by a nagging doubt that art can ever adequately convey meaning, or even 'reality', through an unstable system of language. Or in the jargon of Saussurian linguistics: how can we possibly mediate truth through a language system which is both *arbitrary* (random, non-natural) and *differential* (defined by difference)?

For metafictionalists as historically diverse as Laurence Sterne (*Tristram Shandy*, 1759–7) and Flann O'Brien, language is a hermeneutic circle referring only to itself. Consequently, metafiction sets out to undermine accepted and conventional modes of discourse by concentrating on their inherent linguistic instability. Metafictions focus on representational form, and eschew 'meaning' in favour of poetics, i.e. the ways in which meanings are constructed and transmitted to the reader. In metafiction the intermedium is the message, and such texts endlessly deconstruct and juxtapose a broad spectrum of different discourses in order to reconstruct them in new and startling contexts. This planned incongruity is a self-conscious attempt intended to draw attention to the mongrel composition of literary language in particular, and to the dialogic nature of all language in general.

If realist art traditionally held a mirror up to society, then metafiction holds a mirror up to the mirror. In 1834, for instance, the novelist Maria Edgeworth wrote:

> It is impossible to draw Ireland as she now is in the book of fiction – realities are too strong, party passions too violent, to bear to see, or care to look at their faces in a looking-glass. The people would curse the fool who held the mirror up to nature – distorted nature, in a fever.[11]

In 1907, Synge's playboy sees himself clearly for the first time after killing his father: 'Didn't I know rightly, I was handsome, though it was the divil's own mirror we had beyond, would twist a squint across an angel's brow'.[12] And in 1922, Joyce in *Ulysses* has Stephen Dedalus declare (following Oscar Wilde in *The Decay of Lying*) that Irish art is the 'cracked looking-glass of a servant'.[13] As Declan

Kiberd notes, the cracked looking-glass 'is an apt image [. . .] of Joyce's own escape into modernism, for what a cracked looking-glass shows is not a single but a multiple self'.[14] However, for a metafictionalist like Flann O'Brien in 1940, the mirror itself is less important than the frame which contains it: 'de Selby was obsessed with mirrors and had recourse to them so frequently that he claimed to have two left hands and to be living in a world arbitrarily bounded by a wooden frame' (*3P*, p. 64).

This appropriation of a traditional literary metaphor deliberately draws attention to itself in a self-publicising manner. The mirror is an important metaphor in *The Third Policeman*, laden as it is with literary, scientific and autocritical signification. But in terms of metafictional aesthetics – 'a world arbitrarily bounded by a wooden frame' – it is a perfect example of a self-conscious metaphor, i.e. a radically re-aligned metaphor that emerges from the concrete and objectified images of traditional fiction. These self-conscious metaphors allow us access to *The Third Policeman* as a work of metafictional inquiry: an 'allegory', as it were, of reading and writing practices.

Although no standard definition of metafiction seems to exist, there is in its absence the related – but to my mind archaic and unsatisfactory – category *anti-novel*, a term used by early (and some contemporary) critics to describe *At Swim-Two-Birds* and *The Third Policeman*. Lexicographer Martin Gray defines an 'anti-novel' as a form of 'Modern experimental fiction which deliberately refuses to make use of elements considered essential in the traditional novel, such as plot, characterisation or ordered narrative sequence', and notes that these techniques and preoccupations were historically 'foreshadowed in Sterne's remarkable novel *Tristram Shandy*'.[15]

J.A. Cuddon in *A Dictionary of Literary Terms* is rather more expansive, and reminds us that the 'anti-novel' has its historical origins 'as far back as 1627 [when] Charles Sorel sub-titled his novel *Le Berger Extravagant* an "anti-Roman"', although again he cites *Tristram Shandy* as its first historical incarnation. For Cuddon, the shaping spirit of the anti-novel form is the manner in which it departs from traditional methods of storytelling:

> Often there is little attempt to create an illusion of realism or naturalism for the reader . [. . .] Some of the principal features of the anti-novel are: lack of an obvious plot; diffused episode; minimal development of character; detailed surface analysis of objects; many repetitions; innumerable experiments with vocab-

ulary, punctuation and syntax; variations of time sequence; alternative beginnings and endings.[16]

For the record, all of the above features, as we shall see, are used as metaleptic (or frame-breaking) strategies in the composition of *At Swim-Two-Birds* and *The Third Policeman*. Cuddon also notes that the anti-novel tradition has thrown up some rather extreme physical and typographical features, including 'detachable pages; pages which can be shuffled like cards; coloured pages; blank pages; collage effects; drawings and hieroglyphics',[17] but such radical metaleptic gestures need not concern us here. Of more significance to our present discussion is that under the heading of 'notable and influential contributions' in the anti-novel tradition (most of which are written in French), Cuddon cites *At Swim-Two-Birds*, while conceding that, on the whole, the category anti-novel is itself 'a thoroughly misleading term'.[18]

This problem arises, I think, because the term 'anti-novel' tends to have rather disparaging connotations as a prescriptive label. It views such fiction in terms of its negative qualities (signified by the prefix 'anti'), and dismisses it within a liberal humanist tradition as being somehow nihilistic, cynical and amoral. In his *A Glossary of Literary Terms*, M.H. Abrams conveys his essential distaste when he writes that an anti-novel is 'deliberately constructed in a negative fashion, relying for its effects on deleting traditional elements, on violating traditional norms and playing against the expectations established in the reader by the novelistic methods and conventions of the past'.[19]

The terse tones of the curt lexicographer barely conceal his dismay: 'deliberately [. . .] negative'; 'deleting'; 'violating'; 'playing against' – qualities that would seem to disqualify such work on the grounds of ungentlemanly conduct and for not playing by the accepted rules. In these terms, the anti-novel is something of a non-work which has usurped the value system of art by destroying the logical and syntactical coherence of its own medium, language itself. Whatever it is, the anti-novel is obviously not canonical cricket.

J.A. Cuddon's more liberal definition invalidates this invective by noting the progressive aspects of the form. While it may disrupt traditional expectations, the anti-novel 'establishes its own conventions and a different kind of realism which deters the reader from self-identification with the characters, yet at the same time persuades him to "participate", but not vicariously'.[20]

To label such shamanistic work an 'anti-novel' is misleading.

Anti-novelists are not some arcane cult of book-burners – just creators of fiction with a healthy scepticism. Therefore the distinction here between 'anti' and 'meta' is not chasing a paper dragon but is simply a question of signifying practice, a struggle for meaning within a wider critical context. This distinction is important because it frames two different sets of interpretative priorities. The term 'anti-novel' prescribes the artist as a cultural terrorist who is ideologically devoted to the anarchic disavowal of fiction. On this scheme, the anti-novelist wantonly destroys in a spirit of gleeful abandon, and seemingly fails to offer any alternative aesthetic other than the tactics of aleatory shock.

Defining this process as metafiction goes one step further and replaces the perception of nihilism with reference to metafiction's self-conscious awareness of its own intertextuality. In metafiction, value is shown to be paradigmatic, and all forms of discourse – literary, scientific and philosophic – are historically determined by the forcefield of the hermeneutic circle. Metafiction plays with a blend of genres, re-casting the rules of different linguistic systems within a new contextual zone. This interaction not only draws attention to the essential 'writtenness' of all discourse, but it dynamically creates a new, multi-layered pastiche out of old materials: metafiction does not abandon tradition but critically reappraises and enriches it. By so doing, metafiction strives for greater reader competence and involvement in the consumption of literature; it empowers rather than disenfranchises the reader. Metafiction's self-consciousness does not herald the end of fiction but teaches us to be more critical of the interpretative codes we usually employ and take for granted. In this respect, metafiction is the fictional equivalent of Brecht's alienation effect, 'designed to free socially conditioned phenomena from the stamp of familiarity which protects them against our grasp'.[21]

Metafiction's self-awareness of literary practices is not merely a flashy trick or clever sleight-of-hand but an integral part of a wider post-modernist ethos, as it forcibly reminds the reader of the ineluctable writtenness of 'reality', and, on a macrocosmic scale, that the real world is not 'given' but constructed. The implications of the shamanist worldview has shocking ramifications for all forms of discourse – be they literary, historical or epistemological. It even affects our belief in 'objective' science, itself deconstructed in *The Third Policeman* as a paradigmatic language game.

As a result of the relativism enshrined in metafiction, critics of the form seem to condemn such works as being somehow morally

bankrupt, and estranged from the 'real' world. Not only does metafiction refute moral systems which depend on theories of 'Natural Law'
(these critics would argue), but it is corruptive by virtue of its denial
of objective reality and is essentially 'about' nothing: an abstracted
poetry of estrangement, floating adrift in a chaotic universe.

Brian McHale cites one such critic, Robert Alter, who illustrates
his case by comparing the signifier 'tiger' to the animal it refers to
in the real world, outside of language. If we accept Saussure's
assertion that reality is defined by language, then 'tiger' is an arbitrary and differential sign which refers only to itself. But for Alter
the ontological status of the real world tiger remains unaffected by
the metafictional/post-structuralist textualisation of the signifier,
or as he wittily phrases it: 'We are free to decenter, deconstruct,
decode, re-encode a tiger in a text, but even the hardiest structuralist would not step inside the cage with the real beast, whose
fangs and claws, after all, are more than a semiotic pattern.'[22]

So then, the argument goes, a tiger does exist in the real world,
whatever we decide to call it. McHale offers the simple rebuttal of
this critique by reminding us that all literature is concerned with
'tigers' (reality that is expressed through discourse), as opposed to
the real beast; in other words, be it the romantic 'tyger' of William
Blake (1794) or the metafictional tiger of Guillermo Cabrera
Infante's *Three Trapped Tigers* (1967), the hermeneutic circle of
language is inescapable. Common sense tells us that the fanged
beast exists in the real world but you cannot rationally argue for
its pre-determined reality through a deficient system of language.
Reality is called into being by the process of naming, and is contingent upon the songlines of discourse. For metafictionalists,
language is not unified and monological, but multi-vocal and dialogic. The point is that Humpty Dumpty was never really together
in the first place, so it is disingenuous to pretend that we can
really piece him together again. However, given the same 'semiotic
pattern' that Alter refers to, all literature is 'about' something – if
only about the self-conscious theme of 'unreal', fractured reality.

More specifically, though, and in relation to literary convention,
critic Colin Greenland complains that in its deliberate estrangement from tradition, metafiction has somehow dumped the baby
with the bathwater, or as he pleads: 'Certainly we can do without
the paternalistic Victorian values enshrined in 19th century
realism, but do we have to dump everything they developed, all
those grand techniques, those rich and subtle pleasures?'[23]

The problem with Greenland's banner-waving plea for a return to those 'rich and subtle pleasures' is that he mistakenly equates metafiction with anti-fiction. The very intertextual consciousness that permeates metafiction refutes this if we realise the playful manner in which it re-casts realist conventions, and in the process tells another story. Or as Miles Orvell said of Flann O'Brien: if he 'laid aside the traditional grand schemes of literature, he by no means discarded the sublime conception'.[24]

Every novel generates its own aesthetic, and metafiction sets up a self-conscious intertextual zone governed by its own laws and cosmological design; a verbal playground which resists ritual murmuring (and which refuses to remain silent about this resistance). In place of ritual or silence, metafiction opts for honesty – and this involves the 'laying bare' of its art. Critics like Colin Greenland cannot (or will not) see the integrity of this position, and he rather snidely derides metafiction by reference to realist works which have themselves hardened into conventional cliché. For Greenland, it can only ever be 'decorative, parasitic: meta-parasitic, maybe, as fiction which pre-empts its own criticism by ingesting it'.[25]

In one sense, Greenland is correct: metafiction does pre-empt some criticisms by getting its retaliation in first and autocritically commenting on its own deconstructed design. But the critics who feel most pre-empted tend to be those who privilege humanist interpretations of realist texts, and who cannot see that the exposure of artifice does not necessarily result in the 'death' of fiction. Metafiction is not entirely parasitical but instead recycles new fictions out of old in light of a new consciousness. Or as the nameless narrator of *The Third Policeman* remarks of the imaginary philosopher, de Selby: 'He adopts the customary line of pointing out fallacies involved in existing conceptions and then quietly setting up his own design in place of the one he claims to have demolished' (*3P*, p. 94).

Metafiction then is shamanistic rather than ritualistic; interactive rather than inert; progressive rather than regressive. The metafictionalist is not a nihilist but an alchemist, transmuting leaden convention into golden invention, and by occasion reminding us that we cannot represent 'reality' but only images and symbols of reality. As Roland Barthes has written, 'Realism is always timid, and there is too much surprise in a world which mass media and the generalisation of politics have made so profuse that it is no longer possible to figure it projectively: the world, as a literary object, escapes'.[26] Thus the shaman cuts and sews, cuts and sews . . . and stitches together a new story made out of old material.

These new stories will be the object of this book.

The context

At this juncture we might usefully widen our frame of reference to
include the tricky concept of 'post-modernism' into the equation. As
Patricia Waugh writes, metafiction itself is 'a mode of writing
within a broader cultural movement often referred to as post-modernism', and although it is 'just one form of post-modernism, nearly
all contemporary experimental writing displays some explicitly
metafictional strategies'.[27] Considering that we have already cited
the eighteenth-century *Tristram Shandy* as an early metafiction,
this association may seem anachronistic, although Waugh sees no
inconsistency here: 'If post-modernism shares some of the philoso-
phies of modernism, its formal techniques seem often to have
originated from novels like *Tristram Shandy*.'[28]

Post-modernism is more difficult to define than metafiction. It is
one of those shifting, nebulous and seductive systems of thought
that defy classification – indeed, it takes a provocative delight in
remaining elusive. Look at any critical text on the subject and you
will discover that a whole tribe of academics have made careers out
of talking about the 'post-modern experience', without ever adequately telling us what that actually means. This, they then tell us,
is all part of the post-modern experience. The problem of classification arises because post-modernism is a vast complex of cultural
actions and creative activities. Due to its dependency on parody,
pastiche and irony, any particular trait of this parasitical complex
may find predecessors in other eras and movements, and so its
margins are never neatly cut and dried. Moreover, beyond the
simple problem of pigeon-holing, any liberal humanist discussion of
this topic presents specific problems, not least because post-modernism contests that same liberal humanist paradigm from within.
As Linda Hutcheon writes, post-modernism is, 'if it is anything, a
problematising force in our culture today: it raises questions about
(or renders problematic) the commonsensical and the "natural". But
it never offers answers that are anything but provisional and con-
textually determined (and limited)'.[29]

Therefore, within its own terms, the post-modernist sensibility
resists absolute interpretation. It is neither a closed, homogeneous
entity nor a consciously directed movement, but a big baggy monster
encompassing a new sense of ethics and aesthetics. Above all, it
prides itself on the confusions it engenders: 'post-modernism is a
contradictory phenomenon, one that uses and abuses, installs and
then subverts, the very concepts it challenges.'[30] At the same time

we must be careful not to toss it around too casually. It is not simply a synonym for hypersaturated mass culture but a serious and problematic confrontation with history itself. History is not obsolete in post-modernism, but it is re-thought of as a human construct and not as a natural, temporal progression. Bearing all of this in mind, we might usefully construct for ourselves a brief history of post-modernism, or at least track the basic genealogy of the term.

Ihab Hassan traces its historical usage back to Federico de Onís, who coined the nonce-word 'postmodernisimo' in 1934, as a reaction to the experiments of modernism. In 1947, Arnold J. Toynbee used 'post-modernism' to designate a new historical cycle in western civilisation (beginning around 1875), which went beyond the cultural assumptions of the European renaissance. In 1960, Harry Levin used it as a pejorative expression to describe the perceived decay and decadence that emerged in the aftermath of the great modernist movement(s). However, during the 1960s and 1970s it came to approve a new sensibility, referring to attitudes which, in the years after the Second World War, extended and broke with modernist techniques and conventions, but without reverting to realist or pre-modernist positions.[31] Finally, from the 1980s onwards, 'postmodernism' (without the hyphen) came to be defined in terms of the 'late-capitalist dissolution of bourgeois hegemony and the development of mass culture',[32] and to the world of hyperreal technology and mass destruction which followed in the wake of Auschwitz and Hiroshima. Here it began to develop its own giddy and apocalyptic rhetoric, which already seems generic, fuzzy and oddly archaic: 'Ours is a fin-de-millennium consciousness which, existing at the end of history in the twilight time of ultramodernism (of technology) and hyperprimitism (of public moods), uncovers a great arc of disintegration and decay against the background radiation of parody, kitsch, and burnout.'[33]

The cultural encoding of post-modernity as a socio-historical construct (de-construct?) need not concern us here. Of greater, practical interest is the concept of literary post-modern*ism* as a valuable and proper context in which to critically re-appraise the metafiction of Flann O'Brien. Because of their historical and cultural proximity, O'Brien is usually lumped in together with Joyce, the godfather of modernism – an assumption which is unfair to both writers. Although the premise is rarely questioned, the critical implication always assumes that O'Brien is a late-modernist by default – a kind of 'poor man's' Joyce. Similarly, it conveniently ignores that with *Finnegans Wake* (1939), post-modernism most likely finds its actual point of origin, or, as Hassan notes,

Finnegans Wake is: 'a monstrous prophecy of our post-modernity. [. . .] All the elements of post-modern literature crowd this "novel": dream, parody, play, pun, fragment, fable, reflexiveness, kitsch, [. . .] the edge of pure silence or pure noise.'[34]

Of course it doesn't help that so much of *At Swim-Two-Birds* is obsessed with confronting the Joyce of *Dubliners*, *A Portrait of the Artist as a Young Man* and *Ulysses*, or that critics so far have tended, almost exclusively, to favour *At Swim-Two-Birds* as the primary defining text of the O'Brien *oeuvre*. The central premise of this current work is that *At Swim-Two-Birds* (1939) is best considered as a late-modernist, transitional text which critiques both realism and modernism in an openly deconstructive manner, and in the process comes to the brink of an exciting new aesthetic. I will argue that the metafictional techniques developed publicly in *At Swim-Two-Birds* (the role of the author-god; the self-conscious narrator and the co-creative reader; its frame-breaking topography; its programme of explorative and creative intertextuality) are more deeply imbricated and embedded within the fabric of *The Third Policeman*. This new type of metafiction not only challenges Joyce as he stands, but also develops a progressive genre independent of Joyce's towering presence. To my mind, this makes *The Third Policeman* (composed 1939–40; first published 1967) the first great masterpiece – along with the less accessible *Finnegans Wake* – of what we generally refer to now as post-modernism.

Of course, it could also be argued that *At Swim-Two-Birds* is itself an early expression of post-modernism, and there is certainly some merit in this argument.[35] Nonetheless, I still prefer to see *At Swim-Two-Birds* as a liminal text on the edge of a new paradigm – a proto-post-modernist work which combines elements of modernism and post-modernism, and which lays the groundwork for the full-blown post-modernist concerns of *The Third Policeman*. Indeed, the blurred borderland between these two movements may be more legibly traced on the literary map to coincide with the arrival of *Finnegans Wake* and the composition of *The Third Policeman*. Here we see a more decisive split begin to emerge: where modernism sought coherency and form, post-modernism strives for fragmentation and indeterminacy. Ihab Hassan usefully appropriates the myth of Orpheus to personify this schism. The poet Orpheus represented the mythic unity between the word and nature. On the command of the envious god Dionysius, Orpheus is torn to pieces by the frenzied Maenads, 'the victim of an inexorable clash between the Dionysian principle [. . .] and the Apollonian ideal which he, as a poet, venerated'.[36] Orpheus is savagely dismembered but receives greater energy and power through his fragmentation, and goes on singing.

In a series of seminars at the Yeats Summer School in 1993,[37] Hassan outlined eight central tenets which he believes are characteristic of the post-modernist novel:

1 It avoids symbolism; its reality is phenomenological and on the surface.
2 It promotes indeterminacy; its language slips and slides and resists interpretation. The breakdown of syntax is designed to defer and postpone any absolute translation of the work – it is an open, dialogic, and polyphonic field of possibilities.
3 It seeks fragmentation. It is against holism and reconciliation, and is concerned with irony rather than catharsis.
4 It is self-reflexive, i.e. it is conscious of itself and opposed to realist verisimilitude.
5 It is pluralist. It is a hybrid genre, an unmargined discourse, which privileges intertextuality.
6 It uses topographic variations, i.e. it fragments itself visually and physically.
7 It celebrates parody, play and pastiche. It is anti-Promethean and resists any notion of textuality that promotes possession or genius.
8 It questions the unifying voice and is anti-authorship.

The issue of anti-Promethean authorship is perhaps the central distinguishing feature of post-modernism which sets it apart from its predecessors. Metafictions like *At Swim-Two-Birds* or *The Third Policeman* are the historical successors to the self-conscious tradition of *Tristram Shandy* – which also questioned the primacy of the author, but never with such self-reflexive, thematic violence. As an early post-modernist, O'Brien's repudiation of the author as the central signifying presence of the text rejects certain modernist (as well as realist) premises, and his exploration of this idea in *The Third Policeman* declares a radical departure from ritual convention.

Modernism, for all its radical innovations, had retained and consolidated the key convention of the earlier bourgeois novel, namely the conceit of the author-god. As Patricia Waugh points out: 'Postmodernism clearly does not involve the modernist concern with the mind itself as the basis of an aesthetic, ordered at a profound level and revealed to consciousness at isolated epiphanic moments.'[38] For Joyce (following Flaubert), the author should remain embedded within (and hidden behind) the literary machine: 'like the God of creation [. . .] within or behind or beyond or above his handiwork, invisible, refined out of existence, indifferent, paring his finger-nails.'[39] Through his representation of Stephen Dedalus, Joyce reaches the limits of the modernist aesthetic – Stephen, though conscious of the literary symbolism of his name (the first Christian martyr; the creator of, and escaper from, the mythical labyrinth), is never pushed so far into meta-literary self-consciousness as to consider that he is actually the symbolic 'author' of his own texts. Indeed, as Waugh observes, 'the only strictly metafictional line in *Ulysses* is Molly's: "O Jamesey let me up out of this pooh."'[40]

While modernists may well have envisaged the world as a chaotic flux, they still believed that meaning could be salvaged and inscribed in words. However, these words were still filtered and negotiated through the figure of the author-god, the ultimate arbiter of meaning. Thus the modernist interest in the het-eroglossic text and the possibilities of intertextuality remained firmly rooted on an aesthetic rather than an ontological plane. For critic Brian McHale, this distinction is a crucial one: 'the dominant of modernist fiction is epistemological' (a reality that is *subjectively* structured) while 'the dominant of post-modernism is ontological' (a reality that is *linguistically* structured).[41]

It is the linguistically structured reality of *The Third Policeman* which ultimately defines it as a work of post-modernism, and con-sequently this will be the focus of this present study. One healthy by-product of this contextual model is the way it detaches O'Brien from the paralysing association with Joyce, and aligns him more with a figure like Samuel Beckett. Indeed, J.C.C. Mays establishes a connection between the work of O'Brien and Beckett on similar grounds, and quotes Beckett's comment that 'The more Joyce knew the more he could. He's tending towards omniscience and omnipo-tence as an artist. I'm working with impotence, ignorance'.[42] This is the Brave New World of post-modern literature: gone is the posture of the heroic artist, and in comes an art with an innate fidelity to failure. Gone is the redemptive force and coherent form of mod-ernism to be replaced by the ludic ironies and playful parodies of post-modernism. Gone too are the closed ideological systems, the 'Grand Narratives' of Freudianism, Marxism and even Cartesianism, supplanted by a literature which is happy to exist in a decentred world. Where Eliot and Joyce had gathered fragments to shore against their ruins, O'Brien and Beckett are content to loiter and play in the literary rubble. As Ihab Hassan puts it:

> Post-modernism is the rejection of representation in favour of
> self-reference – the willing rejection of the work as an organic
> whole and the myth of the author; the rejection of character, nar-
> rative and plot as meaningful or artistically defensible concepts
> or conventions; even the rejection of 'meaning' itself as a hopeless
> delusion. Post-modernism takes the subjective idealism of mod-
> ernism to the point of solipsism, but rejects the tragic and
> pessimistic elements in modernism in the conclusion that if one
> cannot prevent Rome burning then one might as well enjoy the
> fiddling that is left open to one.[43]

This is our context.

The method

In the course of researching this book in the 1990s, it became clear
to me that two broad strands of O'Brien criticism seemed to exist at
the time, which I labelled the indigenous versus the international;
or, not putting too fine a gloss on it, the insular versus the decontextualised.

The indigenous school of Irish criticism (which includes a brace
of biographies, a large critical introduction, and a collection of
extrinsic biographical memoirs),[44] is sometimes folksy and anecdotal, and often lacking in critical rigour. The slightly insular tone
of these works – with some notable exceptions – generates a cosiness that would have made Flann O'Brien blush in the way that
they promote certain aspects of value and authorship which his
novels directly assault and subvert. Play and parody are the main
weapons in the O'Brien arsenal, for they possess the innate ability
to confront authority and assert imaginative autonomy. In response
to this maverick subversion, these indigenous critics usually
attempt to place O'Brien's 'comic spirit' within the safe confines of
the Irish Literary Tradition, though without much reference to any
consistent or systematic critical model. At the same time, these
good-natured and well-intentioned nativists manage to cultishly
protect the O'Brien canon against outside critical encroachment,
thus limiting more theoretically-minded approaches.[45]

By far the biggest problem with such traditional criticism is the
way that it tends to bolster the cult of the Author, and the issue of
biography should be addressed here. I have a basic mistrust of the
implicit principles of biographical criticism, which insist that knowledge of an author's personal life – and speculation about his or her
supposed 'intentions' in writing – will in some mysterious way unlock

the 'meaning' of the text. As Myles na Gopaleen himself wrote, 'the entire breed of biographies [. . .] is too devout. [. . .] Biography is the lowest form of letters and is atrophied by the subject's own censorship, conscious or otherwise'.[46] In particular, I distrust the vague psychoanalytical rhetoric used by some biographical critics to resolve the 'problems' of the text. While they may well be entertaining, these off-the-shelf nostrums of pop psychology are not just pseudo-scientific in nature but often downright misleading. Although biography does offer an in-built chronological narrative which occasionally stumbles across textually relevant themes, it still lacks a coherent context in which to explore these issues properly. All biography is selective in that out of a vast continuum of facts it mystically privileges certain features of the life and work over others, or as Roland Barthes' witty epigram has it, 'any biography is a novel that dare not speak its name'.[47]

This kind of biographical criticism frequently heralds a rather reductive type of analysis whereby the 'meaning' of a text is squeezed out of a swamp of textually extrinsic conditions, and deciphered in light of some unspecified and platonic conceptual scheme. Texts like *At Swim-Two-Birds* and *The Third Policeman* seem to me to be so eclectic as to defy such a narrow, monological process, and indeed directly challenge and parody such critiques. In this respect, I adopt the position of Roland Barthes when he writes that:

> We know now that a text is not a line of words releasing a 'theological' meaning (the message of the Author-God) but a multi-dimensional space in which a variety of writings, none of them original, blend and clash. The text is a tissue of quotations drawn from the innumerable centres of culture. [. . .] [The writer's] only power is to mix his writings, to counter the ones with the others, in such a way as to never rest on any one of them.[48]

Barthes' dislodgement of the author-god from his transcendental throne and his attendant emphasis on intertextuality correspond neatly with O'Brien's stated ideal in *At Swim-Two-Birds* (the public manifesto of his art that also governs the more sublimated metafictional poetics of *The Third Policeman*):

> The novel, in the hands of an unscrupulous writer, could be despotic. In reply to an inquiry, it was explained that a satisfactory novel should be a self-evident sham to which the reader could regulate at will the degree of his credulity. [. . .] The entire corpus of existing literature should be regarded as a limbo from which discerning authors could draw their characters as

> required, creating only when they failed to find a suitable
> existing puppet. The modern novel should largely be a work of
> reference. (*AS2B*, p. 25)

Every text then is an intertext: a site of hermeneutical play and
semiotic re-arrangement that is deliberately exploited in works of
metafiction. The concept of intertextuality suggests that a text does
not exist as a self-sufficient, hermetic whole, and therefore cannot
function as a 'closed' system. Intertextuality links a narrative not
so much to the real world as to the world of other stories in which
the reader lives. The theory of intertextuality suggests an interactive, double paradox: the writer 'reads' and the reader 'writes'.
First, the author is a reader before he or she is a creator, and therefore every literary text is inexorably riddled – consciously and/or
unconsciously – with references, quotations and influences from
other works. Second, a literary text is only ever actualised through
some system of reading, and thus becomes the by-product of all the
other texts which a reader brings to it. Although a text's intertextual origins can never be exactly located or reduced to a mere
catalogue of sources, this post-modernist agenda is a progressive
move away from authorship and towards textuality and reader
response, and it provides a refreshing critical antidote to more traditional forms of O'Brien scholarship.

This anticipates the second school of O'Brien criticism, which we
might call the 'International Brigade': a legion of mostly European
critics who have established a more expansive and open-ended set
of post-structuralist priorities.[49] However, given the fact that these
critics tend to locate O'Brien's work within an experimental tradition of avant-garde fiction, their critiques are invariably
decontextualised, and often fail to take account of the uniquely
Irish idiosyncrasies of O'Brien's linguistic experiments. As Rüdiger
Imhof writes in his introduction to *Alive-Alive O!: Flann O'Brien's
At Swim-Two-Birds*:

> Certainly, *At Swim-Two-Birds* is immensely and disarmingly
> Irish. Yet, as with any profound specimen of literature or art, it
> is not as an outstanding specimen of a particular national litera-
> ture – as a supreme instance of the Irish comic tradition, for
> example – that the novel is likely to be appreciated in times to
> come. Despite its unequivocal references to Ireland and Irish lit-
> erature, *At Swim-Two-Birds* should find its proper context as a
> brilliant artistic achievement in the international tradition of
> innovative fiction.[50]

As an Irish critic I feel obliged to at least attempt some sort of tribal retrieval of O'Brien's work, but one which draws on the wealth of literary theory which has emerged in recent times. Moreover, I would hope to show that the two traditions (of writing as well as criticism) – the Irish and the international – are not mutually exclusive, and indeed find a unique point of convergence in *The Third Policeman*. Consequently, this present study will be divided into three phases: the first two chapters will place O'Brien in a native context and show his allegiance/resistance to the Irish tradition; the following three chapters will deal in depth with his metafictional/post-modernist poetics; and the final chapter will address the question of intertextuality and interpretation, and the emergence of O'Brien as a young post-modernist. In order to develop a consistent, coherent and appropriate model – and to nail my own critical colours to the mast – the method applied for much of this analysis is indebted to Russian Formalism.

Formalism originated in Russia around the time of the Russian Revolution. At the time, it was a Copernican revolution in literary studies which foreshadowed structuralist (and later, post-structuralist) critical theory. Nowadays it barely merits attention in critical circles, except as an interesting historical footnote. However, the original theorists retain a particular critical clarity which we might usefully apply to works of metafiction in a post-modernist context. If metafiction is a shamanist repudiation of ritual convention, then we might say that formalist criticism is its critical counterpart, its 'academic wing', and indeed many of its key acolytes have championed metafictional literature for its 'defamiliarising' practices.[51]

Formalism is a set of overlapping ideas about literature, not all of which are shared by its practitioners; as Pavel Medvedev has observed, 'there are as many formalisms as there are formalists'.[52] In general, it studies the organising principles of a work: the 'how' of a text (its poetics) rather than the 'what' (its content). Formalism is a rejection of *extrinsic* conditions – biographical, socio-historical, philosophical, psychological, political – in favour of a more *intrinsic* approach which tackles literature directly, as a phenomenon. On this scheme, there is no extra-literary motivation in a text – no emotional, cognitive or social significance – only the shaping of pure form. As its leading practitioner Viktor Shklovsky declared:

> What is significant is that we approached art as a production.
> Spoke of it alone. Viewed it not as a reflection. Found the spe-
> cific features of the genus. Began to establish the basic
> tendencies of form. Grasped that on a large scale there is a real
> homogeneity in the laws informing works. Hence the science [of
> criticism] is possible.[53]

Two fundamental premises negotiate this formalist enterprise:
first, that we should study the phenomenon of literature and not its
metaphysical essences; and second, that the object of study in literary science is not literature *per se* – after all, who can say with
any certainty what 'literature' actually is? – but what Roman
Jakobson calls 'literariness', i.e. 'that which makes a given work a
literary work'.[54] For Shklovsky, it is simply a return to 'craftsman-
ship', and he adopts the metaphor of the car mechanic: 'The
understanding mechanic scrutinises the car serenely and comprehends "what is what": why it has so many cylinders and why it has
big wheels, where its transmission is situated, why its rear is cut in
a acute angle and its radiator unpolished. This is the way one
should read.'[55]

As Victor Erlich has noted, while all of this may sound suspi-
ciously like 'a refurbished notion of the late nineteenth-century
"art for art's sake" doctrine' – and, indeed, 'formalism' was originally used as a term of opprobrium in early communist Russia – it
is really just a way of analysing what is artful about art.[56]
Moreover, formalists were well aware of the fact that 'literary
texts are semantically charged, and hence involve values, ideas
and other qualities not open to direct, sensory experience. Rather
they would agree that these qualities do not constitute the essence
of literature'.[57] Like Saussurian linguistics, which directly influenced the early formalist agenda, it is a search for the generative
rules which govern the formation and transformation of forms. As
such, this is a joyful and proliferative assumption rather than an
apolitical and reductive one, or as Susan Sontag wisely puts it, 'To
stipulate that there is no understanding outside of language is to
assert that there is meaning everywhere'.[58]

For formalists, art is the systematic displacement of an object
from its customary context, similar to the frame-breaking techniques of metafiction. As Peter Steiner notes, 'Disjunction was the
key logical principle by which mechanistic Formalism organised its
basic concepts. This principle split art decisively from non-art, and
expressed their mutual exclusivity in the following set of polar
opposites':

Art	*Everyday Life*
Defamiliarisation	Automatisation
Teleology	Causality
Device	Material
Plot (*syuzhet*)	Story (*fabula*)[59]

Formalism insists that the synchronic (descriptive) element in criticism must always precede the diachronic (historical): trust the tale and not the teller, and the *syuzhet* (plot devices) not the *fabula* (story). Like metafiction and post-modernism, formalism espouses a reality that is linguistically structured. This has ideological repercussions in the way that it deconstructs naturalised assumptions and makes strange the commonplace conventions of discourse that bind and govern our social behaviour. As Fredric Jameson comments, 'the doctrine of the arbitrariness of the sign eliminates the myth of a natural language'.[60] The formalist critic does not search for the 'meaning' of a story as such – this is a liberating avoidance of the obvious and the obsolete – but rather questions the *discourse* of a text, or how that story is told. Moreover, in later versions of formalist criticism, this approach has been applied to 'everyday life' situations as well as to literary language. Take, for example, Roland Barthes' neo-formalist analysis of an ordinary, mundane conversation about the weather:

> This morning the woman in the bakery said: *It's still lovely, but the heat's lasting too long!* (people around here always feel that it's too lovely, too hot). I add: *And the light is so beautiful!* But the woman does not answer, and once again I notice that short-circuit in language of which the most trivial conversations are the sure occasion; I realise that *seeing the light* relates to a class sensibility [. . .]. In short, nothing more cultural than the atmosphere, nothing more ideological than what the weather is doing.[61]

Within the formalist paradigm, art is perceived as a revolution of form rather than an evolution of substance. As a critique, the revolutionary cut of the formalist stance is primarily ludic as opposed to being directly political – like feminism or Marxism, for example – although it does not preclude the use of such evaluative, diachronic idioms once the synchronic aspect is first established, i.e. formalism is descriptive rather than prescriptive. The key phrase in formalist criticism is 'defamiliarisation':

> If we start to examine the general laws of perception, we see that as perception becomes habitual, it becomes automatic. [. . .]

> Habitualization devours work, clothes, furniture, one's wife, and
> the fear of war. [. . .] And art exists that one may recover the sen-
> sation of life; it exists to make one feel things, to make the stone
> *stony*. The purpose of art is to impart the sensation of things as
> they are perceived and not as they are known. The technique of art
> is to make objects 'unfamiliar', to make forms difficult, to increase
> the difficulty and length of perception [. . .]. *Art is a way of experi-
> encing the artfulness of an object; the object is not important.*[62]

Like metafiction, formalism privileges art which subverts ritual
expression and renews jaded perception – in itself a prerequisite
step towards political clarity and cultural rejuvenation. Or as
Fredric Jameson puts it: 'Art in this context is a way of restoring
conscious experience, of breaking through deadening habits of
conduct [. . .] and allowing us to be reborn to the world in all its
existential freshness and horror.'[63]

For the purposes of this present inquiry, the formalist mind-set
presents itself as the most systematic yet compatible method for
discussing metafictional poetics. Above all, it seems to me that formalism allows for a direct confrontation with literature which
celebrates storytelling and which encourages us to be better
readers. By virtue of its discursive elegance – a flair for aphorism; a
passion for parody, paradox and play – it evades the brutal and
envious distortions that sometimes characterise more contemporary deconstructive methods, and it avoids the ugly apocalyptic
rhetoric that frequently accompanies post-modernist critiques.
Quite often, good criticism is nothing more than an elegant fusion
of empathy, arrogance and charm, which the formalists, at their
best, embodied. As Susan Sontag wrote:

> The formalist temperament is just one variant of a sensibility
> shared by many who speculate in an era of hypersaturated
> awareness. What characterises such a sensibility more generally
> is its reliance on the criterion of taste, and its proud refusal to
> propose anything that does not bear the stamp of subjectivity.
> Confidently assertive, it nevertheless insists that its assertions
> are no more than provisional. (To do otherwise would be . . . bad
> taste.)[64]

This will be our method.

1. The two towers: the Celtic Toilet meets the filthy modern tide

It is the serious lack of commitment in any direction that limits Brian O'Nolan and ensnares him in the second rank, below Joyce and Yeats [. . .].
Bernard Benstock, 'The Three Faces of Brian O'Nolan', 1968[1]

In the best essay so far on the novels of Flann O'Brien – 'Literalist of the Imagination' – J.C.C. Mays makes the telling remark that O'Brien's 'alternatives in prose may be said to have been pointed to by Liam O'Flaherty and by Joyce, either to unsling the camera and follow across the dreary plain or to look abroad to the master of silence, exile and punning'.[2]

From the beginning, the two towers confronting O'Brien were the twin legacies of Joyce's modernism and Yeats's Celtic Revival – and he was nervously uncomfortable with both. For O'Brien, Irish literature was trapped within a Celtic twilight zone – a historical limbo of transitional flux and rapidly fading glory. A Joycean acolyte, O'Brien was conscious that Joyce had irrevocably altered the modern literary map, although the Irish public in general seemed oblivious to this achievement. Meanwhile, back at the ranch, the jaded idealism of Yeats's Celtic Twilight – or 'Celtic Toilet' as Myles na Gopaleen mockingly dubbed it[3] – had, in the aftermath of Irish independence, inspired nothing more than a trenchantly insular and inherently rural literary consciousness, intimately bound to a restrictive Catholic ethos. The 1930s realist school of fiction had further consolidated this paradigm, or as John Montague later expressed it in a Yeatsian parody: 'Puritan Ireland's dead and gone/A myth of O'Connor and Ó Faoláin.'[4] O'Brien too detested this complacent kind of realism, believing it to be sentimental and anachronistic, or as Myles sneered: 'Not to be left out of the picture are Seán Ó Faoláin and Frank O'Connor, with stories about wee Annie going to her first confession, stuff about country funerals, [. . .] will-making, match-making – just one long blush for many an innocent man like me, who never harmed them.'[5]

Myles na Gopaleen/Flann O'Brien was bitterly antagonistic towards this bland brand of post-colonial cosiness, and indeed both of these fictional personas emerged of out his violent contempt for it. In January 1939, controversy had erupted over an Abbey production of a Frank O'Connor play, which was critically slated by *The Irish Times* and subsequently defended by Seán Ó Faoláin. Brian O'Nolan (i.e. Flann O'Brien) used the occasion to mock the entire nativist school by writing to the letters page of that paper under a variety of pseudonyms, attacking and counterattacking his own endlessly shifting position. After O'Brien's voluminous and witty epistolary campaign, the editor of *The Irish Times* was impressed enough by the writer's versatility to offer him a job as a columnist. Thus began Myles na Gopaleen's long-running satirical column, the 'Cruiskeen Lawn' ('Crúiscín Lán: a Full Jug, i.e. of porter or its equivalent').[6]

In itself the 'letter campaign' was an index of O'Brien's emergent ideological position, and demonstrated an aesthetic shift towards a polyphonic, post-realist mode of writing. A crude form of dialectical poetics, O'Brien's letter writing showed the deconstructive potentials of intertextual composition – a potent rhetoric of critical demolition, comic inversion and cultural provocation. It also revealed one of the cornerstones of his personal aesthetic, namely the need for the pseudonymous mask. As Rüdiger Imhof remarks, the 'plethora of pen-names protected his privacy and gained him immunity from possible retaliatory attacks',[7] but more than this the mask established a crucial distinction between the author and the narrative voice. Or as Myles himself wrote in 1964: 'Compartmentation of personality for the purpose of literary utterance ensures that the fundamental individual will not be credited with a certain way of thinking, fixed attitudes, irreversible technique of expression. No author should write under his own name nor under one permanent pen-name.'[8]

During the letter campaign that launched Myles na Gopaleen in *The Irish Times*, one of the pen-names used was 'Flann O'Brien', a name that Brian O'Nolan had previously suggested to Longmans Green publishers for the forthcoming release of *At Swim-Two-Birds* (1939): 'I think his invention has the advantage that it contains an unusual name and one that is quite ordinary. "Flann" is an old Irish name now rarely heard.'[9] The choice of names reveals some of the tensions underlying O'Brien's ambivalent attitude to Irish literature and language. As a scholar of Irish – Brian O'Nolan had written his MA thesis on 'Nature in Irish Poetry' – he was consciously invoking the rich, historical connotations of the name 'Flann', held as it was by several medieval poets, scholars and high kings.[10] At the same time, as John Garvin has argued, it was also a wry, parodic lift from the eponymous hero of a mid-nineteenth-century comic ballad entitled 'Brian O'Lynn' – 'in Irish, Brian Ó Fhloinn, which he turned backwards, taking the nominative of Ó Fhloinn, Flann, as a personal name'.[11] This ballad – a classic piece of paddy-whackery – had first appeared in Dion Boucicault's melodrama *The Colleen Bawn; or, The Brides of Garryowen: A Domestic Drama in Three Acts* (1860), sung by a character called 'Myles na Coppaleen':

> Brian O'Linn had no breeches to wear,
> So he bought him a sheepskin to make him a pair;
> The skinny side out, the woolly side in,
> 'They are cool and convanient', said Brian O'Linn.[12]

In a nice intertextual twist which would have appealed to Flann O'Brien, Boucicault had pirated the figure of Myles from a character in Gerald Griffin's novel *The Collegians* (1829). As John Cronin notes, Griffin's novel was based on a celebrated murder case, where a high-born lover and his henchman were executed for the murder of a young peasant girl in 1819 (early echoes of *The Third Policeman* perhaps?). In this earlier version, 'Myles-na-Coppuleen' is an 'idealised portrait of an Irish mountaineer and horse-dealer, a kind of bluff, Arcadian figure possessed of the gift of the gab and of great natural courtesy'.[13] As Griffin elaborately describes him:

> A broad and sunny forehead, light and wavy hair, a blue cheerful eye, a nose that in Persia might have won him a throne, healthful cheeks, a mouth that was full of character, and a well-knit and almost gigantic person, constituted his external claims to attention; of which his lofty and confident, although most unassuming carriage, showed him to be in some degree conscious.[14]

The Colleen Bawn was first performed in 1860, with Boucicault himself playing the pivotal role of Myles na Coppaleen. In this black comedy of errors, the Boucicault Myles is a slyly comic figure who turns out to be quietly heroic. When we first meet him, though, he seems like the bog-standard stage Irishman, so beloved of the English stage:

CORRIGAN [the 'middle-man']: 'Tis that poaching scoundrel – that horse stealer, Myles na Coppaleen. Here he comes with a keg of illicit whisky, as bould as Nebuckadezzar.

Enter MYLES *singing, with a keg on his shoulder.*

Is that you Myles?

MYLES: No! it's my brother.[15]

Shortly after, Myles and his friends sing a drinking song, 'Cruiskeen Lawn':

> Let the farmer praise his grounds,
> As the huntsman doth his hounds,
> And the shepherd his fresh and dewy morn;
> But I, more blest than they,
> Spend each night and happy day,
> With my smilin' little Cruiskeen Lawn, Lawn, Lawn.[16]

As David Krause has noted, in Boucicault's play the reincarnated Myles becomes a comic anti-hero, the historical literary antecedent to Synge's playboys and O'Casey's paycocks, a 'lazy lying tramp, beyond any hope of reform, a horse thief and ex-convict'.[17] The archetypal stage Irishman had long been a stock caricature of English drama, but Boucicault's achievement was his comic subversion of type by placing the 'Shaughraun' (or fool) within a colonial context, blessing him with native wit and cunning, and reconstructing him as 'a liberated playboy who cavorts outside the ordinary restraints of society'.[18] By this account, putting the Shaughraun back in the Irish landscape was an act of retrieval and appropriation; against the native playboy's excessiveness, the demure English gentry once again become the 'other', or non-native. This establishes a telling opposition whereby the ruling class has power but lacks a real sense of place, while the playboy is empowered by the gentry's very lack of identity (mockingly reflected in his obsequious cap-tipping). This, of course, is a long-established tradition in Irish writing, going back at least to Maria Edgeworth's disingenuous narrator, Thady Quirk, in *Castle Rackrent* (1800).

Such revisionist play-acting, however, did not impress the post-colonial Myles of *The Irish Time*s, whose love of Irish language and literature had been somewhat soured by the nationalist cavortings of Boucicault and, later on, by the Celtic Revival of Yeats *et al*. With Synge's re-vamping of the Shaughraun in *The Playboy of the Western World* (1907), Myles felt that the stage Irishman had become the central, signifying archetype of the Irish literary imaginary:

The set-up is this. These people turn angrily on the British and roar: 'How dare you insult us with your stage Irishman, a monkey-faced leering scoundrel in ragged knee-breeches and a tail coat, always drunk and threatening anybody in sight with a shillelagh? We can put together a far better stage Irishman ourselves, thank you. The Irish Stage Irishman is the best in the world.'[19]

For Myles, the net result of the Revival's nationalist agenda was that it had privileged an imagined peasant lifestyle, and through its promotion of this dubious myth it had inadvertently enshrined the parochial shibboleths of a conservative order. As Hubert Butler has noted:

[I]n that perilous region of half-belief which the sophisticated find charming [. . .] they are more acquainted with its tenderness than its cruelty. It is a no-man's land of the imagination, in which fantasy, running wild, easily turns into falsehood and ruthlessness. It has still in the twentieth century its appeal and highly civilised people, as well as simple ones, claim access to it. [. . .] A great deal of Irish poetry and romance is born of isolation and the nostalgia of those who escape it. Eyes that are dim with tears are not particularly perceptive [. . .].[20]

This unwitting legacy, sold to a successive generation of Irish writers, was for Myles nothing more than a literary pig-in-a-poke: '[the revivalists] persisted in the belief that poverty and savage existence on remote rocks was a most poetical way for people to be, provided they were other people'. In particular, Myles seemed embittered by the public acclaim for Synge's syncretic language: 'Here we had a moneyed dilettante coming straight from Paris to study the peasants of Aran not knowing a syllable of their language, then coming back to pour forth a deluge of homemade jargon all over the Abbey stage [. . .].'[21]

Myles's rage and discomfort are essentially a product of post-colonial cringe, and he appears embarrassed at the leftover perception of Irishness promulgated by Synge and typified by his playboy. Throughout his novels O'Brien exerted a peculiar form of bardic revenge by writing his perceived 'enemies' into fiction, and just as Joyce appears as a character in *The Dalkey Archive*, Synge's Christy Mahon makes a (sublimated) intertextual appearance in *The Third Policeman*. Anne Clissmann has suggested that the parody of *The Playboy of the Western World* in *The Third Policeman* stems from O'Brien's moral revulsion that Synge celebrates patricide as a virtuous act of courage, although the truth seems more complex.[22]

Firstly, this suggestion would mistakenly place O'Brien on the same plane as the nationalists who originally accused *The Playboy* of obscenity and misrepresentation of Irishness in 1907. Underlying that initial reaction was a nationalist ideology that privileged excessive 'purity' – especially sexual purity – and Synge's play provocatively challenged the narrow perceptions on which this nationalist identity was based. O'Brien himself challenges similar ideologies in his novels, so this is hardly his objection to Synge. Secondly, the Oedipal tensions within Synge's play contain a very serious, subtextual critique of colonialism and nationalism, which hinges on the idea of paternity and succession. As Edward Said has written:

> For all its success in ridding many countries and territories of colonial overlords, nationalism has remained, in my opinion, a deeply problematic ideological, as well as socio-political enterprise. At some stage in the anti-resistance phase of nationalism there is a sort of dependence between the two sides in the contest, since after all many of the nationalist struggles were led by bourgeoisies partly formed and to some degree produced by the colonial power. [. . .] The other problem is that the cultural horizons of nationalism are fatally limited by the common history of the colonizer and the colonized assumed by the nationalist movement itself. Imperialism after all is a cooperative venture. Both the master and the slave participate in it, albeit unequally.[23]

Synge was fully aware of this historical dynamic when writing *The Playboy*, and to this end fully exploited the allegorical potential of his Oedipal story. When Christy Mahon 'kills' his brutal father – unbeknownst to Christy, he has merely wounded him – he attempts to discard the nightmare of history, and re-create himself anew. However, his new persona is premised on a dangerous fallacy, and when this comes to light the villagers vengefully seek to destroy him. Ironically, his father returns from the dead at this very point, and is reunited with his son through conflict. At the end of the play they ride off into the sunset, determined to face the future together – but with Christy as the new political master in this ancient feudal relationship:

> CHRISTY: Go with you, is it? I will then, like a gallant captain with his heathen slave. Go on now and I'll see you from this day stewing my oatmeal and washing my spuds, for I'm master of all fights from now.[24]

In its structured series of actions and reactions, *The Playboy of the Western World* thus charts the pilgrim's progress of the nationalist movement: revolt, civil strife and, eventually, post-colonial reconciliation. As a member of the decaying Ascendancy elite, it could be argued that Synge wrote a reprieve for his own class by resurrecting Old Mahon, the former master, and reconciling him with Christy, the former slave – a kind of literary wish-fulfilment for Ireland in the coming times. Again, I cannot see how Flann O'Brien, if he was aware of this allegory, would necessarily disapprove of its sentiments. Instead, it seems to me that his disaffection with Synge is rooted mainly on an aesthetic plane:

> It is not that Synge made people less worthy or nastier than they are, but he brought forward, with the utmost solemnity, amusing clowns talking a sub-language of their own, and bade us take them seriously. [. . .] And now the curse has come upon us, because I have personally met people in the streets of Ireland who are clearly out of Synge's plays.[25]

Behind the Mylesian facetiousness lies a palpable anger. The stereotypical discourse that had evolved from protest and imitation – both attitudes a form of colonial dependency – had remained on after independence and hardened into cliché, thereby sustaining a regressive ideology. O'Brien's rejection of Synge is less *ad hominem* and more a mythological repudiation of the nativist writers who followed in Synge's wake. The inherent subversion of *The Playboy* had opened up questions of sexuality and violence, paternity and identity, which were historically needful at that particular moment in time. It is not the violence *per se* that disgusted O'Brien – in fact, his own novels have a grotesque fascination with male violence as a manifestation of sexual repression. On the contrary, O'Brien saw that in a post-colonial context the angry subversion of Synge's play had been denuded and diluted, leaving behind an empty shell of false lyricism which has been imitated, without irony, by successive generations. Stripped of its historical and revolutionary context, this glib lyricism had become the stock language of a corrupt Irish realism: a Walt Disney perception of Irishness peddled on an impossible vision, like a surreal parody of a tourist board advertisement. O'Brien's discontent is with the limitations of ritual form and language, which continue to uphold the politics of colonialism.

In much the same vein, Myles's 'Cruiskeen Lawn' column sprang from this reactionary platform. Indeed, the persona of

Myles himself is a kind of post-modern stage Irishman, 'as old as Shakespeare's MacMorris, turned melodramatic by Boucicault, poetised by Synge, romanticised by O'Connor and Ó Faoláin, urbanised by O'Casey and Joyce, and made outré by Brian O'Nolan'.[26] The first column appeared on 4 November 1940, in Irish, as a satirical response to a critic who had commented that Irish was an archaic language incapable of reflecting modern Irish culture, as it quite obviously lacked sufficient vocabulary to discuss issues of politics or modern warfare. Myles's riposte involved the construction of an imaginary mealtime conversation, using the Irish equivalents of the very words that supposedly did not exist in the Irish word-stock, including 'air-raid warden', 'incendiary bomb' and 'non-aggression pact'.

This display of linguistic pyrotechnics proved – in a witty and ironic manner – that not only could Irish retain its signifying autonomy in a modern context but that it could also exuberantly express itself using highly charged poetic allusions, loaded with dialogic wit and invention. Myles wished to demonstrate that this type of discourse was necessary to create a healthier climate for the promotion of Irish culture, and at the same time show that the Irish language was the secret ingredient that gave certain forms of Hiberno-English writing their distinct flavour. As he wrote to Seán O'Casey in 1942: '[Irish] is essential, particularly for any sort of a literary worker. It supplies that unknown quantity in us that enables us to transform the English language and this seems to hold off people who know little or no Irish, like Joyce.'[27] (It is interesting to note, in passing, that the two post-modernist authors who most resemble O'Brien – Samuel Beckett and Vladimir Nabokov – also wrote in their second languages.)

Paradoxically, Myles's spirited defence won him few friends among Irish-language revivalists whom he later satirised in *An Béal Bocht* (1941). Many revivalists saw the language purely in nationalistic terms, and had constructed rather staid and sanctimonious attitudes to safeguard their political agenda. Though Myles loved the language he abhorred the purist protectionists, and this particular satirical vein is amongst the most corrosive in the Mylesian canon. One irate correspondent – 'A West-Briton-Nationalist, Ballyhaunis' (O'Brien himself) – complained to the letters page of *The Irish Times* that Myles was 'spewing' on the Irish language.[28] Again, the use of the mask was not just self-publicising but dialectical, allowing the satirist room to condemn absolute dogmatism without appearing sanctimonious himself – a strategy of internal policing used to great effect in O'Brien's novels. This rhetorical manoeuvre creates an impossible flux of shifting perspectives which clash and interact unpredictably; it also provokes different responses in different readers, so as to never rest on any one 'true' meaning. Language itself and reader participation are celebrated, and the centrality of authorship is undermined and reconstructed.

What is most valuable in any critical reading of the Mylesian canon is Myles's observations on language and literature. Though unreliable, contrary and contradictory, these observations have one key advantage over biographical criticism in that they are textually based. Myles's literary pontifications are by turn hilarious, insightful, celebratory, mean-spirited and absurd – but he is still O'Brien's most holistically conceived dramatic persona. As the formalist Boris Tomashevsky has argued, 'what the literary historian really needs is the biographical legend created by the author himself. Only such a legend is a literary fact'.[29] Somewhere between the miasma of brilliant invention and blatant distortion lies Myles's need to say something about the world he distorts. As the modern successor to Jonathan Swift, Myles's comic, epiphanic narratives are ruthlessly underpinned by his acid critiques of the established order. In its twenty-six-year history, his column became a collective monologue of what he called the PPI (the 'Plain People of Ireland') – a mosaic portrait of the Irish Free State in the post-colonial era. Myles became the created conscience of his race, an Irish Everyman whose very style was the epitome of pub-talk at its imagined best: witty, fluid, pedantically erudite, with its underlying seriousness always couched in the mellifluous tones of the clown. Myles was the symbolic, deconstructed personification of the archetypal 'charming begrudger' – a character O'Brien felt was symptomatic of post-colonial Irish culture.

It is not within the scope of this book to explore the Mylesian canon in any great depth, but if I had to choose any one exemplary, representative aspect, it would be the popular and long-running 'Keats and Chapman' series. The root structure of these corny comic parables involved the coining of an ingenious pun out of a common platitude, which then became the punchline of an absurd anecdote, delivered with dead-pan solemnity. The inner landscape of the Keats–Chapman world is a self-conscious intertextual zone, where familiar literary and historical figures freely co-mingle, and much of the comedy arises from these absurd juxtapositions. The technical sleight-of-hand, according to Benedict Kiely, 'lies in drawing out the tale, accumulating the fantasy to the point [. . .] of sadism, then in crashing home with the flat desolating pun'.[30]

The sequence has its origins in Myles's telling of how the poet George Chapman brought a sick pigeon to his friend, John Keats. After Keats cured the ailing bird (by removing a piece of champagne cork that was lodged in its throat), he immediately sat down and wrote his sonnet, 'On First Looking into Chapman's Homer'.[31] The punchline is invariably excruciating but this is all part of the reader's masochistic pleasure, a 'conspiracy between the reader's powers of recognition and Myles's inventiveness and sense for incongruous associations of ideas'.[32] Other vignettes include the story of Chapman training performing frogs for a circus ('It's a wrong toad that has no learning'); Keats and Chapman gazing petrified into Mount Vesuvius ('Will you have a drop of the crater?'); the man who built and slept in his own coffin ('A terrible man for the bier'); and the man who left all his money to a cat's home ('I knew he had an aid-to-puss complex').[33]

The sense of conspiracy between author and reader is vital. The reader is co-opted into the experience, and his or her ability to decode the narrative conventions and allusions becomes an integral part of the verbal play. This echoes O'Brien's technique in the novels, where the author manipulates the elasticity of language – in particular the nuances of Hiberno-English – through pun, malapropism, solecism, double entendre, metonymy and synecdoche. Comic in its own right, this manipulation also facilitates the construction of what the literary theorist Mikhail Bakhtin calls a 'carnival discourse'. For Bakhtin, this carnivalesque challenge is inherently subversive (as opposed to straight parody which intrinsically upholds what it mocks): the power of laughter to destroy authority. Michael Worton and Judith Still describe the carnival process as follows:

> When people speak they use a specific mix of discourses which they have appropriated in an attempt to communicate their intentions. However, they inevitably suffer interference from two sources: the words' pre-existing meanings and the alien intentions of a real interlocutor. Every concrete utterance is intersected by both centrifugal and centripetal, unifying and disunifying forces. [. . .] Writers of literature can attempt artificially to strip literature of others' intentions, a unifying project which Bakhtin calls monologism. [. . .] On the other hand, at certain historical moments, writers have historically elaborated and intensified this heteroglossia, creating what Bakhtin calls the dialogic.[34]

Myles's hybrid reconstruction of literary and colloquial speech creates a dialogic space that autocritically undermines itself by destroying syntax in advance. In the polyphonic domain of the dreadful pun, 'signs no longer mediate, or enter into organic contexts; they float relatively independent of concrete social relations, coded with a genetic programme that can fan out into a near infinity of variations on its model'.[35] Any metalinguistic device – like the humble pun – drives a metafictional wedge between the normal conventions of writing and draws attention to the text *as* text. In this respect, the nonsense value of the pun transcends its immediate comic context, and has ideological value in the way it undermines the monological sanctity of the social languages that shape our world. As one of Myles's great satirical influences, Karl Kraus, wrote: 'A pun, though despicable in itself, can be the vehicle of an artistic intention by serving as an abbreviation of a witty view, [. . .] it can be social criticism.'[36] Punning, in this context, is a democratic gesture which resists authorship and insists that the reader appreciate and absorb the intertextual flux implicit in the word-play, or as Myles wrote in 1951: 'Things will get worse instead of better: ultimately the malady will spread from these pages to the most guarded reader – for this malady is infectious, contagious and pandemic.'[37]

In a notorious interview given to *Time* magazine in 1943, O'Brien mischievously compounded the myth of the author by fabricating events in his own life. Although he later admitted in a 'Cruiskeen Lawn' column that this was a 'superb heap of twaddle that would deceive nobody of ten years of age',[38] biographers have rather comically grappled with the possibility that O'Brien could have been 'signposting a by-way in his life that no-one has since cared to explore'.[39] That said, the semi-fictitious *Time* article does indicate Myles's huge popularity at that time, as well as the inevitable (and ultimately destructive) comparisons with Joyce:

> Like the late James Joyce, O'Nolan is a master of the monstrous pun. Erudite, ironic, he devotes many a column to the hilarious, systematic destruction of literary clichés, to parodies of Eire's leprechaun literature and the red-taped verbiage of government service. [. . .] He is an unsparing, beloved critic of devotees of Irish, who overuse Eire's national tongue; a subtler critic of the clerics who are not unaware of his innuendo.[40]

However, if O'Brien/na Gopaleen does reject the nativist tradition of Yeats and Synge, it does not necessarily follow that he embraces the more cosmopolitan, modernist ethic. In his perceived choice between the two towers of tradition, O'Brien gravitates to Joyce – but not unconditionally. As J.C.C. Mays writes:

> Joyce's world is one in which he delights, for its obeyance only of its own fantastic laws and its appearance of liberation from all dull customary physical restraints; and yet one wherein he conceives art has stepped beyond its prerogatives and lost its hold on reality, which is only too successful as a temptation from the proper path.[41]

O'Brien's position on Joyce is eloquently represented in his intelligent and rambunctious 1951 essay, 'A Bash in the Tunnel'. After mischievously comparing Joyce to Satan – 'both were very proud, both had a fall' – O'Brien relates an apocryphal tale told to him by an archetypal pub bore. The central conceit involves a man stealing a bottle of whiskey from a train's buffet car and secretly drinking it, alone, in the toilet of an empty carriage: 'surely there you have the Irish artist [. . .], resentfully drinking somebody else's whiskey, being whisked hither and thither by anonymous shunters, keeping fastidiously the while on the outer face of his door the simple word, ENGAGED? I think the image fits Joyce [. . .].'[42] This elaborate metaphor introduces more sober reflections, which focus on O'Brien's perception of Joyce's arrogant and tyrannical vision of authorship: 'Joyce spent a lifetime establishing himself as a character in fiction. [. . .] Beginning with importing real characters into his books, he achieves the magnificent inversion of making them legendary and fictional. It is quite preposterous. Thousands of people believe that there once lived a man named Sherlock Holmes.'[43]

O'Brien here is resisting the edifice that Joyce had so carefully built by mythologising himself as Stephen Dedalus, martyr and creator of the fictional labyrinth. Despite his radical experimentation with form, Joyce's allegiance to the concept of authorship merely copperfastened the traditional realist position. O'Brien, as an Irish Studies scholar, would have been aware that as a phenomenon the cult of the author had only emerged during the Enlightenment era; until then the personality of the author was either hidden or irrelevant. However, with the advent of the Romantic movement the poet eventually came to be as important as the poetry, or as Boris Tomashevsky wrote: 'A biography of a romantic poet was more than a biography of an author and public figure. The romantic poet was his own hero [. . .]. A double transformation takes place: heroes are taken for living personages, and poets become living heroes – their biographies become poems.'[44]

In a last, waspish broadside in his essay on Joyce, O'Brien makes a barbed (but still valid) comment about the hermeneutics of the literary-academic complex which has canonised Joyce at the expense of the 'ordinary' reader: 'Perhaps the true fascination of Joyce lies in his secretiveness, his ambiguity (his polyguity perhaps?) his leg-pulling, his dishonesties, his technical skill, his attraction for Americans. His works are a garden in which some of us may play.'[45] In the final analysis, and although O'Brien admires Joyce intensely, he remains suspicious of Joyce's elitism and inaccessibility to the general reading public – a theme he returns to in his Menippean satire, *The Third Policeman*. Elsewhere, commenting on *Finnegans Wake*, Myles wrote that 'Joyce has been reported as saying that he asked of his readers nothing but that they should devote their lives to reading his works. Such a method of spending a lifetime would be likely to endow the party concerned with quite a unique psychic apparatus of his own. I cannot recommend it'.[46]

While still a student O'Brien had become familiar with the works of the international modernist literati – Joyce, Pound, Eliot, Hemingway, Huxley, Kafka – but, in typically garrulous fashion, Myles later dismissed these writers as 'layabouts from the slums of Europe poking around in their sickly little psyches'.[47] As self-appointed literary adviser to the 'Plain People of Ireland', Myles never missed a chance to poke fun at the arrogance of authorship – even at the expense of writers whom he admired: 'I read somewhere recently about George Moore's sneer at Tolstoy for *War and Peace*, saying he had tried to outdo Nature and would wake up screaming in the night: "I forgot High Mass! I forgot a yacht race!" I intend to leave NOTHING out.'[48] Again, Myles is taking another post-modernist swipe at the selective verisimilitude and perceived dishonesty of realist (and modernist) conventions, whereby the disingenuous author pretends to conceal her/himself – Joyce's 'invisible artist' – behind the mimetic artifice of the fictional frame. This attempt to 'outdo Nature' is one of the key metafictional concerns explored in his early novels. Consequently, given O'Brien's revulsion with Irish realism and his reservations towards international modernism, metafiction becomes the paraliterary path he chooses. Using the Enlightenment models of Sterne and Swift, O'Brien attempts to forge a new synthesis, harnessing the energy of modernist experimentation in order to re-vitalise the subdued fire of the Irish comic tradition.

His earliest flirtations with metafictional discourse began in 1934, while O'Brien was still a student. He and others of the UCD literary clique had discussed the possibilities of collaborating together on an intertextual composite of 'The Great Irish Novel', provisionally entitled *Children of Destiny*. According to one of the intended collaborators, Niall Sheridan, the novel was to have been an epic saga following 'the fortunes of an Irish family over a period of almost a century, starting in 1840'.[49] The team effort held obvious comforts for the lazy writer, but it was also intended to prevent the dictatorial presence of the single author-god from asserting his will over the fictional domain. Above all, *Children of Destiny* was to be an honestly crass exercise in cynical market exploitation, conscious of the modern novel as an industrial and intertextual product:

> A vast market was ready and waiting. Compulsory education had produced millions of semi-literates, who were partial to 'a good read'. So it must be a big book, weighing at least two-and-a-half pounds. We must give them length without depth, splendour without style. Existing works would be plundered wholesale for material, and the ingredients of the saga would be mainly violence, patriotism, sex, religion, politics and the pursuit of money and power. *Children of Destiny* would be the precursor of a new literary movement, the first masterpiece of the Ready-Made or Reach-Me-Down School.[50]

Although this novel never transpired, it did lead to a short story by O'Brien, 'Scenes in a Novel' (1934), published in a student magazine under the pseudonym 'Brother Barnabas'. In this early metafictional blueprint for *At Swim-Two-Birds* and *The Third Policeman*, O'Brien first dramatised the possibilities of having fictional characters rebel against their creator, a theme he partly appropriated from James Branch Cabell's *The Cream of the Jest* (1917), as both Anthony Cronin and Anne Clissmann have noted. For the purposes of his proposed novel Brother Barnabas conjures up his protagonist, a 'dyed-in-the-wool atheist' named Carruthers McDaid, 'created one night when I swallowed nine stouts and felt vaguely blasphemous'[51] – the drunken author-god calling a world into being.

Barnabas intends McDaid to be a symbolic personification of degeneracy who, 'starting off as a rank waster and a rotter, was meant to sink slowly to absolutely the last extremities of human degradation'.[52] But Barnabas has inadvertently created a metafictional Promethean monster, and when McDaid discovers that he has been programmed to have free will he decides to transgress the realist boundaries of the plot. Despite the exigencies of his decreed destiny, the amoral McDaid refuses his author's directive to rob a church poor-box, and disobeys his creator. McDaid is a metafictional anti-hero who refuses to be oppressed, or as he says to the incredulous Brother Barnabas: 'Well, I'm old-fashioned enough to believe that your opinions don't matter.'[53]

This is only the start of the revolt. The stock romantic hero, the dashing Shaun Svoolish, decides to reject his arranged marriage to the beautiful Shiela [sic]. The author-god is hurt and outraged: 'I gave her dimples, blue eyes, blond hair and a beautiful soul. [. . .] You now throw the whole lot back in my face.'[54] Shaun, too, is aware of his existential autonomy, and begins to deconstruct his own romantic stereotype: 'I may be a prig [. . .] but I know what I like. Why can't I marry Bridie and have a shot at the Civil Service?'[55] Tyrannical author that he is, Barnabas will have no democratic civil disobedience in his text, and threatens to write Shaun out of existence by having him run over by a train. Dissent quickly spreads, and Barnabas is faced with treason from a host of minor characters, including 'a Burmese shanachy, two cornerboys, a barmaid and five bus-drivers, none of whom could give a plausible account of their movements'.[56]

Here, metafiction becomes an antidote to the tyranny of traditional realist authorship, or as Sean McMahon describes the process in *At Swim-Two-Birds*: 'Author, reader and character are all free. The despotism of the monomaniac author (like Joyce) is disallowed. His self-involvement is replaced by extroversion. The commonplace and the fantastic become two aspects of the one thing in a genial if closed universe of interchangeable parts.'[57]

Eventually the author-god is overthrown and Barnabas begins to fear for his life: 'The book is seething with conspiracy and there have been at least two whispered consultations between all the characters, including two who have not yet been officially created. [. . .] Candidly, reader, I fear my number's up.'[58] The 'dominant' of this text – the governing, representative mode of the intertextual labyrinth which binds together the centrifugal modes of discourse – is the mock Gothic, borrowing its metaphors and tone from Mary Shelley, Sheridan Le Fanu and Bram Stoker. With his last frame-breaking address to the reader, Barnabas re-affirms that Gothic mode by imagining his own impending death in a final diary entry:

> I sit at my window thinking, remembering, dreaming. Soon I go
> to my room to write. A cool breeze has sprung up from the west

[. . . .]. These, dear reader, are my last words. Keep them and
cherish them. Never again can you read my deathless prose, for
my day that has been a good day is past. Remember me and pray
for me. Adieu![59]

This short story encapsulates many of the themes developed in
the early novels. In *At Swim-Two-Birds* the beautiful Shiela [*sic*]
becomes Sheila Lamont, and fulfils a similar, objectified function,
and the metafictional character revolt is developed further. The
intertextual clash of discourses is expanded to enhance the ideological power of such metafictional narratives, or as Jim Collins writes
of this process in general: 'Collisions among quite different forms of
discourse share a common purpose – to demonstrate that our cultures are so thoroughly discourse-based that we cannot even hope
to encounter "real life" unless we investigate the ways discourses
fundamentally shape our experience.'[60] This agenda is best
explored in *The Third Policeman* but anticipated here first in
'Scenes in a Novel': fictional characters who 'seek to police the cor-
ridors'[61] of the building (houses becoming metaphors for textual
structure in both texts); the idea of a 'posthumous' narrator; and
the possibilities of topographical fragmentation with the inclusion
of mock footnotes. Most of all, this early story rips asunder the conventional borders of traditional fiction, and paves the way for a new
and radical genre of literature.

In March 1939 the Longmans Green publication of *At Swim-
Two-Birds* first appeared. After six months it had sold only 244
copies, by which time Longmans' London warehouse had been
bombed during the Blitz, and the book sank into obscurity for over
twenty years. Longmans had initially accepted the novel on the
strength of a wildly effusive report from its reader, the novelist
Graham Greene:

> It is in the line of *Tristram Shandy* and *Ulysses*: its amazing
> spirits do not disguise the seriousness of the attempt to present,
> simultaneously as it were, all the literary traditions of Ireland
> [. . .]. On all these the author imposes the unity of his own
> humorous vigour, and the technique he employs is as efficient as
> it is original. We have had books inside books before but O'Nolan
> takes Pirandello and Gide a long way further [. . .].[62]

Greene was later quoted in the dust-cover blurb of the first edition,
where significantly he pointed out the intertextual nature of its
composition: 'It is a wild, fantastic, magnificently comic notion, but

looking back afterwards one realises that by no other method could
the realistic, the legendary, the novelette have been worked in
together.'[63] Although the term 'post-modernist' had yet to be coined,
O'Brien's poetics anticipate it here. Beyond the obvious technical
flamboyance of the metafictional mode – the self-styled 'aestho-
autogamy', the autocritical deconstruction of narrative conventions,
and so on – *At Swim-Two-Birds* is above all a celebratory exploration of language. The fragmented and playfully digressive style
of the novel deliberately usurps reader expectation, and flaunts its
own eclectic make-up: pub-talk, legend, poetry, parody and pastiche
all co-exist and interact dynamically. The liberated metafictional
imagination runs amok in the ruins of the Joycean playground, and
creates a verbal work which is thematically concerned with fiction
itself. Underlying this carnival revelry is the concomitant self-
doubt engendered by its deconstructions that language is
insufficient in its capacity to generate or mediate reality. It is in
this sense that its earliest critics used the rather derogatory phrase
'anti-novel' to describe it, although its own autocritical label, 'a self-
evident sham' (*AS2B*, p. 25) is closer to the mark.

There are three main levels in this novel that overlap, and
which are used mainly for their comic/ironic interaction. The barest
description of plot is that it is a book (by Flann O'Brien) about a
man writing a book (a nameless student narrator) about a man
writing a book (Dermot Trellis). The framing story involves the
student's attempts to write a novel. In the same way that Stephen's
epiphanies in *A Portrait of the Artist as a Young Man* dictate the
textual dynamics of that book, the student's ordinary experiences
determine the progress of *his* work: fiction becomes criticism, criticism fiction. The base psychodynamics of fiction making are
mirrored in the way that the character of Dermot Trellis is based
on the student's uncle in 'real' life – the uncle himself a parody of
the uncle figure who looms large in Joyce's *Dubliners*. The organic
transference from 'life' (a fiction) to 'art' (a fiction of a fiction) is
reflected in the way that the student's everyday experiences shape
the narrative, e.g. 'I hurt a tooth in the corner of my jaw with a
lump of the crust I was eating. This recalled me to the perception of
my surroundings' (*AS2B*, p. 10).

The hero of the student's novel, Dermot Trellis, is himself
writing a 'clarion-call' to the Irish people on the consequences of
sin, and he has some peculiar notions – inherited from his creator –
about textual composition. While Trellis finds it necessary to create
a villain and a heroine, he cannot be bothered 'creating' any other

original characters. In collaboration with another imaginary author, William Tracy, Trellis plagiarises from a diverse range of genres, populating his text with characters such as the Pooka (an Irish folkloric devil); the legendary Finn MacCool; cowboys extrapolated from paperback Westerns; and the mad King Sweeny, hero of the medieval Irish romance *The Frenzy of Sweeny*.

Trellis keeps these characters locked up in his hotel, 'The Red Swan Inn', but almost vampirically they move independently of Trellis when he is asleep. Trellis had created the beautiful Sheila Lamont in order to have her seduced by the evil Furriskey, believing that the moral authority of his tract would only be digestible if it contained a decent dollop of 'smut' (*AS2B*, p. 35). Trellis, however, grows obsessed with Sheila himself, and rapes her. He then kills her off to cover up his crime, but not before she gives birth to their son, Orlick. Orlick is persuaded by the other characters to exert a bizarre Oedipal revenge by writing his father into a courtroom drama, and Dermot Trellis goes on trial for crimes against literary humanity. The whole affair literally goes up in smoke when Trellis's maid accidentally burns the manuscript of his novel, allowing the student narrator a convenient way of closing his text.

One of O'Brien's aims here is to consciously blur, with autocritical signposts for the harassed reader, the distinctions between the real and projected worlds, and thereby mock the linguistic conventions on which both 'illusions' are constructed. To buttress this mockery he develops multiple parodies of existing literature (especially Joyce), as well as a sustained critique of realism and other forms of professional writing. The success of the novel depends on the ironic and absurd interlocking between these intertextual matrices, and as Anne Clissmann has recorded, 'By the time the book ends it has presented some thirty-six different styles and forty-two extracts'.[64] In a letter to Ethel Mannin, O'Brien himself declared it to be 'a belly-laugh or high-class literary pretentious slush, depending on how you look at it'.[65]

Although *At Swim-Two-Birds* was immediately hailed as a masterpiece by several established writers, the general critical reception derided (and misconstrued) its Joycean undertones, and tended to condemn the work as inferior imitation. The *Times Literary Supplement* declared that the only exceptional aspect was its 'schoolboy brand of mild vulgarity',[66] while the *Observer* critic remarked that it 'has been compared to *Tristram Shandy* and *Ulysses*. It is not equal to either [. . .] and I should reluctantly put him among the bores'.[67] Accusations of Joycean slavishness were the norm, with the *New Statesman* lamenting that its 'Long passages in imitation of Joycean parody of early Irish epic are devastatingly dull, passages slavishly following Joyce's love of snotgreen squalor are worse still'.[68] Seán Ó Faoláin, the leading Irish realist, seemed to sum up the general consensus when he commented that while it had its moments, the book had 'a general odour of spilt Joyce all over it'.[69]

At Swim-Two-Birds had a small re-issue on the American market in 1951, but not until the MacGibbon & Kee edition of 1960 did it get a more favourable critical response. It has subsequently become one of the most revered works in the Irish canon, and something of a case study in scholarly debates on metafiction. The tragedy of its erratic publishing history and the initial critical hostility left O'Brien quite embittered, particularly with the Joycean comparisons. Ironically, Joyce himself had declared O'Brien to be 'a real writer, with the true comic spirit',[70] but when Samuel Beckett met O'Brien in Dublin and passed on Joyce's praise, O'Brien already had enough of the Joycean debate, and reportedly snarled: 'Joyce, that refurbisher of skivvies' stories!'[71]

O'Brien's second novel, *The Third Policeman*, was composed in 1939 and completed by January 1940, and in anticipation of a rejection slip he had already briefed his publishers that 'there will be no question of the difficulty or "fireworks" of the last book'.[72] In the same letter, he described the novel simply as a 'very orthodox murder mystery' – although on the surface it seems anything but. The novel opens with another nameless narrator announcing that he is a murderer. In a rambling, fragmented account he relates how he and his partner, John Divney, had murdered and robbed a farmer, old Phillip Mathers, for the contents of his mysterious black box. The nameless narrator – henceforth known as 'Noman' for the sake of convenience – tells us he needed the money to publish the definitive work on an eccentric idiot-genius philosopher known as de Selby. The novel is elliptical in design and it is only at the very end that the reader discovers that Noman has been dead all along as he narrates his tale, killed by a booby-trap bomb planted in the black box by Divney. The bulk of the tale concerns Noman's punishment at the hands of three absurd policemen: supernatural and devilish characters who inhabit and police 'The Parish', an uncanny hell-world of Noman's own making. At the end of the novel both Noman and the reader understand that he must endure this torment for eternity, repeating his macabre odyssey *ad infinitum*: 'Hell goes round and round. In shape it is circular and by nature it is interminable, repetitive and very nearly unbearable.'[73]

Contrary to O'Brien's assertion that this novel was without the 'difficulty or "fireworks"' of *At Swim-Two-Birds*, this is actually a more radical and involved metafictional fantasy, and it was subsequently rejected by his publishers: 'We realise the author's ability but think that he should become less fantastic and in this novel he is more so.'[74] Disheartened by a series of rejections, O'Brien concocted a bizarre anecdote describing how he had lost the manuscript while on holidays, and shelved the project. After his death in 1966 his wife sent the typescript to MacGibbon & Kee, and it was published posthumously in 1967. As Thomas Kilroy wrote in 1968:

> *The Third Policeman* is a masterpiece. And here is a writer that makes nonsense of conventional categories, [. . .] (with Beckett) the only writer since the days of Yeats and Joyce who is of considerable international importance. It used to be said with a certain amount of native satisfaction that [. . .] the man had failed to fulfil himself. Well, here it is, in case anyone still doubts, a beautifully written, terrifying, comic novel of the first order.[75]

O'Brien's third novel, *An Béal Bocht*, was written in Irish, and first published in 1941. During his lifetime the author continually resisted attempts to have him translate it into English, maintaining that the very texture of the language made it untranslatable, though it was eventually interpreted by Patrick C. Power in 1973, under the title *The Poor Mouth*. Like his previous two novels, it is primarily linguistic and intertextual in design, and is a uniquely imaginative and idiosyncratic take on his beloved Irish language. As Breandán Ó Conaire wrote:

> To appreciate the full force and complexity of this creation it is necessary to have some knowledge of a number of specific themes and modes in Irish literature, a good grasp of modern writing in Irish and a reasonable acquaintance with some of the most characteristic aspects of modern Irish society, say, from the late nineteenth century to the late nineteen-thirties. To savour all the innuendoes, barbs, references, insinuations, and word magic something approaching a running commentary is probably necessary [. . .].[76]

As in some of Myles na Gopaleen's 'Cruiskeen Lawn' columns, the satire is mostly levelled at the woolly-headed, woolly-jumpered *gaeilgeoirs* (Irish-language enthusiasts) who espoused a rather

suffocating view of Irish culture: linguistic Luddites and conservative bigots who, in O'Brien's opinion, inhibited rather than
promoted the survival of the Irish Free State's official 'First
Language'. As O'Brien wrote in a letter to Seán O'Casey (who had
lavishly praised the book): 'it is an honest attempt to get under the
skin of a certain type of "Gael", which I find the most nauseating
phenomenon in Europe. I mean the baby-brained dawnburst
brigade who are ignorant of everything, including the Irish language itself.'[77] Unsurprisingly, the same 'Gaels' failed to be amused
by the satire when it was first published, although it is proclaimed
nowadays as a genuinely new departure in modern Irish writing.
By virtue of its scholarship, satire and verbal ferocity, it forcibly
dragged a decaying tradition into alignment with a more modern
urban consciousness. In so doing, it debunked the anachronistic
myths of a recalcitrant culture, and offered a viable, alternative literary tradition.

The fourth novel, *The Hard Life* (1961) appeared some twenty
years later. Still virtually unrecognised beyond a select cult following, O'Brien's work was beginning to suffer, and this novel is
markedly inferior to his previous experimental fiction. *The Hard
Life* is the story of two orphaned brothers, Manus and Finbarr, who
are in the care of their uncle, Mr Collopy. In picaresque fashion it
charts their bleak and sordid progression through their schooldays
until Manus's emigration to England, where he intends to make his
fortune through various entrepreneurial scams and dubious inventions. This ties in rather loosely with the other parallel plot, where
Mr Collopy and his Jesuit friend, Father Fahrt, go to Rome to plead
the indulgence of the Pope. They wish to receive a papal blessing
for Collopy's dream of social engineering: the construction of more
public toilets in Dublin for women. The novel ends with Collopy's
death, caused by the disastrous side-effects of one of Manus's hare-
brained schemes, the so-called 'Gravid Water' – a weight-control
drug which 'properly administered was calculated to bring about a
gradual and controlled increase in weight' (*HL*, p. 119). Collopy's
weight surges up to twenty-nine stone, and during a violin recital
in Rome he falls to his death through a wooden floor.

This lacklustre and chaotic novel finally crawls to a close with
the brothers less upset over their complicity in this 'tragedy', and
more excited at being the beneficiaries of Collopy's estate. The best
that can be said of this text is that it at least tried to live up to its
ungainly sub-title, *An Exegesis of Squalor*. As a belated response
to initial criticisms of the still unpublished *The Third Policeman*,

The Hard Life involves a dramatic and regressive shift to an uncomfortable brand of comic realism, mixed in with a tentative and confused satire of post-colonial Irish society. The primary narrative – a bleak and sordid comedy – is undermined by its rather drab and long-winded satire of the Catholic Church, and the overall effect remains starkly limited in its horizons, sadly unfunny, and seemingly devoid of any coherent focus. Its structural chaos and rather childish vulgarity are largely a consequence of O'Brien's hidden agenda – an attempt to provoke the Censorship Board into slapping a ban on the book, thus earning him (he hoped) a certain regenerative notoriety. (This rather bizarre state of affairs will be discussed in detail in the next chapter.) At any rate, the book was not banned (much to O'Brien's dismay), just ignored, and it remains a sad testament to a squandered and embittered talent.

The final novel published during the author's lifetime, *The Dalkey Archive* (1964), is a radical re-writing of the still unpublished *The Third Policeman*. In its own right *The Dalkey Archive* is an acceptable improvement on *The Hard Life*, but in terms of the masterpiece from which it is culled it seems structurally flawed and anecdotal, and it lacks the verbal intricacies of the original. *The Dalkey Archive* is essentially a pilfered pastiche of disparate thematic elements from *The Third Policeman*, weakly re-cast in a new context. A more 'realist' version of *The Third Policeman*, this novel is narrated (for the first time in O'Brien's novel writing) in the third person, and located in the physical reality of Dalkey rather than the unearthly, fluctuating interzone of The Parish. Less mythopoeic, it lacks the vibrant linguistic and intertextual cohesion of *The Third Policeman*, and thus loses the controlled, satirical precision that made the original work such a stimulating proposition in the first place.

Many of the idiosyncratic elements of *The Third Policeman* re-emerge, in diluted form: a new version of the 'Atomic Theory' (now the 'Mollycule Theory'); a reconfigured and actualised version of de Selby (now written as 'De Selby'); and a variation of Sergeant Pluck in Sergeant Fottrell. The most notable addition is the inclusion of James Joyce as a character – a retrospective bardic revenge on the author whom O'Brien felt had unfairly overshadowed his own work. O'Brien presents us here with an imagined, deconstructed parody of Joyce, a mild-mannered and feeble-minded caricature who occupies himself by slavishly repairing and washing the clothes of the Jesuit Order he wishes to join. This convoluted metaphor is presumably intended to represent the defrocked high priest of modernism, washing his dirty Jesuitic laundry in public. Leaving aside the comic viciousness of the lampoon, O'Brien's reflections on the value of having the author around to resolve the critical 'problems' of his work make a valid point about criticism in general and about the Joycean industry in particular – or, as the protagonist Mick says: 'I've read some of the stupid books written *about* Joyce and his work, mostly by Americans. A real book about Joyce, springing from many long talks with him, could clear up misunderstandings and mistakes, and eliminate a lot of stupidity' (*DA*, pp. 103–4).

Like Noman in *The Third Policeman*, Mick in *The Dalkey Archive* plans to write a book about a legendary and elusive figure (Joyce), at the eventual cost of his own spiritual well-being. One of the issues autocritically dramatised here is the critical concept known as the 'Intentional Fallacy', i.e. that 'the design or intention of the author is neither available nor desirable as a standard for judging the success of a work of literary art'.[78] O'Brien returns to his suspicion that Joyce is an inaccessible, elitist icon who has become more important than his books. With deliberate irony the O'Brien 'Joyce', instead of cleaning up the interpretative slums of criticism, actually compounds the issue by disclaiming the work and denying authorship entirely. *The Dalkey Archive* thus dramatises the problematic author/text relationship, with O'Brien firmly asserting the primacy of the text over the legend of authorship – plus he gets one final dig in at Joyce. This portrait of Joyce as a retrogressive, Catholic pedant reflects O'Brien's personal ambivalence towards his hero/nemesis. Obviously embittered by the eternal critical comparisons with Joyce, O'Brien makes the sour rebuke that Joyce's much-vaunted complexity is nothing more than the dishonest pedantry of a megalomaniac author, sustained by a sycophantic academic industry.[79]

Before his death in 1966 O'Brien had been working on another novel, provisionally entitled *Slattery's Sago Saga*, an extract of which was later published in *Stories and Plays* (1973). A thinly veiled satire of the Kennedy era, the existing fragment is uninspiring, enormously long-winded, and marred by a cynical and ugly misogyny – a recurrent feature of his previous novels which will be discussed in detail in the next chapter.

In the year after his death O'Brien's reputation underwent something of a revival. In 1967 Penguin published a popular edition of *At Swim-Two-Birds*, and MacGibbon & Kee finally released *The Third Policeman* to a growing readership. Despite the unfortunate series of events that prevented O'Brien from enjoying mainstream success during his lifetime, the release of *The Third Policeman* consolidated and encouraged a new critical appreciation of his work. Until recently the academic focus has been almost exclusively devoted to studies of *At Swim-Two-Birds*, although on the ground the general consensus amongst the Plain People of Ireland is an instinctive awareness that *The Third Policeman* remains the best kept secret of Irish literature, and as of late critics have had to reconsider their position on O'Brien.

2. 'Is it about a bicycle?': censorship, sex and the metonymic code

> *'Is it about a bicycle?' he asked.*
> Last line of *The Third Policeman*

Although formalist expositions of style and structure provide a useful framework of analysis for the metafictional poetics of texts like *At Swim-Two-Birds* and *The Third Policeman*, such critiques invariably decontextualise the work by placing it within a broader-based tradition of experimental writing, with little or no reference to the local constituency that helped shape the writer's vision. Unlike Joyce or Beckett, O'Brien never emigrated to Europe, and so his strategies of 'silence, exile and punning'[1] are, by necessity, of a different order. A civil servant by profession, living and working in Dublin, O'Brien's absorption of continental stylistics developed from discussions of European literature in the pubs of Dublin rather than from direct experience in the cafés of Paris. Moreover, it is an Irish pub-talk culture that partly informs the native idiosyncrasies of his prose – a syncretic tribal language which will not gladly yield its more intimate secrets to the Russian Formalist razor. What we need to develop is an Irish brand of formalism.

As previously discussed, although Flann O'Brien rejects the cosy, cottage-industry idealism of O'Connor and Ó Faoláin, this does not mean that he wholeheartedly embraces the cosmopolitan consciousness of Joyce's modernist aesthetic. As J.C.C. Mays wrote: 'Joyce is inevitably to be preferred on the level of artistry, but on the level of day-to-day and time-to-eternity living Brian O'Nolan looks for his values nearer home.'[2] Ideologically speaking, as a writer whose exile was interior, O'Brien's work reflects the cultural burdens of the indigenous Irish writer better than Joyce's or Beckett's ever could, and so it seems worthwhile to replant him in this Irish context. For critic Rüdiger Imhof this may well be a moot point: 'It would be fruitless to quarrel about which of the two possible traditions – the Irish comic tradition or the international tradition of parodic literature or metaliterature – is the more appropriate one.'[3] However, it is precisely within the space created between the quarrel of these two traditions that the complicated psychodynamics of O'Brien's emergent post-modernism lies. The friction between Irish comedy and European metaliterature produces a fruitful synergy, which has implications for both traditions.

With the benefit of critical hindsight, it seems fair to assert that by 1941 Flann O'Brien had reached his critical zenith as a novelist. By that time he had written three of the most innovative novels of the Irish canon, but in terms of public acclaim it was as if he had never existed: *At Swim-Two-Birds* (1939) remained relatively obscure; *The Third Policeman* (written 1940) was to remain unpublished until after his death; and *An Béal Bocht* (1941), by virtue of its Gaelic mode, was marginalised as inaccessible, even by the handful of people who could have appreciated its nuances. These circumstances would adversely affect both the quantity and quality of his later work, *The Hard Life* (1961) and *The Dalkey Archive* (1964). To begin to understand the ideological forces that shaped O'Brien's writing it is well worth considering the composition and design of *The Hard Life*, and the strange context from which it emerged.

As a strategy to meet his publishers' horizon of expectations, O'Brien's shift to a more realist form of representation in *The Hard Life* is understandable; after all, Longmans had previously refused the manuscript of *The Third Policeman* on the grounds that O'Brien 'should become less fantastic'.[4] This is not to say that *The Hard Life* is without its fantastical elements – the Mylesian 'Gravid Water' for instance – but even this lacks his former inventive panache (both literally and figuratively speaking). Otherwise, the nearest this text gets to the Irish fantastical tradition is in its Swiftian fascination with bodily functions, which was part of the squalid design intended to outrage and offend its readership. According to Anthony Cronin, this rather childish rationale was inspired by O'Brien's active and conscious desire to provoke the Irish Censorship Board into banning his novel, and he manipulated his text in such a way as to gratuitously insert material which he imagined would offend public taste and decency: 'He now began to nourish the hope that this new book would be banned in Ireland. [. . .] Nearly every professional Irish author had had a book banned and [O' Brien's] gleeful anticipation of the prospect makes it clear that he was anxious to join the club.'[5]

It seems absurd that an author should wish to see his own work censored, but for the most part I think Cronin is correct in his assumptions. To understand this strange state of affairs it is necessary to understand the complex censorship codes in operation at that time, and their effect on the production and consumption of literature in Ireland.

The Hard Life (of censorship culture)

One major consequence of Irish censorship culture was that modernism almost passed Ireland by. As the bigoted Mr Deasy says to Stephen Dedalus in *Ulysses*, Ireland was 'the only country which never persecuted the Jews. Do you know that? No. And do you know why? [. . .] Because she never let them in'.[6] Lest we forget, *Ulysses* itself was never officially banned in Ireland, simply kept out. In fact, most state libraries and bookshops maintained this unofficial ban until 1966: the fiftieth anniversary of the Easter Rising and the year of Flann O'Brien's death.[7]

With the establishment of the Censorship of Publications Act in 1929, the newly established Irish Free State embarked on a policy of cultural protectionism – aptly described by Robert Graves in 1950 as 'the fiercest literary censorship this side of the Iron Curtain'.[8] By 1946 over 1,700 titles were proscribed on the grounds of 'indecency', including most of the leading international modernists: Beckett, Faulkner, Greene, Hemingway, Huxley, Joyce (for *Stephen Hero*), Kafka, Lawrence, Mann, Maugham, Nabokov, Proust, Scott Fitzgerald and Steinbeck, to mention but a few.[9]

The 'Censorship of Publications Act' (1929), which still operates (with amendments),[10] provides for the banning of literature on three basic grounds:

1 any book or writing which is deemed to be 'in its general tendency indecent or obscene';
2 if such writings advocate 'the unnatural prevention of conception' (amended by the Health Act of 1979) or 'the procurement of abortion';
3 or if such material devotes 'an unduly large proportion of space to the publication of matters relating to crime'.

There were obvious semantic difficulties in defining such relative concepts as 'indecent', so guidelines were established which defined it as 'suggestive of, or inciting to sexual immorality or unnatural vice or likely in any other similar way to corrupt or deprave'.[11] The key word here, in practice, was 'sexual', for anything signifying even the remotest sexual content was dubbed indecent, and thus liable to be banned. Paradoxically, this obsession with sexual censorship in itself seems fetishistic; as Frank O'Connor – himself a victim of censorship – has noted, 'there is a more than casual affinity between the pathological censor and the pathological pornographer'.[12]

O'Connor's point is well made. In January 1937, Leslie Montgomery – a writer (who wrote under the pen-name 'Lynn Doyle') and a previous opponent of censorship – was appointed to the Censorship Board. A month later Montgomery resigned in despair, and issued the following statement, which outlined the actual mechanisms of censorship:

> The books are sent to the Minister [for Justice] by private objectors in different parts of the country. A permanent official marks, by writing folio numbers on a card, passages that he thinks come under the Act [. . .]. It is nearly impossible to report on 'general tendency' after reading the marked passages. Even when one reads the book through afterwards one is under the influence of the markings.[13]

From this moment on, Flann O'Brien – himself a high-ranking civil servant – would have known that he was, literally and figuratively, a 'marked man'. O'Brien never had a novel banned in Ireland – or at least not yet (the laws remain on the statute books) – but this is far from saying that censorship, and/or a censorship mentality, does not impinge on his writing. The legislation enshrined in the 1929 Act ultimately viewed artistic freedom as a form of cultural terrorism, and its authoritarian ethos cast a shadow over O'Brien's freedom of expression, governing (to a certain degree) what can and cannot be explicitly expressed in his work.

Julia Carlson, editor of *Banned in Ireland: Censorship and the Irish Writer*, points out some of the real problems caused by this intellectual quarantine, but she also suggests that the Censorship Act, although draconian in itself, was merely symptomatic of much greater prohibitions which lurked in the Irish post-colonial mindscape:

> [C]ensorship in Ireland has never been simply the banning of books: the paternalism that perpetuates Irish censorship succeeded for many years in blocking the interchange of ideas between Irish society and its writers. [. . .] Censorship has created a rift in Irish society, fostering the ignorance and

provincialism of the Irish people and the intellectual and moral
alienation of Irish writers.[14]

Moreover, as writers such as Yeats, Shaw, Æ and Beckett were
keen to point out, this situation was largely the result of 'the tri-
umphalism that had infected Irish nationalists after the War of
Independence and the position of authority that the Irish Catholic
Church had assumed in the new state'.[15] Throughout the O'Brien
oeuvre there are both formal and submerged debates about the all-
pervasive nature of Irish Catholicism. On the other hand, under
censorship, there can be no such formal discussion of sex or sexuality, and this is combined with a very marked absence of women
figures. All of these features (or non-features) – Catholicism, sexuality, the representation of women – are intricately interwoven in
the novels and bound together by a male, Catholic worldview which
is sexually anxious and fraught with a dysfunctional misogyny.
These issues dominate the background silences of the texts, and
provide us with an interesting framework for analysis.

Artistically speaking, according to the novelist John Broderick,
two problems seem to arise within a pervasive censorship culture:
'One was that you would write in order to get past the censors;
therefore, you would suppress certain truths which you think
should have been told. The other one was that you would do something in order to shock them, and both these attitudes would upset
the artistic balance.'[16] Both attitudes seem to have affected the
texture of O'Brien's novels.

In terms of suppression, O'Brien once wrote to his publishers
(regarding the manuscript of *An Béal Bocht*) that he had 'cut out completely all references to "sexual matters" and made every other
change necessary to render the text completely aseptic and harmless'.[17] Rendering his texts 'aseptic and harmless' meant emasculating
any formal representation of sexual matters, but this is not to say
that the author has (or is capable of having) 'cut out completely' any
mention of sexuality or sex. Writers will always find ways of cir-
cumventing censorship through imaginative processes of invention,
euphemism and circumlocution, or by resorting to encoded metonymic discourses which allegorically substitute signifying symbols
for what is forbidden. Indeed, some writers may positively thrive
from writing within such restrictive parameters, refining their use
of language by giving a cutting edge to the commonplace.
Incidentally, I use the term 'forbidden' here mindful of both its legal
and moral senses, for this process of sublimation may also be unconscious; in all of O'Brien's novels, certain issues seep into the

background which are not always consciously projected. Such slip-
pages tend to avoid the formal narrative structures, and occupy the
margins of the text. Either consciously or unconsciously the censorship mentality exerts tremendous influence over O'Brien's work,
invariably limiting the freedom of expression available. This, of
course, is anathema to the artist; as Virginia Woolf has said, 'literature which is always pulling down blinds is not literature. All that
we have ought to be expressed – mind and body – a process of
incredible difficulty and danger'.[18]

Beyond artistic suppression, the other problem for Irish writers
working within a censorship paradigm was the perceived need to
provocatively 'shock' the censorship mandarins. In the 1950s and
60s, many professional Irish writers had at least some of their writings banned, and many now-reputable books had been removed
from the bookshop shelves. This situation mushroomed to ludicrous
proportions when it became a badge of distinction to have a book
banned. Thus in 1961, according to biographer Anthony Cronin,
Flann O'Brien actively sought the banning of his own novel, *The
Hard Life*.

To this end, O'Brien invented a character called 'Fr Kurt Fahrt',
and as he gleefully wrote to his friend and editor Timothy O'Keeffe
in 1961: 'The name will cause holy bloody ructions here. It will lead
to wirepulling behind the scenes here to have the book banned as
obscene.'[19] O'Brien intended to appeal any subsequent banning
order in court, protesting that it was neither obscene nor blasphemous, and thereby expose the ethos of the Censorship Board as
archaic, sectarian and lacking in aesthetic acumen.[20] In any event
the book was *not* banned, much to his disappointment, but what is
more important here is the degree of strategic textual manipulation, which goes well beyond scatological naming.

While most critics agree that *The Hard Life* is both structurally
flawed and thematically erratic, it does have a certain integrity in
that there is at least an attempt by O'Brien – textual emasculations
notwithstanding – to formally critique the all-pervasive nature of
Irish Catholicism (this mood of dissent seems to inform the landscape of all of his novels, usually surreptitiously). Where the novel
flounders is in its lacklustre characterisation, especially its depiction of the first-person narrator, Finbarr. Finbarr is never allowed
to develop a believable personality and remains a cardboard caricature, despite O'Brien's attempt to trace his picaresque development
from childhood to adulthood in a rather lame parody of Joyce's
Dubliners and *A Portrait of the Artist as a Young Man*. The

parallels with the Joycean texts stress O'Brien's fascination with the Irish Catholic experience: the brutal cruelties of Finbarr's education at the hands of the Christian Brothers, the pedantic theological debates between Mr Collopy and Fr Fahrt, and the general atmosphere of paralysis (culled from *Dubliners*) that this ideology exerts over all human relationships. Subtitled *An Exegesis of Squalor*, the text reeks of what Joyce called the 'odour of ashpits and old weeds and offal',[21] and this is combined with a Swiftian disgust at bodily functions which constantly alludes to a simmering but repressed sexuality. O'Brien even briefly considers a possible root cause of this dysfunctional sexual discomfort: a society moulded by the eccentricities of religious celibates.

This Joycean framework of Catholic angst lends itself to a succession of one-liners and wisecracks on the twin themes of repression and escape, with mixed success. The duel between craven piety and crass materialism does have its incisive comic moments, particularly in its depiction of Edwardian Dublin's Catholic middle class: 'From his waistcoat [Collopy] extracted two pennies and presented one to each of us. —I cross your hands with earthly goods, he said, and at the same time I put my blessings on your souls. —Thanks for the earthly goods, the brother said' (*HL*, p. 17). Middle-class hypocrisy is foregrounded through the novel's rendering of social institutions such as marriage, which highlights the incompatibility of a redundant but residual Victorian modesty: 'An ill-disposed might suspect that they [Mr Collopy and Mrs Crotty] were not married at all and that Mrs Crotty was a kept-woman or resident prostitute. But that is quite unthinkable, if only because of Mr Collopy's close interest in the Church and in matters of doctrine and dogma' (*HL*, p. 20).

The treatment of these and other related issues is erratic and episodic, and there seems to be no central focus through which the disparate threads of the narrative pull together. Isolating the most incisive and memorable moments of the book one might venture to say that it is meant to be a critique of the Irish Catholic experience, but one that fails through coyness, reticence and the disorganisation of resources. The narrative progression of the narrator and 'the brother' is overtaken (and overwhelmed) by Collopy's messianic mission to Rome, where he pleads Papal indulgence on behalf of the dispossessed women of Dublin. While obviously in keeping with the overall theme, the detail of this subplot radically disrupts the primary narrative of the two brothers.

The comic denouement of Collopy's death in Rome, depicted with characteristically violent imagery, was probably intended to show

the underlying influence of the Vatican in Irish affairs, but its execution is clumsy. Symbolically, this wayward insert seems to
suggest that in the final analysis Home Rule is indeed subverted by
Rome Rule, the final arbiter of social and sexual politics. Although
nominally set in Edwardian Dublin – the novel begins in 1890,
when the narrator is five years old, and ends in 1910 after Collopy's
death – *The Hard Life* is really a post-colonial satire of de Valera's
Ireland (with its anti-pluralist constitution which privileged the
role of the Catholic Church). However, this tentative post-colonial
critique ultimately exposes the novel's soft underbelly, and its constant shirking of its own potential. Its radical possibilities seem
squandered by O'Brien's inability to remain single-minded, and by
his perceived need to play the clown. There is also a strange pruri-
ence that devalues the sincerity of his critique: Collopy's liberal
mission to Rome is neither a progressive reformation nor a feminist
revolution – he merely wishes to provide more public toilets for
women, with the imprimatur of Rome. Anthony Cronin thinks otherwise, and suggests that:

> What makes the book an oddity in the O'Nolan canon is that the
> author seems to be on Mr Collopy's side. He, more than the
> brother or the narrator, is the book's informing spirit, the comic
> creation which makes us remember it with affection. Mr Collopy
> accepts the bodily necessities of woman as a proper subject for
> social concern. Through Mr Collopy the book's author had made
> an act of acceptance too. To the emancipated liberal it will doubt-
> less not seem a great deal; but in terms of Brian O'Nolan's
> general outlook it is both significant and important.[22]

This is a good example of the innate weakness of biographical
criticism. Reading the actual text, it seems clear that Collopy's
humanitarian gestures towards women are portrayed in the novel
as the impotent bluster of the middle-class liberal intellectual (or
pseudo-intellectual), and there is no hidden feminist agenda as far
as I can discern. On the contrary, while Collopy (or Collopy/O'Nolan
if we are to trust Cronin) formally espouses feminist liberation, the
language he uses is completely misogynistic. These qualities
abound in all of O'Brien's novels, but oddly there is an absence of
any sustained feminist criticism of his work. As Sean McMahon has
observed:

> O'Brien is a cultish and vigorously defended national treasure
> which is beyond criticism. The literary historian may merely
> note that the world is a male one, a middle-aged one and an

asexual one, and one in which the place of women is enough to cause even the mildest feminist to choke with spleen.[23]

Given the pervasive male bias of this literature, as well as its apolitical criticism, it is hardly surprising that the experience of being Irish in literature is usually equated with the experience of being male. Therefore it seems important to look beyond the obvious narrative structures for the 'not-said': the silences, gaps and omissions that lurk behind this male epistemology – an epistemology which implicitly assumes that gender differences in culture are natural, and which pretends that these differences do not impinge on our reading. Indeed, as Judith Fetterley notes: 'In such fictions the female reader is co-opted into participation in an experience from which she is explicitly excluded; she is asked to identify with a selfhood that defines itself in opposition to her, she is required to identify against herself'.[24] Certainly, on an anecdotal level, many readers of Flann O'Brien – both female and male – have expressed to me their vague discomfort with the masculinist tone of his writings, but were at a loss to say why specifically, beyond the absence of any realistic women characters. From this general uneasiness alone, I suggest that a feminist reading of O'Brien is long overdue.

Bearing these remarks in mind, there exists in *The Hard Life* (and in the other novels) a surface commitment by O'Brien as a cultural observer to show the structures and ideologies which underlie his society, but in the language and imagery he employs to represent women the background noises are decidedly misogynistic. O'Brien is both observer and participant, and his apparent inability to discuss gender roles and sexuality in a serious fashion leads to a giddy frustration which seems to manifest itself, consciously and/or unconsciously, in a number of unsettling ambiguities and double meanings. As critic Wayne Koestenbaum has observed (in a different but related context): 'Certain desires and dreads follow in the double signature's wake: hysterical discontinuity, muteness, castratory violence, homoerotic craving, misogyny, a wish to usurp female generative power.'[25] As we shall see, all of these desires and dreads are present in O'Brien's novels.

Mr Collopy's humanism, for example – his desire to give women 'fair play' (*HL*, p. 42) – is undermined by an essential linguistic misogyny which continually sees women as either madonnas or whores, and his benevolent patriarchal views become both patronising and sordid. Collopy believes that it is the scandalous lack of public toilets which prevents women's participation in politics, as it prohibits them from comfortably attending political street meetings. In fact, Collopy asserts, the only type of woman likely to attend such meetings would be a prostitute: 'Only men go to public meetings. No lady would be found dead at a public meeting. You know that? You would only find prostitutes hanging around' (*HL*, p. 39). Collopy's theorising is in part a satirical reflection of a popular O'Brien theme, i.e. intellectual misunderstanding, which he typically mocks with a favourite weapon, the *reductio ad absurdum* (or 'absurd reduction'). For Collopy, women are either 'ladies' (passive and genteel) or 'prostitutes' (active but immoral), and indeed there is a peculiar fixation with prostitution throughout the text. For example, when Collopy suspects that Manus has pornographic books in the house he bellows: 'If those books are dirty books, lascivious peregrinations on the fringes of filthy indecency, cloacal spewings in the face of Providence, with pictures of prostitutes in their pelts, then out of this house they will go and their owner along with them' (*HL*, p. 67). Collopy is mistaken (it is *his* fixation), as Manus is more interested in money than pornography, although when Manus emigrates to England his cultural conditioning allows him to see how sex and money can be mutually inclusive: 'if that sort of thing [sexual harassment] was the custom of the country, she might as well get paid for it', he says of one Irish prostitute (*HL*, pp. 102–3).

The virgin/whore dichotomy is perpetually foregrounded in this novel, and at one point Collopy himself actually acknowledges this brutal perception: '[Men] have only two uses for women, Father – either to go to bed with them or else thrash the life out of them' (*HL*, p. 39). Within this binary opposition 'thrashing' becomes a substitute for sex, and Collopy suggests that male sexual anger can easily degenerate into violence – a theme which reverberates throughout O'Brien's fiction. Despite his supposed liberal values, however, Collopy's own misogyny manifests itself again and again in his speech. During one of the tiresome theological debates between Collopy and Fr Fahrt, for example, Collopy's casual mockery of the priest reflects his underlying attitudes in the crude simile he uses: 'An humble Jesuit would be like a dog without a tail or a woman without her knickers on her' (*HL*, p. 35).

Perhaps O'Brien's intention here is to portray Collopy as a typical blustering liberal, guilty of all the sins he professes to abjure. On the other hand, the same could be said of the author, and there seems to be a suspicion on O'Brien's part that feminism and the New Woman are even more dangerous than blustery liberalism. Take the figure of Mrs Flaherty, for example, who, we are told, is a 'friend' of Emmeline Pankhurst. As a representation of feminism, Mrs Flaherty is simply portrayed as a lunatic who wishes to bomb City Hall: 'Blow all the bastards up. Slaughter them. Blast them limb from limb' (*HL*, p. 71).

This scene provides an excuse for yet another Fahrt/Collopy dialectic on Church history, and it is apparent that O'Brien's strategy is to constantly refer these issues back to the idea of a cruel, ruling Catholic dogma. Collopy's incipient but ineffectual liberal compassion is set against the dominant conservative ideology, which sees suffering, including the oppression of women, as necessary and good in itself; or as Fr Fahrt says: 'in a scheme to eradicate serious evil sometimes we must all suffer. [. . .] It is not pleasant but it is salutary' (*HL*, p. 36). This entrenched sado-masochistic absolutism is stressed throughout the novel. In this context, the Church cannot provide a solution for it is part of the problem, and O'Brien is keen to stress the harsh brutality of a doctrine which operates under the guise of compassion. With typical irony he has Finbarr recall his theological instructions from the Christian Brothers, who taught him 'what the early Christians went through in the arena by thrashing the life out of me' (*HL*, p. 23). Again, the repetition of the phrase 'thrashing' reminds us of Collopy's comment which equated sexual repression with male violence. Thus, by implication, O'Brien suggests that the Christian Brothers' institutional violence is a response to the pressures of their celibacy.

Fr Fahrt takes all of Collopy's attacks on the Church lightly, and he makes a telling remark when he reminds Collopy that 'At the back of it all, you are a pious, God-fearing man, may the Lord be good to you' (*HL*, p. 83). Here O'Brien demonstrates the problems of traditional Catholicism in a rapidly changing environment. Collopy is the product of a Catholic ethos, but his personal beliefs are plunged into crisis by emerging liberal values. Although burdened with Catholic guilt, Collopy tries to conceive of his feelings in liberal terms – at times expressing himself with passionate eloquence, but at other times lapsing back into a bigoted but reassuring dogmatism (again, perhaps Collopy *does* have much in common with his author). At his best, Collopy puts his finger on the pulse of the problem: 'They say piety has a smell, Mr Collopy mused, half to himself. It's a perverse notion. What they mean is only the absence of the smell of women' (*HL*, p. 23).

It is significant that Collopy says this only 'half to himself'. Platitudes are often re-invested with new meaning by O'Brien, and in this instance Collopy is addressing his more liberal half. This split personality manifests itself in Collopy's behaviour, and particularly in his attitudes to sexuality and women: at times liberal, at times reactionary. This contemplation of clerical celibacy is important but the point is left undeveloped, and O'Brien seems to merely anticipate the writings of more emancipated Irish authors who would develop these observations further. One such writer, John McGahern, had this to say regarding priestly celibacy:

> One of the things that I resent about my upbringing is that the doctrine was taught to us by celibates, and the very nature of abstinence is that it makes food or whatever it is more attractive than if you have too much of it. I actually think that it elevated a normal human appetite into an importance that distorted the reality of almost the whole of life. I think it was a very dangerous thing and a very twisted thing [. . .]. There was cultivation of sexlessness here as well because of the bachelor, simply because it wasn't economically possible for him to marry until the parents grew too old. Celibacy was admired because of economic necessity, and of course, the Church came along and copperfastened that.[26]

This idea that celibacy leads to sexual mystification and guilt is interesting with regard to Flann O'Brien himself. In his biography of O'Brien, Anthony Cronin refers to the author's prudishness, and suggests that it was simply paradigmatic of the male-orientated pub culture of the time that issues of sexuality and images of women were excluded from ordinary discourse. Again, Cronin links this exclusion to the notion of a Catholic ideology which privileged celibacy and thus made sex a fearful and confused phenomenon:

> Ireland was a country where apparent celibacy was not only accepted as a normal state, but was even encouraged as a way of life. [. . .] Aided by English Victorian prudery and perhaps the monkish asceticism inherent in Irish Christian tradition, what began as an economic imperative for smallholders became an ethos for the country as a whole. The church taught that virginity itself was a form of sanctity.[27]

Collopy's confusion with all matters sexual makes him bitterly aware that Irish Home Rule has been undermined by Rome Rule, and that this theocratic power makes a mockery of nationalist aspirations for self-determination: 'We're as fit for Home Rule here as the blue man in Africa' (*HL*, p. 19) – an ironically racist simile, using the language of colonialism to lament the effects of colonialism. Political independence is often anti-climactic because it does not necessarily lead to social liberation. After the colonial withdrawal in Ireland a power vacuum was created, and this void was filled by the Catholic Church and the urban middle classes, personified in *The Hard Life* by Fr Fahrt and Mr Collopy. The historical tragedy of decolonisation is that it often leads to a nativist ethos which is anti-pluralist, intolerant and repressive. This is ultimately the basis of O'Brien's post-colonial critique of Church power, or to phrase it in Edward Said's terms:

> To accept nativism is to accept the consequences of imperialism too willingly, to accept the very radical religious and political divisions imposed on places like Ireland [. . .] by imperialism itself. To leave the historical world for the metaphysics of essences like [. . .] Catholocism [*sic*] is, in a word, to abandon history. Most often this abandonment in the post-imperial setting has led to some sort of millenarianism, if the movement has any sort of mass base, or it has degenerated into small-scale private craziness, or into an unthinking acceptance of stereotypes, myths, animosities and traditions encouraged by imperialism.[28]

Throughout the novel, Collopy slips uncomfortably between thesis and antithesis: between Holy Catholic Ireland and liberal pluralism. Although he espouses a greater societal role for women, he treats his own daughter from his first marriage, Annie, as an unpaid skivvy, and we are not surprised by the narrator's glib comment that she 'seemed to be in a permanent bad temper' (*HL*, p. 11). The men in her family wish to protect her virginity at all costs, and crisis ensues when she begins 'consorting with cornerboys up the canal' (*HL*, p. 113). Again, remembering that O'Brien's primary intention in writing this novel was to shock his audience, the opportunity to discuss issues of desire is squandered as this episode merely becomes an excuse for a discussion on the dangers of contacting venereal disease – a rather squalid symbol of sex which reappears as a motif throughout the novel.

Annie herself acts as a surrogate mother to the two boys throughout the story, and talk of her carnality is vigorously suppressed. Throughout the entire O'Brien canon, mothers are conspicuous only by their absence – in *The Hard Life* the opening lines simply recall her death. Mother figures for O'Brien must not be tainted with even the slightest hint of sexuality, and are removed entirely; as George Bernard Shaw grimly pointed out, 'assassination is the most extreme form of censorship'.[29] As household skivvy, Annie fulfils all the obligations of wife and mother, apart from conjugal rights (although Manus plans to alter that situation too). Physically she is represented as an object of undesirability – 'a horrible, limp, lank streel of a creature' (*HL*, p. 89). Her ugly body but virtuous soul are compared to Finbarr's sexual fantasy, Penelope (whom he simply describes as a 'good hoult'), so once again the virgin/whore opposition kicks in. Finbarr is 'puzzled to think that she [Penelope] and Annie belonged to the same sex' (*HL*, p. 89), which suggests that a woman can be either sexual or domestic, but not both.

After Annie's fall from virginal grace she is depicted as a prostitute in the way that Finbarr and Manus take ownership of her after Collopy's death. Manus starts paying Annie for the domestic duties she performs, but expects something for his money. He asks Finbarr 'does she look after you all right? [. . .] Grub, laundry, socks and all that?', to which Finbarr replies: 'Of course. I live like a Lord' (*HL*, p. 155). Finally, Manus suggests that Finbarr should marry Annie for the money she has inherited from Collopy's estate, and this provokes the final image of disgust which closes the novel: 'I walked quickly but did not run to the lavatory. There, everything inside me came up in a tidal surge of vomit' (*HL*, p. 157).

In the past critics have queried this ending as being unwarranted and pointless, and imagine that O'Brien is seeking a suitably squalid image with which to close his text. However, it seems to me that this ending is neither gratuitous nor is it a moral awakening by Finbarr, but is specifically an image of sexual disgust. Until her fall from grace Annie is a mother figure to Finbarr (in which case the suggestion is spiritually incestuous), and after her fall she becomes a prostitute; either way, the thought of a sexual relationship with her physically disgusts Finbarr. Above all, sexuality – especially female sexuality – is a dark and unknowable power. As the Pope himself tells the crusading Mr Collopy: 'A good woman is a fountain of grace. But it is themselves whom they should busy about their private little affairs' (*HL*, p. 138).

The Catholic thesis finally asserts itself over Collopy's befuddled liberalism, and the message for Collopy/O'Brien is clear: probing the issue of sexuality is dangerous, and should be left well enough alone. Radical potential is glibly avoided here and O'Brien's treatment of these issues is emphatic: if you do not understand something (or fear it), then it is probably best to make a joke of it.

Vivian Mercier sees this as a common feature of Irish writing where fantasy often becomes a pretext for ribaldry: 'Purely erotic writing does not come naturally to the modern Irish [. . .]. Even in the few modern Irish writers who have treated the erotic with frank pleasure, we find a tendency to lighten the burden of passion with humour and fantasy.'[30]

By the end of *The Hard Life* we become aware of the key scatological motif employed by O'Brien to avoid any open, formal discussion of sexuality: the phrase 'private little affairs' (*HL*, p. 138) ostensibly refers to going to the toilet but symbolically signifies sexuality – a rather literalised form of 'toilet humour'. The stratagems used by O'Brien in his other novels to disguise sexual issues are much more convoluted and intricate, and this constant process of sublimation and transference may allow us a further glimpse of the dialogic evasions and ideological tensions which permeate his vision of Irish Catholic culture. In all of his novels, women figures are marginalised and stereotyped to the point that the reader begins to suspect that their exclusion may well have deeper motives in the ordering of the text. For O'Brien himself though, the exclusion of women from his work was not at all sinister or odd but actually quite straightforward, and in a remarkably disingenuous interview in 1962 he said:

> Well, women are not important in Ireland in any sense of the social determinance, if there's such a word ... What I mean is they make our breakfast and they make our beds, but they are not really formative ... [T]hey're not really a social force in this country ... [Y]ou can't leave them out but you mustn't allow them to intrude too much. It would be a very artificial book that gave women a big role.[31]

None of this, of course, can be accepted at face value. Any basic deconstruction of the values espoused in O'Brien's fiction invariably points to the absence of women as a prime concern in the author's moral universe, and he constantly alludes to the fact that this absence has tragic consequences for his male protagonists. However, the ethical force of this counter-narrative is lodged not on the level of the *fabula* or story but rather in the *syuzhet* or discourse, in what is *not* said, or as Margot Norris writes: '[such fiction] must therefore be read not as one text but as two texts: a "loud" or audible male narration challenged and disrupted by a "silent" or discounted female countertext that does not, in the end, succeed in making itself heard'.[32]

Irish culture for O'Brien does seem excessively and exhaustingly male: in all of his novels men are shown to be aggressive, intelligent and opinionated, but flawed through arrogance, pedantry, alcoholism and their apparent inability to love. Women, on the other hand, rarely feature at all, but if they do it is invariably through male eyes. The most common feature of these cartoon women is their feeble intellect, and their only 'active' attribute is their capacity for deviousness. Generally speaking, though, these voiceless creatures remain passive and objectified, and are usually discussed in the tones of a sniggering schoolboy.

There is also a causal connection made between the absence of the female and the presence of male violence. These scenes of violence are always rendered grimly comic, and even the most repugnant acts of murder (*At Swim-Two-Birds, The Third Policeman, The Poor Mouth*) and rape (*At Swim-Two-Birds, The Third Policeman*) are undercut by macabre and grotesque humour. Indeed, the psychological linkage made between sexual repression and male violence makes it axiomatic that such scenes be painted in a blackly extravagant fashion. O'Brien is above all an exponent of absurdist humour, a twentieth-century moralist of Swiftian descent who resorts to fantasy as a refuge from irrational and terrifying forces. He is also a writer firmly implanted within a certain Irish tradition of cruel humour, and, as Vivian Mercier has argued, it is precisely these macabre and grotesque qualities which give Irish comedy its raw cutting edge:

> It is true that life is cruel and ugly, but the macabre and the grotesque do not become humorous until they have portrayed life as even more cruel and ugly than it is; we laugh at their absurd exaggeration, simultaneously expressing our relief that life is, after all, not quite so unpleasant as it might be.[33]

Moreover, there are frequent overlaps between the macabre and the grotesque elements, suggesting that for the Irish writer both modes seem intimately – and perversely – connected:

> Whereas macabre humour [. . .] is inseparable from terror and serves as a defence mechanism against a fear of death, grotesque humour is equally inseparable from awe and serves as a defence mechanism against the holy dread with which we face the mysteries of reproduction. What provokes our laughter? On the one hand, our aesthetic perception of an ugliness which seems excessive and absurd; on the other hand, a release of sexual repression.[34]

Sex and violence then are intimately bound together in O'Brien's texts. His scenes of lurid violence usually begin as exaggerated parody, but quite often his initial intention gets derailed by his fascination with the act of violence itself. The humour frequently recedes as the graphic imagery takes over, transcending the narrative requirements. These scenes become oddly detached and decontextualised, reaching beyond their ostensible significance within the narrative system. They begin to exist in their own right, becoming self-publicising vignettes independent from the network of associations from which they sprang. Violence, it seems, has its own logic and meaning, and a rhetoric which is both compelling and real, e.g. the strangely cold description of suicide which closes the text of *At Swim-Two-Birds*, or the murder of Old Mathers and the mental torture of Noman awaiting execution in *The Third Policeman*. Even in *The Poor Mouth*, O'Brien's comic exegesis of Gaelic misery, the comedy often gives way to acknowledge violence as a primal energy. In the miserable, rain-sodden world of Corkadoragha there is a prohibition on the redemptive qualities of love, compassion and tenderness. It is inferred throughout the novel that this (exclusively male) brutality is the unavoidable outcome of material, spiritual and sexual deprivation, a world where violent rage becomes the only outlet for expression available, usually fuelled by copious amounts of alcohol.

In *At Swim-Two-Birds*, as in the other novels, there is a preponderance of male relationships, often uncomfortable and fraught with tension and sexual anxiety. Fathers, like mothers, are completely absent from the O'Brien canon – with the exception of a cameo appearance in *The Poor Mouth*, when Bonaparte meets his father for the first and only time during a chance encounter in prison. Father/son relationships are replaced by a variety of substitute set-ups: in *At Swim-Two-Birds* between the student narrator and his uncle; in *The Third Policeman* between the orphaned narrator and John Divney; in *The Poor Mouth* between the narrator and his grandfather; in *The Hard Life* between Manus/Finbarr and their uncle; and in *The Dalkey Archive* a whole series of male relationships between Mick, Hackett, De Selby, Joyce, Augustine, Fr Cobble, and Sergeant Fottrell. Biographical criticism has alluded to this feature sporadically, but without adequately explaining the phenomenon in terms of the texts. As Peter Costello and Peter Van de Kamp write:

It may be significant [. . .] that in O'Nolan's novels there are no identifiable parents, only uncles and brothers, and that in *At*

Swim-Two-Birds the created character is intent on destroying
its creator. Perhaps a father absent from his real world has been
erased completely from his fictional universe. Or perhaps Brian
[O'Nolan] was too close to his father to put him into fiction.[35]

First of all, it must be said that the question of character revolt
against the author in *At Swim-Two-Birds* is an integral element of
the metafictional deconstruction of traditional fiction, and not necessarily some sub-Freudian, Oedipal revenge. Second, the
preference for uncle figures as opposed to fathers can, in part, be
deciphered through a closer intertextual reading of the issue. In all
of O'Brien's work the figure of James Joyce hovers on the horizon,
probing and prodding a fictional response. The uncle/narrator relationship in *At Swim-Two-Birds* and *The Hard Life* is part of
O'Brien's parody of similar relationships in *Dubliners*, in stories
such as 'The Sisters' or 'Araby'. Whatever the psychic origins of
father figures in O'Brien's works, what remains important is the
pivotal role these characters play in their relationship with the
male narrator.

Early on in *At Swim-Two-Birds* a simple binary opposition is
established when the narrator contemplates his fellow students,
both male and female. Here, the women are simply described as
being 'modest', while the men are 'brave' and 'arrogant' (*AS2B*, pp.
33–4), and this dyad is sustained throughout as men are defined by
their active attributes and women are subordinated by their passivity. Furthermore, women are once again classified in terms of
the archetypal virgin/whore dichotomy. In order to construct his
'clarion-call to torn humanity' (*AS2B*, p. 36), Dermot Trellis creates
two characters, the evil Furriskey (who contradicts his depraved
design) and Sheila Lamont, 'a woman of unprecedented virtue
[who] is corrupted, eventually ravished and done to death in a back
lane' (*AS2B*, p. 36). Sheila is a deconstructed stereotype, culled
from the back catalogue of romantic fiction. She is a submissive,
objectified rape victim, and even within the terms of the metafictional character rebellion against the despotic author-god, this
essential passivity remains. She is designed to be raped by
Furriskey, but is raped instead by her creator, Dermot Trellis,
'about an hour after she was born and died indirectly from the
effects of the assault' (*AS2B*, p. 206).

If we assume that this episode is a deliberate deconstruction of
the compositional and ideological make-up of the traditional pot-
boiler romance, then O'Brien's portrayal of literary gender
manipulation is quite incisive. We merely have to look at the

modern equivalent, the best-selling 'Mills and Boon' series, for an illustration of just how crass this manipulation can be. As Rosalind Coward noted in 1985, a strange paradox exists in that 'The Mills and Boon romantic novels are written by, read by, marketed for, and all about women. Yet nothing could be further from the aims of feminism than these fantasies based on the sexual, racial and class submission which so frequently characterise these novels.'[36]

In *The Craft of Writing Romance* – a DIY manual for the composition of a Mills and Boon novel – the author (a woman) declares that rape, though not usual, is permissible within the stringent publishing parameters of such writing. 'Rape', she says, 'will be a shameful thing in the heroine's past, despite her innocence', to which she rather blithely adds: 'a rape scene is not a love scene'. On the other hand, she tells us that scenes of 'drug-taking should be avoided in a romance, [. . .] as well as incest, homosexuality, murder. Mass riots, mass violence or muggings do not fit into contemporary romances'.[37] Thus, according to the rigid Mills and Boon worldview, women can be rape victims but not lesbians.

Of course, it is all too easy to mock the generic strategies of such romantic fiction, but it provides a convenient entry point for an analysis of similar strategies in more critically acceptable, canonical texts. O'Brien's clever deconstruction of such literary matters operates quite effectively on a formalist/metafictional level, but where his own innate misogyny emerges is in the language and imagery used, which is partly motivated by his desire to evoke a cheap laugh. As J. Hillis Miller defines it, 'Deconstruction is not a dismantling of the structure of a text but a demonstration that it has already dismantled itself. Its apparently solid ground is no rock but thin air'.[38] What is needed, then, is a deconstruction of O'Brien's deconstructions.

Disturbingly, rape and sexual assault become ongoing leitmotifs in *At Swim-Two-Birds*. When the narrator and his friend Kelly walk the streets of Dublin for the 'discovery and embracing of virgins' – one of many parodies of Joyce's *Dubliners* – they stalk and intimidate women: 'We walked many miles together on other nights on similar missions – following matrons, accosting strangers, representing to married ladies that we were their friends, and gratuitously molesting members of the public' (*AS2B*, p. 48). Later, when the narrator offers us a comic synopsis of his work in progress – '*FOR THE BENEFIT OF NEW READERS*' – we are reminded of the fate of Sheila: 'Trellis creates Miss Lamont in his own bedroom and he is so blinded by her beauty (which is naturally the type of beauty nearest to his heart), that he so far forgets himself as to assault her himself' (*AS2B*, p. 60).

Men are again ascribed active roles, as Sheila's brother, Antony, is created by Trellis in order to avenge her honour. We also learn that a series of assaults have occurred on Peggy, 'a domestic servant', by Finn MacCool (originally introduced to protect Sheila's virtue) and Paul Shanahan – 'another man hired by Trellis for performing various small and unimportant parts in the story' (*AS2B*, p. 61). Furriskey, whose only 'task is to attack women' (*AS2B*, p. 61) resists his authorial design and falls in love with Peggy, though only after he is assured that she first tried to resist Shanahan's attack.

It is significant that while the male characters are empowered by the principle of 'aestho-autogamy' to resist their design, the female characters never confront their gender stereotyping. In fairness to O'Brien, it could be argued that he does subvert certain male mythologies on the level of the *fabula*. The narrator and Kelly, for instance, despite their constant harassment of women, never get to actually meet any, channelling their energies instead into gambling, playing billiards and sheltering in that bastion of patriarchy, the pub. Sexually frustrated at not conquering any 'real' women, they vent their frustration by collaborating in the composition of the narrator's sub-pornographic and violent fantasies. O'Brien may well be making a valid point here about sexuality and textuality, but it still makes for uncomfortable reading.

The theme of rape is continued right through until the end of the novel, when during a surreal trial-by-fiction Trellis cross-examines a material witness, a dairy cow. The cow is able to give testimony in the first place because she has been 'accorded the gift of speech by a secret theurgic process' (*AS2B*, p. 203). Her main complaint is that Trellis had neglected her as a minor character by leaving her unmilked, and as a result she had suffered great pain. Trellis tries to discredit her testimony by reference to her previous sexual history: 'There is, however, another important office discharged by the cowkeeper, a seasonal rite not entirely unconnected with the necessity for providing milk' – to which the cow retorts: 'I resent your low insinuations. I didn't come here to be humiliated and insulted' (*AS2B*, p. 204).

Trellis is subsequently called to order and chastised for introducing 'into the proceedings an element of smut' (*AS2B*, p. 205). Sex here is indeed 'smut', and as part of the general comedy a woman is casually depicted as a cow. Initially at least, this is in keeping with the author's love of wordplay, where colloquial terms often take on new, and quite literal, meanings. The 'horse-play' of corner-boys, for example, becomes the starting-point for the cowboy extract, and in much the same way the derogatory term 'cow', as a signifier for women, is made literal. There is no doubt that the cow is a fabulist symbol for a woman: she emerges from the ladies' toilet in the courthouse, and women have already been equated with cows during the cowboy sequence. This substitution of cattle for women is also something that appears marginally in *The Third Policeman*. During their visit to 'Eternity', Sergeant Pluck shows Noman the inner workings of the machines that control The Parish, and tells him about a machine which can break down the sense of touch: 'Now there is nothing so smooth as a woman's back, or so you might imagine. But if that feel is broken up for you, you would not be pleased with women's backs [. . .]. Half of the inside of the smoothness is as rough as a bullock's hips' (*3P*, p. 139). (It is doubly strange that O'Brien uses the term 'bullock' – a castrated bull – to describe the feel of a woman.)

This point is important not just in its own right, but also by way of illustrating the key strategy of evasion employed by O'Brien to circumvent direct discussion of women and sexuality. To achieve this, he creates a system of symbols built upon the ambiguities of language, a process best defined as a 'metonymic discourse'. I have appropriated this term from the wealth of feminist criticism which has emerged in recent years. In their reassessment of literary history, feminist theorists such as Elaine Showalter have been keen to stress the distinctions between 'Feminine', 'Feminist' and 'Female' phases of literature. According to Showalter, during the Feminine phase (c.1840–80):

> women wrote in an effort to equal the intellectual achievements of the male culture, and internalised its assumptions about female nature. The distinguishing sign of this period is the male pseudonym [. . .]. This masculine disguise goes well beyond the title page; it exerts an irregular pressure on the narrative, affecting tone, diction, structure and characterisation.[39]

Women writers of this period, such as George Eliot and the Brontës, developed an ingenious antidote to their exclusion by constructing an elaborate system of coded symbols, which quite often resulted in some absurd textual manipulations. According to one feminist interpretation, the main function of the Gothic mode in these otherwise realist texts is to avoid censorship through a clandestine process of euphemism: 'For the "unspeakable" sexual desires of women, Charlotte Brontë returned to [. . .] a metonymic discourse of the human body – hands and eyes for penises, "vitals" or "vital organs" for women's genitalia – often to comic effect.' By way of example, this critique offers an extract from *Jane Eyre* (1847): "'I am substantial enough – touch me". [. . .] He held out his hand laughing. "Is that a dream?", said he, placing it close to my eyes. He had a rounded, muscular, and vigorous hand, as well as a long, strong arm.'[40]

Almost a century later, Flann O'Brien employs a similar metonymic discourse as a central evasive tactic. While there were certainly very stringent codes of censorship imposed on the author in 1939 which inhibited sexual frankness, his evasion also stems from a cloistered male attitude which ultimately manifests itself as sexual nausea. Consequently, all formal discussion of the subject is deferred, with the author preferring to bask in the anonymity that the metonymic mask allows. By limiting his role in this manner he avoids direct commentary and eludes censorship, but he also tacitly accepts (and participates in) this Irish evasion of the erotic.

Another simple example of this metonymic discourse in *At Swim-Two-Birds* is Byrne's description of his bed, a symbol again for women:

> I'm not ashamed to admit that I love my bed, said Byrne. She was my first friend, my foster-mother, my dearest comforter . . . He paused and drank. Her warmth, he continued, kept me alive when my mother bore me. She still nurtures me, yielding without stint the parturition of her cosy womb. She will nurse me gently in my last hour and faithfully hold my cold body when I am dead. She will look bereaved when I am gone. (*AS2B*, p. 98)

There is tenderness within this coded extract towards the stabilising and compassionate influence of women, yet its very coded nature – stemming as it does from the juvenile sexual association between women and beds – does tend to devalue it somewhat. In the final analysis, women are either 'foster-mothers' or objects of desire; either beautiful like the passive Sheila Lamont, or repulsive if she happens to be a wife, like the 'hag' who shares the Pooka's bed: 'a black evil wrinkle in the black sackcloth quilts' (*AS2B*, pp. 103–4).

Metaphysically, this is the crux of O'Brien's attitude to sexuality – the ironic discrepancy between the spiritual ideal and the physical reality. During the debate on angelic carnality between the Pooka and the Good Fairy, the Pooka imagines what would happen as the result of union between a spirit and a human.[41] He concludes that the offspring would be invariably traumatised, 'severely handicapped by being half flesh and half spirit [. . .] since the two elements are forever at variance' (*AS2B*, p. 106). Indeed, for O'Brien, these elements must have seemed forever at variance: a spiritual and idealised notion of sexuality fuelled by mystification and denial; and a real, physical carnality which cannot be spoken of.

One typical characteristic of metafiction is the author's use of autocritical intrusions, and in this context O'Brien intervenes to teach us the code, just in case we miss the double-voiced discourse (he assumes, of course, that the more literal-minded censor will miss it). Take, for example, the narrator's description of college clubs and societies, which he suggests are pretexts for men and women to come together socially. These clubs are, he states, 'concerned with the arrangement of ball games' (*AS2B*, p. 48). The metonymic discourse is launched by the sniggering ambiguity of a single signifier – 'balls' – formally representing billiards but metonymically signifying testicles. When Brinsley admiringly comments on a billiards shot – 'Gob, *there*'s a kiss' (*AS2B*, p. 51) – O'Brien exposes his device by sending his uninitiated narrator to a dictionary to unravel the double signification: '*Extract from Concise Oxford Dictionary*: Kiss, n. Caress given with lips; (Billiards) impact between moving balls' (*AS2B*, p. 51).

Even college literary societies are an excuse for crude puns and metonymic codes, and once again the text instructs us, autocritically: 'Some [societies] were devoted to English letters, some to Irish letters and some to the study and advancement of the French language' (*AS2B*, p. 48). The metonymic displacement depends on the reader's understanding that 'French letters' is a colloquialism for condoms, and the comedy is achieved by this word play on language/letter. It is important to remember that, until 1979, literature which 'advocated' the use of contraception was likely to be banned in Ireland.[42] Such clever manipulation of language evades censorship, but tacitly affirms the censor's legitimacy by that very cleverness: O'Brien delights in linguistic game playing, but ethical integrity is sometimes sacrificed for the glory of the pun. Most of these metonymic codes do, in fact, develop from simple scatological puns, and all tend to reinforce the paradigm that men are powerful and women submissive.

Beyond the commitment to coded titillation, the sexual act itself is strenuously resisted, and even the facts of life leave the characters aghast and incapable of utterance. This distaste for the mystified subject of fascination is reflected throughout the novel, particularly in the discussion of 'aestho-autogamy'. Trellis, a moralist and a rapist, is so appalled by sex that he 'at last realized his dream of producing a living mammal from an operation involving neither fertilization nor conception' (*AS2B*, p. 40). Aestho-autogamy becomes the satirical ideal of a celibate utopia, where there would be no need for sex, contraception, or feminism: 'Those mortifying stratagems collectively known as birth control would become a mere memory if parents and married couples could be assured that their legitimate diversion would straightaway result in finished breadwinners and marriageable daughters' (*AS2B*, p. 41). This is literary genetic engineering for an Irish Brave New World, producing, asexually, women for domesticity and men for work and public life, but without the confusion that desire creates.[43]

Silence and evasion are inevitable when the text is faced with the real question of reproduction and birth, and when the Good Fairy tells the Pooka about Sheila's pregnancy, the language is faltering and hesitant: 'She is suffering at the moment, said the Good Fairy with the shadow of a slight frown on the texture of his voice, from a very old complaint. I refer now to pregnancy' (*AS2B*, p. 111). This anxiety is echoed by the narrator, who is unable to describe the birth of Orlick Trellis: 'The task of rendering and describing the birth of Mr Trellis's illegitimate offspring I found one fraught with obstacles and difficulties of a technical, constructional, or literary character – so much so, in fact, that I found it entirely beyond my powers' (*AS2B*, p. 144). Similarly, in *The Third Policeman*, Sergeant Pluck cannot bring himself to say the word 'pregnancy' but talks about a woman in 'a very advanced state of sexuality' (*3P*, p. 57). As Vivian Mercier wrote:

> When these absurdities [of sex] are found tolerable at all by Irishmen, they are found so primarily because they serve that great end, the perpetuation of the human race. But to a number of Irish Manicheans – including Beckett, Swift and Shaw [and, I would include, O'Brien] – they are not tolerable. Irish lovers live in constant terror of being laughed at [. . .].[44]

Given this Manichean perspective, sex is viewed with uncomfortable distaste, with the result that the author either foregrounds its essential 'ugliness' by making it grotesque, or else he deliberately remains silent. The student narrator's theory of 'aestho-psychoeugenics' (the creation of characters without reference to birth or sex), for instance, combines both the grotesque and a self-imposed form of censorship. On the advice of his (all-male) cronies, the narrator considers killing off the pregnant Sheila

Lamont by writing her 'a violent end to herself and the trouble she was causing by the means of drinking a bottle of disinfectant fluid usually to be found in bathrooms' (*AS2B*, p. 145). However, he concludes that Sheila's creator, Dermot Trellis, would be too lazy to carry out this character assassination, and the narrator is content that this 'ingenious' answer to a knotty narrative problem earns him the admiration of his male peers. In the silences disclaiming sex and the noises proclaiming violence, O'Brien is desperately trying to come to terms with the social tragedy of stunted Irish attitudes to sex and sexuality (including, perhaps, his own).

Another metafictional quality used to evade censorship is the intertextual licence to plunder at will from the historical canon, i.e. the belief that the 'entire corpus of existing literature should be regarded as a limbo from which discerning authors could draw as required, creating only when they failed to find a suitable existing puppet' (*AS2B*, p. 25). In this respect, intertextual extracts are often borrowed for their dialogic implications. For example, the narrator presents us with an extract – by an unnamed author – from a second-hand book entitled *The Athenian Oracle*:[45]

> *Extract from Book referred to*: 1.Whether it be poffible for a woman fo carnally to know a Man in her fleep as to conceive, for I am fure that this and no way other was I got with Child.
> 2.Whether it be lawful to ufe Means to put a ftop to this growing mifchief, and kill it in the Embryo; this being the only way to avert the Thunderclap of my Father's Indignation. (*AS2B*, p. 102)

In metafictional terms the author is showing us the oblique psychodynamics of fiction making, as these pseudo-theological ideas are later transformed, on a narrative level, into the principle of 'aesthoautogamy', and the associated question of how to excise troublesome characters from the text such as the pregnant Sheila Lamont. On the level of the counter-narrative, however, these plunderings fulfil another function. They stress the ideological obsessions of a Catholic culture which privileges the ideal of virgin birth, and which denies even the mention of abortion through its rigid censorship laws – 'the Thunderclap of my Father's Indignation'.[46] Alluding to abortion by quoting another text – seemingly more 'authoritative' and beyond reproach (hence the deliberate elision of its real satirical author, John Dunton) – is a clever evasion of this.

O'Brien never borrows in order to create a web of pretty pastiche for its own sake; on the contrary he is smartly selective, and constantly alludes to the spectre of censorship itself. In this regard, the books on the narrator's shelves are certainly strategic: 'ranging from those of Mr Joyce to the *widely read* books of Mr A. Huxley' (my emphasis) (*AS2B*, p. 11). The irony is clear (albeit coded): among the books banned at the very first meeting of the Censorship Board in 1930 was Aldous Huxley's *Point Counter Point* (1928), a key intertext in *At Swim-Two-Birds*.[47]

Many of the extracts and ideas plundered by O'Brien for use in his novels operate in this way. While they contribute formally to the metafictional structure, these selected extracts also manage to speak on a subtextual level. Wayne Koestenbaum, in his critical study *Double Talk: The Erotics of Male Literary Collaboration*, out-lines what can happen when male authors collaborate on a single text. I do not think I am taking any major licence by adopting some of Koestenbaum's observations, and applying his model to the implicit 'collaboration' between O'Brien and the exclusively male authors whom he appropriates from history. This pirating is an actively collaborative act by O'Brien, and by proxy on behalf of the male author being pirated. The intermedium is the message here, and we can learn something of the author's agenda by studying the specific, intertextual borrowings which he employs.

In terms of the male collaborative process, it is worth noting how Dermot Trellis, the 'author-god' of *At Swim-Two-Birds*, first devel-oped aestho-autogamy: 'Much of the credit for Mr Furriskey's presence on this planet today must go to my late friend and col-league William Tracy [. . .]. The credit for the achievement of a successful act of procreation involving two unknown quantities is as much his as mine' (*AS2B*, p. 41). Autocritically, the text reveals the process of male collaboration as an act of 'procreation', or as Wayne Koestenbaum has argued in general: 'men who collaborate engage in a metaphorical sexual intercourse [and] the text balanced between them is alternatively the child of their sexual union and a shared union'.[48]

A revealing source of misogynistic collaboration in O'Brien's work is the debate between De Selby and St Augustine in *The Dalkey Archive*. Despite the comedy of Augustine's Dublin idiom, there is little of what O'Brien's Augustine says which cannot be found in his own autobiographical *Confessions* (AD 397). In one scene, the dialogue between De Selby and Augustine is used to coyly introduce the topic of homosexuality – a taboo topic which roams surreptitiously throughout all of O'Brien's novels. De Selby, questioning Augustine on his legendary lasciviousness, asks: 'Were all your rutting ceremonials heterosexual?', to which Augustine replies: '*Heterononsense! There is no evidence against me beyond what I wrote myself. Too vague. Be on your guard against this class of fooling. Nothing in black or white*' (*DA*, pp. 34–5).

Augustine warns us to be on our guard against accusations that excessive heterosexual posturing and overt misogyny might be understood as an attempt to mask homosexual inclinations. Augustine is right to be so wary, for as Koestenbaum writes in his analysis of such macho behaviour: 'Deconstruction has taught us that any monolithic body of ideas and habits contains the very difference it condemns; within male texts of all varieties lurks a homosexual desire, which, far from reinforcing patriarchy, undermines it, and offers a way out.'[49]

A universal feature of any male collaborative text – like that between Trellis and Tracy or between the student narrator and his various male friends – is its overt homophobic posturing, created in order to distance the author(s) from accusations of homoeroticism. Throughout O'Brien's novels there is a more discreet mocking of homosexuality to serve this end. In *At Swim-Two-Birds*, with its typical male relationships and its denial of the female, he again resorts to a metonymic discourse, in this case punning on the ambivalence of the signifiers 'fairy' (defined by the *Oxford English Dictionary* as 'a mythical small being with magical powers' or 'slang for male homosexual') and 'queer' (defined as 'odd' or 'slang for homosexual').[50]

The Good Fairy is bodiless and therefore technically androgynous, although male gender is conferred by the use of the pronoun 'he'.[51] When he slips invisibly into the Pooka's hut his voice is described as 'a small voice that was sweeter by far than the tinkle and clap of a waterfall and brighter than the first shaft of day' (*AS2B*, p. 104). It is eventually made clear that his voice is rather effeminate, and this becomes the starting point for a complex homosocial subtext: 'Welcome to my poor hut, said the Pooka as he surveyed the floor, and it is a queer standing' (*AS2B*, p. 104). Just in case we miss O'Brien's verbal dexterity he underlines his intention with ruthless repetition, to stress that it is a coded referent. When the Pooka feels that he must be hallucinating due to 'overeating at bed-time', he recalls that the previous night he had finished off a 'portion of a queer confection'. This 'queer confection', he then tells us, was 'the loins of a man' (*AS2B*, p. 105).

After this introductory episode, various other characters attest to the 'queer' speaking voice of the Good Fairy: the cowboy, Slug, tells the Fairy, 'no offence, you have a queer way of talking' (*AS2B*, p. 115); Orlick Trellis, just after his birth, points to the Fairy who is nestled in the Pooka's trouser pocket and says, 'That is a very queer little mouth you have in your clothes' (*AS2B*, p. 146); and eventually, during the mock trial-by-fiction, Mr Justice Casey tells the Good Fairy 'That is a queer thing to say' (*AS2B*, p. 201), in response to the Good Fairy's evasive answer on the nature of his relationship with Dermot Trellis.

Earlier, in the Pooka's hut, the Pooka and the Fairy have a convoluted discussion on the nature of sex and gender. The Fairy has decided against conducting this conversation in the bed where the Pooka and his wife lie, to which the Pooka cryptically responds: 'if your departure from my poor bed was actuated solely by a regard for chastity and conjugal fidelity, you are welcome to remain within the blankets without the fear of anger in your host, for there is safety in a triad, chastity is truth and truth is an odd number' (*AS2B*, p. 106). The Fairy *is* an 'odd number', not just numerically but colloquially: he is bodiless, effeminate of voice, and refuses categorically to declare his gender. When the Pooka probes the gender question further, the texture of the language reveals its metonymic subtext: 'Whether you are a man-angel, that is a conundrum personal to yourself' (*AS2B*, p. 110). It is significant that this is the only time that the synonym 'man-angel' appears for the expected 'man-fairy', and the displacement is another lesson on how to read this dialogic discourse.[52] Homosexuality is finally conferred upon the fairy and we understand that he is in fact neither gender within a sexually conservative paradigm, but an 'odd number', a homosexual.

Perhaps it was the rather snide texture of such prose which led the anonymous critic of the *Times Literary Supplement* (March 1939) to condemn O'Brien for his 'schoolboy brand of mild vulgarity'.[53] No doubt the author himself found this mild vulgarity to be the perfect self-mocking antidote to his own serious Manichean worldview. In *At Swim-Two-Birds* the personifications of these Manichean extremes – the Pooka and the Good Fairy – both appear as sexual deviants. While his mockery of extremism may be valid within the aesthetic and ethical codes of the novel, it also depends upon a vilification of homosexuality to achieve this end. But why go to such lengths to broach this subject in the first place? On the one hand, it may simply be a mischievous attempt to sneak yet another taboo topic past the censor, at a time when the mere hint of homosexuality was grounds enough for suppression.[54] On the other hand, this relentless fascination with homosexuality –

which runs throughout O'Brien's novels in coded form – might well betray a more personal anxiety. Of the man behind the mask, Brian O'Nolan, whereof one cannot speak, thereof one must be silent. But as far as Flann O'Brien goes, that particular mask does seem more than a little queer. Interestingly, biographer Anthony Cronin is both suggestive and evasive on this issue:

> It was not axiomatic in Ireland that those who were apparently uninterested in heterosexual relationships were interested in something else. A lack of interest in the opposite sex could be accounted for by religious zeal, circumstances, natural indifference or a combination of all three; but it was so common that most did not feel it necessary to account for it at all. Most of Brian O'Nolan's friends regarded him as a natural celibate, even a kind of anchorite, fierce and formidable rather than effete and emasculated, the cells of whose hermitage were the pubs, from which women for the most part were debarred.[55]

Even the language used by Cronin here colludes in what Wayne Koestenbaum calls the 'homosocial discourse' – a form of male-ordered writing which excludes women and makes men complicit in that exclusion. O'Nolan is 'fierce and formidable' as opposed to being 'effete and emasculated', and Cronin's description reveals as much about ideology – he was a contemporary of O'Brien's – and the tensions of biography as it does about its subject. By its very nature biography is intrusive and speculative, yet Cronin – as friend and sympathetic recorder – feels obliged to protect his subject's privacy on sexual matters. This loyalty seems laudable and fair-minded, although in critical terms its selectivity is an act of closure. Cronin resists any form of criticism which would engender speculation of homosexuality on O'Brien's part, and in the language of the tribe refuses to even utter the dread word 'homosexual', preferring to call it 'something else'. Thus, by trading signifiers such as 'anchorite' for homosexual, and by refusing to address the homoerotic aspects of the texts, Cronin effectively attempts to pre-empt any such critique.[56]

In any case, the sexual orientation of the author is immaterial to this current study. What *is* important, however, are the many loaded references in O'Brien's writings to homosocial relationships, which seem to be a key element in the architecture of his novels.[57] In the opening page of *The Third Policeman*, for example, the nameless narrator's only real recollection of his mother is that she owned a cat and that 'her face was always red and sore-looking from bending at the fire; she spent her life making tea to pass the time' (*3P*, p. 7). In contrast, his father, who owned a dog, 'was a strong man and did not talk much except on Saturdays when he would mention Parnell with the customers and say that Ireland was a *queer* country' (my emphasis) (*3P*, p. 7). Nonetheless, Noman says, 'We were all happy enough in a *queer* separate way' (my emphasis) (*3P*, p. 8), until both parents mysteriously disappear, leaving Noman a 'poor misfortunate little bastard' (*3P*, p. 8). After returning from boarding school at the age of nineteen, the only relationship in Noman's life is with the factotum John Divney, with whom Noman eventually shares a bed:

> I said it was foolish for us to sleep in different beds in such bitter weather and got into his bed beside him. He did not say much, then or at any other time. I slept with him always after that. We were friendly and smiled at each other but the situation was a *queer* one and neither of us liked it. The neighbours were not long in noticing how inseparable we were. [my emphasis] (*3P*, p. 13)

Noman later explains that these 'peculiar terms of physical intimacy' (*3P*, p. 19) came about through mutual distrust and suspicion. After the murder of Old Mathers, Noman and Divney hide the black box and agree not to open it until the murder trail goes cold. They are helped by the fact that Old Mathers lived alone and was 'a *queer* mean man and that going away without telling anybody or leaving his address was the sort of thing he would do' (my emphasis) (*3P*, pp. 18–19). Until then, though, they worry that one will betray the other and abscond with the money.

In the language used to describe this strange state of affairs, we know from our reading of *At Swim-Two-Birds* that the repetition of the word 'queer' insinuates exactly what the neighbours think: it *is* a queer situation. We also know, even from a cursory reading of the opening chapter, that the unreliable narrative voice cannot be trusted or taken literally – there is always an odd dislocation in Noman's speech which makes us question his surface meaning. Furthermore, unlike the nameless narrator of *At Swim-Two-Birds*, the nameless narrator of *The Third Policeman* bears no obvious autobiographical resemblance to his author. On the contrary, Noman is 'a heel and a killer',[58] and so O'Brien feels safe in conferring deviance upon him through insinuating a homosexual relationship. Sexuality for O'Brien is always dark, secretive and perverse, and often used to condemn the moral standing of his characters.

The characterisation of de Selby also hints at an underlying sense of misogyny, homosociality, and sexual unease. In one of the exaggerated mock footnotes on de Selby, Noman declares that the great idiot-savant had a number of physical 'failings and weaknesses' which occasionally left him a hostage to fortune. One such weakness was his narcolepsy, and 'on at least one occasion in a public lavatory' (*3P*, p. 166, fn) he fell asleep. Noman records how one de Selbian commentator, Du Garbandier, gave this incident 'malignant publicity in his pseudo-scientific "redaction" of the police court proceedings to which he added a virulent preface assailing the savant's moral character in terms which, however intemperate, admit of no ambiguity' (*3P*, p. 166, fn). Nothing further is added, but the insidious cocktail of phrases – 'public lavatory', 'court proceedings' and 'moral character' – convey the intended smutty atmosphere (all of which foreshadows the grotesque 'toilet humour' of *The Hard Life* years later).

De Selby's character is further impugned by another physical failing, namely 'his inability to distinguish between men and women' (*3P*, p. 167, fn). The resultant blurring of gender categories at one stage led to de Selby referring to his mother as 'a very distinguished gentleman'. This 'pardonable error' may be excused, Noman tells us, but 'the same cannot be said of other instances when young shop-girls, waitresses and the like were publicly addressed as "boys"' (*3P*, p. 167, fn). Again, Du Garbandier uses these episodes to produce 'a pamphlet masquerading as a scientific treatise on sexual idiosyncrasy in which de Selby is arraigned by name as the most abandoned of all human monsters' (*3P*, p. 167, fn). Just what makes him such a monster is left to the reader's imagination, and it seems a pity that yet again the possibilities of sex and sexuality are squandered to achieve a cheap, coarse and purely grotesque effect.

In terms of the metafictional structure of the text, these mock footnotes play a vital autocritical function. Masquerading as academic commentary, the footnotes actually do assist us in our decoding of the primary narrative; gradually, we begin to notice that de Selby's eccentric theories help shape the fabric of the narrator's hell. Similarly, the violent fallout from the feuding critics – who perpetually vie for interpretative 'truth' – mirrors the sordid tale of violence and dysfunctional sexuality in the body of the text. The footnotes are also deeply homosocial, although again they contain an inbuilt self-defence mechanism for the author. By showing the reader how literary and philosophical ideas can be

easily misinterpreted, O'Brien implicitly warns us against deconstructing the value systems of his own work in biographical terms.
O'Brien seems anxious that his particular depiction of social and
sexual conduct may be misconstrued, and used against him. Once
again, his insistence on the protective mask of pseudonymity goes
well beyond his use of a *nom de plume*.

In yet another discussion of de Selby's eccentric theories, Noman
informs us of the philosopher's attitude to love and interpersonal
relationships: 'In the *Layman's Atlas* he deals explicitly with
bereavement, old age, love, sin, death and the other saliencies of
existence. It is true that he allows them some only six lines, but
this is due to his devastating assertion that they are all "unnecessary"' (*3P*, p. 93). Certainly love is absent from The Parish – along
with women and children – and O'Brien may be suggesting that
this absence is indeed a characteristic of hell.

Other de Selbian ideas which impinge on the primary narrative
tend to emphasise male violence and sexual nausea. De Selby's
theory of names, for example, where names become 'crude ono-
matopaeic associations with the appearance of the person or object
named' (*3P*, p. 40, fn), directly affects the naming of some of the
characters in the story, e.g. the nameless narrator who is actually
dead, or the crafty Policeman Fox. Moreover, de Selby drew up
'elaborate paradigms of vowels and consonants purporting to correspond to certain indices of human race, colour and temperament'.
Noman then tells us that:

> An unhappy commentary on the theory was furnished by the
> activities of [de Selby's] own nephew, whether through ignorance
> or contempt for the humanistic researches of his uncle. The
> nephew set about a Swedish servant, from whom he was com-
> pletely excluded by the paradigms, in the pantry of a Portsmouth
> hotel to such purpose that de Selby had to open his purse to the
> tune of five or six hundred pounds to avert an unsavoury law
> case. (*3P*, p. 40, fn)

The 'paradigms' drawn up by de Selby showed 'certain groups' to be
'universally repugnant' (*3P*, p. 40, fn) to each other. According to
these culturally imposed codes, men are prohibited from engaging
with certain types of women – carnal women in this case, suggested
by the Swedish stereotype – and typically they react with violence
to that prohibition.

The only female character who actually appears in this novel is
Pegeen Meers, whom Divney eventually marries. According to the

parodic code which dictates some of the ethical assumptions of the text, we might usefully assume that Pegeen Meers is derived from J.M. Synge's Pegeen Mike (and, to a lesser extent perhaps, the Irish-language author Peig Sayers, who is a rich source of parody in *An Béal Bocht*). Pegeen Meers is mentioned by name in the first chapter but only physically appears at the end of the novel for a brief cameo, when she is pregnant with Divney's second child: 'She seemed to have grown old, very fat and very grey. Looking at her sideways I could see that she was with child. She was talking rapidly, even angrily' (*3P*, p. 195).

No other female character appears directly in the novel, although a number of women are alluded to in characteristically crude sexual terms (or, conversely, in strangely coy terms). MacCruiskeen, for instance, when first thinking about what he should contain in his beautifully intricate chest, considers 'them letters from Bridie, the ones on the blue paper with the strong smell but I did not think it would be anything but a sacrilege in the end because there was hot bits in them letters' (*3P*, p. 70). The 'hot bits' or erotica cannot sully the beauty of this magical creation, which is especially interesting when we consider that the chest itself is a self-conscious metaphor for the creation of fiction. Within the context of the overall structure of the novel, the chest-within-a-chest represents metaphysical mystery, and is just one in a whole series of images of infinite regress, which transcend and confound rational thought: 'It was so faultless and delightful that it reminded me forcibly, strange and foolish as it may seem, of something I did not understand and had never even heard of' (*3P*, p. 72). The chest is thus an image of impenetrable beauty, and in its very essence it transcends the human domain. Sexual desire, in the form of a woman's love-letters, has no place in such a tabernacle; it would indeed be 'sacrilege'. Again, in this context, sex, love and desire become dirty, shocking and secretive.

Throughout the novel, the language used by the Policemen is unrelentingly phallocentric, and women are always represented negatively. For instance, when Sergeant Pluck and Mr Gilhaney debate the merits of the three-speed gear on a bicycle, Pluck condemns the crankiness of such gadgetry, which is worse than 'a skinny wife in the craw of a cold bed [. . .] or porter in a sick stomach' (*3P*, p. 76). The value system here is exclusively male, with nagging wives and hangovers the most abominable punishment a man can suffer. However, it is only when the characters in the barracks discuss the pros and cons of the 'high saddle' (*3P*, p.

79) that we realise that an elaborate metonymic discourse is being developed, which will eventually lead to Pluck's celebrated 'Atomic Theory'. Beginning with a basic scatological pun, this discourse evolves into a very complex code, which will imagine bicycles in sexual terms. Again, to employ the model proposed by Wayne Koestenbaum, the male characters develop this 'patter to obscure their erotic burden, [and] the ambiguities of their discourse give the taboo subject some liberty to roam'.[59]

It begins with Pluck's pronouncement that the high saddle is '"very sore on the internal organs". "Which of the organs?", [Noman] inquired. "Both of them", said the Sergeant' (*3P*, p. 79). Before Pluck outlines his 'Atomic Theory', he directs Mr Gilhaney to the bush where Gilhaney's stolen bicycle lays hidden (later on we discover that Pluck had stolen it himself, for reasons which the 'Atomic Theory' explains). The bush is described in female terms by Noman, who tells us that it was 'a small modest whin-bush, a lady member of the tribe as you might say' (*3P*, p. 78). Crudely, Gilhaney roots around in this female bush and eventually finds his 'pump' – a fine phallocentric image if there was ever one (remember, too, that John Divney had used a similar pump to kill Old Mathers with). The foreplay with the pump in the bush eventually leads to full intercourse at Pluck's excited prompting: 'put your hands in under its underneath and start feeling promiscuously', says the Sergeant (*3P*, p. 80). Pluck is a master of malapropism but in the inverted world of The Parish, and according to O'Brien's dialogic construction, 'promiscuously' is the appropriate adverb here. In response to Pluck's exhortation, 'Gilhaney lay down on his stomach on the grass at the butt of a blackthorn and was inquiring into its private parts with his strong hands and grunting from the stretch of his exertions' (*3P*, p. 80).

Shortly afterwards, Pluck explains his theory of atomic transfer to a bewildered Noman:

> The gross and net result of [the Atomic Theory] is that people who spent most of their natural lives riding iron bicycles over the rocky roadsteads of this parish get their personalities mixed up with the personalities of their bicycle as a result of the interchanging of the atoms of each of them and you would be surprised at the number of people in these parts who nearly are half people and half bicycles. (*3P*, p. 85)

This theory becomes a central satirical thread in the novel, demonstrating how fallacious reasoning and spurious syllogisms can lead people astray. Metonymically, though, this bicycle motif also initiates a series of misogynistic jokes centring around the notion of a man riding a woman's bicycle and, later on, it sponsors an oddly tender and homoerotic description of Noman's relationship with the Sergeant's bicycle. This metonymic discourse has its simple scatological origins in the signifier 'bicycle' – at the time, a colloquial term of abuse for both a 'loose woman' and a bisexual – and punning also on the term 'riding' as a colloquialism for sexual intercourse.[60]

Once the basic code is understood, the elliptical sexual pattern becomes clear: 'Of course there are other things connected with ladies and ladies' bicycles that I will mention to you separately some time [said Pluck]. But the man-charged bicycle is a phenomenon of great charm and intensity and a very dangerous article' (*3P*, p. 87). Once again this simple binary opposition proclaims female sexuality as something secretive which cannot be spoken of, while male sexuality is 'charming', 'intense' and 'dangerous'. When the Sergeant recalls the flagrant 'immorality' of Gilhaney riding a lady teacher's 'female bicycle' (*3P*, p. 89), Joe (the narrator's soul) 'urgently' initiates a theological debate on the sinfulness of such an action: '*I have never heard of anything so shameless and abandoned. Of course the teacher was blameless, she did not take pleasure and she did not know*' (*3P*, pp. 89–90).

Joe invokes a Catholic casuistry here – it is the 'knowing' and the 'pleasure' which makes sexuality sinful – and once again the woman is passive, virginal and ignorant, while the traditional values of male sexuality are reasserted. This is an important image for the novel as a whole, in that the question of sexual pleasure and knowledge becomes the nexus for a series of interwoven thematic concerns: aggressive male sexuality, a repressive religious dogma, and a casual objectification of women. The importance of this image is further emphasised when Noman begins his adulterous affair with MacCruiskeen's bicycle – a lengthy scene which, on the surface at least, seems brittle with the language of male domination and female submission:

> I knew that I liked this bicycle more than I had ever liked any other bicycle, better even than I had liked some people with two legs. I liked her unassuming competence, her docility, the simple dignity of her quiet way. She now seemed to rest beneath my friendly eyes like a tame fowl which will crouch submissively, awaiting with out-hunched wings the caressing hand. [. . .] How desirable her seat was, how charming the invitation of her slim encircling handle-arms, how unaccountably

competent and reassuring her pump resting warmly against
her rear thigh! (*3P*, pp. 170–1)

Given the use of the pronouns 'she' and 'her', the bicycle here
would seem to be encoded, anthropomorphically, as a female sex
object. However, as Andrea Bobotis has recently pointed out in a
perceptive queer theory reading of *The Third Policeman*:

> Overlooked by most critics, the bicycle on which the narrator flees
> is Sergeant Pluck's, which he keeps in the cell of the police bar-
> racks. The bicycle, following the rules of Atomic Theory at play in
> the parish, has exchanged atoms with Pluck and is, in turn, gen-
> dered male. The narrator re-imagines the bike as female. [. . .] The
> narrator in fact recognises the bicycle's male gender and his sub-
> sequent reinterpretation of it: '*Notwithstanding* the sturdy
> cross-bar it *seemed* ineffably female' [Bobotis's emphasis].
> Misogyny is a necessary condition for his kind of triangulation:
> the woman is trafficked between the two men as a mere place-
> holder for their own desire. I do not intend to invalidate a
> misogynistic reading of the passage: the female imagined *is* docile,
> submissive, a 'tame domestic pony'. But the re-gendering of the
> bicycle also reveals O'Brien's willingness to extend possibilities.[61]

The 'willingness to extend possibilities' is all-important here.
Despite the multiple ambivalences of the language used, the reader
cannot help but notice the bittersweet tone of the description,
which is made even more poignant by the fact that it is the only
scene in the entire novel that depicts any kind of interpersonal tenderness or love, beyond the usual self-absorption and greed of the
characters. Thus it would seem that the bicycle fulfils another role
in this multi-dimensional, shape-shifting text, by proposing a possible redemptive alternative to the lonely, existential bleakness of
The Parish.

The only problem with this belated awareness of the importance
of love (be it heterosexual, homosexual or otherwise) is the way in
which it is represented. *The Third Policeman* operates on several
interwoven levels, with multifarious allusions to literary mythologies and philosophical systems to help develop its own idiosyncratic
impulses. The denouement of the novel is a terrible vision of existential nausea, inspired by a host of ghostly collaborators, including
the French symbolist J.K. Huysmans and the Renaissance drama-
tist Christopher Marlowe. However, the key difference between
these two intertextual sources mirrors the tensions between theme
and style in O'Brien's own text. The existential outcome of

Huysmans's 1884 novel À Rebours (Against Nature) is quite similar in mood and tone to The Third Policeman, and tends to serve the same moral and spiritual theme. Moreover, each novel employs a mechanistic, metonymic discourse of sexuality: in Huysmans's text, the obscure object of desire is symbolically represented as a train; in O'Brien's text, by a bicycle.[62] As Huysmans wrote:

> [She was] an adorable blonde with a shrill voice, a long slender body imprisoned in a shiny brass corset and supple catlike movements; a smart gold blonde whose extraordinary grace can be quite terrifying when she stiffens her muscles of steel, sends the sweat pouring down her steaming flanks, sets her elegant wheels spinning in their wide circles, and hurtles away, full of life, at the head of an express or boat-train.[63]

Compare this with its parodic appropriation in The Third Policeman:

> Her saddle seemed to spread invitingly into the most enchanting of all seats while her two handlebars, floating finely with the wild grace of alighting wings, beckoned to me to lend my mastery for free and joyful journeyings, the lightest of light murmuring in the company of the swift groundwinds to safe havens far away, the whir of the true front wheel in my ear as it spun perfectly beneath my clear eye and the strong fine back wheel with unadmired industry raising gentle dust on the dry roads. (3P, pp. 171)

Parody is a difficult type of comedy in that it demands an intimate knowledge of the source material. Huysmans's hero Des Esseintes – a progenitor of de Selby – has exhausted the gamut of human physical pleasure in his decadent pursuit of sensual experience. Following the loss of his sexual passion (for men as well as women) – 'he had tasted the sweets of the flesh like a crotchety invalid, with a craving for food but a palate which soon becomes jaded' – he develops an impatient contempt for women, resenting what he calls their 'innate stupidity'.[64] Des Esseintes's adoration of artifice and machinery eventually channels this misogynistic energy into his erotic and fetishistic description of trains. By incorporating Huysmans's observations and style into his own text, O'Brien automatically reinforces his own misogyny. It is unclear whether this is a deliberate narrative ploy on O'Brien's part – after all, Huysmans's novel is famously homoerotic, and was a key influence on Oscar Wilde's The Picture of Dorian Gray (1891)[65] – or just an unintentional side effect of intertextuality. In any case, the

metonymic discourse slightly undermines O'Brien's thematic point
about the redemptive power of love.

The other dominant intertextual framework underlying the existential outcome of *The Third Policeman* is that of the Faustian
myth, and here the redemptive theme fares better. With the help of
Marlowe (and Goethe), *The Third Policeman* becomes a tale of a
scholar who sells his soul to attain the book of knowledge (the black
box containing 'omnium', or omniscience). On this scale of values,
the female bicycle becomes the equivalent of Marlowe's Helen of
Troy in *The Tragical History of Doctor Faustus* (1594), who briefly
offers a vision of hope through the power of human love and desire:

> Sweet Helen, make me immortal with a kiss:
> Her lips suck forth my soul, see where it flies!
> Come Helen, come, give me my soul again.
> Here will I dwell, for heaven be in these lips [. . .].[66]

Implicit in this appropriation is the idea that the love of another –
be they male or female – could have provided an antidote to the
brutal self-absorption which ultimately condemns both Faustus
and Noman to an eternity in hell.

Allegorically, of course, 'The Parish' of *The Third Policeman* can
be read as a microcosm of the Irish Free State and the tragedy of
Irish male attitudes to sexuality. As Albert Camus once wrote:
'Tragedy is born in the West each time that the pendulum of civilisation is halfway between a sacred society and a society built around
man.'[67] Flann O'Brien is writing at the cusp of a new, emergent
society where gender roles are slowly coming under scrutiny. The
'sacred society' – the patriarchal, Catholic hegemony of post-colonial
Ireland – is beginning to creak at its joints, and a more cosmopolitan
consciousness is beginning to emerge from the colonial legacy of
Victorian prudery. Tellingly, the nightmare vision of The Parish is
one that is exclusively male, and one where sexlessness and love-
lessness lead to physical and spiritual annihilation. However, while
O'Brien seems fully conscious of this allegorical vision, his language
is sometimes unable to transcend its boundaries: thus, the dominant
ideology is subverted and reinforced, both at the same time.

The radical re-working of *The Third Policeman* – *The Dalkey
Archive* (1964) – is interesting from this ideological point of view.
Written some twenty-four years after *The Third Policeman*, this final
novel is a much more self-conscious attempt to address these representational issues of women, homosociality and Catholicism, and,
certainly in terms of the earlier novels, *The Dalkey Archive* is a

revealing index of a shift in cultural values. However, sincerity is once again sacrificed on the altar of sensationalism, and O'Brien's correspondence with his publisher, Timothy O'Keeffe, makes it clear that the censorship mentality which impinged on his previous work is still alive and kicking:

> I have a sub-plot. No doubt you know of the funny Censorship of Publications Board here. They ban books they don't like and that's all about it. [. . .] In the case of the ARCHIVE the nitwits will consider part of it blasphemous and ban it without further thought. There is no blasphemy whatever but assuming there was, the Board has no power whatever to ban a book on that ground; their only two statutory grounds are obscenity and the advocation of unnatural birth control. Given the ban (D.V.) [*Deo volente*: God willing] I cannot see that there would be any answer to a writ for libel in the High Court. If there was an attempt at defence, the hearing might put the Lady Chatterley case in the ha'penny class.[68]

As with the publication of *The Hard Life* two years earlier, O'Brien's intention was to provoke the Censorship Board into putting a ban on his novel. Not only would he gain a cherished notoriety but he also believed that he could reveal the underlying ethos of the Board. Like *The Hard Life*, though, *The Dalkey Archive*'s hidden agenda failed to provoke the censorship mandarins, much to O'Brien's disappointment.

In this novel, women finally begin to emerge from the margins of the text, although their narrative input is still quite trivial or else tends towards caricature. Three women appear directly here: Mary, Mick's mother, and Mrs Laverty. Of these, the mother figure's contribution is negligible, and the pious Mrs Laverty is merely the butt of O'Brien's mockery. When Mrs Laverty – who owns the Colza Hotel – discovers that the votive light in churches is fuelled by Colza oil, 'she piously assumed that this was a holy oil used for miraculous purposes by St Colza, V.M. [Virgin Martyr], and decided to put her house under this banner' (*DA*, p. 25). When we consider that the greater part of this novel concerns itself with a series of (male) theological debates between characters as diverse as De Selby, St Augustine, Fr Cobble, the resurrected figure of James Joyce (who wishes to join the Jesuits), and Mick (who wishes to join a Trappist order), the depiction of Mrs Laverty seems unfairly derogatory. Female piety, it suggests, is based on simple-minded theological ignorance, whereas male faith is built on rigorous (if long-winded) debate.

Generally speaking, the depiction of men and women in this novel depends greatly on O'Brien's intertextual borrowings. The Joycean parallels, for example, are many: Mick, like Stephen Dedalus, is intellectually arrogant and nurtures designs on the priesthood, and his friend Hackett equates – on this parodic scheme at least – with the usurper, Buck Mulligan. Anne Clissmann has pointed out some of the more obvious Joycean correspondences: 'When we first meet Mick and Hackett they are swimming, like Stephen and Buck Mulligan in the first episode of *Ulysses*. Mick drinks a good deal as Stephen does, and he intends to join the church but is deflected by a woman.'[69] The correspondences go further, as Hackett – like Mulligan – disparagingly hails his friend as the 'Prince of Denmark' (*DA*, p. 199), and just as Mulligan mocked Stephen's dead mother, so Hackett mocks Mick's (living) mother, to which Mick replies: 'If you mention my mother again, he snarled, I'll smash your dirty mouth' (*DA*, p. 202).

Hackett continually regards women as material possessions – 'Our personal squaws' (*DA*, p. 24) – and goads Mick about his 'pious Mary' (*DA*, p. 8). Mick himself reinforces this negative view of his girlfriend by referring to her as his 'virgin Mary' (*DA*, p. 118), because she refuses to sleep with him. By the end of the novel, however, we discover that Hackett has been conducting a secret, sexual affair with Mary. Moreover, Mary is now pregnant, and so the virgin/whore label would seem to be complete.

Thematising the madly disjointed strands of philosophy, science and religion that punctuate this novel, Anne Clissmann believes that the central message of this text is its critique of rationalism, with the author warning us to 'accept the presence of mystery and miracle, without question':

> In it O'Brien emerges as a deeply religious man, trusting that the questions which are unanswerable will one day be answered completely, that they will not remain half-believed bits or doubts [. . .]. In O'Brien's view, all men who separate faith and intellect and who try to solve the mysteries of the universe without recourse to faith can be described as 'idiot-savants'.[70]

The loaded references throughout the novel to the 'virgin Mary' – all evidence to the contrary – signify for Clissmann that what is intended here is a deliberately ambiguous conundrum: is this pregnancy, ironically, the virgin birth of a new messiah who will bring hope into a desolate wasteland? Of course, the realist alternative to this view is that Mary is simply pregnant by Hackett, with O'Brien having made it perfectly clear that she and Mick have not been sexually active. The choice we are left with at the end of the novel is not necessarily, as Clissmann proclaims, a 'comic question',[71] but a chauvinistic dualism: Mary is either a virgin who has conceived immaculately or, in Mick's eyes, a whore who has betrayed him. Either way, the mythical categories of the virgin/whore dichotomy have become actualised, and, in keeping with his overall theological theme, O'Brien deliberately plays on biblical archetypes. As Penelope Shuttle and Peter Redgrove note:

> In the New Testament the image of woman is, as it were, cas-trated. It is at any rate split into two halves. The two women principally important in the New Testament are Mary Magdalene, the prostitute: the woman who had sex without having a child; and Mary Virgin: the woman who had a child without having sex. This splits the power and completeness of woman into two quiescent halves [. . .].[72]

Throughout the course of the novel the character of Mary fades in and out of the picture, subordinated always to the male relation-ships which dominate the narrative. Mick's relationship with her is uncomfortable and lacking, and yet she constantly preys on his mind: 'She was really a nuisance yet never far away' (*DA*, p. 8). Mary rarely speaks for herself and is largely spoken of through Mick's meandering thoughts, thus creating an image of an over-bearing, selfishly ambitious and cantankerous woman. Mick's conflicted feelings for her betray an unreflective misogyny: 'He was, he thought, very fond of her and did not by any means regard her as merely a member of her sex, or anything so commonplace and trivial' (*DA*, p. 55). While this description of Mary may be intended as ironic commentary on O'Brien's part, other descriptions of her suggest that the author himself seems in general agreement with Mick. In one revealing passage at the beginning of chapter six, O'Brien seems to consciously confess his difficulty when it comes to writing about women: 'Mary was not a simple girl, not an easy subject to write about nor Mick the one to write. He thought women in general were hopeless as a theme for discussion or discourse' (*DA*, p. 55). At the heart of this confusion is the traditional male fear of an active and intelligent woman:

> She read a lot, talked politics often and once even mentioned her half-intention of writing a book. Mick did not ask on what subject, for somehow he found the idea distasteful. Without swallowing whole all the warnings one could readily hear and read about the

> spiritual dangers of intellectual arrogance and literary free-
> booting, there *was* menace in the overpoise that high education
> and a rich way of living could confer on a young girl. (*DA*, p. 56)

The 'menace' posed by this new type of independent and educated
woman hangs over Mick throughout, and threatens to destabilise
his fragile ego. In his mind, fear easily turns to loathing: 'Her *own*
ideas? How home-made in fact were they? No doubt glossy maga-
zines abounded in her little palace of fashion, and the art of
learning to talk smart was no new one. [. . .] What was she, really,
but a gilded trollop, probably with plenty of other gents who were
devout associates' (*DA*, p. 142). The background noises of the novel
reveal the dramatic shift in cultural ideology that confronted Irish
men at that time. Mary, representing the new feminist woman, is
brutally dismissed by Mick as a 'trollop'. O'Brien ultimately links
this fear to Mick's decision to join the priesthood, where he can
embrace the comforts of celibacy. At this point, Mick becomes
increasingly sanctimonious, and in a revealing passage he reflects
on his unhappy relationships with both men and women:

> What possible benefit had he derived from, for instance, his asso-
> ciation with Hackett? Or, for that matter, with Mary? The one
> stimulated alcoholism, the other concupiscence. What of the
> dozens of people of both sexes he knew in the civil service? They
> were pathetic, futile nobodies, faceless creatures, and – worse –
> they were bores. [. . .] As an intending Trappist, he would have to
> turn his back on pleasure but that would not be so easy because
> he knew of practically nothing which could be called pleasure.
> (*DA*, p. 198)

Mick's decision to become a priest – significantly, perhaps, he
wishes to join a 'silent' order – has little to do with his faith, and
everything to do with his terror of sex. To reinforce this point,
O'Brien's intertextual borrowings strategically generate a psychic
echo of Mick's predicament. When De Selby interviews the under-
water reincarnation of Augustine, some of the questions asked
reflect Mick's sexual anxieties; indeed, at one point, Augustine
refers to Origen of Alexandria who, when faced with carnal temptation, castrated himself. But De Selby's questioning of Augustine's
heterosexuality – and the homosocial discourse it initiates – is even
more revealing in terms of Mick's sexual unease. In the original
draft manuscript of *The Dalkey Archive*, O'Brien had intended to
suggest that Mick was actually homosexual. In a letter to Cecil
Scott of Macmillan publishers in 1964, O'Brien wrote:

> Yes, Mary is also unsatisfactory, though she had not been
> intended as very much more than a 'fringe benefit'. A friend to
> whom I showed the MS said she puzzled him until, in a blinding
> flash, he got the point. MARY was a surname, and the emer-
> gence of Mr Mary at the [end of] the book would have shown the
> story to have taken, unnoticed, a quite new direction chez
> Proust. With infinite regret I decided not to get awash in this
> brainwave . . .[73]

Although the extant text is obviously quite different to this
early conception, both the finished product and the original
scheme show O'Brien grappling with topics that weighed heavily
on him. Mary, undoubtedly the most fully realised female portrait
in the O'Brien canon, was initially intended to be a male homosexual; instead, in the finished work, she becomes a devious
portrait of emancipated womanhood who is eventually declared a
whore. Thus, in one complex but fluid image, all of these underlying ideological and personal tensions – a fear of women, an
anxiety about sex and sexuality, and a genuine fear of hell and
damnation – come to the fore.

In the extant version, Mick relents at the end of the novel, and
resigns himself to marriage with this treacherous woman.
Significantly enough, though, there is a strange coda just before the
end of the book when Mick wonders 'what sort of a job [James Joyce]
would make of the story of Mary and me' (*DA*, p. 202). To which
Mary, the aspiring writer, says: 'I don't think that's a story I'd like to
try to write. One must write outside oneself. I'm fed up with writers
who put a fictional gloss over their own squabbles and troubles. It's
a form of conceit, and usually it's very tedious' (*DA*, pp. 202–3).

Conclusion

> Was Hamlet mad? Was Trellis mad? It is extremely hard to say.
> Was he a victim of hard-to-explain hallucinations? Nobody
> knows. Even experts do not agree on these vital points. (*AS2B*,
> final section, p. 217)

The question of gender representation and sexual identity in
O'Brien's work is obviously very complicated. In all of his novels
there is a painful awareness that a cloistered Catholic ethos has
damaged Irish male attitudes to these issues. At times O'Brien
gamely attempts to deconstruct certain cultural taboos within the
restrictive parameters of an oppressive censorship code (itself a
reflection of socio-sexual anxiety), but in the process he sometimes

loses track and reveals himself to be a participant as well as an observer. Language leaks, and the texture of his own writing is often inflected with an ugly misogyny and homophobia, which he cannot always transcend. He evades censorship by constructing a coy metonymic discourse, which by virtue of its sniggering tone sometimes reneges on its possibilities. Paradoxically, his critique of censorship degenerates into a cheap, lurid exploitation of sexuality: simultaneously enshrining yet strangely subverting the conservative, patriarchal assumptions of his time.

What does this mean (*enshrining yet subverting*), and how are we to evaluate these contradictory critical observations – if at all? As Margot Norris points out, two broad strands of feminist literary criticism seem to exist: the Anglo-American school, exemplified by Sandra Gilbert and Susan Gubar, which is representational and polemical (it 'pays attention to *what* is said'); and French feminism, exemplified by Hélène Cixous and Julia Kristeva, which is performative and rhetorical (it 'pays attention to *how* saying works').[74] On the first level of representational politics, O'Brien's novels are obviously disappointing. But in terms of his counterrealist discourse there is another version of this story:

> Post-structuralist feminism pays relatively little attention to what writers say about women, or how women are represented, in favour of exploring how the activity of saying may itself act as a gendering of a text. [. . .] The inauthoritative textuality of *Finnegans Wake* [for example], which proclaims itself as having nothing significant to tell the reader, acts out a set of values (anti-dogmatism, undecidability, playfulness) that can be designated as feminine writing (*écriture feminine*), in distinction to a patriarchal writing that arrogates truth, knowledge, and authority to itself.[75]

The anti-dogmatic playfulness of Flann O'Brien's Menippean satire is predicated on its resistance to 'truth, knowledge and authority'. As Yeats famously put it, 'Great hatred, little room, maimed us from the start', but the dialogic carnival of O'Brien's metafictions offer themselves up as a gesture of healing within the oppressive, fetishistic culture of Irish censorship.

3. Character building:
the role of the self-conscious narrator

The answer to all questions of life and death [...] was written all over the world he had known: it was like a traveller realising that the wild country he surveys is not an accidental assembly of natural phenomena but the page in a book [...]. Thus the traveller spells the landscape and its sense is disclosed.

Vladimir Nabokov, *The Real Life of Sebastian Knight*, 1941[1]

The analytical focus so far has been concerned with context, and the rather emotive issue of metonymic codes – those complex strategies of evasion that skirt around the fringes of ideologically sensitive taboos. We saw how at times these metonymic codes exploited the basic instability of language in a coarse, Rabelaisian manner. Within a censorship culture, any material that cannot be talked about openly tends to become sublimated within the fabric of normal, acceptable discourse. The forbidden lodges itself within the familiar by infiltrating language at the syntactical level, and plays on the dialogic potential that emerges when a single sign is forced to take on multiple meaning. This playfulness is liberating in the way that it disturbs the monological sanctity attached to traditional realism. Yet at other times it becomes uncomfortably schizoid, as the encoded material staggers beneath the burden of its anxiousness and undermines the cohesion of the surface plot. A mythic dualism thus emerges between Apollonian needs (rational, linear) and Dionysian urges (irrational, tangential) of the text. At such times the author and the reader are seduced by the forbidden and trapped by the familiar, like wasps crawling into a watery jam jar. Finding our deepest satisfaction in the subtextual margins, we can be easily deflected from the bigger story; the politics of seduction invariably become a poetics of suggestion and innuendo.

While this suggestiveness might be understood as tragic necessity, formalist critics would regard issues such as the erotic or the

grotesque as purely technical devices, and would have no immediate or specific interest in the ideological conditions which
produced these devices. As Brian McHale notes, 'The function of
such materials [. . .] is [to] intensify ontological instability, titil-
lating or horrifying the reader (it works equally well either way) so
that he or she will resist having to "surrender" to the reality of
these materials'.[2] For such critics the erotic is decontextualised out
of existence and functions merely as a device for 'making strange'
the reading process; as Viktor Shklovsky wrote: 'Art is a way of
experiencing the artfulness of an object; the object is not important.'[3]

What *is* important from a formalist perspective is the frame: the
essential organising principle which distinguishes the object as art.
In his book *Framing the Sign*, Jonathan Culler explains why he
favours the term 'frame' over the more conventional synonym
'context'. For Culler, the frame is not given but produced:

> The expression 'framing the sign' has several advantages over
> context: it reminds us that framing is something we do; it hints of
> the frame-up [and] it eludes the incipient positivism of 'context'
> by alluding to the semiotic function of framing in art where the
> frame is determining, setting off the object or event as art.[4]

We have previously mentioned the image of the mirror in fiction
– a traditional literary symbol for the relationship between art and
society – and how in *The Third Policeman* it becomes a self-conscious metaphor for this framing process: 'a world arbitrarily
bounded by a wooden frame' (*3P*, p. 64). As Susan Stewart notes,
'there is no place in which one can escape metalanguage or framing.
An activity that was not framed would be completely natural, would
be prelapsarian'.[5] This present chapter will look specifically at the
key *metaleptic* (frame-breaking) strategy of *The Third Policeman*,
namely the role and function of the self-conscious narrator.

On a metafictional plane, the picaresque journey in *The Third
Policeman* is a quest to discover the borderland between reality and
fiction. As a character, Noman wavers between metafictional self-
consciousness and 'realist' passivity, flickering between an awareness
that he is a character trapped within a fictional order and his own
realist belief that he is a 'real-life' person. Throughout the novel,
Noman's hellish punishment is his growing realisation of the gulf
between language and the 'real world' it refers to, and his awareness of the frame which contains him:

[T]here are no suitable words in the world to tell my meaning. [. . .] It took me hours of thought long afterwards to realise why these articles were astonishing. *They lacked an essential property of all known objects.* [. . .] Simply their appearance, if even that word is not inadmissible, was not understood by the eye and was in any event indescribable. That is enough to say. (*3P*, p. 135)

This is a meta-narrative description (i.e. a narrative which refers to itself and its own procedures), dramatised by Noman's struggle for meaning in his own life. The problem of even describing this problem of description in itself defies description – 'there are no suitable words' – yet paradoxically he must use words to describe his word-lessness. In the end he concedes defeat: 'That is enough to say.' This novel portrays a world in a state of impossible flux, where language becomes an impotent poetry of improvisation. Out of this funda-mental ontological crisis emerges a highly self-reflexive language, typified by the use of the *self-conscious metaphor*. A self-conscious metaphor is a traditional literary metaphor which has been actu-alised or made literal within a metafictional universe, what Henri Bergson calls 'the comic effect obtained whenever we pretend to take literally an expression which was once used figuratively, or once our attention is fixed upon the material aspect of the metaphor'.[6]

This technique has an analogue in – and is directly inspired by – the meta-theatre of Pirandello and Brecht, whereby the metaphors of the stage, acting and playwrighting (the ontological 'real' that pre-determines drama), become powerful metaphors in themselves. As Martin Esslin describes it in *The Theatre of the Absurd*, this meta-theatre tends 'toward a radical devaluation of language, toward a poetry that is to emerge from the concrete and objectified images of the stage itself', where the element of language 'still plays an important part in this conception, but what happens on the stage transcends, and often contradicts the words spoken by the characters'.[7]

Here, language is contradicted by action and becomes pure, abstracted, compulsive poetry: an exuberant blend of cliché, collo-quialism, pun, slang, literary language and repetition, which is constantly questioning its own worth but chattering on regardless, like the tramps in Beckett's *Waiting for Godot*. In meta-theatre the search for identity is found in the concrete metaphors of the stage itself. Again this is not new – Shakespeare constantly uses metaphors such as 'All the world's a stage' – but as Esslin perce-tively notes, in the modern theatre such metaphors 'transcend the purely ethical plane that they occupied in the Renaissance

synthesis. [. . .] Modernism took these notions and applied them to
the realm of aesthetics, where the real was opposed to the illusory,
the mask to the face, the stage to the auditorium'.[8]

Pirandello and Beckett employ these metaphors to challenge the
audience's perception of what is 'real' and what is 'fictional', and to
undermine the tired conventions of naturalism by deliberately
playing across the footlights. Given the material, physical parameters of live drama, this metaleptic technique can become quite
sophisticated: 'The fundamental ontological boundary in theatre is
a literal, physical threshold, equally visible to the audience and (if
they are permitted to recognise it) the characters: namely the
footlights, the edge of the stage.'[9] In this form of theatre, acting
becomes a metaphor for the fractured, alienated individual; the
stage a metaphor for the limits of the knowable world; the play-
wright a metaphor for authority. As it applies to the novel, of
course, the author becomes the author-god, a metaphor for the
prime mover of a fictional universe. Life thus becomes a metaphor
for fiction; fiction becomes a metaphor for life.

Poetry, by its very nature, has always been a self-conscious
pursuit aware of the dance between signifier and signified, but the
realist tradition of the novel – with notable anti-realist exceptions
such as Laurence Sterne – had always tended towards verisimilitude
and away from self-consciousness. Realist conventions try to disguise
the framing structure by presenting an unbroken, seamless narrative. Semiotically, the codes of perception used by an audience
viewing a live play and by a reader reading a novel are obviously
quite different, and therefore the metaleptic methods needed to
expose these codes must be of a different order. Indeed, this very
topic is explored by the student narrator of *At Swim-Two-Birds* – the
novel itself being a critical manifesto of sorts for the emergent post-
modernist ethos:

> It was stated that while the novel and the play were both
> pleasing intellectual exercises, the novel was inferior to the play
> inasmuch as it lacked the outward accidents of illusion, fre-
> quently inducing the reader to be outwitted in a shabby fashion
> and caused to experience a real concern for the fortunes of illu-
> sory characters. The play was consumed in a wholesome fashion
> by large masses in places of public resort; the novel was admin-
> istered in private. (AS2B, p. 25)

In *At Swim-Two-Birds* O'Brien deals with this problem by giving
his characters varying degrees of self-consciousness – what he calls

'aestho-autogamy'. The aesthetic backlash against traditional authorship is dramatised by the characters' revolt against the despotic Dermot Trellis. The god-like hubris of the 'author' – including that of the student narrator – is continually destabilised throughout the text, in the deliberately flagrant manner that befits a 'self-evident sham' (*AS2B*, p. 25).

The recursive structure of *At Swim-Two-Birds* thus consists of a series of flickering ontological levels: a book (by Flann O'Brien) about a man writing a book (a student narrator) about a man writing a book (Dermot Trellis). Before the text proper begins, O'Brien draws our attention to the relationship between author and narrator by his re-working of the traditional disclaimer (a typical form of metafictional frame-breaking): 'All the characters represented in this book, including the first person singular, are entirely fictitious and bear no relationship to any person living or dead' (*AS2B*, p. v). Ironically, some the details of the (deliberately nameless) narrator's existence seem close enough to the biographical details of the author's life to allow critics enough room to make dubious connections, but O'Brien's disclaimer neatly foregrounds the distinction between the 'I' of writing and the 'I' of the real world. As Patricia Waugh writes:

> [Metafictions] reject the traditional figure of the author as a transcendental imagination [. . .]. They show not only that the 'author' is a concept produced through previous and existing literary and social texts, but that what is generally taken to be reality is also constructed and mediated in a similar fashion.[10]

The ultimate irony of this 'Chinese-box' pattern is that the author-narrator represented in the act of creation (or destruction) is himself inevitably a fiction. Should O'Brien go one step further – as, for instance, Kurt Vonnegut does in *Breakfast of Champions* (1973) – and declare himself as 'Flann O'Brien' inside his own novel, then he himself is fictionalised, or as Brian McHale writes (discussing post-modernism in general): 'the real artist always occupies an ontological level superior to that of his projected fictional self – puppet-master behind puppet-master, ad infinitum.'[11] Thus the self-conscious narrator is an image for ontological determinism, or, as Patricia Waugh puts it, 'a concern with the idea of being trapped in someone else's order'.[12] All characters in fiction are puppets, but metafiction draws attention to this fact, autocritically. As the narrator of *The Third Policeman* tells us: 'de Selby likens the position of a human on the earth to that of a man on a tight-wire who must continue walking along the wire or perish, being, however, free in all other respects. Movement in this restricted orbit results in the permanent hallucination known conventionally as "life" [. . .]' (*3P*, pp. 94–5).

What makes *The Third Policeman* a difficult text for analysis is that its strategies of metalepsis are more deeply embedded than in *At Swim-Two-Birds*. *At Swim-Two-Birds* is so determined to lay itself bare that it invites us to decentre it in a straightforward manner, with signposts clearly provided. But the metalepsis of *The Third Policeman* is less immediately obvious and more disconcerting. As a result we can read it on a 'realist' level, yet we are disturbingly – almost sub-consciously – aware of the lurking meta-narrative that gradually renders our 'realist' reading untenable.

While the concept of the self-conscious narrator and the question of authorship is central to both novels, the styles of presentation are quite different. In both texts the problem of authorship is fic-tionalised by foregrounding the gap between what is real and what is illusory, 'in such a way as to model the discontinuity between our own mode of being and that of whatever divinity we may wish there were'.[13] Both *At Swim-Two-Birds* and *The Third Policeman* concre-tise the image of the author as the god of a fictional universe by questioning the ontological status of their nameless narrators, but *The Third Policeman* destabilises the process entirely with its final revelation that Noman is actually dead as he narrates his tale.

O'Brien's tactic of posthumous narration first surfaced in the early metafictional story 'Scenes in a Novel' (1934), which ends, sig-nificantly, with the 'author', Brother Barnabas, preparing for his own death: 'I am penning these lines, dear reader, under conditions of great emotional stress, being engaged as I am in the composition of a posthumous article.'[14] This reference to 'posthumous' authorship is not a casual, throwaway remark but one which autocritically ini-tiates a post-modernist motif in O'Brien's work, where authorship is often equated with death. In many ways, this morbid motif fore-shadows Roland Barthes' famous post-structuralist manifesto, 'The Death of the Author' (1968) – a seminal essay which stresses the need to overthrow the myth of the author (analogous to the char-acter revolt in metafiction) in order to assert the interpretative role of the reader. For Barthes, 'To give a text an Author is to impose a limit on that text, to furnish it with a final signified, to close the writing'.[15] As far as Barthes and O'Brien are concerned, authorship is a pernicious fallacy; we must turn away from the historical centrality of the Author as the final arbiter of meaning and look instead to the text itself, the meaning of which is inscribed in an infinite, intertextual space. The ultimate beneficiary of this re-alignment of the literary matrix is the previously disregarded component, the reader: 'The reader is the space on which all the quotations that make up a writing are inscribed without any of them being lost; a text's unity lies not in its origin but in its destination.'[16]

The Third Policeman plays with these issues by employing a very complex series of self-reflexive devices, in particular the use of a self-conscious narrator who also happens to be dead: 'When you are writing about the world of the dead – and the damned – where none of the rules and laws (not even the law of gravity) holds good, there is any amount of scope for back-chat and funny cracks.'[17] Within a fictional zone all traditional laws can be contravened, and characters can even become aware of their fictional identity. Noman's feelings of existential angst – beyond the implicitly moral implications of the Faustian theme – have a self-conscious aesthetic function: we can read Noman's predicament, metafictionally, as a critique of literary procedures – a kind of allegory of writing. Throughout the novel, Noman feels tremors of doubt regarding the strength of his own existence: his relationship to his world (the text) seems flimsy and dislocated, and he is half-conscious of a large shadow manipulating him (an author). Through Noman the novel remains in a constant state of narrative flicker, where, according to Brian McHale, 'a world of fixed and discrete objects is given and then taken away, with the dual effect of destabilising the ontology of this projected world and simultaneously laying bare the process of world construction'.[18]

Noman automatically assumes – out of realist convention – that he is both author of his own tale ('in the story I am going to tell' [*3P*, p. 9]) and author of his own destiny ('I had long-since got to know how I was situated in the world' [*3P*, p. 9]). But, as the story unfolds, Noman's eventual awareness of his predicament – that he is dead – also becomes a metafictional awareness of his own fictionality: that he is not, as he imagines, the author of his story or his destiny but simply a character; not the puppet-master but merely a puppet.

In the opening chapter of the novel the narrative proceeds in a relatively realist fashion – apart from the time-shifts in memory and a disconcerting narrative tone. In a parody of the 'Bildungsroman', Noman recalls his early life, the gruesome murder of Old Mathers, and his friendship with John Divney. The moral/ontological crisis of identity begins at the end of this chapter, as Noman retrieves the black box that he and Divney have killed for. As he is about to enter the house where the box is hidden, Divney gives him some advice: 'If you meet anybody, you don't know what you're looking for, you don't know in whose house you are, you don't know anything' (*3P*, p. 20). This appeal for secrecy evokes a strange response in Noman, which surprises even him: '"I don't even know my own name", I answered. This was a very remarkable thing for me to say because the next time I was asked my name I could not answer. I did not know' (*3P*, p. 20).

Initially Noman's remark – 'I don't even know my own name' – is intended sardonically, as a reaction to Divney's lecture. But in typically exploitative fashion O'Brien literalises this common colloquialism for secrecy and renders it fact – Noman cannot actually remember his own name. Later on we shall see how Divney's advice can be interpreted as an autocritical comment – 'house' being a recurrent self-reflexive metaphor for the textual frame – which rewrites Divney's comment as 'you don't know in whose [text] you are; you don't know anything'. With the benefit of hindsight (i.e. having read the novel and discovered that Noman is dead), we see how his account of life in 'The Parish' (another metaphor for the fictional zone) is laden with irony; we evade the deferred decoding of the novel's ellipsis and enjoy that irony in full. Initially, though, on our first reading, we travel the journey with our unreliable narrator, and are unaware of the coded significance.

In the meantime, the loss of his identity is a feature which Noman returns to sporadically. In the beginning this amnesia does not bother him too much, but as the novel progresses it becomes more and more of an issue. Significantly, and from the outset, his lost name is deliberately linked to his greedy pursuit of the mysterious black box, which he has lost. When Noman meets the ghost of Old Mathers in chapter two, Noman demands to know where the black box is, to which Mathers sharply replies: 'What is your name?' (*3P*, p. 31). Noman is aware of the illogicality of this question, but not of its implications: 'I was surprised at this question. It had no bearing on my own conversation but I did not notice its irrelevance because I was shocked to realise that, simple as it was, I could not answer it. I did not know my name [. . .]' (*3P*, p. 31). On the contrary, though, within the metafictional zone of The Parish, this question has a very direct bearing on Noman, as the black box itself is an image rich in self-reflexive design. On a 'realist' plane, the box supposedly contains enough money to allow Noman to publish his book on de Selby (metafictionally translated as 'the self' or 'the same person'); for him the box represents a possible book. However, on a metafictional plane, the box is later revealed to contain a substance called 'omnium' (translated as 'omniscience'), i.e. knowledge. This conjures up the Faustian myth of a man who has sold his soul for the book of knowledge. Whichever way you look at it, though, Noman's loss of identity is intrinsically linked to the black box, i.e. the text.

Even before this episode, Noman has started to notice his strange surroundings and remarks on their uncanny artificiality – 'I remember that I noticed several things in a cold mechanical way' (*3P*, p. 24) – yet he still cannot make any connection between his own manner of 'seeing', and his subsequent description of Old Mathers' eyes: 'Looking at them I got the feeling that they were not genuine eyes at all but mechanical dummies animated by electricity or the like' (*3P*, p. 24). What animates the dead eyes, of course, is the author – Mathers is indeed a dummy, and although it 'disturbed [him] agonisingly' (*3P*, p. 24), Noman cannot yet see that he too is a fictional construct.

Interestingly, this mechanical description – which is typical of virtually every character in the novel at key strategic points – is a textbook example of the Freudian concept of the *uncanny*: 'that class of the frightening which leads back to what is known of old and long familiar.' As Freud acknowledged, this condition was first identified by Ernst Jentsch in his 1906 essay, 'On the Psychology of the Uncanny'. Jentsch defines the uncanny as 'doubts whether an apparently animate being is really alive; or conversely, whether a lifeless object might not be in fact animate' – in fact, both of these uncanny processes are at work throughout *The Third Policeman* – and he expands upon its use in fiction:

> In telling a story one of the most successful devices for easily creating uncanny effects is to leave the reader in uncertainty whether a particular figure in the story is a human being or an automaton and to do it in such a way that his attention is not focused directly upon his uncertainty, so that he may not be led to go into the matter and clear it up immediately.[19]

At this point, significantly, Noman has the first in a long series of epiphanies on the theme of infinite regress, a metafictional motif for the Chinese-box pattern of the novel as a whole:

> [His eye] gave rise in my mind to interminable speculations as to the colour and quality of the real eye and as to whether, indeed, it was real at all or merely another dummy with its pinhole on

the same plane as the first one so that the real eye, possibly behind thousands of these absurd disguises, gazed out through a barrel of serried peep-holes. (*3P*, pp. 24–5)

The motif of infinite regress (the chest-within-a-chest, spears with points to infinity, houses within houses, souls within souls, etc.) is a Zenoist paradox which subverts the dictates of reason, as well as being another case of narrative flicker. The pattern of repeating structures, according to Brian McHale, interrupts and compounds 'the ontological horizon of a fiction, multiplying its worlds and laying bare the previous operation'.[20] The image of infinite regress mirrors the way in which the primary text is continually interrupted by secondary worlds – representations within representations – which serve to upset and resist any absolute interpretation of the primary material. Secondary representations – digressions, dreams, repetitions, footnotes, etc. – fragment the reality of the primary text by scattering and dispersing concrete images which would normally stabilise meaning. The recursive structure of the entire novel echoes this motif, as the text itself moves towards infinite regress when we discover that it is circularly looped, and that Noman is cyclically bound to re-enact his crime and punishment, *ad infinitum*: 'Hell goes round and round. In shape it is circular and by nature it is interminable, repetitive and very nearly unbearable.'[21]

After his meeting with the ghost of Old Mathers, the mechanical universe of the created text begins to cast its shadow over Noman's awareness of himself and everything that previously defined his own sense of reality. Even his voice sounds tinny and hollow as he becomes aware of the flimsy fabric of his own speech: 'Words spilled out of me as if they were produced by machinery' (*3P*, p. 26). But Noman's cerebral torture has just begun, and the cruel author-god is not yet prepared to show his hand, and pulls Noman back from the brink of the ontological abyss. Noman begins to re-assert himself, ironically by reference to the black box/text: 'I found I was sure of nothing save my search for the black box' (*3P*, p. 31).

Critic Wim Tigges has casually suggested that Noman's loss of identity is not a governing factor in his struggle for meaning – 'It is true he has lost his name', writes Tigges, 'but that does not bother him much'.[22] On the contrary, identity is contingent upon naming in this novel. As the familiar system of common sense begins to degenerate and real-world logic continues to flicker like a faulty light bulb, the importance of anchoring his identity in a name – any name – becomes paramount for the distressed Noman. With superbly absurd logic, Old Mathers points out that if Noman has no name then how could he ever hope to sign a receipt for the black box, to which Noman replies (with a growing sense of despair): 'I can always get a name. [. . .] Doyle or Spaldman is a good name and so is O'Sweeny and Hardiman and O'Gara. I can take my choice. I am not tied down for life to one word like most people' (*3P*, p. 31).

This is true in one sense: as a fictional character invented by a despotic author-god he can be called any name or none – it is entirely at the discretionary whim of the author. Old Mathers drops a hint to the beleaguered Noman that perhaps a greater power shapes their identities and their destinies: 'everything you do is in response to a request or suggestion made to you by some other party either inside you or outside' (*3P*, p. 30). Noman regains his good spirits after he leaves the haunted house, and once he forgets his fears his normal arrogance re-asserts itself: 'I did not know my name or where I had come from but the black box was practically in my grasp' (*3P*, p. 37). Again, though, just as he gets comfortable with himself, Noman becomes strangely aware of his artificial environment but cannot pinpoint its cause: 'My surroundings had a strangeness of a peculiar kind, entirely separate from the mere strangeness of a country where one has never been before. Everything seemed almost too pleasant, too perfect, too finely made' (*3P*, p. 39).

Despite his acute rationalist perception, Noman cannot explain this strange 'country'. In fact, what he has intuitively experienced is the limits of the intertextual zone he inhabits, i.e. the text. The alert intertextual reader, on the other hand, might notice the literary appropriation from Shakespeare – in part, this is an episode from *Hamlet*, concretised. Like Hamlet, Noman has just emerged from his meeting with the dead ghost of a father figure, and his description of the countryside recalls 'the undiscovered country, from whose bourn no traveller returns', i.e. death, or, metafictionally, a country created entirely from literary tradition. While it may mimic reality, even the most realist of texts remains mimetic – an artificial remake of reality or a literary machine. Recognising the intertextual borrowing simply makes us more conscious of that machine, or as Brian McHale puts it, 'the machine does not have to be fully visible in order for the foregrounding to work; it only has to be conspicuously present, conspicuously in place'.[23] In the perverse but well-ordered design of The Parish, Noman is trapped within a literary machine – a metaphor which becomes concretised later on when Noman travels into the bowels of the machine in the 'lift to Eternity' (chapter eight) and sees its actual workings: '"Do you not see the wires?", MacCruiskeen asked' (*3P*, p. 138).

In the meantime, Noman exercises doublethink and refuses to accept the implications of his flickering existence. All he wants, he says, is the black box, which 'would secure me for life in my own house' (*3P*, p. 39). Again, if we accept for the time being – more conclusive proof will be offered later – that 'house' is a metonymic code-word for 'text' then we see how the metafictional ontological struggle and the 'realist' moral struggle collide: Noman seeks the black box (the book of knowledge) which will make him secure in his own house. Noman's existential struggle is that of a metafictional character who wishes to transcend his condition – Noman seeks the power (omnium) to create his own world where he shall reign as author-god. Noman then is a metafictional version of Faust; a fallen angel whose pride forces him to challenge the omnipotence of his creator. Fiction thus imitates the human desire for transcendence; desire for transcendence imitates fiction.

These dark thoughts on the artificiality of his world refer him back to the question of his lost identity. He realises that a name has magic power; that it differentiates him from his surroundings; and that it confers meaning, however arbitrary: 'Even a dog has a name which dissociates him from other dogs' (*3P*, p. 40). Without a name he is intangible and vaguely unreal in a world which calls things into being by naming them. Without language we cannot talk about 'reality', and without a name we do not fully exist:

> All people have names of one kind or another. Some are arbitrary labels related to the appearance of the person, some represent purely genealogical associations but most of them afford some clue as to the parents of the person named and confer a certain advantage in the execution of legal documents. (*3P*, p. 40)

Interestingly, this theme is reflected in modern Saussurian linguistics and is a cornerstone of post-structuralism (the academic wing of post-modernism). According to Saussure, language is both arbitrary and differential: 'without the help of signs we would be unable to make a clear-cut, consistent distinction between two ideas. Without language, thought is a vague, uncharted nebula. There are no pre-existing ideas and nothing is distinct before the appearance of language.'[24] Names, despite being 'arbitrary labels' (*3P*, p. 40) which just differentiate one thing from another – 'even a dog has a name which dissociates him from other dogs" (*3P*, p. 40) – serve to define one's place in the ruling framework. Moreover, in traditional folklore and fairytales, names are vitally important elements in the ontological quest. As Sue Asbee notes:

> We name things, and people, in order to 'know' and thus exert control over them. Countless legends and folktales turn on the hero's need to discover his adversary's name in order to tame or neutralise the adversary's influence. O'Brien's protagonist eludes us because we do not know what to call him.[25]

Metafictionally, we can take Asbee's comment further. It is not so much that Noman 'eludes us because we do not know what to call him' – this is a slightly fanciful way of saying that the texture of the narrative language is shifting and polyphonic. As readers we all adopt reading strategies and fill in the gap – in my case I call him 'Noman', and this suffices. The real point is that Noman's *own* identity eludes him: he has no name within the text because he is (a) dead and (b) merely a fictional character within a text – he lacks ontological significance. As the narrative progresses, however, we learn alongside Noman. Although we cannot always trust his solipsist narration, his journey of discovery is also our journey, and we are helped in our understanding of the situation by the autocritical array of clues scattered about like breadcrumbs by the self-conscious text.

The horrible truth of his own condition slowly unfolds for Noman as he searches for a clue to the 'parents of the person named' (*3P*, p. 40), which in his case is his literary father, the author-god of the text. To fill in the ontological gap stemming from this 'blank anonymity' (*3P*, p. 40), Noman proposes a list of ten names – in the manner of *Rumplestiltskin* – 'which for all I knew, I *might* hear' (*3P*, p. 41). The construction of lists is itself a common and useful metaleptic device in metafiction, as any list draws attention to its own incompleteness and so becomes an impossible struggle to classify the infinite range of names available. Indeed, Noman gives up after a list of ten seemingly arbitrary names, the enormity of his hopeless task apparent.

Shortly after, Noman gets diverted from his existential reflections by the picaresque vagaries of his journey and he meets the bizarre Martin Finnucane, the robber captain of the one-legged men. Finnucane himself is obviously a mechanical puppet, with 'an arm that's as strong as an article of powerful steam machinery' (*3P*, p. 45). Finnucane is also a mirror image of Noman, a generic product of the same literary machine: 'A black murderer also. Every time I rob a man I knock him dead because I have no respect for life, not a little' (*3P*, p. 46). And, like Noman, Finnucane has a wooden left leg, a perverse mirror image of a topsy-turvy world where the normal laws of reality are transgressed and overwritten by the internal laws of the fictional zone. Finnucane, like Joe the soul, is a fragmented reflection of his Noman's ontological instability and essential fictionality. Their deliberate similarities remind us of their creation and their creator – the hand of the author-god who creates his characters with the simple stroke of a pen or a tap of a typewriter key.

In this way, description in the novel becomes meta-descriptive with everyday events revealing themselves as mimetic patterns. Language foregrounds itself as language, flickering between mimesis and diegesis, and ordinary words pick at the seams of the projected world. For example, Finnucane smokes a pipe – a normal, real-world event – but the description of this draws attention to the framing context rather than the smoking itself, and colloquial language takes on unearthly qualities: 'He lay back and filled himself up to the ears with dark smoke and when he was nearly bursting he let it out again and hid himself in it' (*3P*, p. 47). We read the figurative language literally – meta-literally – and are once again reminded that what we are reading is all an illusion; a trick conjured up with smoke and mirrors.

Before Finnucane helpfully points Noman in the direction of the police barracks – a convenient narrative progression – an interesting change comes over Finnucane's diction, which is unexpected and, initially at least, unexplained. His colloquial and poetic diction suddenly becomes artificial, cold and awkward with verbose malapropisms and solecisms (devices that formally proclaim their essentially ludic nature). This linguistic transition anticipates the language of Sergeant Pluck, the first policeman and next character we shall meet. Moreover, in this topsy-turvy world of repetition and inversion, every malapropism and solecism becomes semantically relevant: 'Have you a desideratum?' (*3P*, p. 47), asks Finnucane, i.e. a 'thing lacking but needed' (*OED*), to which Noman replies: 'To find what I am looking for' (*3P*, p. 48). 'Have you an ultimatum?' asks Finnucane – 'I have a secret ultimatum' (*3P*, p. 48) replies Noman. The dialogue here is cagey and secretive, and both characters speak in abstract codes rather than specifics. Yet the codes also point to the metafictional subtext, e.g. Noman's secret 'ultimatum' is the ultimate revelation of the text, or as he describes it much later: 'Why was Joe so disturbed at the suggestion that he had a body? What if he had a body? A body with another body inside it in turn, thousands of such bodies within each other like the skin of an onion, receding to some unimaginable *ultimatum*?' (my emphasis) (*3P*, p. 118).

These are typical metafictional devices: the use of verbal echoes and the way in which the author subverts the commonplace. As Patricia Waugh writes, 'attention is drawn to the formal organisation of words in literature and away from their referential potential'.[26] This linguistic deconstruction continues with Noman's interview in the barracks by Pluck. As Noman enters further into the hellish, fictional labyrinth, the tenuous logic of the real world comes under increasing pressure. Pluck asks Noman his name, but the signifiers for name in the policeman's vocabulary are again a series of malapropisms and solecisms: 'pronoun', 'cog' and 'surnoun'. Noman quickly realises that to communicate in this strange world he must adapt to the new system of signification: '"I have no pronoun", I answered, hoping I knew his meaning' (*3P*, p. 56).

The most interesting phrase is Pluck's use of 'cog' as a synonym for name, and it best illustrates O'Brien's multi-levelled, polyphonic exploitation of words. Presumably 'cog' is a clipped form of 'cognomen' (a nickname or surname), though it also suggests a cog in a machine (a character in a literary text) and a bicycle cog (Pluck speaks ontologically in terms of bicycles). It also suggests the concept of the Cartesian 'cogito' (*cogito ergo sum*), the principle which establishes the existence of a being from the fact of its thinking or awareness of itself. All meanings are equally valid and deliberately open-ended, so that the reader will imagine some or all of the possible referents. The Cartesian implication is certainly intended: five pages later Pluck demonstrates that 'cog' and 'name' – or 'knowing' and 'naming' – are intimately related when he tells the now despairing Noman: 'If you have no name you possess nothing and you do not exist and even your trousers are not on you although they look as if they were from where I am sitting' (*3P*, pp. 61–2).

Beyond the immediate truth of this statement – that Noman is both dead and fictional – Pluck sums up perfectly the post-modernist crisis of language, namely, that how we respond to the world depends on how our language conventionally chooses to classify it. Common sense tells us that objects exist in the real world, but we can only refer to these objects through language. Language is ultimately self-referential, and you cannot argue the pre-determined reality of 'trousers' through a faulty system of communication. This is the fundamental aesthetic principle of post-modernist texts which are obsessed with the theme of 'unreal' reality, and they exploit the gap between the real and projected world to metaphorically explore that predicament.

The legal wrangling over the illegitimacy of having no name (literally and figuratively speaking) continues with Pluck's topsy-turvy syllogisms: Pluck once knew another nameless man, he says, ergo 'you are certain to be his son and the heir to his nullity and all his nothings. What way is your pop today and where is he?' (*3P*, pp. 56–7). Noman goes along with this story, fabricating an alibi that his father had emigrated to America, or as Pluck calls it, the 'Unified Stations' (*3P*, p. 58). Again, this coinage is structurally significant as it refers to the textual nature of the zone they inhabit, expressed in the idiomatic language of that zone. Later on in the novel we will be confronted by Policeman Fox, the mysterious Third Policeman and structural architect of The Parish. Fox inhabits a miniature version of the police station, located between the walls of Old Mathers' house – the core controlling station of the 'Unified Stations'.

Michel Foucault coined the phrase 'heterotopia' to describe such mysterious zones, and argued that such heterotopias are intrinsically disturbing in the way 'they secretly undermine language [and] make it impossible to name this and that, because they destroy syntax in advance [. . .] which causes words and things [. . .] to hold together'.[27] Heterotopias are zones of the middle heartland that shatter the fragile syntax of everyday language. The Parish is a re-imagined space comprising the world of literature, myth and philosophical ideas on the one hand, and the more mundane, everyday world of 1940s Ireland on the other. The created space is the interface of two seemingly incompatible structures, each destabilising the other through linguistic friction. This juxtaposition of two idioms – one real, one fictional – simultaneously deconstructs and reconstructs our perception of language.

Within this heterotopia, words take on new, ulterior or allegorical meaning, usually autocritical in nature. Thus, when MacCruiskeen tells Noman that he has 'never encountered a more fantastic epilogue or a queerer story' (*3P*, pp. 66–7), he is alluding not just to the narrative of Noman's personal history (and his queer relationship with Divney) but to the metanarrative of the text itself, and to Noman's ontological status: 'Surely you are a queer far-fetched man', he says (*3P*, p. 67).

Pluck and MacCruiskeen see life almost exclusively in terms of bicycles, and both echo the same question on first meeting Noman:

'Is it about a bicycle?' (Pluck, *3P*, p. 54; MacCruiskeen, *3P*, p. 58). The bicycle metaphor continues the self-reflexive revelations: 'the no-bicycle', says MacCruiskeen, 'that is a story that would make your golden fortune if you wrote it down in a book where people could pursue it literally' (*3P*, p. 69). Irony and repetition are rampant here: Noman himself is a writer and the 'golden fortune' that the policeman refers to is an echo of John Divney's remark in the opening chapter when he first implanted dark, murderous thoughts in Noman's mind: 'It might make your name in the world and your golden fortune in copyright', says Divney (*3P*, p. 14). The observant reader notices the echo; Noman does not. Noman still sees himself as an author and not a character, a creator and not a creation. The policemen confront Noman with a generic mirror image of his own fictionality, in the same manner as the physical descriptions of Old Mathers and Martin Finnucane did earlier. When we first encounter Pluck – significantly, gazing into a mirror – Noman's description emphasises the policeman's unreality:

> Again I find it difficult to convey the precise reason my eyes found his shape unprecedented and unfamiliar. [. . .] Ordinary enough as each part of him looked by itself, they all seemed to create together, by some undetectable discrepancy in association or proportion, a very disquieting impression of unnaturalness, amounting almost to what was horrible and monstrous. (*3P*, p. 54)

Much later, Noman nearly chokes at the sound made by Pluck tapping his head, 'a booming hollow sound, slightly tinny, as if he had tapped an empty watering-can with his nail' (*3P*, p. 154) – a typically arresting and concrete simile which draws attention to his mechanical design. And in his final encounter with the Sergeant, Noman's description makes Pluck's ontological status (and by extension his own) abundantly clear: he is nothing but a 'toy man' (*3P*, p. 163). Pluck is a fictional composition of features and characteristics borrowed from other texts – most notably James Stephens' policemen in *The Crock of Gold* (1912) – all cobbled together in a 'monstrous' (*3P*, p. 54) physiological pastiche.

To consolidate our intertextual reading – and to remind us of the 'writtenness' of the text – O'Brien puts words in Pluck's mouth which not only echo other characters within the novel but which also evoke characters from other novels. For example, the first words that Pluck utters are muttered 'abstractly and half-aloud': 'It's my teeth. [. . .] Nearly every sickness is from the teeth' (*3P*, p. 54), which, as J.C.C. Mays has noted, is just one of many incidental borrowings lifted from J.K. Huysmans's *À Rebours* (*Against Nature*, 1884).²⁸ Parody, of course, is a problematic form of comedy because it demands familiarity with both texts as well as the interpretive ability to make sense of the interrelationship. By itself this partic-ular parodic borrowing is a marginal intertextual detail, which registers only if we compile a whole network of similar borrowings from Huysmans's text, and so it is hardly surprising that this mar-ginal detail is uttered 'abstractedly and half-aloud' (*3P*, p. 54).

Such intertextual details reaffirm one of the key metafictional principles espoused in *At Swim-Two-Birds*: 'The entire corpus of existing literature should be regarded as a limbo from which dis-cerning authors could draw their characters as required, creating only when they failed to find a suitable existing puppet' (*AS2B*, p. 25). Again, though, where metalepsis is apparent in *At Swim-Two-Birds* it is encoded within the fabric of *The Third Policeman*. In this respect, it does not matter so much exactly where Pluck's words are borrowed from as long as we sense that they *are* borrowed. This confronts us with the fact of Pluck's fictionality, and that he is merely a 'suitable existing puppet' (*AS2B*, p. 25). Every text is thus an intertext, or as Roland Barthes declared: 'Any text is a new tissue of past citations. Bits of code, formulae, rhythmic models, fragments of social languages, etc. pass off into the text and are redistributed within it for there is always language before and around the text.'²⁹

Lest we somehow imagine that by charting the intertextual sources we will in some way 'unlock' the mysteries of the text, Barthes adds a codicil to his statement: 'Intertextuality [. . .] cannot, of course, be reduced to a problem of sources or "influences"; the intertext is a general field of anonymous formulae whose origin can scarcely ever be located; of unconscious or automatic quota-tions, given without quotation marks.'³⁰ This is not to mention the fact that metafiction would never allow us to reduce the text so easily to a mere catalogue of sources. In metafiction, as Ninian Mellamphy notes, an awareness of intertextuality allows the author to 'reject the traditional *mythos*, or plot, in favour of an Eisensteinian principle of montage'.³¹ The interwoven fabric of any text is impossible to disentangle, and O'Brien seeks to remind the reader of this. Therefore we may say that the relationship between Huysmans *À Rebours* and O'Brien's *The Third Policeman*, for example, embodies a number of metafictional principles: first, it expands the levels of reading by aligning the primary text with a secondary text which contains similar themes or characteristics (both texts explore the possibilities of synaesthesia; both texts have an interest in the philosophy of colour; and O'Brien co-opts Huysmans's misogynistic and homoerotic interest in machines). Second, with parody popularly considered a form of literary flattery, the degree of intertextual borrowing seems to operate in direct ratio to the significance attached to the original work. Thus the long list of textual borrowings from *À Rebours* testifies to O'Brien's identification with its themes,[32] right down to the existential/ontological crisis at the closure of both texts.

In the same intertextual fashion as Sergeant Pluck, the second policeman, MacCruiskeen, becomes an agent of metalepsis – his characterisation *proclaims* rather than conceals its textuality – and is also another reflection of Noman's identificatory search for significance. Noman describes his first meeting with MacCruiskeen and comments that he was 'more like a poet than a policeman' (*3P*, p. 57), and in a metafictional sense this is quite true. MacCruiskeen's excruciating inventions, like the spear with the point to infinity and the series of infinitely small chests, not only confound 'normal' world logic but also echo the recursive Chinese-box design of the entire novel. Moreover, MacCruiskeen's mechanical inventions are very obvious symbols for artifice and fiction making, e.g. Noman describes the infinite series of chests as possessing 'the dignity and the satisfying quality of true art' (*3P*, p. 70). MacCruiskeen, then, is indeed more poet than policeman, a mechanical creator of fiction.

Significantly, when MacCruiskeen tells Noman about the problems he had in deciding what to actually put inside the first, perfectly crafted chest, he employs the traditional language of storytelling: 'I will tell you a story and give you a synopsis of the ramification of the little plot' (3P, p. 70). In the end, 'to put myself right with my private conscience', MacCruiskeen does what any decent post-modernist would do in a similar situation – he draws attention to the frame itself: 'the only sole correct thing to contain in the chest was another chest of the same make but littler in cubic dimension' (*3P*, p. 71).

At this point in the narrative we could be easily led into believing that MacCruiskeen, with his strange mechanical inventions, could in fact be the architect of The Parish and not just a policeman who 'polices' its internal workings. But this is a typical metafictional trap or 'tangled hierarchy', where the reader is deliberately misled and tempted into regarding a secondary, embedded representation as the primary one, or, in this particular instance, into imagining that MacCruiskeen is the previously unseen phantom of the text, the author-god lurking in the background. (Realistically, of course, the 'real' author can never appear in his own text, for to reveal the author's position within the narrative structure is merely to introduce the author into the fiction as a fictional character.) At any rate, O'Brien is not yet ready to play this metafictional trump card, and continues to engage in more literary brinkmanship with the harassed reader. MacCruiskeen, more a 'poet than a policeman', is certainly more 'real' than the almost robotic Sergeant Pluck, but he is still a puppet nonetheless. Indeed, as Pluck says of MacCruiskeen, he is – in the manner of his own inventions – 'a walking emporium, you'd think he was on wires and worked with steam' (*3P*, p. 76).

O'Brien again resorts to a little intertextual pirating in order to construct this portrait of MacCruiskeen, a device which metaleptically reminds the reader of the character's fictionality. Pluck's repetitive refrain – 'nearly all sickness comes from the teeth' – has its parodic double and counterpoint in MacCruiskeen's pet phrase 'unless I am a Dutchman' (*3P*, p. 110). For J.C.C. Mays, this catchphrase is an 'ironic counterpart to the creator of Des Esseintes', presumably alluding to the Dutch surname 'Huysmans' (Huysmans, though French, was of Dutch origin).[33] Mays may be stretching the point here a little, I think. A much likelier and more telling intertextual influence is Luigi Pirandello's *Six Characters in Search of an Author* (1921) where the producer figure of the play utters a similar catchphrase: 'We've got something in that first act [. . .] or I'm a Dutchman.'[34] This appropriation, though again fairly marginal, pays due homage to one of O'Brien's key theoretical sources. While the Huysmans text may impinge more directly on some of the details of *The Third Policeman*, Pirandello's seminal work of meta-theatre is the perfect model for the metafictional estrangement between character and author (a post-Nietzschean trope for the relationship between humanity and God). The alignment between O'Brien's policeman and Pirandello's producer is quite deliberate: both characters imagine that they exert a certain control over the running of their (fictional) worlds – one polices, one produces – with the ontological irony that despite their illusions of grandeur both are obviously just characters in a text.

The relationship between Noman and the three policemen is an interesting one, because it establishes a series of carefully constructed narrative levels which playfully inflate and deflate reader expectation. Infuriatingly, O'Brien tends to assign a seemingly fixed position to the policemen, only to immediately cancel out that

closed perception and replace it with another. The first two
policemen, for example, initially seem to control the workings of
The Parish but are subsequently revealed to be puppets, controlled
in turn by someone else. Similarly, the very title of the novel serves
to frame our expectations of the mysterious 'Third Policeman', but
before we actually meet Policeman Fox in chapter eleven, O'Brien
lays a false trail by introducing a 'mock' third policeman, in the
spectral shape of Inspector O'Corky in chapter seven. O'Corky
appears for literally two pages, briefly threatens to become a character of significance – he is after all the superior officer – but then
disappears from the text for good. O'Corky's presence foregrounds
his inclusion as a literary device, and unveils the contrived manner
of realist fictions which often introduce minor characters simply as
a means of furthering the plot. Indeed, O'Corky's appearance does
reactivate the narrative (which has become rather static at this
point) by announcing that Noman is to be hung for murder, based,
ironically, on the flimsiest of circumstantial evidence, or as Pluck
tells him: 'It was your personal misfortune to be present adjacently
at the time' (*3P*, p. 98). Here, the concept of 'framing' takes on a
new and more sinister connotation.

Inspector O'Corky's brief appearance confirms the innate
strangeness of the first two policemen, not least in the way that his
language seems to be an extreme version of his subordinates'
speech: 'See that you regularise your irregularity instantaneously',
he tells Pluck, 'and set right your irrectitude and put the murderer
in the cage before he rips the bag out of the whole countryside' (*3P*,
p. 97). With this brief cameo O'Corky vanishes completely from the
text, or as Noman blithely (but autocritically) notes: 'After that he
was gone' (*3P*, p. 97).

Noman's relationship with the policemen had begun before he
actually meets them in the 'flesh', as it were. In chapter two the
ghost of Old Mathers first mentions their existence, and immediately their supernatural/meta-literary status is established: 'The
first two are down in the barracks and so far as I know they have
been there for hundreds of years', says Old Mathers, although the
mysterious and elusive Policeman Fox seemingly 'disappeared
twenty-five years ago and was never heard of after' (*3P*, p. 35).
According to Old Mathers, these policemen have the gift of 'wind-
watching', i.e. reading the colours of the winds: 'A record of this
belief will be found in the literature of all ancient peoples. There
are four winds and eight sub-winds, each with its own colour. [. . .]
People in the old days had the power of perceiving these colours

and could spend a day sitting quietly on a hillside watching the beauty of the winds [. . .]' (*3P*, p. 32).

Again, J.C.C. Mays argues that this colour theory 'takes off from Des Esseintes' theories [in] *À Rebours*'.[35] This is only partially correct – as part of his experiments with synaesthesia, Des Esseintes develops an eccentric theory of colour whereby 'there exists a close correspondence between the sensual make-up of a person [. . .] and whatever colour that person reacts to most strongly'.[36] A more significant intertextual borrowing is the medieval Irish poem 'Saltair na Rann' (trans. 'The Psalter of Quatrains'), which Brendan McWilliams believes is the primary source material for O'Brien:

> The four principal winds – well known to us as the four cardinal points – were called the 'primgaetha', and there were two secondary winds – or 'fogaetha' – interposed between each two. A separate colour was assigned to each direction. A purple wind blew from the east, and a white wind from the south; between these two the secondary winds were red and yellow. The north wind was black and the west wind brown – and so on, to assemble the full kaleidoscope of the twelve directions.[37]

This description, with some minor modifications – for O'Brien the west wind is 'amber', not brown – dictates the base structure of this scene. O'Brien is ascribing to the policemen not the theories of an eccentric, fictional, nineteenth-century dandy (or at least not *only* those theories), but the folkloric beliefs of the ancient Celtic druids. The policemen, then, are the resultant interface of several intertextual worlds: the plodding, lumbering policemen from a novel by James Stephens, and mythical beings from the Irish folkloric tradition – a potent fusion of the banal, the literary and the supernatural.

Where Des Esseintes' theory of colour might enter the intertextual equation is in Old Mathers' contention that everyone has their own personal colour, 'the colour of the wind prevailing at his birth' (*3P*, p. 33). According to Mathers, knowing one's own colour is a useful thing to know because 'you can tell the length of your life from it. Yellow means a long life, and the lighter the better' (*3P*, p. 33). Furthermore, 'a certain policeman' who was present at the birth of Old Mathers had made him the gift of a fine yellow gown, 'very thin and slight like the very finest of spider's muslin' (*3P*, p. 33). Each birthday thereafter another gown was added, each new gown darkening the overall colour until eventually 'the addition of one further gown will actually achieve real and full blackness' (*3P*, p. 34), i.e. death.

The textual ramifications of this theory are manifold. The policemen themselves are said to be 'operating on a very rare colour' (*3P*, p. 35), i.e. they are supernatural – perhaps even immortal – creatures. The colour theory also affects Noman: in chapter eight, when he undresses for bed he notices that 'When all my clothes were laid on the floor they were much more numerous than I had expected and my body was surprisingly white and thin' (*3P*, p. 115). The truth of Old Mathers' story about gowns is borne out literally here: Noman has used up his collection of birthday gowns, i.e. he is dead, and the supernatural policemen have predetermined his destiny. (Intertextually, this scene also evokes *Tristram Shandy*, when Tristram compares the Cartesian dualism of mind and body – rather like the split between Noman and Joe the Soul – to a 'gown' of sorts, namely a jerkin: 'a man's body and mind, with the utmost reverence to both, are exactly like a jerkin, and a jerkin's lining – rumple the one, – you rumple the other'.[38])

Significantly, once Noman sheds his clothes/gowns he becomes dramatically aware of the plastic boundaries of his strange universe, noticing how 'the outside night framed neatly in the window as if it were a picture on the wall' (*3P*, p. 116). These thoughts on the artificiality of night inspire a convoluted de Selbian footnote on theories of night, blackness, sleep and death – a *mélange* of interrelated issues which have a direct bearing on Noman's circumstances and Old Mathers' original theory of colour. Night for de Selby 'was simply an accretion of "black air", i.e. a staining of the atmosphere due to volcanic eruptions'; sleep was a 'succession of fainting-fits brought on by semi-asphyxiation' induced by this corrosive climate; and eventually death itself results in a 'collapse of the heart from the strain of a lifetime of fits and fainting' (*3P*, p. 116, fn). Thus de Selby's theories of blackness and death are a pseudo-scientific analogue of Old Mathers' belief in wind-colours and gowns, both themes elaborately interwoven. As always, Noman treats de Selby's theories with scornful scepticism, and describes his ruminations in a mocking tone. The irony is, of course, that both sets of colour theories directly impinge on the primary text. De Selby's eccentric theories and the policemen's sinister machinations directly affect and control what happens to Noman – he is their puppet and their plaything.

All the characters, but especially the policemen, are designed to hover around the central protagonist and reflect his situation in some way: Finnucane mirrors Noman in that he is a self-confessed

murderer with a wooden left leg; Finnucane's speech changes mysteriously to anticipate Pluck; some of Pluck's phrases ('golden book')
echo earlier comments made to Noman by John Divney; and so on.
As J.C.C. Mays succinctly sums it up: 'Structure and style in this
way come to mirror a vision of infinite recession which appals, fas-
cinates and amuses, resting as it does on an ultimate assertion of
unmitigated selfhood. The book's method is its theme [. . .].'[39]

As previously discussed, the first two policemen are obviously
metafictional characters charged with varying degrees of aestho-
autogamy, yet still also fictional puppets. Their intertextual design
establishes a series of different ontological levels – Pluck is obviously a puppet, MacCruiskeen too but less dramatically so – but
what of the crafty Policeman Fox: who (or what) does the (real)
third policeman represent? This is the same question that Noman,
anticipating the reader's question, puts to Sergeant Pluck at the
start of chapter six, to which Pluck replies:

> 'Policeman Fox is the third of us', said the Sergeant, 'but we
> never see him or hear tell of him at all because he is always on
> his beat and never off it and he signs the book in the middle of
> the night when even a badger is asleep. He is as mad as a hare,
> he never interrogates the public and he is always taking notes'.
> (*3P*, p. 77)

This is an image of the Joycean 'invisible author' ('we never see
him'), concealing his presence from the reader ('he never interro-
gates the public'). Indeed, it could even be an image of Joyce
himself, author of *Finnegans Wake*, who 'signs the book in the
middle of the night'.

We know from the outset that the third policeman operates on a
different level to the others – his physical absence and the framing
title of the novel encourage this perception. Later on, when Noman
threatens to escape from custody, Pluck gives him a sinister warning
that there is no escaping the confines of The Parish: 'Policeman Fox
would be sure to apprehend you single-handed on the outskirts.
There would be no necessity for a warrant' (*3P*, p. 99). Fox patrols
the 'outskirts', the limits of the text within which Noman, as a fictional character, is trapped. Ominously for Noman, Fox needs no
'warrant', i.e. he is above the laws of The Parish. Ontologically, Fox is
a powerful figure, a transcendent character with greater self-awareness than either Noman or the other policemen.

As the narrative progresses, it moves closer and closer to the
heart of darkness: Noman's realisation of his own death (and innate

fictionality) will coincide with his inevitable confrontation with Fox, the dark god of The Parish. In the meantime, Noman grows more anxious all the time, and by chapter eight the stark implication of the motif of infinite regress is finally beginning to dawn on him: 'Was I in turn merely a link in a vast sequence of imponderable beings, the world I knew merely the interior of the being whose inner voice I myself was? Who or what was the core and what monster in what world was the final uncontained colossus? God? Nothing?' (*3P*, 118).

Noman is getting frightened now, half-conscious of the metafictional determinism at work as he faces the 'final uncontained colossus' – Policeman Fox, the apparently fictionalised 'author-god'. Now, more aware of the heterotopic zone, Noman begins to scrutinise the strange idiom of The Parish, seeing how monologic, 'real-world' meaning is deconstructed and reassembled in dialogic patterns. In a discussion with Joe the Soul, for instance, Noman debates the possible meaning of the word 'lift' (in the context of a 'lift to Eternity'). From Noman's strictly monological viewpoint the word could only signify 'elevator' – unless, as Joe morbidly reminds him, 'the word "lift" has a special meaning. Like "drop" when you are talking about a scaffold. I suppose a smash under the chin with a heavy spade could be called a "lift"' (*3P*, p. 126).

Nothing now can be understood in realist, monological terms. When Noman does descend in the lift to Eternity he directly encounters the inner workings of the literary machine, although as yet he cannot (or will not) accept its implications. Among the strange, cruel wonders of Eternity is a strange hammering sound in the background which repeats itself several times, but without explanation: 'another burst of hammering, then silence, then a low but violent noise like passionately-muttered oaths, then silence again and finally the sound of heavy footsteps from behind the tall cabinets of machinery' (*3P*, p. 132).

Noman cannot decipher the importance of this and so forgets about it, although three pages later the observant reader notices that MacCruiskeen approaches one of these 'cabinets of machinery', and 'pressed two red articles like typewriter keys' (*3P*, p. 135). The detail is marginal yet visible, and it signposts clues for the alert reader. The giant cabinets of machinery in the bowels of The Parish are thus revealed to be some kind of cosmic – or hellish – typewriter. This knowledge allows us to refer back to the mysterious 'burst of hammering' and 'passionately-muttered oaths' of a few pages before – the sound of the invisible author, hammering away at his typewriter keys, 'writing' The Parish into existence.

Later, in the opening lines of chapter nine, Noman is 'awakened the following morning by sounds of loud hammering' (*3P*, p. 144) – ostensibly the hammering of a carpenter erecting a scaffold to hang Noman, but metafictionally the hammering of the author-god who shapes the narrative. Immediately this initiates a de Selbian footnote on the theme of hammering, but despite his philosophical reflections Noman cannot grasp the irony of his own commentary. He tells us that in the course of his experiments de Selby was engaged in an enormous amount of hammering, although the cause of this was unknown: 'Unfortunately the hammering was always done behind locked doors and no commentator has hazarded even a guess as to what was being hammered and for what purpose' (*3P*, p. 144, fn).

The reader, as commentator, can indeed 'hazard a guess' – it is the sound of typing, of literary creation. In his autocritically entitled work *The Layman's Atlas* (suggesting a reader's map of the text), de Selby himself argues that 'hammering is anything but what it appears to be' (*3P*, pp. 144–5, fn) – which is metafictionally true – although Noman suggests that this statement, 'if not open to explicit refutation, seems unnecessary and unenlightening' (*3P*, p. 145, fn). From a rigidly materialist point of view, of course, it is 'unenlightening' – but not for the reader. Irony runs riot here as Noman unwittingly describes the carpenter 'hammering at a wooden frame' (*3P*, p. 149) – more echoes of the word 'frame' – and notices, when the hammer falls on the carpenter's foot, that he too has a wooden left leg, like Noman and Martin Finnucane.

In chapter ten, as Noman awaits the hangman's noose, his thoughts turn naturally to the question of God and the afterlife. In a probing conversation with Pluck he learns more about the nature of the world the policemen inhabit: '"And where do you sleep then?" "Down below – over there – beyant". He gave my eyes the right direction with his brown thumb. It was down the road to where the hidden left turn led to the heaven full of doors and ovens' (*3P*, p. 152). The policemen sleep in Eternity to preserve their supernatural yet apparently finite lives. Pluck cannot find the appropriate word to describe their habitat, and prefers to point. The words he does use are open-ended, abstract, and must be interpreted by the reader: 'Down below' (Hell perhaps?), 'over there' (Eternity itself, a kind of purgatory?) or 'beyant' (beyond in Heaven?). The 'hidden left turn' reminds us of Pluck's 'rules of wisdom' in chapter four, the fourth rule being to 'Take left turns as much as possible' (*3P*, p. 60). Noman was originally sceptical of this gnomic advice, although

Pluck entreated him then to take it seriously: 'If you follow them [. . .] you will save your soul and never get a fall on a slippy road' (*3P*, p. 60). Eternity is just a left turn away but it is too late, it seems, for the fallen Noman.

Policeman Fox himself is described by Pluck as living 'beyant', and indeed he does seem to be 'beyond' the ontological limits of the others, and operates in 'a separate ceiling in a different house' (*3P*, p. 152); the omnipotent Joycean artist 'beyond or above his handi-work, invisible, refined out of existence'. Pluck is rather vague on the subject, but seems critical of Fox's behaviour and blames him for the current state of flux in The Parish which the policemen keep in order: 'indeed the unreasonable jumps of the lever-reading would put you in mind that there is unauthorised interference in the works. He is as crazy as bedamned, an incontestable character and a man of ungovernable inexactitudes' (*3P*, p. 152). Pluck suspects that Fox is interfering with the reality of The Parish (the text), and that these 'jumps of lever-reading' (metaleptic intrusions) are 'unauthorised'. Fox, it seems, is more than just the realist author-god but is the metafictionalist personified; a literary saboteur challenging the normative reading codes and writing practices expected in a 'realist' text.

Unlike Pluck or MacCruiskeen, Fox does not want to preserve his life for ever, but wants to 'get rid of as much as possible, under-time and overtime, as quickly as he can so that he can die as soon as possible' (*3P*, p. 153). The first two policemen, though supernat-ural (or self-conscious) seem aware of their fictional limitations, and want to preserve their existence within the text – 'you don't fade when you are inside your sleep', says Pluck (*3P*, p. 152). As long as our reading preserves them, then, they will exist but Fox, on the other hand, has a different urge. He is an author of sorts who wants to die, to escape his duty to his creations, to remove himself from the labour of writing. Thus it seems that Fox *is* the dark-god of the text – not just a traditional realist author-god but also a metafictional 'author', and O'Brien's fictional ambassador.

Noman asks one final question of Pluck: 'And why is Fox crazy?' (3P, p. 153). Apparently – although Pluck seems unsure – Fox had opened a box in MacCruiskeen's room, looked into it, and, upon seeing a colour in it beyond the normal realm of perception, went insane: 'It was not one of those colours a man carries inside his head like nothing he ever looked at with his eyes. It was . . . different' (*3P*, p. 154). Noman offers a typically materialist response and thinks it an 'unlikely story' that this new, uncharted colour could 'blast a man's brain to imbecility by the surprise of it' (*3P*, p. 155).

The colour motif which punctuates the text at regular intervals challenges the nineteenth-century beliefs of the rigidly materialist Noman. Interestingly, this notion of colour also reflects Saussurian linguistics – colour being the most frequently cited illustration of Saussure's radical linguistic theory. According to Saussure, an individual colour is not a distinct material essence that exists independently but is, in fact, culturally constructed from an infinite colour continuum – a rainbow is a continuum, for example, which our western culture has cut up into seven arbitrary 'colours'. Language cannot name a pre-existing colour but rather decodes it as a system of differentiation. A particular colour, say red, depends on its difference by defining it against the rest of the continuum; there is no essence of 'redness', only a differentiation, so red is red simply because it is not yellow or orange. As Saussure wrote: 'Linguistics then works in the border land where the elements of sound and thought combine; *their combination produces a form, not a substance*'.[40]

Similarly, the famous Sapir-Whorf hypothesis – an experimental variant of this linguistic phenomenon – used colour as a means of testing the cultural encoding of language. People speaking different languages were asked to sort out piles of different coloured chips into piles of 'similar' colours. The result indicated that the number of resultant piles corresponded to the number of basic colour terms in the language spoken by that person, thus proving that how we respond to the world corresponds to the way our language classifies it. As Edward Sapir wrote in 1929:

> Human beings do not live in the objective world alone, nor alone in the world of social activity as ordinarily understood, but are very much at the mercy of the particular language which has become the medium of expression for their society. It is quite an illusion to imagine that one adjusts to reality essentially without the use of language and that language is merely an incidental means of solving specific problems of communication or reflection. The fact of the matter is that the 'real world' is to a large extent unconsciously built upon the language habits of the group.[41]

Unaware that colour is a socially determined construct and not an independent essence in nature, Noman himself is 'at the mercy' of the language of his society – the fabulous heterotopia of The Parish where naturalised linguistic concepts frequently dissolve. Fox, by discovering an 'unnamed' colour, opens the Pandora's box of post-modernist thought and realises that reality is contingent upon language – a concept that could very easily drive one 'crazy' (*3P*, p. 153). Thus the colour motif in the novel becomes yet another metafictional trope for the writtenness of reality. Noman is a staunch traditionalist who conceives of the world in pre-Saussurian terms, and thinking the story 'unlikely' (*3P*, p. 155) he drops the subject, refusing as ever to contemplate some hard metaphysical truths.

Pluck continues with the existential tone of this debate and presents Noman with yet another mirror image of his fictionality with the story of Quigley the balloon-man, who floated skywards in a hot-air balloon in order to 'make observations' (which are left unspecified). Quigley, like Noman, sought to transcend geographical and physical boundaries, and similarly was 'a man of great personal charm but a divil for reading books' (*3P*, p. 158). The moral of the parable concerns Noman quite directly: 'When the time-limit for the observations was over they pulled down the balloon again but lo and behold there was no man in the basket and his dead body was never found afterwards lying dead or alive in any parish ever afterwards' (*3P*, p. 158). The 'time-limit for observations' refers to the reading limits of the text. Once we reach the end of the novel we discover that Noman is dead, although it is a peculiar brand of 'deadness' – 'his dead body was never found afterwards lying dead or alive' – for in truth Noman is both things simultaneously: alive and dead, 'real' yet illusory.

Interestingly, as an intertextual source, the story of Quigley the balloon-man evokes images from the 1939 film *The Wizard of Oz* – a film that was released during the writing of *The Third Policeman*.[42] Quigley, like Professor Marvel in the film, disappeared over the rainbow in a balloon and lands in a strange country. There are many correlations between novel and film: a central protagonist (Dorothy/Noman) is transported with a travelling companion (Toto/Joe the Soul), inside a house (belonging to Auntie Em/Old Mathers), to a magical world (Oz/The Parish) where the common-sense rules of logic are continually violated. To return home safely both protagonists enlist three companions (one a tin man like Pluck); both travel down a road (an important motif in *The Third Policeman*); both have killed (The Wicked Witch/Old Mathers); and both come face to face with the magical ruler of the heterotopic zone (the Wizard/Policeman Fox), who is later revealed to be a fraud, hiding behind a mask. As an early post-modernist work *The Third Policeman* is fascinated with the intertextual and aesthetic implications of cinema, and both de Selby and Pluck debate the possibilities of the 'cinematograph' (*3P*, pp. 50, 59). In any case, Noman continues his journey towards his inevitable confrontation with Fox, the Wizard of The Parish, and begins to realise that, wherever he is, he's not in Kansas any more.

In chapter eleven Noman returns to Old Mathers' house – the site of his own death and the place where he had first encountered the ghost of Old Mathers. Although only three days have elapsed in The Parish, 'It seemed a long time ago now and doubtless was the memory of a bad dream' (*3P*, 174) – an ironic allusion to Noman's eventual discovery that sixteen years have elapsed in the 'real world' during his stay in The Parish. Within a fictional zone, spatial and temporal laws are governed by different principles, and The Parish is a relativistic world prefigured by diverse intertextual influences from Einsteinian physics to medieval Irish epics such as *The Voyage of Maeldoon* (*c.* ninth century), both of which shape the temporal pattern of Noman's hell world.[43] Noman dismisses this time shift as a 'bad dream', not realising that in this fictional world dreams have as much 'reality' as reality itself. Within a fiction the boundaries between dreams and the waking consciousness are easily violated, and dream reality occupies as much space as non-dream reality. A page describing a dream moment occupies the same material, textual space as a waking moment, and unless it is clearly signposted the reader makes no distinction between the two states of being (both fictional).

In the fictional zone of The Parish different levels of reality collide. Quite often the reader is misled by these shifting boundaries (in the manner of Noman's dream of his own death in chapter seven) and seduced into imagining that a secondary, nested representation – dreams, anecdotes, false trails, etc. – is in fact the primary representation. Because of the delayed decoding process of this most elliptical of texts, the reader, like Noman, has been constantly tripped up by false levels of representation. Now, as he returns to Old Mathers' house for the final confrontation with Policeman Fox, all of these tangled hierarchies seem to mesh together under the roof of the key structural motif, the house itself: 'a lonely place, with no life or breath in it' (*3P*, p. 174). Initially at least, Noman is happy to recognise a familiar landmark, but he soon senses an unearthly presence, a shadow: 'a feeling came upon me that the house had changed the instant my back was turned. [. . .] I think I had made up my mind to go and had taken a few faltering steps forward when some influence came upon my eyes and dragged them round till they were again resting upon the house' (*3P*, p. 175).

This statement is loaded with encoded, yet autocritical, significance. As a narrator, Noman is a self-centred, egocentric solipsist, trusting only in the subjective evidence of his senses and particularly his sight, what Stephen Dedalus in *Ulysses* calls the 'ineluctable modality of the visible'.[44] Now, though, 'some influence came upon [his] eyes' (*3P*, p. 175), and directs his gaze. The author-god is close to bringing his fiction to an end, and manipulates his puppet accordingly. As revelations are about to unfold, the descriptive language becomes laden with self-consciousness, and even starts decoding itself: 'I stopped thinking, closing up my mind with a snap as if it were a box or a book' (*3P*, p. 178).

Throughout the narrative, the word 'box' has been a metaphor for the word 'book', and now both terms become concretely synonymous as the fictional frame buckles under the pressure. Noman has been archly monological in his thinking, resolutely refusing to accept the polyphonic and shifting nature of human language. Only when he 'stopped thinking' and closes up his rational mind can he finally begin to understand this intuitively. In fear and anger Noman hurls a stone at the lighted window of Old Mathers' house, testing the very fabric of the text: 'The shadow was so incomplete that I could not recognise any part of it but I felt certain it was the shadow of a large being or presence who was standing quite still at the side of the window and gazing out into the night to see who had thrown the stone' (*3P*, pp. 179–80).

The shadow is, of course, the invisible artist: the god of creation who lurks behind every fictional frame, making a metafictional appearance. Appropriately enough he hides at the 'side of the window', behind the framing structure of the text. Conscious of his own stuttering language and 'expecting an onslaught of indescribable ferocity', Noman is surprised by what happens next: 'Then I heard words' (*3P*, p. 180). The author-god, Policeman Fox, finally deigns to speak: 'This is a brave night!', he says, commenting not just on the narrative events but on his own realist frame breaking. Unsurprisingly, Fox's presence overwhelms Noman: 'nothing was clear to me except his overbearing policemanship, his massive rearing of wide strengthy flesh, his domination and his unimpeachable reality' (*3P*, p. 180). Fox's 'unimpeachable reality' now reigns over Noman's every response: 'He dwelt upon my mind so strongly that I felt many times more submissive than afraid' (*3P*, p. 180).

Fox, as might be expected, knows all the secret tricks of the text, the hidden trapdoors and conventions of his created world. This knowledge allows him to use the window as a door, 'putting his immense body in through the tiny opening. I do not know how he accomplished what did not look possible at all' (*3P*, p. 181). Anything is possible for the creator of the fictional world, and what is dramatised in this scene is of fundamental importance to our understanding of metafictional poetics. When Fox squeezes through a space too small to possibly contain his bulk, it is not only an affront to the commonsense logic of the 'real world' but a challenge to the conventions of realist discourse. Realist verisimilitude demands that described objects in the projected world should be conveyed in a discreet, unassuming fashion that will not draw undue attention to their created fictiveness. As Susan Stewart writes: 'Realism attempts to recoup the measurements of everyday discourse, [and] a balance of signification and significance is sought after [which is] borrowed from common sense.'[45]

The illogical horrors of *The Third Policeman* disrupt the tenuous balance of the literary system by foregrounding the creative/descriptive dichotomy of textuality. In fictions conscious of their own composition the very idea of dimensions – both spatial and temporal – is laid bare. Descriptions of objects often take on a chillingly detailed aspect, so that the object is foregrounded as words rather than embedded and naturalised. The success of this technique lies in the way that the details publicise the presence of the object as discourse, and test the parameters of description. It is like an abstract study in still life: what concerns us is not the fruit in the bowl (or even the bowl), but the formal composition of the picture within its arranged frame. What makes this particular form of metalepsis so radical is that it invites the reader into the literary process, thereby replacing the outmoded concept of the author as the primary interpretative centre. Readers of fiction bring their own experience to the story and thus animate objects by investing them with significance. Brian McHale describes this process in general: 'Real-world objects have no indeterminate points, ontologically speaking [. . .] while presented objects in fiction have ontological gaps, some of them filled in by readers in the act of concretising the text.'[46]

Retrospectively, we now begin to see how these 'ontological gaps' of descriptive paradox have been used to harass and torture Noman throughout the narrative. As far back as Noman's descent into Eternity, this flickering and uncanny meta-narrative description haunts him as he notes the simultaneous 'reality' and 'non-reality' of objects:

> It took me hours of thought long afterwards to realise why these
> articles were astonishing. *They lacked an essential property of all
> known objects.* [. . .] Simply their appearance, if even that word is
> not inadmissible, was not understood by the eye and was in any
> event indescribable. That is enough to say. (*3P*, p. 135)

Consequently, Fox squeezing his immense body through tiny
gaps not only tests the dimensions of objects but also the limits of
described bodies in discourse. Alice can descend down the rabbit's
hole and Fox can slip through the window not by magic but because
within the heterotopic universe (Wonderland; The Parish) size is
measured differently than it is in the real world, or, as Susan
Stewart writes: 'In everyday life our size is determined by measurement to context, to those things in the surrounding environment
[. . .] but in nonsense, size becomes determined by those things
within the boundary of the text.'[47]

As with objects in the physical world, measurement is not fixed
but relative to context; all units of measurement have an arbitrary
(and conventional) reference point or frame, and when the fictional
world collides with the commonsense world this reference point
shifts, and becomes meaningless. Metafictional texts use the
devices of traditional fiction as basic building blocks, showing how
life is a series of reference points, frames and contexts, without
which, as Saussure tells us, thought would be a 'vague, uncharted
nebula'.[48] It all depends on a system of difference, or, as Pluck says
of Eternity: 'It has no size at all [. . .] because there is no difference
anywhere in it and we have no conception of the extent of its
unchanging coequality' (*3P*, p. 133).

Fox brings Noman, and the reader, to his own personal police
station – a perfect, miniature replica of the 'real' barracks. The
recursive image makes Noman conscious of the tangled secondary
representations that have been deluding both him and us: 'I knew
that I was standing, not in Mathers' house, *but inside the walls of it*'
(*3P*, p. 182) – yet another of the Chinese-box motifs of infinite
regress. Now that he is near his journey's end (the end of the novel)
primary and secondary levels of representation start collapsing furiously, as if of their own volition. Noman is sucked into the verbal
vortex of the compositional design where the centre cannot hold, and
the thin, transparent membrane between the rational and the irrational starts dissolving. Words and images start leaking from one
representation to another, metamorphosing into grotesque hybrid
monsters as Fox's voice becomes the voice of Old Mathers, and Fox
assumes Old Mathers' face. In his disbelief Noman stammers an

anguished cry: 'I escaped' (*3P*, p. 183). But fictional characters cannot escape the boundaries of the text, no more than real people can escape the boundaries of their world. Noman now must realise that he is a character simply programmed to play a role, a puppet trapped within the pages of a fictional universe. His senses begin to spin and the workings of his body go haywire, like a robot malfunctioning: 'Each eye fluttered like a bird's wing in its socket and my head throbbed, swelling out like a bladder at every surge of blood' (*3P*, p. 183). Finally, the voice of the 'author-god' intrudes upon the proceedings, and addresses both Noman and the reader: 'I am Policeman Fox [. . .] and this is my own private police station and I would be glad to have your opinion on it because I have gone to great pains to make it spick and span' (*3P*, p. 183).

Though inscribed within the idiom of The Parish, this is obviously a metafictional intrusion by the 'author'. We must distinguish here between the 'author' (a metafictional representation) and the Author (Flann O'Brien). This distinction is vital because it underpins the ultimate irony of infinite regress in that an 'author' appearing in a text is nothing more than a fictional representation of authorship. We can pre-suppose an authorial first cause or prime mover, but we can never capture it through discourse. In this sense, while post-modernist fictions privilege the text over the Author, the Author still hovers above the text like an unknowable god, or, as Foucault describes it, in 'transcendental anonymity'.[49] Metafiction, it seems, is not entirely atheistic but rather agnostic in its attitude to authorship.

Metafictional narrative intrusions also parody the narrative intrusions of nineteenth-century realist texts, to underline the difference between realism and post-modernist meta-realism. Patricia Waugh makes an important distinction when she notes that the Dickensian 'Dear Reader' intrusions, although meta-lingual, function mainly in order to 'aid the readerly concretisation of the world of the book by forming a bridge between the historical and fictional world'.[50] Realist intrusions ultimately serve the mimetic order and seek to close the ontological gap between the real and the fictional (the whole point of verisimilitude) – it is really a case of emergency bridge making rather than subversive frame breaking. Contrary to this, metafiction seeks to co-opt the reader as an active player in textual composition, 'in a new conception of literature as a collective creation rather than a monologic and authoritative version of history'.[51] Metafictional intrusions remind the reader of the artifice that shapes a text. The 'author', by drawing attention to his/her existence reminds us of our shaping roles – a text is not just written but read into existence. This is why Fox declares his share in this literary nexus: 'I would be glad to have your opinion on it because I have gone to great pains to make it spick and span' (*3P*, p. 183).

Noman, no longer imagining himself as 'author' now becomes the voice of the active reader, and demands to know some of the tricks of fictional construction. Noman's struggle for identity in terms of the machinations of plot mirrors the struggle of the reader. Allegorically, Noman now represents the 'reader' in conversation with the 'author', and demands to know the significance of the station inside the walls of the house, to which Fox replies: 'It is a very rudimentary conundrum [. . .]. It is fixed this way to save the rates because if it was constructed the same as any other barracks it would be rated as a separate hereditament [. . .]' (*3P*, p. 184).

This is a direct critique of the realist tradition by a metafictional author, indicated by the deliberate verbosity of the term 'hereditament', i.e. 'a property that can be inherited' (*OED*). If the novel did not operate on this self-conscious level of representation (houses-within-houses), it would invariably represent a single, straightforward house – the realist text – and would fail in its metafictional duty to the reader. Thus it would indeed be rated a 'separate hereditament', a property (or text) inherited from an archaic and discredited tradition of realist representation.

In a final flourish, the revelation that Fox is his 'author' does not close the final page on Noman's life. Noman has sufficiently recovered his old hubris, and is determined to 'get out of this hideous house' (*3P*, p. 185), i.e. escape the enclosing parameters of the text. After all, given the ontological gap between 'author' (a character) and Author (the transcendent figure outside the text), Noman shares the same ontological plane as his erstwhile 'author', and this new-found knowledge of aestho-autogamy inspires a plea for self-determination: 'There were many things to be thought about but I would not think of them at all until I was secure in my own house' (*3P*, p. 185).

Noman briefly fantasises about the possibility of transworld migration; after all, if the metafictional author can import characters from other texts (Huysmans, Pirandello, Synge *et al*), then why not have aestho-autogamous characters who can emigrate? With this sense of powerful rebellion growing in Noman, Fox begins to look almost childlike: 'He now looked so innocent and good-natured and so troubled by the writing down of simple words that hope began to flicker once again within me' (*3P*, p. 185). Like Tristram Shandy, the author-god of Sterne's *Tristram Shandy*, Fox is 'so troubled by the writing down' that he seems distracted. Noman is about to tiptoe off the page completely and slip out of the fiction, unnoticed. Like the flickering narrative itself, hope begins to 'flicker' again in Noman. Unfortunately, as always, Noman's greed for power and knowledge overtakes him and he cannot resist one last question as to the whereabouts of the black box (the book of knowledge), the object that had landed him in such trouble in the first place. However, Fox seems evasive in his response and slips unexpectedly into a rather weird and banal discussion about 'strawberry jam':

> 'Do you like strawberry jam?' he asked. His stupid question came so unexpectedly that I nodded and gazed at him uncomprehendingly. His smile broadened. 'Well if you had that box here', he said, 'you could have a bucket of strawberry jam for your tea and if that was not enough you could have a bathful of it to lie in [. . .]'.
> (*3P*, p. 186)

Noman's debates with the policemen often degenerate into banal obscurity, a rhetorical device which Brian McHale calls the 'rhetoric of contrastive banality', i.e. a situation where 'the characters' failure to be amazed at paranormal happenings serves to heighten our amazement'.[52] The net result is a levelling effect whereby formal discourse (Noman's line of questioning) co-exists on the same semantic plane as a seemingly banal discourse (discussions about jam), and the juxtaposition undermines the commonsense legitimacy of the question. Once decoded, though, the metonymic language of the banal has an ulterior meaning. The bizarre analogy of the 'strawberry jam' refers to the latent power of the black box and the limitless possibilities of fictional creation, where anything can be true if the writer says so: 'I will put it another way', says Fox, 'you could have a house packed full of strawberry jam, every room so full that you could not open the door' (*3P*, p. 186).

Despite continuing his discussion of jam, Fox says he 'will put it another way' – an invitation to the reader to decipher it as a metafictional comment. Given the power of the box (Faustian omniscience), Noman has the power to create whole new universes of fiction. Noman is tantalised by the possibilities, but in his eagerness does not recognise the intertextual pirating of the analogy, which is taken from Lewis Carroll's *Through the Looking-Glass* (1871) when the White Queen says: 'The rule is, jam tomorrow and jam yesterday – but never jam today.'[53] As with the lift to Eternity, Noman can take out of his projected world only what he brings in with him. He can have anything he desires – as much jam as he pleases – except the one thing that he most needs: the freedom to transcend his ontological limitations, and to escape the hell of The Parish.

With this revelation of the black box's meaning, the Faustian theme is actualised. The secret of the black box is that it is the book of knowledge, with the power to manipulate all the other puppet-characters of the text, including the other policemen. Noman describes Fox's use of this power: 'calmly making ribbons of the natural order, inventing intricate and unheard of machinery to delude the other policemen, interfering drastically with time to make them think they had been leading their magical lives for years, bewildering, horrifying and enchanting the whole countryside' (*3P*, p. 188). This is the magic of fiction revealed: the author cuts and sews the natural order and re-shapes it into words, using intricate fictional devices to interfere with 'real' concepts such as time and space, and all to bewilder, horrify and enchant the reader. Now that Noman understands this he dreams of becoming a god himself, intoxicated by the 'foreshadowing of creations, changes, annihilations and god-like interferences. Sitting at home with my box of omnium I could do anything, see anything and know anything with no limit to my powers save that of my own imagination' (*3P*, p. 189).

With overreaching arrogance Noman's mind is glutted at the thought of becoming the godhead of the fictional world, with the ability to 'destroy, alter or improve the universe at will' (*3P*, p. 189). Thoughts of omnipotence rattle through his excited mind: 'I would bring de Selby himself back to life' (ironic given that de Selby translates as 'the self' or 'the same person'); or 'I would make myself invisible' (an appropriation from Marlowe's *Doctor Faustus*). Fox interrupts these frenetic reveries, and undercuts the fantastic by juxtaposing it against the mundane: 'it is very handy for taking the muck off your leggings in winter' (*3P*, p. 189). Noman is exasperated by this banal intrusion upon his megalomaniac dream of re-ordering dull reality into creative paradise, and mocks the policeman: 'Why not use it for preventing the muck getting on your leggings at all?' (*3P*, p. 189), to which Fox replies: 'You are very intellectual, and I am certain that I am nothing but a gawm' (*3P*, pp. 189–90) – a timely reminder of the Menippean satire at the heart of the novel. Noman the overreacher reacts angrily to Fox's more simplistic vision of art, and condemns the traditional conventions of fiction:

> It was clear that he was not the sort of person to be entrusted with the contents of the black box. His oafish and underground

> invention was the product of a mind which fed upon the adven-
> ture books of small boys, books in which every extravagance
> was mechanical and lethal and solely concerned with bringing
> about somebody's death in the most elaborate way imaginable.
> (*3P*, p. 190)

As the novel moves towards its close, O'Brien makes a valid critical point concerning the artificiality of narrative closure, in the
way that texts are often 'solely concerned with bringing about
somebody's death in the most elaborate way imaginable' (*3P*, p.
190). These words are not just a commentary on his own narrative
but also a critique of the way in which many realist texts tend, by
expedient convention, to end in either death or marriage: the heroic
fatal finale (the limits of consciousness) or the happily-ever-after
conclusion of romantic love. Metafictions have always grappled
with such convenient narrative closures, reflected in Sterne's
famous self-reflexive ending in *Tristram Shandy*: 'Lord!, what is all
this story about', asks Mrs Shandy after the convoluted anecdote of
Obadiah's pregnant wife and Walter Shandy's bull: 'A cock and a
bull, said Yorick – and one of the best of its kind I ever heard.'⁵⁴

The formalist Viktor Shklovsky noted how Sterne 'worked
against the background of the adventure novel with its firmly
established form and its rule of ending a story with a wedding'.⁵⁵
Paradoxically, and while this critique is doubtless intended by
O'Brien, *The Third Policeman* itself comes dangerously (and mischievously) close to a similar realist denouement. The theme of
marriage is re-enacted in the love affair between Noman and the
bicycle (Faustian redemption through love), but this scenario is
strategically abandoned almost as soon as it is set up – after all,
Noman is dead and his loved one is a bicycle.

A possible closure is the revelation of Noman's death, but what
pulls it all back from the brink of realism is the final circular loop:
Noman is dead but it is a living death of infinite regress, destined as
he is to cyclically re-enact his adventures for all eternity. As Noman
enters the barracks for the 'last' time (now with Divney in tow),
Pluck's catchphrase from chapter four – '"It's my teeth", I heard him
say, abstractedly and half-aloud. [. . .] "Nearly every sickness is from
the teeth"' (*3P*, p. 54) – is repeated almost verbatim, taking account
only of the added presence of Divney: '"It's my teeth", we heard him
say, abstractedly and half-aloud. "Nearly every sickness is from the
teeth"' (*3P*, p. 199). O'Brien avoids any conventional ending by
forcing Noman (and the reader) to begin again, the tale repeating
itself, *ad infinitum*. The repetition invites the reader to start the

novel once again, but this time conscious of the ironic ellipsis which has deferred our decoding of the narrative all along. We have come close to a realist ending – a possible death and a possible marriage – but that realist conception of the world is no longer tenable. Noman had hoped to escape the limits of the final pages by running away with the bicycle, but now that hope had faded: 'I could not quite convince myself beyond all doubt that I would ever again see the house where I was born' (*3P*, p. 194). That house belongs to an older, realist tradition; the house that confronts him now is a self-conscious metaphor for textual structure:

> Suddenly I found myself noticing my own existence and taking account of my surroundings. [. . .] About a hundred yards away was a house which astonished me. It looked as if it were painted like an advertisement on a board on the roadside and, indeed, very poorly painted. It looked completely false and unconvincing. (*3P*, 198)

This description – 'painted like an advertisement on a board' – advertises its own ontological incongruity: a picture on a two-dimensional plane, painted in by an artist – the artificiality of all mimetic discourse, revealed as discourse. Like all objects created in fiction a house is an arbitrary line drawing, sketched by the artist and coloured in by the reader, or, as Noman now sees it, 'uncertain in outline like a thing glimpsed under ruffled water' (*3P*, p. 198). As he draws closer to the 'shadow of the structure', Noman finally sees the real boundaries that lock him into the Parish – the final page of the novel:

> It seemed ordinary enough at close quarters except that it was very white and still. It was momentous and frightening; the whole morning and the whole world seemed to have no purpose at all save to frame it and give it some magnitude and position so that I could find it with my simple senses and pretend to myself that I understood it. (*3P*, pp. 198–9)

Noman gets his final fright as time ('the whole morning') and space ('the whole world') are revealed to be constructs and that he is trapped within a fictional order. There is 'no purpose' or meaning behind the structure of the house except to 'frame it'. Reality is a fiction which is framed by convention in order to 'pretend to myself that I understood it'. Existential and metafictional ontologies finally blend as one: Noman's consciousness of his own 'death' and his awareness of his own fictionality become the same thing, woven together in a grim, post-modernist joke. As Brian McHale has said of this post-modernist conceit: 'The connection between awareness of fictionality and awareness of death [. . .] is highly suggestive [and] often functions as a kind of master-trope for determinism – cultural, historical, psychological determinism, but especially the inevitability of death.'[56]

For the post-modernist everything is fiction: history, psychology, language. O'Brien's fascination with death is not just a macabre or morbid personal excitement but a powerful metaphor for the limits of human consciousness. Noman's final horror is that he is eternally locked into an endlessly repeating cycle because, as Susan Stewart notes, 'closure can only be imposed on infinity by an arbitrary stop rule'.[57] Appropriately then, the novel ends with a repetition of the opening description of Pluck, which brings us right back to our initial discussion of mirrors and frames: 'He was standing behind a little counter in a neat whitewashed day-room; his mouth was open and he was looking into a mirror which hung upon the wall' (*3P*, p. 199).

4. This is not a pipe:
frame-breaking strategies

[N]ever do I hit upon any invention or device which tendeth to the furtherance of good writing, but I instantly make it public; willing that all mankind should write as well as myself.
Laurence Sterne, *Tristram Shandy*, 1759–6[1]

According to the narratologist Gerard Genette, metalepsis is 'the transition from one narrative level to another [that] can in principle be achieved only by the narrating, the act that consists precisely of introducing into one situation, by means of a discourse, the knowledge of another situation'.[2] Metaleptic transition is an act of transgression, a cross-border violation of the usual narrative boundaries which serves to make the reader conscious of 'another situation'. In the preceding chapter we discussed the metaleptic significance of the self-conscious narrator, and saw what this other situation might entail. Broadly speaking, the device of the self-conscious narrator has two important functions: first, an aesthetic function, a formal deconstruction of fictional – and in particular realist – conventions; and second, a moral function, whereby the self-conscious narrator becomes a metafictional trope for ontological determinism.

The relationship between these two functions is basically a pedagogic one, i.e. a belief that an aesthetic awareness of fictional conventions has wider ideological repercussions because it forcibly reminds us of the artificiality of *all* discourse, literary or otherwise. Metaleptic techniques transfer action from the devices in a story to the reader of the story, or as Ninian Mellamphy puts it: '[The reader], no longer duped into conventional expectations, no longer needing to suspend his disbelief, casts a cold eye on every word, line and passage, recognises influences, archetypes, parallels, plagiarisings, and thus, perceives the love-hate relationship between the narrative and the tradition.'[3]

As a metafiction, *The Third Policeman* is an ontological mnemonic puzzle, a literary labyrinth complete with autocritically signposted clues to its own methods of construction. Like a trail of breadcrumbs in a dark forest, it reminds us of where we came in, and it offers us a way back out. Although metalepsis lays bare the historically contingent conventions of literature, it does not entirely abandon them; instead, it burns up some the clichés of the novel while perversely retaining all its privileges. It is not anti-realist or anti-modernist for its own sake but is rather a reconstruction of fictional conceits in light of a post-modernist consciousness. Frame-breaking techniques in fiction help us map the inescapable 'writtenness' of reality through self-awareness of literary practices. Metalepsis helps smash the fragile illusion that not only is a text a series of formal conventions but that all discourse is a conventionalised set of forms, enshrined by history and culture.

The focus of this present chapter will be a discussion of *The Third Policeman*'s primary frame-breaking devices – a series of semiotic signs and topographical arrangements that deliberately intrude on the fiction's narrative structure to remind us of its own textuality. Such classical metafictional devices include the use of lists; the deconstruction of naturalised semiotic patterns such as the days of the week and number systems; and the use of maps, graphs, tables and different kinds of typeface. The most important of these devices in *The Third Policeman* is the imaginative use of mock footnotes, and this will be considered in detail. For the moment, though, it is sufficient to note the allegorical nature of the relationship between the primary narrative and these footnotes. The body of the text, as a metafiction, is chiefly concerned with the nature and problems of authorship and textuality – a ludic allegory of writing practices. The footnotes are, literally, commentaries on that text, and teach the reader how to decode its intricacies. The footnotes then are simultaneously a guide to the reader and a critical satire of that guide, becoming, in effect, an allegory of reading practices. Nearly all the topographical arrangements in *The Third Policeman* operate according to this set of principles. If the self-conscious narrator is the master trope for determinism in the novel, then the mock footnote is its key metaleptic device.

Post-modernist metafiction – a self-reflexive, dialectical and parodic form of literature – is often, by its very nature, on the cutting edge of literary practices: a reactive antidote to established mainstream modes of discourse (including scientific, philosophical and cinematic modes, as well as popular and more formal literary genres). As such, this genre is often aligned with an avant-garde, experimental tradition, and indeed some metafictional texts occasionally employ quite radical, even eccentric, metaleptic devices of disruption, e.g. the use of blank pages as in *Tristram Shandy*. At the same time, metalepsis does not have to be quite so anarchic to be successful, or as Brian McHale comments: 'The machine does not have to be fully visible in order for the foregrounding to work; it only has to be conspicuously present, conspicuously in place.'[4]

In fact, it could be argued that this 'conspicuous' yet discrete self-conscious presence better serves the polyphonic carnival which is central to the post-modernist aesthetic. Unlike the openly deconstructive format of *At Swim-Two-Birds* – a late-modernist transitional text – the sublimated metaleptic strategies of *The Third Policeman* simultaneously mimic the surface patterns of traditional narratives, while subtly undermining these patterns by 'making strange' key textual conceits. The reader's horizons of expectations are quietly displaced as traditional configurations are progressively disassembled. If we are to fully participate in the riotous carnival of reading then we must absorb both narrative and alter-narrative – the revealed realist mimesis, and the latent metafictional diegesis.

Consequently, the concept of metalepsis will be discussed over two chapters. This present chapter will deal with its more overt, autocritical forms, which usurp the authority of the text *from without*, by intertextually employing recognisable devices from other fictions or modes of representation such as maps, graphs, footnotes, etc. These visible (but still discrete) patterns not only invoke the intertextual spirits which inhabit the fictional text, but because they operate on a more analytical level they also allow us a way into the meta-narrative maze, and help us to understand the novel as an allegory of discourse. Chapter five will then expand on this argument and focus on more covert subtextual disruptions which operate *within* the idiomatic zone of the projected world itself.

In his essay 'Two Meta-Novelists: Sternesque Elements in Novels by Flann O'Brien', Rüdiger Imhof makes a valuable comparison between *Tristram Shandy* and *At Swim-Two-Birds* which, beyond 'superficial similarities, shows an enormous amount of compositional and thematic correspondences'.[5] Imhof is wary of stating that O'Brien deliberately or consciously imitated Sterne, or used his work as a direct source. Given the infinitely expansive nature of intertextuality – in its broadest sense all discourse is intertextual – such caution is understandable. For Imhof, the purpose of the comparison is simply to show that O'Brien 'belongs to the tradition of the comic-experimental, or, preferably, meta-novelists'.[6] However, from my own reading of these texts it seems clear that Sterne is an abiding influence on O'Brien's work – not just in *At Swim-Two-Birds* but in the compositional design of *The Third Policeman* as well. I also believe that the debt goes further, and that O'Brien very consciously steals key metaleptic devices from Sterne, and also adapts certain stylistic idiosyncrasies which are important from a thematic point of view. To pretend otherwise is to hedge one's bets, and the depth of these Sterne/O'Brien parallels should become evident over the course of this analysis.

In terms of the relationship between *At Swim-Two-Birds* and *Tristram Shandy*, Imhof draws at least one conscious stylistic parallel which suggests deliberate imitation, in the form of topographical arrangements or, more specifically, alphabetical charts. In *Tristram Shandy* Tristram tells us that 'love is certainly, at least alphabetically speaking, one of the most

    A gitating
    B ewitching
    C onfounded
    D evilish affairs of life' . . .[7]

This acrostic arrangement has a direct parallel in *At Swim-Two-Birds*. When Orlick Trellis is poised to recite a long list of his father's sins, the other characters, in the interest of reader-friendly brevity, suggest that he catalogues them. Orlick duly obliges:

> ANTHRAX, paid no attention to regulations governing the movements of animals affected with.
> BOYS, corner, consorted with.
> CONVERSATIONS, licentious, conducted by telephone with unnamed female servants of the Department of Posts and Telegraphs.
> DIRTINESS, all manner of spiritual mental and physical, gloried in. (*AS2B*, p. 171)

Any alphabetical list underlines the essentially arbitrary ordering of the world into conventional, methodical categories. The strategic re-ordering of the verb–object word order – 'BOYS, corner, consorted with' – parodies the formal tone and style of supposedly 'authoritative' and non-fictional texts, such as dictionaries or telephone directories. The alphabetical list also foregrounds the artificiality of discourse (fiction or non-fiction) by deconstructing written language as a semiotic system of symbols, namely individual letters. Above all, such lists proclaim their own textuality, or, as Susan Stewart has noted: 'Alphabetical order epitomises the elimination of hierarchy, the levelling of elements in the list. It provides a gesture of resistance to any attempt to interpret significance in the particular arrangement of textual elements.'[8]

Alphabetical lists are a perfect illustration of the way that metaleptic devices foreground the duality of metaphor, by giving metaphors both a literal and figurative function. This emphasises the importance of context or framing, and expresses the tension between what language refers to and its own volatile, unstable make-up. By drawing attention to the constituent letters in a word this form of metalepsis 'takes the words of the continuum literally, to the letter'.[9]

In a broader context, alphabetisation as a formalist strategy immediately places *At Swim-Two-Birds* within a recognisable generic tradition, or, as Brian McHale notes, it is 'especially characteristic of [. . .] Menippean satire; hybrid fictional–non-fictional discursive narrative texts made up of fragments'.[10] Alphabetisation illustrates the primary concern of post-modernist Menippean satires, namely that reality will always be fragmented because any discourse is fundamentally a process of 'metaphorical substitution', i.e. 'the application of a name to an object or action to which it is not literally applicable' ('Metaphor', *OED*).

Other conventional systems of classification are foregrounded in this manner, such as the use of non-alphabetical lists. Unlike the obviously metaleptic list in *At Swim-Two-Birds*, the lists used in *The Third Policeman* typically tend to be buried deep within the fabric of the text itself, almost naturalised by the 'realist' surroundings – but not so much that we fail to notice their distracting displacement. In *The Third Policeman* there are no blank pages, no chapter synopses, no flagrant authorial intrusions or transworld travelling (like the obviously textual Finn Mac Cool in *At Swim-Two-Birds*). Though less violent in its disruptions, *The Third Policeman* better exploits the reflexive potential of such methods by deliberately striving for polyphony and multiple reading strategies. The net result is that it renders our normative reading strangely disconcerting; we sense that something is amiss but must delve deeper to analytically chart its estranging structures.

Such cloaked forms of metalepsis achieve their success by repeated levels of nested representation. Repetition formally estranges and dislodges these devices from their naturalised positions. It makes strange the 'normal' and the 'natural', and

shows us the methods by which simple, everyday codes of signification are socially structured. Delaying the impact of metalepsis can
strengthen its epiphanic value. Other metafictions – *At Swim-Two-
Birds* included – sometimes foreground their 'tricks' to such a
degree that they fail to truly 'alienate' (in the proper Brechtian
sense) the reader sufficiently. We marvel at the ingenuity and .
applaud the intricate playfulness, yet may fail to recognise the
wider philosophical implications. Metalepsis can trip itself up by its
very cleverness, and the dazzling displays of technical virtuosity
can become indulgently self-gratifying and therefore extrinsic to
thematic concerns. In this respect, the metalepsis of *At Swim-Two-
Birds* can seem rather mechanical whereas in *The Third Policeman*
it operates more organically.

An example of this is the repetitious use of lists in *The Third
Policeman*. In chapter three, Noman, in a 'mocking inquiry' (*3P*, p.
41) – which it literally is, although Noman misses the irony – puts
forward a list of ten names which he might conceivably bear:

> Hugh Murray.
> Constantin Petrie.
> Peter Small.
> Signor Beniamino Bari.
> The Honourable Alex O'Brannigan, Bart.
> Kurt Freund.
> Mr. John P. de Salis, M.A.
> Dr. Solway Garr.
> Bonaparte Gosworth.
> Legs O'Hagan. (*3P*, p. 41)

Beginning with an arbitrary though apparently ordinary name –
'Hugh Murray' – the referential scope of the list broadens geometri-
cally to show the impossibly limitless range of choices. More exotic,
even absurd names are put forward, such as 'Constantin Petrie' and
'Signor Beniamino Bari'. Significantly, the list of names follows de
Selby's 'theory of names', outlined in a footnote on the previous page,
which proposed that names had 'crude onomatopoeic associations
with the appearance of the person or object named' (*3P*, p. 40, fn),
which would explain a name such as 'Peter Small'. This is a perfect
example of the many tangled hierarchies that litter the text whereby
secondary representations – like the set of footnotes – directly
impinge on the primary narrative, instructing the reader how to
'order' the text.

The primary list of names widens exponentially to include
foreign names, titles and puns – 'Kurt Freund' suggesting 'Curt

Friend' perhaps. (Interestingly, Kurt Freund (1914–96) was also the name of a Czech sexologist famous for his studies of male homosexuality. The fact that this is the only name on the list that seems to be taken from real life is surely significant.) Academic titles establish themselves in a false hierarchy ('M.A.', 'Dr.'), and this gives way to the realisation of historical names ('Bonaparte'). The infinite possibilities and permutations of the list are copperfastened by the inclusion of nicknames – 'Legs O'Hagan' (legs being an important motif in the text as a whole).

In part, the semiotic significance of such a list is its infinite range – the fact is that it can go on forever yet still be incomplete proclaims its open-endedness and essential emptiness. Despite its formal attempt at structuring and cataloguing, the list has no real subordination of order and in the end is anti-hierarchical and hopelessly arbitrary. Most of all, the topographical design of the list usurps normative reading codes, and in the process foregrounds the materiality of the text. Normally we tend to read (by conventional decree) from left to right and from top to bottom, across and down the page. The composition of a list alters this normal process, or, as Susan Stewart notes, 'the list is vertical, it runs against this dynamic'[11] and so we are forced to revise our reading habits and improvise a new dynamic. All topographical arrangements in metafiction operate like this, or, as Shari Benstock writes of *Tristram Shandy*: 'The various encrustations on the textual surface include drawings, musical scores, asterisks, ellipses, and changes in typeface; there are also dislocations such as the Dedication and various chapters – another means of reminding us of the textuality of the work.'[12]

The repetition of similar lists on successive pages reinforces the metaleptic condition with ruthless efficiency. For example, Noman proposes a list of possible occupations for Martin Finnucane (becoming fearful when Finnucane answers only in the negative) (*3P*, p. 45); Pluck provides a list of possible crimes that Noman may wish to report, and when Noman ticks none of the above Pluck declares it to be 'a very difficult piece of puzzledom' (*3P*, p. 56). Later still, MacCruiskeen initiates yet another list when he asks Noman an apparently absurd question: 'Can you notify me of the meaning of a bulbul?' (*3P*, p. 65). Noman is perplexed but humours him by giving him a list of possible answers, and the game ends only when MacCruiskeen gives the correct definition – 'a Persian nightingale' (*3P*, p. 66). The point here is that all language is a game, and all signs arbitrary and differential. A little-known word like 'bulbul' – infrequently used outside of its specialised field or cultural context – could equally be applied to any number of phenomena which lack specific designated signifiers – like the 'brass knobs on a German steam organ' (*3P*, p. 65), or the 'lather in a cow's mouth' (*3P*, p. 66) also proposed in Noman's sarcastic but imaginative list of possible meanings.

In chapter seven a final list of some twenty-eight possible names is offered to Noman as the Sergeant tries to name him, but to no avail. As Pluck says, it is an 'astonishing parade of nullity', and on completion of his proposed list (which playfully includes O'Brien's real name, 'Nolan'), Pluck declares: 'there are very few more names that you could have [. . .] different to the ones I have recited' (*3P*, p. 101). The ironic autocriticism here is that, no matter how long Pluck's random list is, there will always be more names that could be added to it, and so on *ad infinitum*. Imposing any system of order on an infinite plane – no matter how seemingly exhaustive and methodical (Pluck's is neither) – is an exercise doomed to failure. Metalepsis then is a way of testing the parameters of conventional framing procedures, a way of short-circuiting the random nature of any system of signs and exploding the concept of fixed, stable order. Similarly, all the topographical arrangements and physical trappings in the novel function as short-circuit signs: tables, footnotes, maps, etc., all proclaim themselves as text. Less obvious, though, is the way that the novel tends to disrupt more commonplace categories of arbitrary order, like the days of the week, the names of the months, or even simple number systems.

In the opening chapter, for example, all the days of the week are enumerated in a seemingly haphazard fashion. Noman recalls, from a child's point of view, the death of his mother, believing in childish fashion that she had merely gone away, and 'might be back on Wednesday' (*3P*, p. 8). His confusion is understandable but his choice of that particular day is unexplained and seems arbitrary, in the way that children often confuse the order of days and cannot differentiate change until they successfully master the conventional pattern – pointing out in fact that it *is* a conventional pattern, culturally acquired.

When Noman returns to the farm from boarding school, Divney announces his imminent departure now that his work is done and his services are no longer required, but he keeps putting off that departure by randomly changing the designated date:

> The next day was Thursday. John Divney said that his work was
> now done and he would be ready to go home to where his people

were on Saturday. [. . .] But on Saturday he said there were a
few things to finish and that he could not work on Sunday but
that he would be in a position to hand over the place in perfect
order on Tuesday evening. On Monday he had a sick pig to mind
and that delayed him. (*3P*, p. 10)

Divney's promises are empty and the day of leaving is perpetually deferred. Unless he fulfils his promise to leave, the naming of
the day becomes quite meaningless. Divney's inaction strips his
speech of any possibility of meaning, and renders the names of the
days purely self-referential and abstract. As Susan Stewart has
observed, this is a typical strategy of metafiction, where nonsense
and absurdity confront 'the institutions of everyday life and
rearrange them according to another, incongruous set of principles
[which is] a radical shifting of form away from content'.[13]
    Several pages later Divney disappears on business, and when he
returns he promises that 'four barrels of better porter could be
expected on Friday' (*3P*, p. 12). At this point the reader is allowed a
little knowing smirk at the fact that the porter arrived 'punctually
on that day' (*3P*, p. 12) – the only promise kept by the manipulative
Divney. Conscious of this fact, we might wonder whether 'Friday'
held any special significance for Divney. The answer is no, not particularly, although the inclusion of that particular day means that
all seven days of the week get a mention in the first chapter. This
manipulation of the text makes us realise that at least two voices
'tell' the story: Noman's mimetic voice and a textual voice which
arises from the physical text itself – a semiotic discourse exclusive
of represented speech or the narrative speaker.
    Later on in the novel this re-arrangement of socially natu-
ralised categories is textualised further when Noman fantasises
about the limitless power of the black box: 'I could get rid of John
Divney [. . .]. I could write the most unbelievable commentaries
[. . .]. I would improve the weather [. . .]. Every Tuesday I would
make myself invisible' (*3P*, p. 189). Having realised the possibilities of omnipotence – destroying or creating life, altering the fabric
of the universe – we are not surprised that Noman imagines
becoming invisible, but why on Tuesday? Why not any other day?
Again, no reason at all save to foreground the capriciousness of a
most mundane yet customary system of order. Noman can play
God it seems, yet still be trapped within a simple temporal order.
Time is an ideological construct which figures his existence, literally, on a daily basis, yet is not deemed important enough to be
altered or transformed.

In a similar vein, the seasons, an index of change in the 'natural' world, can be conceived of only through non-natural categories of thought. In chapter one, Noman's memories of that time record 'an evening in a happy yellow summer' (*3P*, p. 10), changing a page later to 'One day in early winter' (*3P*, p. 12). Given the absolutely nebulous and relative time-changes in the projected world of the novel, such categories no longer have any real concrete function. When they lose their signifying ability as temporal reference points in the real world they become self-publicising and self-referential; evocative words which evoke only their emptiness.

Months of the year are also rendered obsolete. In chapter one, for example, Noman tells us about how he discovered the works of de Selby while still in school: 'I was about sixteen then and the date was the seventh of March. I still think that day is the most important in my life and can remember it more readily than I do my birthday' (*3P*, p. 9). It seems so important for Noman to record his discovery that he gives the reader a specific date, but having no more information the date is meaningless to us and we are more interested in the fact that he cannot remember his birthday. Out of its framing context the specific date, by itself, has no meaning. Dates, like all words, depend on a contextualising system for their relevance. Throughout the novel a total of seven months is recorded, but at no time do they ever further our knowledge of the situation, or locate the shifting narrative within a specific time frame.

Numerical systems are similarly foregrounded, and for the most part serve to impede rather than enlarge our understanding of the narrative. In chapter five, for example, numbers appear with alarming and noticeable frequency, referring to a wide range of measurements, times and quantities: 'two left-hands' (p. 64, fn), 'three-speed gear' (p. 66), 'seven inches' (p. 68), 'ten minutes' (p. 69), 'two years' (p. 70), 'five mins' (p. 70), 'two thin butter-spades' (p. 72), 'two straight-handled teaspoons' (p. 72), 'two knives' (p. 72), 'twelve little chests' (p. 72), 'three years' (p. 72), 'thirteen', 'twenty-eight' and 'twenty-nine' chests (p. 73), 'two wrinkled cigarettes' (p. 74), 'Number twenty-two' (p. 74), 'six years ago' (p. 74), 'the last five' (p. 74), 'Number One' (p. 74), 'a million of them' (p. 74).

This preponderance of numeric detail does nothing to enhance our understanding of The Parish, save to remind us of its textual make-up. So many different numbers are cited that we can imagine the author just pulling them out of the air at random. We become casually aware of the author's hand by realising that numbers in this text are fictitious and purely self-referential. Systems of order that are useful in the real world become distracting in the projected zone, emphasising the difference between the two worlds. Again this is achieved by repetition – concepts that would normally evade our notice insistently proclaim their presence by intrusion – on page 88, for example, some eighteen different figures are quoted, all quite meaningless, except for the way in which they retard the reading process.

The only number in the novel with any real narrative relevance is the number three, which earns its significance both as a structural motif and an intertextual 'magic' symbol. In the space of one page in the first chapter that number is repeated several times, which makes us conscious of its presence. We are told that Old Mathers lives in a house 'three miles away' and always carried no less than 'three thousand pounds with him' (*3P*, p. 15). After Noman and Divney discuss their murderous plan, 'three further months passed before I could bring myself to agree to the proposal', Noman tells us, 'and three months before I openly admitted to Divney that my misgivings were at an end' (*3P*, p. 15).

The near-mantric repetition of this number reminds us of the mysterious title of the book, *The Third Policeman*. The principle of verisimilitude underlying realist fiction would naturally tend to avoid such self-conscious references, not only because they remind us of the textual frame but also because they suggest the shaping hand of an author. In this novel we are deliberately made aware that the apparently random and marginal numbers described (referring to distance, quantity and time) are being manipulated to some further end by the author-god.

On an intertextual level the number three is a highly significant 'magic' number in folklore and fairytale. As Bruno Bettelheim wrote in his seminal work *The Uses of Enchantment: The Meaning and Importance of Fairy Tales*, three is not only a traditional symbol for sexuality but also for 'finding out who one is biologically':

> Three also stands for the relations within the nuclear family, and efforts to ascertain where one fits in there. Thus, three symbolises a search for who one is biologically (sexually), and who one is in relation to the most important persons in one's life. Broadly put, three symbolises the search for one's personal and one's social identity.[14]

Three, then, represents Noman's search for his identity, and his eventual discovery that he is, in fact, a fictional character; the 'child' as it were of the union between text and author (that author represented by the dark god of the novel, the third policeman). Three has always been an important symbol in O'Brien's fiction. In *At Swim-Two-Birds* he opens his novel with the frame-breaking notion that 'A good book may have three openings entirely dissimilar and inter-related only in the prescience of the author' (*AS2B*, p. 9). This stylised triadic opening (constructed by the author for all to see) ends appropriately with a triadic conclusion, and a reprise of this triadic coda symbolised by the grotesque tableau of a suicide which ends the novel proper:

> Numbers, however, will account for a great proportion of unbalanced and suffering humanity. [. . .] Well known, alas, is the case of the poor German who was very fond of three and who made each aspect of his life a thing of triads. He went home one evening and drank three cups of tea with three lumps of sugar in each, cut his jugular with a razor three times and scrawled with a dying hand on a picture of his wife, good-bye, good-bye, good-bye. (*AS2B*, pp. 217–18)

Structurally, the triadic demands of the texts are symmetrically closed ('good-bye, good-bye, good-bye' to the three sub-narratives) and in his description of the schizoid perceptions which inspired the suicide, O'Brien makes one last thematic gesture as a Menippean satirist. O'Brien represents here the kind of cabalistic thought that isolated individuals resort to in a hopeless attempt to impose some vestige of order on a random, chaotic universe, where 'normal' verbal language has become devalued. Within this paradigm all reality is a series of constructs, and numerology just one extreme example of how futile such systems of thought can be once deconstructed. Emphasising the number three in *The Third Policeman* breaks the frame and reveals the plastic artifice of all discourse, literary or otherwise.

It is within the material trappings of the text itself, however, that metaleptic procedures function best by constantly exposing the framing conventions of the primary mimetic narrative. The primary narrative of *The Third Policeman* – Noman's picaresque journey of discovery – is most effectively destabilised at the *margins* of its discourse, that is to say, on the flickering boundaries between the text as mimesis, and the text as text. The mimetic integrity of Noman's tale is continually violated by the intrusion of secondary, nested levels of representation which confuse the true status of the overt, primary narrative. Quite often, a series of tangled hierarchies is introduced into the story without warning, and these serve to alienate the reader from the apparently 'real' text: dreams, nightmares, hallucinations and different modes of rhetoric undermine the mimetic authenticity *from the inside. The Third Policeman* is a novel in a constant state of internal contradiction. These tangled hierarchies can also be topographical: graphs, maps and footnotes, for example, fulfil a similar function in meta-novels.

Such devices are not unique to post-modernism: Sterne employs them liberally in *Tristram Shandy*, but to slightly different effect. In the closing chapter of Book VI for example, Tristram presents the long-suffering reader with a series of graphs which, he says, represent the narrative progress, digressions included: 'except at the curve, marked A, where I took a trip to Navarre, – and the indented curve B, which is the short airing when I was there with the Lady Baussiere and her page, – I have not taken the least frisk of a digression':[15]

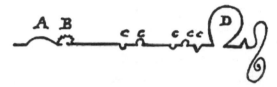

Comically, insofar as it can, Tristram's narrative graph does actually map the general narrative terrain with all its glorious twists and turns. More important is the way in which it uses the raw materials of traditional storytelling to reveal its own poetics, or, as Viktor Shklovsky describes it: '[This] novel's characteristic trait is precisely the unusualness of the pattern of deployment often even of its typical elements.'[16]

By juxtaposing two levels of discourse – and subsequently two modes of rhetoric – in the one textual space, Tristram transgresses the framing boundaries of each, and simultaneously deconstructs both. The narrative discourse of fiction and the scientific discourse of graph analysis destabilise each other. The various components of the work (graph, footnotes, etc.) appear to support the supposed 'authority' of the primary narrative, thus making the fictional aspect of *Tristram Shandy* the means of undercutting the work's authority.

A similar deconstruction occurs in chapter seven of *The Third Policeman*, with the footnoted inclusion of a table of figures which purports to be a reconstruction of MacCruiskeen's 'readings' of the eternal machine that controls the workings of The Parish:

PILOT READING	READING ON BEAM	READING ON LEVER	NATURE OF FALL (if any) with time
10.2	4.9	1.25	Light 4.15
10.2	4.6	1.25	Light 18.16
9.5	6.2	1.7	Light 7.15 (with lumps)
10.5	4.25	1.9	Nil
12.6	7.0	3.73	Heavy 21.6
12.5	6.5	2.5	Black 9.0
9.25	5.0	6.0	Black 14.45 (with lumps)

(*3P*, p. 103)

In pseudo-scientific fashion Noman re-creates for the reader a table of 'the relative figures for a week's reading' (*3P*, p. 103, fn). In a moment of supreme metaleptic irony the author has Noman (in his dual role as mimetic narrator and textual 'editor') issue a traditional but mock disclaimer – 'For obvious reasons the figures themselves are fictitious' (*3P*, p. 103, fn). Metafictionally, the reason for these 'fictitious' figures is obvious – we *are* reading a fiction, albeit one with clues to its own poetics. Noman, however, as a classical positivist scholar, cannot share in the irony, and this for him is merely a conventional disclaimer for unverified (and unverifiable) data. Having got only a brief look at the policeman's notebook (significantly a black book, which recalls the black box), Noman is presenting us with a reconstructed model, and not the 'real' figures. The fact that Noman here adopts a textual voice, and talks directly to the reader, is itself an effective schizoid split. On the one hand, Noman as mimetic narrator cannot see that he is merely a character in a fiction; on the other, he squarely addresses a reader from the footnoted margins of the text – a perfect example of the way in which mimetic and textual voices interface at the margins of discourse.

The readings on the graph, from a formalist perspective, are less important than the graph's material inclusion in the work, though in themselves these figures and classifications have inevitably evoked speculation amongst O'Brien critics. In a fascinating essay on the use of scientific rhetoric in the novel – 'Beyond the Zone of Middle Dimensions: A Relativistic Reading of *The Third Policeman*' – Charles Kemnitz proposes a 'four-dimensional table analogous to the table of readings'.[17] For Kemnitz, the table titles – 'Pilot Reading', 'Reading on Beam', 'Reading on Lever' and 'Nature of

Fall' – correspond respectively to his own titles of 'Newton', 'Relativity', 'Morals', and 'Language':

NEWTON	RELATIVITY	MORALS	LANGUAGE
Chapt. 1	Chapt. 2–12	soul	analogues
de Selby	narrator	execution	map
bicycle	bicycle	bicycle	bicycle

(Kemnitz, p. 72)

How Kemnitz arrives at this conclusion is never adequately explained, either in the context of his essay or in terms of the novel itself, and the kindest conclusion to be reached, given the spirited, tongue-in-cheek tone of the essay, is that Kemnitz is being deliberately playful here, and is celebrating the comic spirit of the satire.

If we must venture some interpretative speculation – a strong temptation which in itself is to willingly succumb to the metaleptic lure – it seems saner to decode these categories in terms of the metafictional pattern. On this scheme, the three different categories of reading ('pilot', 'beam' and 'lever') point to the matrices of literary composition, i.e. author, text and reader. Specifically, let us assume that 'pilot' is a metaphor for 'author', the person in the controlling cockpit of the work. Then, let us construe 'beam' as a metaphor for the text, the word itself defined by the *Oxford English Dictionary* as: '1. Long piece of squared timber supported at both ends, used in houses' [house being a metaphor for text in the novel]; 'lever in engine connecting piston-rod and crank' [a key component in the literary machine]; or '2. Ray or pencil of radiation; this as guide to aircraft' [the pencil of light which guides the pilot]; 'directional flow of particles' [particles being an image for words in this novel]. Indeed, later on in the text, Joe the Soul (Noman's ontologically superior alter ego, and another textual voice) tells us that 'beam' does, in fact, represent the fictional life of the projected world when he lectures Noman that 'Humanity is an ever-widening spiral and life is the beam that plays briefly on each succeeding ring. All humanity from its beginning to its end is already present but the beam has not yet played beyond you' (*3P*, p. 119).

On this scheme, if 'pilot' represents 'author' and 'beam' the 'text', then it is fair to assume that 'lever' symbolises the reader, or, as the *Oxford English Dictionary* again defines it: 'a device consisting of [. . .] a rigid structure of which one point (fulcrum) is fixed, another is connected with the force (weight) to be resisted or acted upon, and a third is connected with the force (power) applied' – a good analogy of the way that the text operates on the reader. Figuratively speaking, the dictionary describes the lever as the 'means of exerting moral force', i.e. the co-creative reader.

Finally, the fourth category – 'Nature of Fall (if any) with Time' – could be understood as the gradual fall of Noman himself as the story evolves, analogous both to the Faustian fall (the moral theme) and ontological fall (metafictional theme). This interpretation is validated in the following chapter when MacCruiskeen and Pluck tell the baffled Noman the significance of the readings, though again it is encoded within the language of The Parish:

> 'You would be astonished at the importance of the charcoal' [the physical marks of writing], the Sergeant said. 'The great thing is to keep the beam [text] reading down as low as possible and you are doing very well if the pilot-mark [writing] is steady. But if you let the beam [text] rise, where are you with your lever [reader]? If you neglect the charcoal feedings [writing] you will send the beam [text] rocketing up and there is bound to be a serious explosion.' (*3P*, p. 138)

Not to be outdone, MacCruiskeen weighs in with his own words of wisdom: '"Low pilot, small fall", MacCruiskeen said. He spoke neatly and wisely as if his remark was a proverb' (*3P*, p. 138). MacCruiskeen's remark is a reconstructed proverb within the idiom of the zone, a textual perversion of real-world proverbs, and as Susan Stewart has noted, 'proverbs, those last bastions of common sense, are often the victim of [metalepsis]'.[18]

Finally, the Sergeant tells Noman that the literary machine has 'helical gears' (*3P*, p. 138), i.e. a spiral system, which equates with Joe the Soul's previous comment that 'Humanity is an ever-widening spiral' (*3P*, p. 119), confirming that the readings of the machine do relate to the literary process. Deciphering the table of readings in this manner is at least consistent with the 'fictitious' (*3P*, p. 103) range of figures in the graph. The seven sets of readings ostensibly relate to a week's daily readings, but also correspond to the seven chapters of the novel consumed at this point, the graph itself appearing in the seventh chapter. The 'lever' readings (i.e. reader awareness and participation) are the only readings which consistently rise, from 1.25 to the final reading of 6.0 (while the other categories of reading vary erratically), with the exception of the sixth lever reading, which drops slightly. There is in fact a textual explanation for this. The sixth chapter of the novel concerns itself with Pluck's atomic theory, and is the only chapter of the seven which is not annotated by de Selbian footnotes (with the exception of the first 'realist' chapter which discusses de Selby in the primary narrative). These footnotes, being both a guide to the reader and a satire of that guide are, as I shall shortly discuss, an allegory of reading. In chapter six, where the reading level dips slightly, there is no such autocritical aid provided, so that the fabricated coefficient for that reading drops in relation to the other factors, which rise slightly (the primacy of the author and the text over the reader).

If the set of seven readings does correspond to the narrative progress of the seven chapters, we can visually chart the growing instability of Noman's precarious ontological status, as the 'Nature of Fall' readings slide from 'Light' to 'Heavy' to 'Black'. This reminds us again of the theories of colour which run throughout the novel: from Mathers' theory of gowns (which darken as death approaches), to de Selby's belief that night is an accumulation of black particle pollution which eventually leads to death.

It is unimportant whether my allegorical reading of the table is the 'correct' one – although I certainly had fun trying to work it out – what *is* important is that O'Brien teases us into making such interpretations in the first place. Reading the graph deflects us from reading the text; we get diverted from the task at hand. We can, of course, choose to ignore the graph, but fear that we might miss some vital clue in the textual jigsaw puzzle. Either way we are faced with a divisive topographical arrangement, and a choice between reading two competing blocks of discourse. The spatial displacement of this split-text format frustrates our attempt at linear, monological absorption – either we read one or the other but we cannot assimilate both at the same time. The simultaneity of two co-existent events in mutual contradiction is the antithesis of the seamless linearity demanded by realist narratives, and is therefore a powerful form of metalepsis. Not only does a split-text format represent two different modes of discourse in a disruptive and mutually deconstructive manner, but it forces us to radically alter the normative reading dynamic. We manipulate the text as a physical object and notice its materiality as an industrial product composed of pages, typeface and so on. We begin to see the book as object and ourselves as readers, or, as Brian McHale wittily put it, 'post-modernist texts are typically spaced-out, literally as well as figuratively'.[19]

The use of maps in a metafiction constitutes a similar form of spatial displacement – and again O'Brien seems indebted to Sterne. In Book I of *Tristram Shandy*, Tristram attempts to describe the boundaries of his own 'Parish', but the details accumulate exponentially like a fractal configuration. Realising its infinite expansion, Tristram breaks off mid-sentence and tells us that 'all this will be more exactly delineated and explain'd in a map, now in the hands of the engraver, which, with many other pieces and developments of this work, will be added to the twentieth volume'[20] – part of the joke being that there are only nine volumes in total. This violent break in the narrative itself is a convenient way of ending the infinitely widening spiral web of description, and it makes us aware of the shaping hand of the author. More important is the implication that the discourse of cartography is somehow superior to the verbal discourse of the text itself. Although the actual map never transpires, and does not materially cause a spatial disruption (as the graph did), the allusion splits the narrative on an analytical level by juxtaposing two possible modes – one 'real', one imagined – on the same conceptual plane. This, of course, informs us of the artificial boundaries of each discourse.

In similar fashion, O'Brien presents us with an image of a map of his Parish, though again the physical map is not materially represented but suggested verbally, which defeats the purpose of a map altogether. It is also worth considering, briefly, the difference between these two metafictional 'maps': in Sterne it serves to counterpoint and undermine the narrative voice, while in typical post-modernist style the 'map' and 'The Parish' in O'Brien's novel become self-reflexive metaphors for the metafiction itself.

In reply to Noman's final request before he is due to be hanged – that the figures in MacCruiskeen's black book (from which Noman had extrapolated his tabular model) be explained – Pluck decides to show Noman a map of The Parish, which is etched out of the cracks in the ceiling of MacCruiskeen's room, or, as Pluck says: 'it is easier to show you than to tell you verbally' (*3P*, p. 122). This in itself is a clever illustration of the creative/descriptive paradox: quite simply, pointing to the object itself in reality is closer (semiotically speaking) to describing that object than by attaching arbitrary and differential verbal signifiers to it, i.e. a physical map in the real world is more 'real' than the word 'M-A-P' which describes it. Thematically this scene has a parallel in *Tristram Shandy*, when Dr. Slop's secret instrument is signified as '******', or, as Tristram remarks: 'It is a singular stroke of

eloquence [. . .] not to mention the name of a thing, when you had
the thing about you in petto, ready to produce, pop, in the place
you want it.'[21]

The analytical split between 'map' as discourse and map as
physical object is a very clear-cut way of exposing the relationship
between signifier and signified (separable only on this analytical
level), and by extension the ontological differences between the
projected and 'real' worlds. The 'map' (as a signifying acoustic
sound or visual symbol) is a metaphorical substitution (or linguistic map) for the signified concept of 'map-ness'. To underline
the arbitrariness of the signifier even further, O'Brien's map of
The Parish is formed out of cracks in the ceiling, yet according to
Noman 'it was a map of the parish, complete, reliable and astonishing' (*3P*, p. 123).

As a short-circuit sign, a map is the epitome of artifice – an
obviously functional chart of the continuum of the landscape
etched on a two-dimensional plane. But O'Brien's map is a metafictional blueprint, a map of a fictional zone where commonsense
laws are continually transgressed. As Pluck tells Noman, this map
is drawn up by a cosmic cartographer, the author-god of the fictional territory: 'I did not [make it] and nobody else manufactured
it either. It was always there and MacCruiskeen is certain that it
was there even before that' (*3P*, p. 123). This map is an intertextual, heterotopic map, a meta-map designed by the author-god
himself to remind us of the textuality of both modes of discourse –
cartography and the primary mimetic narrative. Above all else it is
a striking reminder, as Charles Kemnitz has noted, of the 'relationship between signifier and signified: "The map is not the
territory."'[22] (Kemnitz believes that this scene may be a reference
to Alfred Korzybski's famous comment that 'The map is not the
territory'. This comment originally appeared in Korzybski's
*Science and Sanity: An Introduction to Non-Aristotelian Systems
and General Semantics*, first published in 1933. There is no direct
evidence that Flann O'Brien actually read Korzybski's book, but it
does seem a likely intertextual source.)

This brings us finally to the last but most overt (and distinctive)
frame-breaking device of the text, the de Selbian footnotes. The
notion of writing a critical commentary, footnotes and all, on a
Menippean satire which implicitly mocks such critical practices is
one that is not lost on this present writer – like trying to explain a
joke, you invariably fall flat on your face. Indeed this ironic collision between critical and fictional discourses has not gone

unnoticed by other commentators, including, most notably, O'Brien's friend and editor Timothy O'Keeffe.*

---

* *One of the tests that I should like to set for any potential thesis writer is to call for an analysis, at de Selbian footnote length perhaps, of the comedy of Myles's description of a particular Dublin flower trough as 'The Tomb of the Unknown Gurrier'.* (Timothy O'Keeffe, Preface, *Myles: Portraits of Brian O'Nolan*, 1973, p. 12)

Myles na Gopaleen bestowed this salubrious sobriquet in solemn commemoration of the ill-fated 'Bowl of Light' monument which was erected (and subsequently dismembered) during the inaugural 'An Tóstal' tourist festival of 1953. To savour the aptness of the Mylesian moniker it is first necessary to consider the nature of 'An Tóstal' itself. On New Year's Day, 1953, *The Irish Times* carried a full-page advertisement which proudly proclaimed:

> On next Easter Saturday morning, An Tóstal – 'Ireland at Home' – will be inaugurated throughout the land with full religious and state ceremonial. During Easter week and the two weeks following, Ireland will be at home to the world with a very special welcome [. . .] to portray the richness of our culture, the variety of our pastimes, and the traditional hospitality of Ireland.

And the subtext to this unique cultural extravaganza? – 'We want more and more tourists to come in the springtime' (*The Irish Times*, 1 January 1953). The three-week festival was under the overall command of Major-General Hugh Hyacinth McNeill, and planned with meticulous military precision. Hundreds of local 'An Tóstal' councils were established all over the country to assure the co-ordinated success of this Cultural Revolution. Public support was essential, and the PPI (Plain People of Ireland) were drafted into the cause because, as Major-General McNeill himself declared, 'Although "An Tóstal" was initiated by the government, it was really the people's project' (*The Irish Times*, 29 January 1953).

Civic spiritedness became the order of the day, and Dubliners in particular were urged to paint their house fronts, erect flower boxes, and keep the streets clean. Almost immediately the cultural legitimacy of the festival came under sustained attack. Dr Roger McHugh, a lecturer in English at UCD, felt uneasy about some of the planned events, especially the 'Rose of Tralee' carnival which included a pilgrimage to a 'clear crystal fountain': 'That', observed Dr McHugh, 'is the kind of thing that discredits the country' (*The Irish Times*, 27 January 1953).

Myles na Gopaleen was equally wary of the public relations machine promoting the festival, and he entered the fray with a series of five 'Cruiskeen Lawn' articles entitled 'Titostalatinarianism': 'I am convinced that there is a connexion between the Tito visit [to London] and the Tóstal – and possibly the coronation [of Queen Elizabeth]. We must further consider these matters' ('Titostalatinarianism', *The Irish Times*, 28 January 1953).

Doubtful of the cultural value of the enterprise, Myles posed a simple question: 'Who invented this thing? [. . .] I will give you my wild guess. It was invented by The Crowd Who Are Going To Clean Up' ('Titostalatinarianism 2', *The Irish Times*, 30 January 1953). In the succeeding column, Myles exclusively exposed the secret identity of this Crowd: 'I can reveal that this Tóstal idea was conceived by a group of Dublin hotel owners [who] expect every Irishman to do his duty: Shoneenism will not be tolerated. We must all paint our houses; a box, gay with spring flowers, must grace each windowsill' ('Titostalatinarianism 3', *The Irish Times*, 3 February 1953).

As Susan Stewart has written, the frame of any discourse is a scene of transformation, the formal structure which 'lies between the external space of the commonsense world and the internal space of representation'.[23] A frame then is a formal border lodged between the real and fictional domains, the crossover point between the given and the projected. Realist texts naturally wish to downplay the existence of this partition and ideally seek to create a seamless passage of movement where the reader travels from the given to the projected with a minimum of fuss and travel restrictions.

Consequently, the most difficult hurdle to be overcome in the creation and consumption of realism is the entry to the projected zone – the reader picks up the book, looks at the title, notes the blurb and the publishing details, gets comfortable, and settles down to embark on a journey. Until the reader actually gets caught up in

---

*(cont.)   The fourth article in this series is sometimes credited with the distinction of being the offending article which led to Brian O'Nolan's eventual removal from his civil service position. In it, Myles roundly condemned the 'Shaymuses' of Dublin Corporation for having wasted scarce resources on 'An Tóstal', at the expense of the Health Services: 'The Shaymuses recently reached down into our pockets and voted thousands of pounds – or the price of many ambulances – for the purposes of this Tóstal, including the construction of two elongated troughs of water on O'Connell Bridge' ('Titostalatinarianism 4', *The Irish Times*, 5 January 1953).

This is the first mention by Myles of the 'Bowl of Light' monument, the centrepiece of the 'An Tóstal' decorations. Gifted with a native flair for architectural flamboyance, the Corporation had decreed that a traffic island on O'Connell Bridge would be the site of a permanent reminder of the first 'An Tóstal':

> A copper bowl, with a diameter of about four feet, is fitted to a semi-circular bridge of tubular girders which spans an octagonal basin, measuring about fifteen feet by eighteen feet, and containing about a foot depth of water. The many coloured plastic 'flames', which could revolve, were set in the bowl, and at night were illuminated. The remainder of the decorative scheme in the bridge consists of oblong artificial ponds, with small fountains, the entire structure being surrounded by banks of flowering plants. (*The Irish Times*, 20 April 1953)

The opening ceremony of the festival was marked by the hoisting of the 'An Tóstal' flag, followed by an army parade. From Dublin, a flight of carrier pigeons was released from the roof of the GPO to carry greetings to 'An Tóstal' councils all over Ireland, and in the evening symbolic bonfires were lit on the historic hills of Tara and Slane. The President of Ireland, Seán T. O'Kelly, made the opening address: 'The central theme of An Tóstal [. . .] is epitomised in the phrase "Ireland at Home", which was chosen as a free translation of the Irish title. I think the choice was a happy one, for the words express ideally the intention underlying the three weeks of national celebration' (*The Irish Times*, 6 April 1953). Myles na Gopaleen, polyglot and deconstructionist *avant la lettre*, did not think the choice all that happy:

the fictional web, s/he cannot but notice the materiality of the book itself, or as Brian McHale describes the process:

> A book is a thing, and its material qualities and physical dimensions invariably interact with the world [but] realist fiction tends to deny this technical reality. It does so by conventionalising space out of existence. Nothing must interfere with the fiction's representation of reality, so the physical dimensions of the book must be rendered functionally invisible.[24]

Self-conscious genres like metafiction transgress the commonsense world either by presenting paradoxes of framing which proclaim its textuality, or by juxtaposing different rhetorical modes which splinter the linear, monological pattern of realism. Such strategies of metalepsis and polyphonic composition both share a common purpose: the erasure of the commonsense context and paradigmatic beliefs which normally smooth the transition from the real to the fictional.

Nothing is unified in a heterotopic zone and the physically schizoid text is reflected in its own characterisation. In *The Third Policeman* all the characters are shadows or mirror images of each

---

*(cont.) What unfortunate poor scholar dug out this word 'Tóstal' which – never mind the foreigners – was ever heard of by more than half a dozen people alive in Ireland today? It is clear that he mined it out of that Golden Treasury of Rawmaysh, *Dineen's Dictionary*, because Dineen says the word means 'pageant, parade'. Unfortunate indeed, and it doesn't. Anybody interested should look up a book called *Fuinn na Smol*, where he will find a poem in which the word connotes an all-out debauch on POITÍN. ('Titostalatinarianism 2', *The Irish Times*, 30 January 1953)

Subsequent events proved Myles's interpretation more semantically correct. The night before the official opening ceremony, people spilled out of pubs at closing time and gathered together to see the wooden hoarding being removed from the Bowl of Light. A crowd of several thousand soon jostled and pushed to witness this unofficial unveiling, but this spontaneous spirit of celebration quickly degenerated into a clash between police and gangs of hooligans: 'Baton charges were made [. . .] and flowers, shrubs and earth from the flower beds at the O'Connell monument were thrown at the police, and plate-glass windows were smashed' (*The Irish Times*, 6 April 1953). In later court proceedings, Inspector J. Callinan recalled some of the unsavoury scenes: 'Some of the crowd were endeavouring to open the doors of motor cars and shouting into the cars "capitalists" and [. . .] when being moved on by the civic guards they shouted: "we want work, not flowers"' (*The Irish Times*, 27 May 1953).

Dr Roger McHugh had previously echoed these revolutionary sentiments in his critique of the Bowl of Light, declaring that there was 'little good in putting a plastic wreath on an Ireland drained by emigration [and] unemployment' (*The Irish Times*, 13 April 1953). In his post-mortem of the riot, Myles na Gopaleen gleefully reflected: 'I did not have the pleasure to be in Dublin last Saturday night but absence did not deny me a glow of pride when I learnt what the citizens did. [. . .] Here we had Cathleen Ni Hooligan in person' ('Postostal', *The Irish Times*, 9 April 1953).

other; even Noman himself is split between his narrative persona (itself split between mimetic and textual voices) and the persona of his soul – the Cartesian dualism rendered literal. As a means of actualising this split, even typographical uniformity is splintered: Noman's language is presented in traditional roman typeface (with the notable change in the footnotes) *while Joe's language is presented in italics*. The use of footnotes as a metaleptic device operates within similar technical parameters, or, as Susan Stewart has noted, 'as a depiction of a voice splitting itself, the footnote is from the beginning a form of discourse about discourse'.[25]

The use of footnotes in fiction is a historically well-established convention, used to great effect in a handful of critically acclaimed texts: Swift's *A Tale of a Tub* (1704); Fielding's *Tom Jones* (1749); Sterne's *Tristram Shandy* (1759–67); Joyce's *Finnegans Wake* (1939); Beckett's *Watt* (1944); and Nabokov's *Pale Fire* (1962). What makes the device more 'naturally' acceptable as a form of metalepsis (and thus gives it greater re-usable currency) is its peculiarly literary quality: footnoting is an established branch of discourse that has a practical scholarly usage – citing influences, avoiding plagiarism, offering background information – that does not seem out of place within a text, albeit a fictional one. The inclusion of footnotes in a fiction – though mischievously disruptive – is not entirely anarchic; it merely stretches the convention beyond the usual parameters, and in the process questions the arbitrary

---

*(cont.)   However, the story of Cathleen Ní Hooligan and the Bowl of Light was not yet over. On Sunday, 19 April 1953, 'a man was seen to climb on to the foot of the parapet of the basin underneath the Bowl of Light, [. . .] wrench out the cluster of plastic flames, run to the parapet of the bridge and hurl it into the Liffey' (*The Irish Times*, 20 April 1953). The culprit, an engineering student, made his escape down Aston Quay, pursued by a police detective, several civic guards, a newsvendor, a taxi-driver, and a posse of other civic-minded individuals. When he was apprehended, some members of the public were reported to have shouted 'throw him in the river!' (*The Irish Times*, 20 April 1953), as the man was led away. The offender was later charged with causing malicious damage to public property. The plastic flame was not recovered, although the *The Irish Times* reported that 'divers may be employed to try and find it' (20 April 1953).

Myles na Gopaleen was delighted that his public criticism of the monument had ultimately crystallised into this symbolic (and literal) overthrow by the PPI. As he wrote in the 'Cruiskeen Lawn': 'Last Sunday a public-spirited gentleman put the plastic flame [. . .] into the Liffey. Lawlessness? Maybe so, but I am delighted. I think I was the first to voice publicly Dublin's feeling of outrage at the despoilment of the city centre by its wretched corporation' ('Splarge', *The Irish Times*, 22 April 1953).

The dust of years is long settled upon this affair, and it now joins the pantheon of other legendary Dublin uprisings. Years later Myles recalled these events, and ceremoniously re-named the desecrated monument 'The Tomb of the Unknown Gurrier'.

borders between 'fiction' and 'non-fiction'. Even in critical non-fiction there is a genuine discursive ambivalence between footnotes and the primary text. By convention, footnotes are meant to be brief and pithy although, in practice, this secondary line of rhetoric frequently carries writers away. As any reader or writer will attest, footnotes are a handy functional tool but can also be an annoying distraction from the fluid consumption of the primary material. Consequently, footnotes become the perfect ready-made form of metalepsis: textually common yet still intrusive; conventional yet still capable of estranging the reading process by their very nature. The new context of fictional usage derives from these conditions, or, as Shari Benstock writes: 'The referential and marginal features of these notes serve a specifically hermeneutic function [and] in a literary work highlight the interplay between author and subject, text and reader [. . .] giving us occasion to speculate on self-reflexive narration as an aspect of textual authority.'[26]

Footnoting in fiction operates by inversion. Instead of bridging the gap between the projected and real worlds, as it would normally do, it draws attention to the bridge as frame, or, as Susan Stewart describes it, the footnote 'stands on the interface between the fiction and reality. To enter into an agreement with the fictive footnote is to stand outside and inside at the same time'.[27] Footnoting is a dispersal of the real, a form of transworld flicker. The keynote here is 'at the same time' – two texts are presented simultaneously but you cannot read both: you must read one or the other.*

This playful interaction is typical of how the primary narrative and secondary footnotes autocritically impinge on each other in *The Third Policeman*. If footnotes in critical works allow for extended commentary on themes explored in the primary text, then in metafiction footnotes help the reader understand textual strategy, and paradoxically fulfil their traditional function. If the text of a metafictional work can be said to be a ludic allegory of writing practices, then metafictional footnotes can be said to be an allegory of reading practices.

Again, the use of this device in *The Third Policeman* resembles the footnoting pattern of *Tristram Shandy*, in the way that a footnoted digression sometimes outstrips (in terms of sheer volume) that portion of the text it annotates in the first place. The reader is taken outside the bounds of the primary narrative frame and

---

* Like so. The keynote here is 'at the same time' – two texts are presented simultaneously but you cannot read both: you must read one or the other.

remains there for several pages – long enough in fact to become involved in a new, counter-narrative. The reader is co-opted into the metaleptic act and becomes an active frame-breaker by abandoning the primary story, and stands, literally, at the margins of discourse: inside the frame of the work but outside the frame of the text.

In *The Third Policeman*, O'Brien gradually dismantles the textual apparatus to a point where the footnotes and the text compete for space and signifying supremacy. Twenty-seven footnotes in all appear in eight of the twelve chapters, beginning in chapter two. There are four relatively brief footnotes here, occupying some twenty-three lines of text, which is not unduly excessive. Two of these are simple citations – e.g. '*Golden Hours*, ii, 156' (*3P*, p. 21, fn) – which serve to lend credence to the ontological status of the imaginary de Selby.

In chapter three a single footnote occupies some nineteen lines of textual space, but after this the footnote length returns to conventional proportions. By chapter eight, however, a single footnote, spread over the space of four pages, threatens to spiral out of control, and overpower the point it initially set out to develop. The various commentators cited – with Noman acting as 'editor' – gradually begin to attack each other's reputations and the primary text begins to recede. This coincides with an extreme spatial displacement – having read this meandering footnote we have to skim back through the pages of the book to find the spot where we last left the primary narrative.

This is followed in chapter nine by a series of five footnotes in succession which account for some 138 lines of text, including a full page of commentary that completely displaces the primary text off the page. The final footnote appears in chapter eleven and consists of 160 lines spread out over six pages; a sub-narrative demanding a completely separate reading from the main body of the work – in fact, for a while, it *is* the main body of work. All pretence towards assuming the brisk, measured and unobtrusive tones of the conventional apparatus is finally abandoned. The sub-narrative tale of the feuding critics gains its own momentum, seemingly independent of the text which spawned it. It even acquires its own rhetorical mode, cast in a style reminiscent of nineteenth-century Gothic romance. Contravening accepted academic practice, the primary text is replaced as pretext. The change has been so gradual that by the time we read the final footnote we find ourselves willingly abandoning the 'primary' text, and this seems to be one of the desired effects. As Brian McHale wrote:

> Whenever a text is split into text proper and gloss, whether
> marginal or in footnotes, questions arise about the relation
> between the two parallel texts. According to the conventions
> [. . .] the gloss ought to be accessory or supplemented to the text
> proper; in practice however, the post-modernists often flout this
> convention.[28]

Simultaneous narratives collide and force us to make a crucial
choice: whether to read text or glossary. To our simultaneous
shame and delight we tend to go with the glossary, and in so doing
we defer or at least suspend our reading of the more serious or
'authoritative' text, preferring to indulge our pleasures and privileges as free, creative participants, manipulating the work to suit
our needs and comforts. Not only is the ultimate authority of the
primary text successfully overthrown by the liberated reader, but
this pattern actualises normal reading habits not usually considered – the way perhaps we are tempted sometimes to sneak a look
at the final page; the way we might scan a page quickly and skip a
line or paragraph here and there to cut to the chase; and so on.

Above all, though, we find ourselves manipulating the physical
text like a puzzle, jumping forwards and backwards through the
novel's spatial and temporal arrangements, and improvising an
order. (Thematically, of course, this is echoed in the work itself, and
this notion of 'time-travel' will be discussed in the final chapter of
this book.) The split between text and glossary has a fundamental
metaleptic value then in the fact that we never lose sight of the
ontological cut between the projected world and the material text.
If the self-conscious narrator is the master trope for determinism,
then the footnotes in the novel are the master technique of metalepsis, helping to restore the freedom of the reader who empowers
the text with her/his imagination.

Perhaps the most fascinating aspect of the footnotes is the intricate way they impinge on our understanding of the primary text
and help us to decode the metonymic mysteries of The Parish. On
this semantic level, two narrative voices are represented: Noman
as mimetic narrator of the primary fiction and Noman as textual
editor of the footnotes. The relationship between these two voices
parallels the relationship between the two forms of discourse as a
whole, and their interaction in the overall work.

Chapter one of *The Third Policeman* ends on a quizzical note,
with Noman about to enter Mathers' house to reclaim the black box.
Divney warns Noman to maintain secrecy – 'If you meet anybody,
you don't know what you're looking for, you don't know in whose

house you are' (*3P*, p. 20) – followed by Noman's strange declaration that the next time he was asked his name he 'did not know' (*3P*, p. 20). This puzzle sparks our interest, but narrative developments delay further debate. Chapter two opens immediately, and begins with a discussion of de Selby, and his eccentric theory of houses. The seemingly marginal detail of the house is foregrounded and over-takes the question of Noman's lost identity, but we also get the first hint that 'house' is a vitally important self-reflexive metaphor for textual structure that will, eventually, bring us back to the vexed question of identity.

The body of the text in chapter two tells us that de Selby regarded a block of houses as 'a row of necessary evils' and that he variously defined a house as 'a large coffin', 'a warren' and 'a box' (*3P*, p. 21). The sources for these quotations are footnoted in a formal manner, citing de Selby's *Golden Hours* and *Country Album*, and thereby supporting the notion of de Selby as a 'real' if eccentric philosopher. As the novel progresses, we begin to see how de Selby's theories of houses are clues in our solving of the metafictional mys-teries: Noman is murdered while looking for a box, so that the house is literally transformed into his coffin. And later on, with the appearance of Fox's police station between the walls of the house, the house literally becomes a warren, a symbol of the Chinese-box pattern of the novel.

The details of de Selby's theories often remind the observant reader of its intertextual source. De Selby's drawings of '"houses" without walls' (*3P*, p. 21) proclaims a debt to Swift's *Gulliver's Travels* (1726), recalling Gulliver's description of the Grand Academy of Lagado, and the 'ingenious architect who had contrived a new method for building houses, by beginning at the roof and working downwards to the foundation, which he justified to me by the like practice of these two prudent insects, the bee and the spider'.[29]

Other marginal borrowings confirm this particular intertextual agenda: Swift's inventor who extracted sunbeams out of cucumbers has an analogue in MacCruiskeen's light mangle (*3P*, p. 110); and Noman's description of his artificial environment and a 'fine island of clouds anchored in the calm' (*3P*, p. 86) recalls Gulliver's journey to the floating Island of Laputa. Again, this is not just a question of literary trainspotting but an invitation to the reader to identify with the parodic double. By aligning the mysterious de Selby with the mad inventors of the Swiftian academy, O'Brien underscores with ruthless intertextual efficiency the Menippean subtext by historical identification, using Swift to remind us that 'there is nothing so extravagant and irrational which some philosophers have not maintained for truth'.[30]

This first series of footnotes also reveals the autocritical significance of the footnote device by introducing us to the first of de Selby's quarrelling critics, the 'severe Le Fournier' (*3P*, p. 22, fn), who suggests that de Selby's 'absent-minded' doodles in the margins of his original manuscript of the *Country Album* were later misinterpreted by de Selby himself: 'The next time he took it up he was confronted with a mass of diagrams and drawings which he took to be the plans of a type of dwelling he always had in mind and immediately wrote many pages explaining the sketches' (*3P*, p. 22, fn).

Satirically, this mocks the eccentricity of philosophers and critics and undermines the traditional monolithic power of authorship, but it is metafictionally loaded as well. 'Doodles' on the side of a page (like footnotes or marginalia), though merely random scribbles, are misinterpreted and subsequently transformed into houses, i.e. text. In the topsy-turvy world of nonsense everything is inverted. The seemingly nonsensical footnotes or doodles are not just a diverting sideshow which displace the narrative, but a critical commentary on how to read that narrative.

As the footnotes begin to expand (both in volume and scope), it becomes clear that a whole new sub-narrative is emerging which competes with, and enlarges, our appreciation of the text. It appears almost as if the twelve-chapter structure of the novel has in fact an embedded, hidden chapter, a secret compartment which mirrors the Chinese-box motif pattern of the work itself. The footnotes essentially constitute a thirteenth chapter (thirteen, of course, being a powerfully symbolic wild-card number in numerology and folklore). Describing the footnotes as such is in no way fanciful or overdetermined: in chapter five, when MacCruiskeen shows Noman his infinite series of chests (a powerful motif of the recursive structure), he arranges thirteen of them 'in a row upon the table' at which point Noman autocritically remarks: 'These are the most surprising thirteen things I have ever seen together' (*3P*, p. 73). The interplay between this internal thirteenth chapter (part of the allegory of reading) and the primary text (an allegory of writing) reflects the polyphonic composition of the novel's language and the vast range of secondary forms – anecdotal digressions, cut-up narrative, dreams, etc. – which continually invade the text, causing it to fold back in on itself in hierarchical violation.

The second footnoted block in the novel in chapter two increases our awareness of the metaleptic versatility. The description of the policemen's gift for 'wind-watching' in the body of the text (*3P*, p. 33), for example, coincides with de Selby's theory of night in the footnotes, which suggests that 'night, far from being caused by the commonly accepted theory of planetary movements, was due to accumulations of "black air" produced by certain volcanic activities' (*3P*, p. 32, fn). Much later, we discover that this insanitary pollution induces 'fainting fits' – i.e. sleep – which will eventually lead to death: 'the collapse of the heart after from the strain of a lifetime of fits and fainting' (*3P*, p. 116, fn). Thus de Selby's bizarre observations echo, in a different rhetorical style, the action of the primary narrative which tells us that when a person's natural birth-colour turns to black, death will come. At this juncture it just seems like a recursive echo; later on, we realise that Noman is actually trapped inside a hell-world constructed from the disparate fragments of de Selby's theories.

Interestingly, this fourth footnote in chapter two on de Selby's theory of night quotes one of the feuding critics, 'Le Fournier',[31] in French – and infuriatingly this passage is left untranslated:

> On ne saura jamais jusqu'à quel point de Selby fut cause de la Grande Guerre, mais, sans aucun doute, ses théories excentriques – spécialement celle que nuit n'est pas un phénomène de nature, mais dans l'atmosphère un état malsain amené par un industrialisme cupide et sans pitié – auraient l'effet de produire un trouble profound dans les masses. (*3P*, p. 32, fn)

The content of this note is unimportant from a formalist perspective, although the gist of it is a suggestion by Le Fournier that de Selby's eccentric theories were in some mysterious way responsible for starting 'la Grande Guerre' (*3P*, p. 32), presumably the First World War. From a formalist point of view, the inclusion of another language has several strategic functions: first, it contributes a degree of conventional verisimilitude to the footnoting proceedings by invoking the annoyingly snobbish habit in certain critical texts whereby foreign commentators are quoted in their original language, but often without any translation provided. This becomes an index of traditional authorial arrogance, as the author presumes that readers are capable of translating the material by themselves. Second, it suggests that the precious material is in itself untranslatable – or that it would invariably lose something of value in the translation process – and it therefore guarantees the authoritativeness of the 'original' text by implying that it is somehow inviolable, or intrinsically sacred. Foreign language inserts thus create a false hierarchy of linguistic privilege, or, as Shari Benstock has observed:

> They refer to something totally foreign, and their inclusion in the 'original' language assumes a degree of untranslatability, a problem examined briefly by Derrida, suggesting that the inclusion of language either untranslatable or wholly translatable ensures for the text a certain disappearance, 'as text, as writing, as a body of language'.[32]

In chapter seven a similar problem of translation arises. In the body of the text Noman quotes a critic, 'Du Garbandier', on the quality of de Selby's prose style: 'the beauty of reading a page of de Selby is that it leads one inescapably to the happy conviction that one is not, of all nincompoops, the greatest' (*3P*, p. 92). As far back as the opening chapter Noman had told us that he had learned French and German 'in order to read the works of other commentators in those languages' (*3P*, p. 11), and he subsequently footnotes this passage with the original quotation by Du Garbandier: 'Le Suprême charme qu'on trouve à lire une page de de Selby est qu'elle vous conduit inexorablement a l'heureuse certitude que des sots vous n'êtes pas le plus grand' (*3P*, p. 92, fn).

This is a variation on the first foreign insert presented in chapter two. In that first case, where no textual translation was offered, the insert had a palpable effect on the reader in the way it distracted us from the text and frustrated our attempts at decoding. Either we ignored it and hoped that we did not lose anything of any great significance, or we attempted to translate it. If, like this present writer, your school French is a little rusty (and not up to much to begin with), this involves having the passage translated by someone else, and completely ceding interpretative control. This is possibly the most violent form of metalepsis in that another reader has been co-opted into the reading experience. Even then, that particular version of events will be open to debate, depending on the fluency and idiomatic subjectivity of the translator.

In the second case, where Noman's translation is counterpointed by Du Garbandier's 'original', this process is inverted, and interpretation becomes more problematic rather than less. We find ourselves distracted from the main body of work and concerned with making detailed comparisons between the two versions, looking for revealing discrepancies or ideological insights. As a device it encapsulates the mock-footnoting process as a whole: two blocks of visually distinct discourse organised in the same space and competing with each other for authority, thereby fragmenting the narrative voice into mimetic and textual components.

In any event, it would seem that our linguistic labour is in vain. There is no discernible difference between the two versions, and even Noman's colloquial translation of 'nincompoops' can be construed as an appropriately idiomatic translation of Du Garbandier's 'des sots' (*3P*, p. 92, fn). The intermedium is the message, and the semantic difference lies in the topographical arrangement of the split-text format. The collision of styles at the margins of discourse mostly provokes questions concerning authorial ordering, textual authority, and reader participation.

This splintering of monological and monolingual discourse is further echoed in the repetitious use of macaronic language by the characters, i.e. 'a burlesque form containing [. . .] foreign words' (*OED*). Usually it is the policemen who utter these macaronic phrases, as part of their garbled idiom of malapropism, solecism, spoonerism and cliché, e.g. '*sub-rosa*' [meaning 'in secrecy'] (*3P*, p. 69), '*pari passu*' ['with equal step'], and '*nolle prosequi*' ['unwilling to pursue'] (*3P*, p. 105). Noman himself is not beyond employing intellectually pretentious diction – '*roi-s'amuse*' (*3P*, p. 67) – although, ironically, unlike the policemen's macaronic phrases, which mostly relate to legal jargon, this phrase is essentially meaningless.[33] In order to communicate within the heterotopia of shifting signification, Noman has slowly begun to acquire the local language habits: 'The Sergeant gave me a look which I am sure he himself would describe as one of *non-possum* and *noli-me-tangere*' (*3P*, p. 84).[34]

Macaronic language is a typical metaleptic device because it increases our awareness of the polyphonic composition of the text, and it problematises the process of decoding for the harassed reader. Above all, it declares its own textuality, or, as Susan Stewart has suggested: 'The attack on univocality that the macaronic undertakes has to do with the beginning of a tear in the fabric of any singular way of organising the world. [. . .] The confrontation with another language is a confrontation with the limits of the everyday world.'[35]

This 'confrontation with the limits of the everyday world' is something that Noman will have to face at the end of the novel. In the meantime, it should be clear that, as the footnotes serially progress as a sub-narrative, there are essentially two ways of looking at them: first, reading them on an independent, literal and comic level; and second, reading them on an ironic and interactive level, where the secondary material impinges on the structural design of the primary text. In chapter three, for example, there is a footnoted discussion on de Selby's theory of names. Although comic in its own right, and part of a growing and autonomous Menippean satire of philosophical traditions, it becomes increasingly obvious that the mock footnotes provide us with a means of standing on the margins where we can observe the framing or organising poetics of the primary text. Following protracted debates on the importance of personal names as a semiotic indicator of identity within a social system, we come across de Selby's assertion that 'the earliest names [have] crude onomatopoeic associations with the appearance of the person or object named' (*3P*, p. 40, fn). Ironically, this theory is mocked by Noman, who resorts to biographical and textually extrinsic critiques of de Selby himself to usurp the authority of his ideas. In this respect, O'Brien seems to pre-empt some of his own critics by parodying their methods: Noman is the archetypal positivist scholar who ignores the text (at a cost to himself) and instead privileges the author (de Selby – 'the self') as the key arbiter of meaning. This parody reminds us that how we decipher a literary text often depends on the model of criticism used. For example, we are told that in his theory of names de Selby had drawn up

> elaborate paradigms of vowels and consonants purporting to correspond to certain indices of human race, colour and temperament and claiming ultimately to be in a position to state the physiological 'group' of any person merely from a brief study of the letters of his name after the word had been 'rationalised' to allow for variations of language. Certain 'groups' he showed to be universally 'repugnant' to other 'groups'. (*3P*, p. 40)

Before this episode degenerates – as it so often does in this novel – into ridiculous comic farce, we could be tempted to interpret this scene in terms of a wider, political context. Composed as it was in 1940, this passage could be understood as a critique of right-wing fascist movements that espoused social theories based on 'race, colour and temperament' (*3P*, p. 40). While there is no doubt some validity to this interpretation, it ultimately leads us into a critical cul de sac, and diverts us from our formalist reading. Infra-textually, de Selby's theory of names lies within the cabalistic tradition of *themura*, i.e. the activity of finding the hidden and mystical meaning of names, on which many fairytales turn. Autocritically, de Selby's themura provides us with a framework for understanding the naming of characters within the fictional world of the novel: practically all the characters (but especially the nameless narrator and the three policemen) have 'associations with the appearance of the person or object named' (*3P*, p. 40). Again, the footnotes instruct our reading.

In the opening pages of chapter four – an annotated discussion of de Selbian theories of travel – the interactive dynamic between the primary text and its 'explanatory' footnotes becomes much clearer. With typical sarcasm, Noman mockingly describes de Selby's assertion that a 'journey is an hallucination' (*3P*, p. 50), and, using biographical criticism, he paints a portrait of an eccentric, even lunatic, philosopher, noting that: 'It is a curious enigma that so great a mind would question the most obvious realities [. . .] while believing absolutely in his own fantastic explanations of the same phenomena' (*3P*, p. 52.) As a Menippean broadside the point is well made, but ironically we also realise that Noman himself could do worse than question his own 'obvious realities'. The irony is double-edged by virtue of the de Selbian footnotes – whose philosophical eccentricities Noman so casually derides – bearing a striking resemblance to Noman's mimetic world.

As the main text informs us, human existence for de Selby was 'defined as a "succession of static experiences each infinitely brief", a conception which he is thought to have arrived at from examining some old cinematograph films' (*3P*, p. 52). The subsequent footnote expands upon the bizarre details of de Selby's discovery, noting how he 'had examined them patiently picture by picture and imagined that they would be screened in the same way, failing at that time to grasp the principle of the cinematograph' (*3P*, p. 52, fn).

The literal comedy of Noman's snide account is again fairly obvious, but the ironic value of the description operates at a more profound level, where it offers a valid epistemological critique of the cinematic apparatus. Intertextually, it should be noted that many of de Selby's ideas – including his conception of cinema – are comic re-workings of J.W. Dunne's theory of Serialism, although this is not important here. (On a wider intertextual level it is also worth noting that the montage composition of *The Third Policeman* is inherently cinematic in style, and indeed it incorporates certain cinematic motifs and citations – in particular its borrowings from *The Wizard of Oz*.)

The formal value of this particular footnote rests with its critique of the problematic relationship between art and reality. Semiotically, realist cinema approximates reality much more than the novel ever can by presenting the viewer with dynamic and iconic visual images, rather than static and symbolic verbal images.

Quite simply, a cinematic portrait of a bicycle can be said to be much 'closer' to a physical, real-world bicycle than the word 'bicycle', as it appears on the printed page or in speech. This is also the inherent danger of cinema from a metafictional perspective: although much closer to reality than verbal artifice, cinema is still just artifice but mediated in a highly sophisticated way. As a character in Jean-Luc Godard's *Le Petit Soldat* famously put it, 'cinema is truth twenty-four times a second'[36] – an allusion to the mechanics of cinema whereby the illusion of reality is created by running twenty-four frames per second past the human eye (at a speed faster than human visual comprehension). De Selby deconstructs the magic of cinematic technology by examining each frame individually, and accurately concludes that human experience – as trapped through the magic lantern of cinema – is a 'succession of static experiences each infinitely brief' (*3P*, p. 50). The key word here is 'infinitely'. Between each of the twenty-four frames per second we could equally imagine another twenty-four frames (invisible to the human eye) and still not adequately capture the continuous human dynamic. We could repeat this process to infinity but the gulf between art and life remains a Zenoist paradox – we will never capture a finite plane of representation between these successive, infinitely brief moments. Cinema, despite its heightened verisimilitude, remains mimetic and therefore can never be 'real'.

In chapter twelve Noman comments on de Selby's *Layman's Atlas*, a book dealing 'explicitly with bereavement, old age, love, sin, death and the other saliencies of existence' (*3P*, p. 93) – an autocritical summary of the themes of the novel itself. Comically, Noman undercuts the noble solemnity of this philosophical enterprise: 'It is true that [de Selby] allows them only six lines but this is due to his devastating assertion that they are all "unnecessary"'(*3P*, p. 93). With this broad sweeping gesture, O'Brien gruffly declares the central philosophical theme of his Menippean satire: a condemnation of any rationalist tradition that excludes any consideration of spiritual matters. At heart, perhaps, O'Brien remains a Catholic thinker, albeit in a rather Manichean manner. The corresponding footnote, though primarily comic, suggests as much: 'The sardonic Du Garbandier makes great play of the fact that the man who first printed the *Atlas* (Watkins) was struck by lightning the day he completed the task' (*3P*, p. 93, fn).

The conscious affiliation with the Faustian myth throughout *The Third Policeman* (and the overt recognition of St Augustine in its re-write, *The Dalkey Archive*), confirms the existence of this broadly Christian ethic. This ethic is combined with a peculiar use of religiose language, e.g. the structure of the entrance to Eternity 'looked exactly like the porch of a small country church' (*3P*, p. 127), and as Pluck metonymically advises in chapter eight, 'attend to your daily readings and your conscience will be as clear as a clean shirt on Sunday morning' (*3P*, pp. 138–9). The Catholic conscience at the deep core of this novel quietly confronts the relativist ethos more formally espoused by the post-modernist concerns, and perhaps offers a way out of the ontological labyrinth.

Interestingly, the same footnote in chapter twelve continues the critique of authorial arrogance by questioning the authenticity of de Selby's *Atlas*: 'the otherwise reliable Hatchjaw has put forward the suggestion that the entire Atlas is spurious and the work of "another hand", raising issues of no less piquancy than those of the Bacon-Shakespeare controversy' (*3P*, p. 93, fn). The irony here is that the de Selbian commentators (including Noman) have dedicated their lives to writing about a writer who may not have written his ascribed works, and who may not have even existed. Given the inclusion of Joyce himself in *The Dalkey Archive* (denying authorship of anything after *Dubliners*), it seems clear that this is largely modelled on the legion of Joycean scholars who, in O'Brien's opinion, have deified the author at the expense of the work.

In the same block of footnotes in chapter twelve, there is a brief one-line note that beautifully captures the deconstructive potential of mock footnotes. During a particularly convoluted discussion of de Selbian theory in the primary text, Noman quotes de Selby saying 'It can be safely inferred' (*3P*, p. 94) – only to abruptly intrude with a sarcastic, footnoted counterpoint: 'Possibly the one weak spot in the argument.' De Selby's observations are, for the most part, exaggerated variations of real-life historical writings, including Augustine, Descartes, Wittgenstein, Dunne, Einstein and Vico, amongst others, but where these ideas become truly absurd is in de Selby's insane 'inferences' (even if these inferences are the same ones that help shape the projected world of The Parish).

The most extreme use of the mock footnote occurs in chapter eleven, where O'Brien explores the metaleptic possibilities of spatial displacement. As Hugh Kenner describes the process in general:

> The footnote's relation to the passage from which it depends is established wholly by visual and topographical means, and will typically defeat all efforts of the speaking voice to clarify it without visual aid. [It is] something analogous with counterpoint; a way of speaking in two voices at once, or of ballasting

or modifying or even bombarding with exceptions his own discourse without interrupting it.[37]

Over the space of five pages, six lengthy footnotes interrupt the
primary text (with five of these interruptions occurring mid-sentence). If we break away from the body of the text to read the first
lengthy footnote, we are tempted to stray on to another page, and
move further away from our original point of departure. In the
second footnote, the sheer volume of the commentary overtakes the
primary text completely as a full page of glossary spills over on to
another leaf. To return to the primary text we have to turn back a
page and locate our reference point, only to depart again after
another disruptive footnote, and so on. Our reading thus becomes a
constant process of disruption, both physical and mental.

The footnotes themselves, for the most part, tell of the con-
flicting and self-cancelling critiques of a de Selby manuscript
simply known as the 'Codex' – some 'two thousand sheets of
foolscap closely hand-written on both sides. The signal distinction
of the manuscript is that not one word of the writing is legible' (*3P*,
p. 145, fn). This illegibility causes utter confusion to erupt amongst
the de Selbian commentators, who begin to feud viciously over the
one 'true' meaning of the de Selby manuscript: 'One passage,
described by Bassett, as being "a penetrating treatise on old age" is
referred to by Henderson (biographer of Bassett) as "a not unbeau-
tiful description of lambing operations on an unspecified farm"'
(*3P*, p. 145, fn). Elsewhere, Du Garbandier claims to have defini-
tively deciphered the same text, revealing it to be 'a repository of
obscene conundrums, accounts of amorous adventures and erotic
speculation' (*3P*, p. 146). This is a mocking critique both of creative
fiction and of critical practices. Whatever the author's intentions
in a text, readers will invariably insist on bringing their own experiences to bear and will interpret the text according to their own
biases. All literature, for O'Brien, is heteroglossic and self-
reflexive, a lesson that Noman himself must learn.

Yet another footnote uses biographical criticism to attack de
Selby, noting the savant's 'forcible medical examination' (*3P*, p.
147, fn) after some imprudent, possibly insane, comments made by
him during a court case. Throughout the course of the footnotes,
Noman continually debases de Selby's character. Amongst the
litany of physical and mental ailments ascribed to de Selby is narcolepsy, and his habit of falling asleep, 'on at least one occasion in
a public lavatory' (*3P*, p. 166, fn). This illness has a strange inter-

textual echo in other Menippean satires which employ footnotes, such as haemophilia in Beckett's *Watt* and sciatica in Sterne's *Tristram Shandy* – all ailments which attack the body from within, in much the same way that footnotes attack the main body of the work.

The only footnote in chapter eleven is the final footnote in the novel, which occupies some 160 lines of text. In this final note, not only is the primary narrative abandoned but so too is the ostensible object of inquiry in the footnotes, namely de Selby. This extensive glossary follows the exploits of his devoted and demented apostles, the 'commentators', including Le Fournier, Du Garbandier, Bassett, Hatchjaw, Henderson, Kraus, Barge and Le Clerque. The megalo-maniac feuding between these rivals – full of intricate twists and turns that are virtually impossible to disentangle – completely dis-places the primary tale, both spatially and thematically. Du Garbandier, we are told, had published 'a pamphlet masquerading as a scientific treatise on sexual idiosyncrasy in which de Selby is arraigned by name as the most abandoned of all human monsters' (*3P*, p. 167, fn). Rival critic Hatchjaw, however, is convinced that the mischievous Du Garbandier is in fact a pseudonymous cover for the 'shadowy Kraus' (*3P*, p. 168, fn), another de Selbian critic. Meanwhile, Bassett is convinced of the opposite view, i.e. that Kraus is a pseudonym for Du Garbandier, while Noman himself feels that both names do refer to one individual who (in the histor-ical manner of the Danish philosopher Søren Kierkegaard) presented contradictory arguments under different pen-names, thus setting up a dialectic with himself.

At any rate, Hatchjaw is incensed, and, heavily armed, he sets off for Hamburg in search of Kraus/Du Garbandier, to 'end once and for all a cancerous corruption which has become an intolerable affront to the decent instincts of humanity' (*3P*, p. 169, fn). The account of this cites Barge's work on Hatchjaw, *The Man Who Sailed Away: A Memoir* (*3P*, p. 172, fn), and is narrated in a mock-Gothic mode. Noman describes how Hatchjaw eventually disappeared for good, although several apocryphal legends remain: that he converted to Judaism; that he became a drug dealer or brothel keeper; 'that he returned home in disguise with his reason shattered' (*3P*, p. 172, fn). To collapse the ontological levels alto-gether, Noman quotes Du Garbandier's suggestion that 'Hatchjaw was not Hatchjaw at all but either another person of the same name or an impostor who had successfully maintained the pre-tence, in writing or otherwise, for forty years' (*3P*, p. 172, fn).

With these tangled, contradictory ruminations, the mock footnotes came to an end, leaving in their wake a world of radical
inversion and dispersion. Initially, in the paratextual apparatus, de
Selby is presented as a 'real' character, sharing as he does an epigraph with Shakespeare – although, as Noman later suggests, it is
doubtful whether Shakespeare ever wrote his ascribed works. The
critical footnotes add a further sense of verisimilitude to the character of de Selby, but, as the narrative of the margins unfolds, not
only is de Selby's sanity doubted but the very authenticity of his
works is questioned (not least by Hatchjaw, who is prepared to lay
down his life for de Selby, although Hatchjaw himself may not exist
either). Indeed, the identities of all the main de Selbian commentators (including Noman) are called into question as a whole series of
ontological and narrative levels collapse, at the stroke of a pen. All
the events in the footnotes are called into being by Noman, who
presents the arguments of the feuding critics in conventional,
matter-of-fact terms. So much is contradictory that nothing at all
can be accepted at face value, and we are thus left with the distinct
possibility that the entire footnoted sequence is a marvellous con-
fabulation: a fictive product of Noman's unstable – even psychotic –
mind. This, in the end, is the principal intention. The novel is, of
course, nothing more than a fiction, and Noman's insanity is the net
result of his greedy pursuit of de Selby ('the self' or 'the same
person'). Thus, in itself, the device of the mock footnote is the
perfect vehicle for a Menippean satire: a condemnation of rationalist methodologies, using those very methodologies as its main
satirical weapon.

5. Paradise lost, Paradise regained: Flann O'Brien and the dialogic imagination

'If you lived here for a few days and gave full play to your observation and inspection, you would know how certain the sureness of certainty is.'

Sergeant Pluck, *The Third Policeman*, p. 87

If the success of *The Third Policeman* depended solely on structural estrangement (overt frame-breaking strategies or topographical displacements), then the novel would quickly degenerate into a rather tiresome parade of affected gimmickry: amusing but indulgent party pieces fully deserving of the demotic 'anti-novel' label. Where post-modernist writings make their most decisive break with realist and modernist traditions is in their attitude to language itself, and this is the pivotal defining factor of post-modernist poetics.

The Third Policeman, as an early post-modernist novel, bears out this general observation. Consequently, this chapter will focus on the more 'covert' and intrinsic metaleptic operations in the novel which defamiliarise conventional linguistic patterns *from within*. Given the limitations of space I will concentrate on the polyphonic composition of chapter one of the novel – ostensibly the most 'realist' chapter – which gives a seemingly straightforward account of Noman's early life before he enters the topsy-turvy, fantastic world of The Parish.

In his seminal essay 'Discourse in the Novel', Mikhail Bakhtin opens by stating his fundamental premise – that there is no distinction between 'form' and 'content' in fiction. For Bakhtin, 'form and content in discourse are one, once we understand that verbal discourse is a social phenomenon'.[1] All fiction is governed by this relationship, but the real value of metafiction lies in its particular treatment of language as a series of different discourses trapped within a relative universe. Bakhtin invites us to imagine how each and every utterance operates within a textual system, where

169

multiple heteroglossic forces are brought to bear on every word in that system: 'The word, directed towards its object, enters a dialogically agitated and tension-filled environment of alien words, value judgements and accents, weaves in and out of complex interrelationships [that] complicate its expression and influence its entire stylistic profile.'[2]

The world of any fiction is a chaotic carnival, but metafiction exposes this essential chaos by stripping away the false veneer of respectability normally imposed by realist structures. The metaleptic disorder of metafiction – its interruptions, its instabilities, its flagrant contraventions of established codes – is a premeditated attempt to show that form exists for its own sake, and for no other reason. Just as all texts are in reality intertexts, all language is a metalanguage. Nobody is free from the hermeneutics of discourse, or, as Bakhtin wrote: 'Only the mythical Adam, who approached a virginal and as yet verbally unqualified world with the first word, could really have escaped from start to finish this dialogic inter-orientation with the alien world that occurs in the object.'[3]

This is the inescapable circularity of discourse that informs all works in the post-modern Paradise Lost: after Adam there is no original, prelapsarian thought, merely a language that is culturally inherited. Awareness of Bakhtin's dialogic inter-orientation on this analytical level is one thing, but it is quite another issue to organically dramatise its implications within a fictional work. More than any other genre, though, metafiction is designed for this venture. If the self-conscious narrator is the metafictional master-trope for determinism, and the mock footnote the topographical metalepsis *par excellence*, then we might say that it is the polyphonic composition of *The Third Policeman* which best explores the dialogic nature of language.

Susan Stewart defines 'polyphonic composition' as the 'juxtaposition of two or more systems of sense [that] will point to the nonsensical character of one or more of them, for such a juxtaposition undermines the suspension of doubt needed to engage in at least one of the domains of reality'.[4] Polyphony is the resultant collision between different 'domains of reality' or 'systems of sense' which disrupts normative reading patterns. It produces a deliberate disjunction between what is actually said and how we are expected (or tend) to interpret that utterance. Polyphony is a feature of all forms of writing, although 'realist' texts usually endeavour to suppress or disguise this fact by projecting a linear, unified world that is intended to be read monologically.

With the advent of modernism this monological presentation came under closer scrutiny, although there remains a crucial difference between the symphony – or cacophony – of different voices employed by T.S. Eliot in *The Waste Land* (a formally cut-up heteroglossia), and the ideological polyphony of post-modernism. While modernists certainly confront us with a plurality of voices, modernism was still 'held in check by a unifying, monological perspective [. . .] – a unified projected world'.[5] Polyphony is not the dominant of modernism but an unintended side effect – the inevitable outcome of presenting different points of view within the one textual space. Post-modernists, however, use polyphony quite deliberately, and dramatise its multiple confusions. As Brian McHale wrote: 'Instead of resisting centrifugal tendencies, post-modernist fiction seeks to enhance them [by] breaking up the unified projected world in a polyphony of worlds of discourse.'[6]

This subversion of monological authority makes the reader more conscious of her/his input in the re-ordering and consumption of literary texts. The very texture of language becomes the arena of conflict where Bakhtin's dialogic potential is actualised – a field of play where all utterances resist absolute resolution. In *The Third Policeman* this is dramatised by the fact that Noman understands language monologically, while the reader is invited to read it dialogically.

In a letter to his publishers in 1939, Flann O'Brien offered a thematic abstract of his linguistic concerns in *The Third Policeman*, and noted how the 'most casual remarks create a thousand other mysteries'.[7] The very success of the novel as a post-modernist text depends on the tight interlocking of seemingly disparate syntactical matrices – 'casual remarks' – to form a cohesive narrative. As with *At Swim-Two-Birds* the author is passionately concerned with expanding the formal, conventional boundaries of ordinary 'commonsense' language. A favoured technique in the O'Brien/na Gopaleen canon is the deconstruction of clichés, which are then reconstructed in new and startling ways. Not only do these reconstituted phrases take on new signification but they also retain recognisable features from their previous identity. Such deliberate fragmentation of language is not entirely anarchic, but serves to create a new polyphonic idiom within the cosmological design of the text as a whole.

The structural undermining of a word, phrase or image informs the reader that language is pre-eminently the social instrument that binds and maintains the everyday world. O'Brien subverts convention to highlight the paradigmatic provisionality of discourse, or, as Patricia Waugh describes this metafictional deconstruction in general: 'Everyday language endorses and sustains [social] power structures through a continuous process of naturalisation whereby forms of oppression are constructed in apparently innocent representations.'[8]

In all of his writings O'Brien plays continually with the elasticity of words, giving multiple or subtextual meaning to what is formally signified. It is an impressionistic worldview comparable in theme and style to the work of Vladimir Nabokov, who wrote: 'It is as if a painter said: look, here I'm going to show you not the painting of a landscape but the painting of different ways of painting a landscape, and I trust their harmonious fusion will disclose the landscape as I intend you to see it.'[9] The polyphonic language of *The Third Policeman* sculpts a similar kind of landscape, but our comprehension of its meaning is compounded by the delayed decoding implicit in its elliptical composition – only when certain codes are broken do the ciphered commonplaces take on ironic tones.

The opening chapter of *The Third Policeman* is thus deceptively simple: what seems to be a standard, biographical account of Noman's life (and the events leading up to the murder of Old Mathers) becomes a coded introduction to the novel's theme. For example: the second paragraph of the opening page begins with a conventional and mundane gambit of realist storytelling – 'I was born a long time ago' (*3P*, p. 7). Yet as the novel progresses we become aware that Noman is no more than thirty years of age, and not an old man as the opening would suggest. Of course, once we finish the novel and understand that this is a tale told by a dead man, endlessly reliving the cycle of his life, then this commonplace opening takes on a whole new meaning. If the cycle is eternally looped then we cannot say how many times he has re-lived it, and he could conceivably have been born a 'long time ago'.

The ambiguity is only mildly disconcerting, and indeed can only make sense once the elliptical code has been cracked. But because we are presented with a whole series of such polyphonic imponderables, we are constantly put on our guard. Beyond the secrets of ellipsis, the spare detail of the prose style is vaguely unsettling in a quiet, unassuming way that is difficult to pin down. We imagine that we are competent enough to close these epistemological narrative gaps through lateral thinking (and by applying simple principles of causality), yet we are disturbed that we may be taking too much licence in our reading.

Noman's narrative style – based on his limited, empirical system of information gathering – is perpetually at odds with what the reader feels they need to know. This fundamental tension in the novel stresses that there are no fixed truths, merely impermanent structures, or, as Patricia Waugh notes: 'The materialist, positivist and empiricist worldview on which realist fiction is premised no longer exists.'[10] Noman is a personification of this anachronistic worldview, and the novel operates on the margins between Noman's ordering of the world in a realist fashion, and the reader's awareness of the meta-realist modes of discourse at play elsewhere. We become aware that the traditional communicative codes between text and reader are being perpetually violated, and realise that understanding this text demands a large degree of interpretative risk-taking.

In the style of the *Bildungsroman* (reminiscent of the opening chapter of Joyce's *A Portrait of the Artist as a Young Man*), Noman recalls his earliest memories of his parents. However, these flat and splintered recollections of his mother and father are syntactically interwoven, and often in semantic conflict with each other. The childlike string of associations sets up claim and counter-claim, thesis and antithesis, and the resultant synthesis renders both portraits strangely abstruse. It is worth quoting the passage at length:

> I was born a long time ago. My father was a strong farmer and my mother owned a public house. We all lived in the public house but it was not a strong house at all and was closed most of the day because my father was out at work on the farm and my mother was always in the kitchen and for some reason the customers never came until it was nearly bed-time; and well after it at Christmas-time and on other unusual days like that. I never saw my mother outside the kitchen in my life and never saw a customer during the day and even at night I never saw more than two or three together. But then I was in bed part of the time and it is possible that things happened differently with my mother and the customers late at night. My father I do not remember well but he was a strong man and did not talk much except on Saturdays when he would mention Parnell with the customers and say that Ireland was a queer country. (*3P*, p. 7)

Whatever about Ireland, Noman certainly inhabits a 'queer country'. The syntactical pattern consists of a series of clauses, interconnected by a string of prepositions. These clauses alternate between descriptions of the mother and the father, disrupted by the inclusion of banal or bizarre qualifying clauses, all of which makes for a rather meandering account. The juxtaposition of two sets of memories (one for the father; one for the mother) establishes a series of strange binary oppositions that equate a person with an object – the adjective 'strong' describes both the father himself ('a strong farmer'; 'a strong man') and the mother's public house ('not a strong house'). Presumably this entangled series of fractured memories makes sense to Noman, but to decipher it ourselves we have to impose some system of order, and detach certain motifs and themes. If the father is strong but the pub is not, we wonder if one is at the expense of the other. He works during the day when the pub is closed, except for Saturdays when the pub is open and he drinks with the 'customers' (a word repeated four times). Then again, we are thrown by the obscure linkage of association – do we literally accept that he only really talked on Saturdays, and then only of Parnell?

Similarly, the portrait of the mother is fraught with epistemological gaps which we plug by commonsense assumptions. As critic Sue Asbee has noted:

> How literally are we intended to take the statement that his mother was 'always' in the kitchen? The word *and* is used here very much as a child might use it, simply to join ideas together, but we may wonder whether there is a logical – indecent – association in the linking of mothers and customers implied [. . .].[11]

Noman (like the reader) is a rational observer making simple cause-effect assumptions. If he is in bed then it is more than possible that 'things happened differently [. . .] late at night', but does this necessarily imply a sordid relationship between the mother and the customers? And does this statement tie in with the succeeding sentence which recalls how the father 'did not talk much except on Saturdays when he would mention Parnell'? The mention of Parnell is the only specific historical allusion in the chapter, yet it does not help us locate Noman's memories within a particular time frame. The allusion then is purely literary, evoking comparisons with the first chapter of *A Portrait of the Artist as a Young Man*, and it also reinforces, intertextually, the possibility of his mother's adultery by association with Parnell (assuming, of course, that the reference *is* to Charles Stewart Parnell, and not some other Parnell).

From the outset then, before the retrospective ellipsis of Noman's ontological status comes into play, Noman's oblique style of narration makes us doubt the 'truth' of his narrative. Several 'truths' seem to co-exist simultaneously, each jockeying for position. The language is structured like a riddle which ceaselessly shuffles the boundaries of potential meaning. As the levels of textuality shift from a realist mode of representation to a more polyphonic mode, there occurs what Susan Stewart calls 'surpluses of signification', i.e. where the author 'overloads the text with information that the reader will organise along a hierarchical interpretative scheme, whether or not that scheme is appropriate'.[12] The dialogic disorientation this induces provocatively delights in making us unsure of what we normally take for granted when we read – that the narration, however oblique, is at least attempting to guide us towards a point of trusting acceptance. Noman is the archetypal unreliable narrator, an incorrigible solipsist whose external world has been fabricated by the subjective perceptions of his limited consciousness. We have no way of verifying the reliability of his narrative voice but, in the absence of any other authority, we must grudgingly accept what is given.

The net result of this incipient distrust is that we begin to scrutinise the text for other dialogic clues, of which there are many. Our reading dissolves into discord as these coded textual possibilities, furtive insinuations and metafictional intrusions challenge our commonsense perceptions of language by throwing up various ontological oppositions. We may decide to read it literally (accepting the mimetic narrative) but this seems insufficient; or we may decide to read it allegorically (accepting the textual contradictions) but this seems rather unnerving. As Brian McHale notes of this process in general: 'Allegorical reading is possible, perhaps even tempting, but it is not in any sense necessary: the literal level [. . .] seems perfectly self-contained, quite able to do without an allegorical level. We may well wonder whether an allegorical reading here would not be an imposition of our own.'[13]

On the second page, Noman recalls the deaths of his parents. Again the descriptions of these events are fractured and confused, and filtered through the solipsist memory of the narrative voice. The poignant memories are tinged with sadness, and the reader must assume to know more than the innocent mimetic voice: 'I was young and foolish at the time and did not know properly why these people had all left me, where they had gone and why they did not give explanations beforehand' (*3P*, p. 8). Equally we have no 'explanations beforehand' to help us resolve the casual mysteries of the text, though if we choose to empathise emotionally with a young child's bewilderment it makes a certain limited sense. This tension reflects the dialogic pattern of the text as a whole, as we make a distinction between the unreliable mimetic voice and the textual voice which arises from the written discourse, exclusive of represented speech. We waver between accepting the narrator's representation and receiving the text's presentation – the autocritical and contradictory clues etched between the lines.

Noman explains his confusion over the parents' disappearance from his life as follows:

> My mother was the first to go and I can remember a fat man with a red face and a black suit telling my father that there was no doubt where she was, that he could be as sure of that as he could be of anything else in this vale of tears. But he did not mention where and as I thought the whole thing was very private and that she might be back on Wednesday, I did not ask him where. (*3P*, p. 8)

Again the dialogic potentials of interpretation are unnerving. On a literal level we presuppose that the man in the 'black suit' who talks about a 'vale of tears' is a priest (or perhaps an undertaker), comforting Noman's father. Consequently, we smile sadly at the child's innocent misconception that 'she might be back on Wednesday'. On the other hand, this is taking a huge leap of faith on very flimsy evidence – can we be so sure that this is what actually happened? Nowhere in the novel does Noman definitely tell us that the 'black suit' was a priest, nor does he mention death – just that she was gone. The textual possibility remains that the child's perception is accurate – perhaps the mother has simply gone away, and it is not inconceivable that she will return 'the next Wednesday' (*3P*, p. 8).

Our doubt is reinforced when the father also 'went' – dead? left? – and the 'man in the black suit was back again' (*3P*, p. 8). Two more nameless men arrive, and he recalls one saying to the other, 'The poor misfortunate little bastard' (*3P*, p. 8). Naturally we assume this refers to Noman, now an orphan, but the textual voice autocritically warns us not to presume so much, and has Noman say: 'I did not understand this at the time and thought that they were talking about the other man in black clothes' (*3P*, p. 8). Infuriatingly for the reader, the choice of dialogic possibilities is never resolved. Despite Noman's final remark that he 'understood it all clearly afterwards' (*3P*, p. 8), he never fully clears it up for the reader. A page later he tells us: 'I had long-since got to know how I was situated in the world. All my people were dead' (*3P*, p. 9), and it would seem the dialogic alternatives of this small puzzle are resolved: the parents died, Noman is orphaned, the 'black suit' is a priest. But at this point O'Brien is only beginning to play with the reader's smug complacency. Once we decode the text in light of the final revelation – that Noman is dead as he recounts his story – we can recast these casual remarks within a huge field of irony. Noman thinks he now knows how he was 'situated in the world', but the savage irony is that in the dead zone he inhabits all his 'people' are indeed dead.

This is a perfect illustration of how O'Brien re-invigorates colloquial language and cliché and gives it an ulterior, *textual* meaning distinct from a literal, *mimetic* meaning. The phrase 'all my people were dead' takes on ironic significance (other than its literal translation that his family were dead) by playing on the simple signifier 'people'. The polyphonic language of this novel is further complicated by its use of delayed decoding, giving a commonplace utterance an ironic, subtextual meaning which is only gradually revealed over time.

Critic Ian Watt first coined the term 'delayed decoding' to describe this aspect of Joseph Conrad's impressionistic narratives, where the author attempts 'to present a sense impression and to withhold naming it or explaining its meaning until later. [. . .] This takes us directly into the observer's consciousness at the very moment of the perception, before it has been translated into its cause'.[14] Indeed, such is the frequency and intensity of this device in *The Third Policeman* – not to mention the dark irony attached to the text's final, morbid revelation – that it might be more appropriate to refer to it here as 'deferred decoding', where perception is never fully translated into its cause.

Irony itself is a form of meta-communication, which pre-empts any fixed meaning. As Susan Stewart commented on the use of irony in metafiction: 'With irony commonsense begins to be undermined. [It is] a presentation of the relative nature of points of view, of the incomplete and only partially predictable nature of experience.'[15] This destabilising field of irony runs riot throughout the novel, constantly revelling in its own withheld knowledge. Later on this irony practically degenerates into farce, as when the Sergeant informs Noman that he is to be hung, to which Noman absurdly replies: 'I will resist [. . .] to the death and fight for my existence even if I lose my life in the attempt' (*3P*, p. 98). This is the multiple irony of a man who will 'resist to the death' to save his life, unaware that he is already dead.

After the death (?) of his parents, Noman is sent to a boarding school. Expecting some details of his life at this juncture, we are slightly disturbed at the abrupt and dramatic manner in which he breaks off from his own story: 'My life at this school does not matter except for one thing. It was here that I first came to know something of de Selby' (*3P*, p. 9). This melodramatic revelation creates an air of expectancy, but Noman immediately digresses to consider other matters. This dissolves, or at least defers, the tension – a typical narrative ploy. Throughout the opening chapter O'Brien cuts up his narrative into an arrangement of dislocated time shifts – a method of delayed decoding which frustrates linear reading while drawing attention to its own apparent disorder. As Viktor Shklovsky described this process in *Tristram Shandy*, 'causes are given after effects after deliberately implanted possibilities of false conclusions'.[16]

The metaleptic effect of time-shift operations is that they underline the way in which literary worlds are constructed. Time-shifted narratives give birth to a series of digressions that split the linear narrative into its constituent thematic components. The progression of the basic narrative is constantly interrupted, delayed, resumed, then interrupted again; or, as Tristram himself describes it in *Tristram Shandy*: 'By this contrivance the machinery of my work is of a species by itself; two contrary motions are introduced into it, and reconciled, which were thought to be at variance with each other. In a word, my work is digressive, and it is progressive too, – and at the same time.'[17] These digressions are another aspect of polyphonic composition whereby a linear text is deliberately de-centred and fragmented, producing interesting juxtapositions between one fragment and the next and between one phrase and its successive phrase.

When Noman tells us how he 'first came to know something of de Selby' (*3P*, p. 9), and that nothing else mattered except this discovery, we presume that this is an important revelation (even if its significance is ultimately deferred). Nothing in this text can be blindly accepted at face value, though, and our attention is drawn to the oddness of the name 'de Selby', which J.C.C. Mays has deconstructed etymologically as a variation of the German 'der selbe', which he translates as 'selfhood': 'The book's method is its theme: the dizzying indulgence in the abyss of selfhood (*der selbe*), the regardless pursuit of omniscience (*omnium*).'[18] If this interpretation is correct, then another dialogic problem presents itself: do we accept de Selby as the name of a 'real' person, or do we read it allegorically (following Mays) as: 'I first came to know something about [selfhood/the self]'?

To complicate things further (and to underscore the intricacies of translation and interpretation), Rüdiger Imhof – in a review of the first edition of this present book – suggests a more nuanced translation of the name: 'The name of the idiot savant de Selby is said to be derived from the German "der Selbc" meaning "the Self". No, "der Selbe", or rather "derselbe", means "the same (person)".'[19] From this perspective, the name conjures up a more sinister set of possibilities, namely that Noman and de Selby are the same person (echoing the feuding critics later on in the narrative) or, echoing the uncanny tone of the novel's characterisation in general, that de Selby is Noman' s *doppelgänger* – the ghostly double of a living person that haunts its living counterpart – or even vice versa, i.e. that Noman is de Selby's ghostly twin.[20] In any case, Noman himself should at least be aware of the German origins of the name – on page eleven he tells us how he had learned 'French and German thoroughly' in order to translate de Selby's commentators. Despite this, he never registers the significance of the name, even though he is fully aware of de Selby's self-reflexive theory of names (*3P*, p. 40).[21]

The ontological status of de Selby is further complicated by the lengthy series of footnotes which contribute to a sense of verisimilitude. Paradoxically, the absence of de Selby as a physical character in the text serves only to strengthen his ontological authority, as a legion of critics furiously debate his work, giving further credence to his existence. Our own perception of de Selby is informed by the epigraphs to the novel that quote de Selby and Shakespeare side by side, thus violating the boundaries between 'fictional' and 'real' characters. In terms of the textual space they occupy in these epigraphs, de Selby is at least as ontologically 'real' as Shakespeare.

Noman goes on to tell us how he stole a first edition of de Selby's '*Golden Hours*' from the school library, which had 'the two last pages missing' (*3P*, p. 9). In its immediate context the fact of the missing pages seems an odd detail, though it confronts us with the essential materiality of the novel itself, and anticipates the revelations unveiled in the last two pages of the text. *The Third Policeman* is a murder mystery of sorts, and like any good 'whodunit' the real murderer is not revealed until the final few pages. This seemingly marginal (yet quietly foregrounded) detail therefore becomes highly self-reflexive, even if its significance is elliptical and its decoding delayed or deferred.

Noman is conscious that his stealing of the book is immoral:

> Nevertheless I packed it in my bag without a qualm and would
> probably do the same if I had my time again. Perhaps it is impor-
> tant in the story I am going to tell to remember that it was for de
> Selby that I committed my first serious sin. It was for him I com-
> mitted my greatest sin. (*3P*, p. 9)

'If I had my time again' is another example of a reconstructed, dialogic cliché. Once the elliptical irony and metalinguistic code are
deciphered, this utterance reminds us that Noman is dead as he
speaks. It is also one of the many allusions to time in the opening
chapter, and highlights the fact that time moves differently in this
fictional world. For example, Noman has already described his
mother as having 'spent her life making tea to pass the time and
singing snatches of old songs to pass the meantime' (*3P*, p. 7). The
hackneyed phrases 'pass the time' and 'meantime' are deliberately
differentiated, presenting us with an image of temporal dualism or
relativity – a central motif in the novel as a whole. Polyphony also
operates on individual words in a system and 'meantime' can be
deconstructed as a portmanteau word, signifying either the
present temporal moment (literal), or a 'mean' and grim time (figurative), or both.

   The structural logic of Noman's syntax also leaves its semantic
meaning open to interpretation. Noman has yet to reveal his motive
for the murder of Old Mathers (to get the money to produce the definitive index of de Selby), although he has already confessed to the
gruesome murder in the abrupt opening line of the novel – 'Not
everybody knows how I killed old Phillip Mathers' (*3P*, p. 7).
Consequently, Noman's stealing of a book from a school library
'without a qualm' (*3P*, p. 9) is logically linked to 'it was for [de Selby]
that I committed my greatest sin' (*3P*, p. 9). Presumably his 'greatest
sin' refers to the (then motiveless) murder, but the syntactical composition leaves an uneasy impression in the reader's mind that this
self-confessed murderer considers the stealing of a book to be his
'greatest sin.' And again, if we decide to allegorically substitute
either 'the self' or 'the same person' in place of 'de Selby', other possibilities emerge: 'It was for [the self/the same person] that I
committed my first serious sin' – be that sin either murder or theft.

   As the narrative progresses, we become alive to the multiple
levels of reading (split between the mimetic and textual voices), but
at the same time we realise that Noman himself does not have this
same capacity. He is a strict positivist, trusting only in the empirical

evidence of his blinkered senses and in the rationalist principle of cause-effect deduction. Noman is also a victim of what Roman Jakobson terms 'aphasia': the incapacity to 'name' objects or manipulate language through substitution, or, as the *OED* defines it, a 'loss of speech, or of understanding of language, owing to brain damage'.[22] All fictional characters suffer from this type of 'brain damage', as they are programmed within a text to obey the dictates of their author-god. Noman is doggedly monological and does not understand the operations of the metalanguage. He cannot see that language can operate outside its own intended referential context, and can have ironic, multiple meanings. Noman thus interprets language monologically, whereas the reader is invited to read it dialogically. This difference causes an important split between the projected world of the text and the real world of the reader, in the way that Noman's steadfast ignorance contrasts with our ontologically superior status as co-creative reader. Patricia Waugh has characterised this metafictional split as a 'schizophrenic' construction, 'where information is not processed, where metalingual insufficiency results in a failure to distinguish between hierarchies of messages and contexts'.[23]

Noman, it would seem, is a conventional construction lifted out of realist tradition and thrown into a metafictional world. Aphasia dislocates and prescribes his language, and we sense that in his mimetic description of objects and events he misses the wider implications of his own speech. Take, for example, his description of the accident which cost him his leg:

> In one of the places where I was broadening my mind I met one night with a bad accident. I broke my left leg (or, if you like, it was broken for me) in six places and when I was well enough again to go my way I had one leg made of wood, the left one. I knew that I only had a little money, that I was going home to a rocky farm and that my life would not be easy. (*3P*, pp. 9–10)

What is immediately disturbing about this off-hand and brief disclosure – beyond its digressive incongruity – is the grotesquely cold exactness of marginal detail: 'six places', 'the left one', and we slowly begin to question the reliability (and eventually the sanity) of our narrator. We are not shocked by the disclosure of the amputation *per se* (if indeed that is what actually occurred), but by his cosmic indifference to the loss of his leg, illustrating, as Wim Tigges has noted, the strange 'absence of emotional involvement on the part of the narrator'.[24] The absence of emotion is made strange through the planned incongruity of the scene, what Denis

Donoghue in a study of Jonathan Swift calls 'the imposition of a proper perspective by putting gross perspectives in lurid proximity'.[25] In good Swiftian fashion, O'Brien severs the relationship between facts and moral ideas by flitting in and out of context. The facts are fine in themselves but the forcing of a square word into a round sentence tends to warp their shape. Language becomes a lurid and sinister poetry which travesties form *and* content, and so *discourse* (how we are told what happens), as well as *story* (what happens), comes under closer scrutiny.

The polyphonic composition of this scene has an important metaleptic aspect. The complex syntactical arrangements make us conscious that a dialogic pattern of language can never have fixed, referential value. The phrase 'I broke my leg' is deconstructed by O'Brien himself as having several possible meanings: either as a passive, metaphorical coinage (implying an accidental breakage); or as an active, literal phrase whereby Noman might have broken his leg, deliberately, by his own hand – signposted by the bracketed insert '(or, if you like, it was broken for me)'.

This grammatical exactitude is autocritical and informs the reader that even simple and seemingly straightforward statements must be treated with interpretative scepticism. The self-deconstructed phrase examines minutely the social conventions of speech, and shows the deductive causality that underlies our most mundane reading assumptions, i.e. if there is smoke there must be fire; if Noman says 'I broke my leg' then it must be accidental. This parenthesis reveals how meaning is culturally conditioned, and it also initiates a critique of rationalism which has significant implications for the moral/ontological themes of the novel.

We could also posit a third possibility, namely that some other agent broke Noman's leg: 'it was broken for me.' If Noman is a character in a fictional world (unbeknownst to himself at this stage) then we could say that his leg is broken because it simply suits the machinations of plot – later on Noman will meet Martin Finnucane, leader of the 'Hoppy men' (a gang of similarly handicapped bandits). This scene can thus be read as an establishing shot, providing us with information that will be crucial to later plot developments. By framing such structurally relevant information in a strange context, O'Brien exposes his methods of textual construction. This creates a disingenuous sense of immediacy on the author's part, which overrules the primacy of the mimetic narrative. Though seemingly unstructured and undisciplined it is, of course, deliberate, and it breaks the delicate frame.

The oddness of his grotesque disclosure – amputation and a wooden leg – fulfils other structural functions as well. On an inter-textual level, it recalls the scene in Marlowe's *Doctor Faustus* when the horse-courser pulls off Faustus's leg, and later tells him: 'I'll drink a health to thy wooden leg,' thereby identifying Noman in terms of the Faustian archetype.[26] Of more significance to our present discussion is the way that the wooden leg foregrounds the artificiality of physical description. This aspect of the novel has been previously discussed – the way, for instance, that Policeman Fox squeezes his enormous bulk through a small window. However, what is most interesting about the description of Noman's leg is that it is the first description of his body in the text, and the artificial limb makes us conscious that all limbs and bodies in a text are essentially artificial, i.e. created descriptions only partially specified by the author. From a formalist perspective, characters in a text are functions of composition: achromatic outlines sketched by the artist but coloured in by the reader who brings his or her experience to the text. As Patricia Waugh writes: 'Descriptions of objects in fiction are simultaneously creations of that object. [. . .] The ontological status of fictional objects is determined by the fact that they exist by virtue of, whilst also forming, the fictional context which are finally the words on a page.'[27]

Any description of an object in fiction calls that object into being through words. Metafictions split the conventional links between reality and representation, and remind us that, even if objects pre-exist in the real world before description, they can be conjured up on the page only through language. In the nightmare sequence in chapter eight, Noman becomes intensely conscious of his wooden leg, which in turn makes the reader conscious of his described physique: 'I had a curious feeling about my left leg. I thought that it was, so to speak, spreading – that its woodenness was slowly expanding throughout my whole body, a dry timber poison killing me inch by inch' (*3P*, p. 115). The image of artificiality is thus literalised, and Noman becomes surprised by the fragile, almost translucent outline of his 'white and thin' body (*3P*, p. 115). As he lies in bed his description of his body is made strange by a grotesque metaphorical exaggeration that is overtly and self-consciously lyrical – 'My knees opened up like rosebuds in rich sunlight' (*3P*, p. 115) – and traditional literary conceits become monstrously bloated: 'My eyelids, each weighing no less than four tons, slewed ponderously across my eyeballs' (*3P*, p. 116).

As darkness falls on Noman (complicated by an elaborate footnote on de Selby's theories of night), he is denied the use of his primary descriptive sense, his eyesight, and so he becomes keenly aware of his other senses, and how they help construct his bodily make-up:

> Robbing me of the reassurance of my eyesight, [the night] was disintegrating my bodily personality into a flux of colour, smell, recollection, desire – all the strange uncounted essences of terrestrial and spiritual existence. I was deprived of definition, position and magnitude and my significance was considerably diminished. Lying there, I felt the weariness ebbing from me slowly, like a tide retiring over limitless sands. (*3P*, p. 116)

Sight is the principal sense used by Noman to describe his world to the reader. Like Stephen Dedalus in the 'Proteus' chapter of *Ulysses*, Noman is conscious of what Stephen calls the 'ineluctable modality of the visible: at least that if no more, thought through my eyes'[28] – and the imagery of the beach consciously parodies Stephen's torturous wanderings on Sandymount Strand. In *Ulysses*, Stephen closes his eyes to experience reality more forcibly through his other senses, but in *The Third Policeman* Noman is deprived of his sight and feels his 'bodily personality' disintegrate. Ontologically deconstructed, Noman realises that he is nothing but a 'flux of colour, smell, recollection, desire' – feelings and qualities assigned to him by his creator, the author-god. Formally denuded of the glossy details – 'deprived of definition' – which make up his written character outline, Noman feels that his 'significance was considerably diminished.' In good old-fashioned Brechtian style, the reader is alienated from the co-creative process through which the reader and the words on the page subconsciously interact to help construct fictional characters. Remove subconscious reader input from the equation (by making it conscious) and what is left is a few words marked out on a flat page – the ineluctable modality of fiction; thought through discourse.

Later on, in the zone of Eternity (the subterranean machinery which controls the workings of The Parish and the text itself), Pluck tells Noman of machines that break down sense experiences into their constituent components. 'A smell is the most complicated phenomenon in the world', he tells Noman, 'and it cannot be unravelled by the human snout' (*3P*, p. 139). But in Eternity there is a machine that 'splits up any smell into its sub- and inter- smells the way you can split up a beam of light with a glass instrument' (*3P*, p. 139), as well as a 'machine for tastes' and a machine for disentangling touch. In this openly deconstructive manner O'Brien reveals the literary machine, showing us that the sense experiences through which the narrator mediates his story are merely mechanical devices. O'Brien lays bare the fact that our knowledge of this textual world depends on the solipsism of our narrator as well as our ability as intertextual readers to flesh out his bare description.

Physiological deconstruction is brutally honest in this scene, almost to the point of clumsiness. Far more subtle is the way that O'Brien cuts up simple utterances (often with the unwitting complicity of the reader) to refine our reading habits. A perfect illustration of this occurs just as Noman is about to depart from Eternity, and he sees MacCruiskeen lift up a bag: 'Without lifting my head I looked across the floor and saw MacCruiskeen's legs walking away with my bag' (*3P*, p. 141). This form of metalepsis depends on the reader's dialogic disorientation for its effect. Noman's rationalist belief in causality is rigidly over-developed – from his subjective viewpoint he can see only a pair of legs, and describes it so. Presumably the rest of the policeman's body is firmly attached to these legs, although in this topsy-turvy world of illogic anything is possible. Noman sees only the legs, so only the legs walk away with the bag; only the legs are given but the reader rationally assumes the rest.

The strength of this richly suggestive language lies in the way it heightens our consciousness of the nature and origin of interpretation. *The Third Policeman* is a text that lies between what Susan Stewart calls 'the external space of common sense and the internal space of representation'.[29] Interpretation thus becomes a battleground, or, as Sterne writes in *Tristram Shandy*: 'the life of a writer, whatever he might fancy to the contrary, was not so much a state of composition as a state of warfare'.[30]

This polyphonic warfare is most subtly at work in the opening chapter, with a whole series of structural forces at play that disturb readerly expectations. Again, O'Brien makes great use of cut-up and time-shift to delay and impede any absolute interpretation. In the opening line of the novel, for instance, Noman begins to tell us about the murder – 'Not everybody knows how I killed old Phillip Mathers' – but this initial tension dissolves by digression – 'but first it is better to speak of my friendship with John Divney' (*3P*, p. 7). Six pages later Noman attempts to explain about the murder, but the telling becomes excessively convoluted, and bound up yet again with his memories of Divney. The mental associations between the murder and Divney are reminiscent of Sterne's appropriation of the Lockean principle of duration. This concept of associative time-shift parallels Tristram's transgressing of conventional narrative

schemes that usually report temporal events in chronological succession. As Walter Shandy paraphrases Locke: 'men derive their
ideas of duration from their reflection on the train of ideas they
observe to succeed one another in their own understanding'.[31]

A few pages later, Noman tells us that 'It was about this time,
when I was nearing thirty' – ten years after his return to the family
farm – 'that Divney and I began to get the name of being great
friends' (*3P*, p. 12). Rather than tell us outright the reason for this,
Noman begins a long-winded digression on the degree of closeness
between him and Divney, which culminates with both of them
sharing the same bed: 'I slept with him always after that. We were
friendly and smiled at each other but the situation was a queer one
and neither of us liked it. The neighbours were not long noticing
how inseparable we were' (*3P*, p. 13).

The logical explanation for this – that they had killed Old
Mathers but Noman did not trust Divney to share the contents of the
hidden black box – is delayed for another five pages: 'And that is why
Divney and I became inseparable friends' (*3P*, p. 18). In the meantime, there is a split between cause (their mutual mistrust) and
effect (their sleeping together) which foregrounds the physical relationship. Without prior knowledge of the actual circumstances, the
reader is forced to interpret the scene out of context, and makes the
supposition that Noman and Divney are homosexual lovers. The
polyphony here has two catalysts: the positioning of this scene out of
context, and the metonymic instability of the word 'queer'. We are
forced to make an uncomfortable choice: is the situation 'queer'
because it is odd or because it is homosexual? Do the neighbours
'notice' in a malicious, disapproving fashion, or do they quite simply
applaud a laudable friendship?

In a similar way, O'Brien delays our decoding of key thematic
sequences in chapter one by shifting and displacing scenes out of
their 'natural' context, and juxtaposing them against other scenes
which then intersect in a curious configuration, thus guaranteeing
deliberate misreadings. In this reconstructed roundabout pattern,
Noman finally tells of the 'peculiar situation' (*3P*, p. 14) between
himself and Divney. Both of them, it transpires, needed an urgent
injection of capital – Noman to publish his work on de Selby and
Divney because he intends to marry a local woman, Pegeen Meers.
Consequently, they hatch their murderous plan to kill Old Mathers
and rob him of the contents of his black box.

Several self-conscious elements emerge in our reading of this
murder plot that point to the artifice of the novel, including the

name of Divney's intended wife. In a chapter so doggedly ephemeral and shifting, the specificity of the name – 'Pegeen Meers' – automatically grabs our attention. In terms of intertextual play her name can be broken down into two components: a nod in the direction of Peig Sayers (1873–1958), one of the Gaelic autobiographical writers whom O'Brien admired (but also parodied) in *An Béal Bocht*, and a variant of Pegeen Mike from Synge's *The Playboy of the Western World* (1907). We can safely assign Pegeen Meers this latter transworld identity by virtue of a series of parallel associations. Old Mahon, Christy's father and supposed murder victim, here equates with Old Mathers, and the descriptions of both murders share parallel correspondences: 'I went forward mechanically, swung the spade over my shoulder and smashed the blade of it with all my strength against the protruding chin. I felt and almost heard the fabric of his skull crumple up crisply like an eggshell' (*3P*, p. 16). The murder in *The Playboy* is the prototype for this description: 'I just riz the loy and let fall the edge of it on the ridge of his skull, and he went down at my feet like an empty sack, and never let a grunt or groan from him at all.'[32]

Parody is always a problematic form of wit by virtue of its dependency on connotation and parallelism, and this presents the reader with certain interpretative obstacles. As Vivian Mercier writes: 'Parody makes [. . .] greater demands on a reader: first of all, he must recognise the work or the genre parodied, then he must see the parody by comparison with the original; finally this absurdity must be reflected back from the parody to the original.'[33] Consequently, O'Brien's use of *The Playboy* is quite complex, as it is not just a critique of Synge's synthetic language but a creative intertextual process as well. In this respect, the Synge parody typifies the construction of *The Third Policeman* as a post-modernist, schizoid text. In the novel, the dual nature of the original Christy Mahon is split into its two base components: the Oedipal Christy who 'kills' his father in order to take control of his destiny (represented by Noman himself), and the later Christy who uses the 'gallous story' of the murder to win the affections of Pegeen Mike (represented by Divney, who murders so that he can marry Pegeen Meers). Once again this highlights the artifice of character construction in the way that most of the minor characters in the novel seem to echo the narrator, or else recall other characters appropriated from the wider literary tradition.

Furthermore, both Christy Mahon and Noman labour under similar delusions. In Christy's case the victim (his father) is not dead at all, and metaphorically returns from the grave. *The Third Policeman* concretises this Oedipal metaphor in the way that Noman's victim – Old Mathers – returns from the dead to haunt him in the second chapter. This is typical of the way that parody functions in many metafictional texts where a 'metaphoric substitution is forced into an on-going metonymic plane'.[34] As Susan Stewart has noted in general: 'Once irony makes a split with reality by means of its double voices, parody can set in, opening the wound between discourse and the world, between discourse and discourse.'[35] Whereas realist texts would seek to disguise such splits between the real and the fictional, metafictional texts exaggerate them by signposting their intertextual dependence.

During the actual murder of Old Mathers, which is rather graphically recounted, it is Divney who strikes the first blow with his 'iron pump' (*3P*, p. 16). This recalls the strange opening of the novel that had piqued our curiosity in the first place:

> Not everybody knows how I killed old Phillip Mathers, smashing his jaw in with my spade; but first it is better to speak of my friendship with John Divney because it was he who first knocked old Mathers down by giving him a great blow in the neck with a special bicycle-pump which he manufactured himself out of a hollow iron bar. (*3P*, p. 7)

This is a classic example of the principle of delayed decoding used throughout the opening chapter. The opening clause is a dramatic revelation: a killer, it seems, is about to confess his story. But then the focus of the action switches abruptly with the introduction of another qualifying clause – 'but first it is better to speak of my friendship' – as if his friendship with Divney is of greater interest than the details of his self-declared murder. It is a question, ultimately, of syntactical order: the positioning of clausal sequences speak to us *textually* while Noman's voice speaks *mimetically*. Teasingly, we get some of the detail we seek but the action has temporarily shifted to Divney's part in the murder, and to the cold, flat description of the murder weapon (a pump) that we presume had been fashioned for that very purpose (signifying a cold-blooded, premeditated crime). It also, of course, initiates the first in a long series of bicycle motifs which have an important bearing on later events.

The point of this convoluted opening is that it cuts up the linear consumption of the narrative: effects are given prior to cause and interrupted by a series of often banal digressions, which in turn initiate other digressions, and so on. Like Sterne in *Tristram Shandy*,

O'Brien often tells the end of a story first, then the beginning, then the middle; sometimes he may even tell the beginning but abandon the story for a few pages or so. Both authors manipulate, place, displace and replace events as it suits them – the narrative moves along a picaresque line but is constantly modified by flashback and interruption. This fragmentation makes nonsense out of traditional storytelling methods and interpretative procedures by 'reversing or inverting them, shifting their boundaries, repeating them to infinity and/or exhaustion, co-joining them in time, or fracturing them in their members and recombining them'.[36]

This Shandean principle of digressive-progressive narration is employed to great effect throughout *The Third Policeman*. The murder scene is declared, interrupted, then resumed, and all according to the solipsist imagination of the untrustworthy narrator. As Rüdiger Imhof has written: 'this device, in addition to its riddle or surprise effect, generates tension; it appeals to the reader's curiosity; he wants to know how the presumable "whodunit" will be continued.'[37] In fact, from the announcement in the first line of the novel that Noman has murdered Old Mathers, ten pages elapse before he actually recalls the murder itself. Even then the details are fractured and oblique, and fluctuate continually between grotesque, detailed disclosure and abstruse, dialogic disorientation. As Old Mathers falls from Divney's blow he mutters something in a muted dying whisper, 'softly, in a conversational tone' (*3P*, p. 16). Noman is not quite sure what Mathers mutters, and this confusion is allowed to filter down to the reader. We are torn between delaying our reading to make sense of the dying man's words and between continuing to read this gripping tale. Noman himself is petrified with fear and fascination – 'I had been watching the scene rather stupidly, still leaning on my spade' – until Divney roars at him to wake up and 'Finish him with the spade!' (*3P*, p. 16).

Then comes the graphic description of Noman's spade crunching into Old Mathers' skull, and a real sense of visceral horror is evoked by the descriptive detail. In between Mathers being struck down by Divney and Noman finishing him off, the depiction of the killing frenzy – 'I do not know how often I struck him after that but I did not stop until I was tired' – is interrupted by the victim's mysterious last words: 'something like "I do not care for celery" or "I left my glasses in the scullery"' (*3P*, p. 16). What does Old Mathers mean here? Has Noman misheard him begging for mercy, or uttering a black curse perhaps? Is this comment significant for the reader, anxious to accumulate clues to solve this dark murder mystery? We feel obliged, somehow, to at least attempt some kind of formal decoding. Is it yet another act of intertextual pirating, or can it be deciphered like a riddle? It could even be the invisible author intruding on his text, feeding us useless titbits of information like his taste in food, or the fact that his glasses, as he writes his novel, are in the kitchen – the secular psychodynamics of the writing act.

Whichever way we look at it, from a formalist point of view it is certainly a strategic intrusion. Its inclusion deliberately impedes our emotional involvement with the murder scene, and it alienates us from becoming too absorbed in the local pleasures and horrors of the text. What makes this intrusion strategically valuable is that it diverts us from the orgiastic violence described. We are embarrassed that we are reluctantly torn away from enjoying the pulsating account of violence, and we become conscious of our own complicity. If we do eventually decide that Old Mathers' dying words are meaningless (in a semantic sense at least), then we are quietly reminded of our co-creative role. Consequently, this scene has several functions: first, it reminds us that we are constantly mapping out and conceptualising the text in terms of what is useful to our monological reading habits; and, second, it points the finger at our voyeuristic participation – it is we, as readers, who are titillated by the violence; it is we who conjure it into being.

The description of Noman's involvement in the murder has been anticipated by the reader from the opening line, but the narrative process by which it is revealed has been so convoluted that by the time it eventually comes we are highly aware of the text which frames it. The graphic description is disturbing because it organically dramatises for us the violence of the act in the very language it uses, re-enacting a horrific, nightmarish sense of slow motion. Noman is petrified into inaction until Divney's animal roar pushes him forward 'mechanically' (*3P*, p. 16), and he raises his spade to crush the fragile skull. The word 'mechanically' is itself polyphonic, as it captures both Noman's critical distancing of himself from the dreadful act, and it metaleptically points out that Noman is a puppet being manipulated by the author-god. Like the reader, Noman 'felt and almost heard the fabric of his skull crumple up crisply' (*3P*, p. 16). This method of polyphonic representation foregrounds the callous violence of the murder and Noman's lack of compassion, and it also makes strange the representation. From a formalist perspective, the grotesque becomes a technical device of defamiliarisation which impinges directly on the reader, making us conscious of our complicity. Above all, what is sought here is a sense of disorientation, which seems appropriate to the circumstances.

After this scene, the remaining pages of chapter one seem anti-climatic. Divney hides the black box in a 'safe place', and they decide to wait 'until things have quietened down' (*3P*, p. 18) to split the proceeds. The mystery of the 'peculiar terms of physical intimacy' (*3P*, p. 19) between Noman and Divney – formerly eroticised – is simply revealed to be a state of intense paranoia between the two. We are a little disappointed in the flatness of the general description – at least until the final page of the chapter when Noman goes back into Old Mathers' house to reclaim the box, months or even years later. Time has become so fractured in the telling of this tale that we have lost track of it, as the narrative jumps forwards and backwards almost at random.

Finally, Divney brings Noman to the house and proposes to send him in alone: 'I would like you to get the box with your own hands because it is only simple justice after not telling you where it was' (*3P*, p. 20). Noman accepts this explanation, although the reader is less sure of Divney's altruism. Throughout the chapter Divney has been revealed as an untrustworthy, Machiavellian character, and now he asks Noman to trust him. The issue of trust has in fact become crucial to this scene, as Divney gives the naive Noman a 'long hurt look and asked me sadly did I not trust him' (*3P*, p. 19). Divney repeats the word 'trust', and swears an oath to heaven, and, although Noman has some doubts, Divney's face 'seemed to wear a look of honesty' (*3P*, p. 20).

Paradoxically, the repetitious use of words like 'honesty' and 'trust' makes us conscious that we do not, in fact, trust Divney. As Noman prepares to enter the house, we have a strong sense of foreboding that surpasses that of the mimetic narrator. Just before he goes in (to his death) Divney gives him what seems to be, on the surface, some commonsense advice: 'If you meet anybody', he says, 'you don't know anything' (*3P*, p. 20). The chapter would appear to be ending rather conventionally, but suddenly any sense of stability is overthrown by one final, dialogic twist – 'I don't even know my own name,' replies Noman with mild sarcasm, but this phrase is abruptly concretised by the final, mysterious revelation of chapter one: 'This was a very remarkable thing for me to say because the next time I was asked my name I could not answer. I did not know' (*3P*, p. 20). Immediately the dramatic tension is re-established by the polyphonic juxtaposition between the realist and the fantastic, or, as Brian McHale describes this process in general: 'The fantastic has been co-opted as one in a number of strategies of an ontological poetics that pluralises the "real" and problematises representation, [. . .] a sort of jiu-jitsu that uses representation itself to overthrow representation.'[38]

In this way, a casual, throwaway remark has suddenly been revitalised and enriched with dialogic mystery. The polyphonic composition of *The Third Policeman*'s language bears out O'Brien's initial comment to his publishers that in this novel 'casual remarks create a thousand other mysteries'.[39]

6. Relative worlds:
Kit Marlowe meets Philip Marlowe in the fourth dimension

All literature is a footnote to Faust.
                    Woody Allen, 'Conversations with Helmholtz', 1980[1]

Thematically and stylistically, *The Third Policeman* is a parabolic text, i.e. 'displaying the infinitely open curve of a parabola, and forming parables for an infinite number of propositions'.[2] In using the term 'parabolic' within a literary context, I am conscious of overloading an already crowded critical space with yet another neologism. But this term is born out of a personal frustration with the conventional categories of genre – should *The Third Policeman* be labelled as metafiction, satire, fantasy, whodunnit or even as sci-fi? It can certainly lay claim to all but can derive complete satisfaction from none. 'Parabolic', then, suggests two things: a story which strives towards parable (a narrative of imagined events illustrating a moral or spiritual lesson – in this case a satire of epistemology); and in a technical sense it refers to an open plane curve formed by a series of intersections, i.e. an open narrative which is shaped intertextually. As Jeremy Hawthorn notes: 'A parabolic text is *open* rather than *closed*, receiving and transforming varied approaches to it as a parabolic dish antenna "captures" a range of different signals, but it also has the quality of a parable, supporting a succession of never-ending applications.'[3]

The concept of intertextuality is crucial to our understanding of this parabolic novel. As Michael Worton and Judith Still note, 'The theory of intertextuality insists that a text [. . .] cannot exist as a hermetic or self-sufficient whole, and so does not function as a closed system'.[4] Intertextuality is a bridge between the words and images of a text and the world of words and images in which the reader lives. A writer is a reader before ever being a creator, and every literary work is riddled (consciously and unconsciously) with references, quotes and influences – every text, then, is an intertext.

193

The reader also participates in this intertextual arena in the way that a text can only be understood by some active process of reading, which is shaped by all the other texts a reader brings to it. The promiscuous poetics of intertextuality are deeply enshrined within the post-modernist paradigm. It is an interactive paradox: the writer 'reads' and the reader 'writes'.

The intertextual construction and polyphonic language of *The Third Policeman* operate on an open plane where multiple modes of discourse and reading strategies converge, and vie for signifying supremacy. The post-modernist author is an intertextual tailor stitching together a pastiche of eclectic languages that compete for privilege in a relative universe. The novel itself is a heteroglossia of shifting, irresolvable meaning: a series of multiple representations that cancel, contradict or collude with previous representations. 'Sense' is prescribed according to the interpretative potentials of the co-creative reader, who is forever conscious of the precarious balance between the novel's 'multiplicity of meaning and absence of meaning'.[5] What Flann O'Brien seeks in the composition of *The Third Policeman* is a dialogic disorientation where, as Mary A. O'Toole notes, both 'the narrator and the reader are unable to grasp any basis for temporal or spatial stability in this queer universe'.[6]

Given this disorientation, the intertextual reader is obliged to improvise a system of reading, and although it may be tempting to interpret O'Brien's work allegorically, this is ultimately a crude and provisional gesture. Traditional allegories are stories with a simple and obvious double meaning, e.g. George Orwell's *Animal Farm* (1945). Here the primary, surface narrative (a fairytale) informs and interacts with a secondary, subtextual narrative (a critique of totalitarianism). Such allegories must adhere to established codes of conduct. The author makes a narrative contract with the reader that promises to recognise a fixed and stable universe, with familiar patterns of meaning which are then rearranged through irony: pigs equate with politicians, farms with countries, and so on. Such classical allegories involve a relatively straightforward conflict of Manichean principles, or a personification of semantic opposites.

Post-modernist narratives, however, lack the realist certitudes of old, and have no such stable order to refer to. A parabolic text is by nature unstable, and refers only to a flickering, fragmented world. In fact, if *The Third Policeman* can be considered an allegory at all, its allegorical thrust is its attempt to destabilise the general structures on which conventional narratives depend. In this sense, *The*

Third Policeman is an indeterminate allegory of a relative world: an open network of irony *and* paradox that invites the reader to participate, but which resists any absolute interpretation.

Very often in this novel, false hierarchical structures are suggested by the author's establishment of conventional contours – a deliberate implantation of recognisable codes, metaphors and representations. The topographical landmarks deliberately seduce the reader into making false assumptions about the 'true' meaning of the text. But then the lines of the allegorical map flicker and disappear, leaving the hapless reader stranded in no-man's-land: the author-god giveth and the author-god taketh away.

The danger of such seductive rhetorical strategies is the way they tease the reader into constructing an absolutist model of interpretation, which the text suddenly undermines and exposes as a self-serving delusion – a dramatic re-enactment, if you will, of its own picaresque narrative and solipsist narrator. The reader, disturbed by the shifting field of focus, tends to latch on to a particular theme, only to watch their allegorical reconstruction being deconstructed before their very eyes. More sensible readers accept these pluralities and discontinuities, and enjoy its mischievous playfulness. The critic, however – a more obsessive kind of literary trainspotter – often unearths a specific intertextual borrowing and immediately scurries off to decipher the text in light of their discovery, crucifying the text under their critical microscope and pillaging it for confirmation of their brilliant insight. Triumphant, the critic descends the ivory tower, thesis in hand, having successfully reduced the novel to an allegorical heap of ashes.

This final chapter will view *The Third Policeman* as a post-modernist Menippean satire – 'official literature's dialectical antithesis and parodic double'[7] – and as a parabolic text which specifically satirises reductive forms of critical thought. Rather than isolate one monological, allegorical theme or intertextual 'key', I will trace the general intertextual flux and refer to the 'dominant' of the work – the governing component of the intertextual labyrinth which acts as a skeletal framework for the various modes of discourse. The dominant binds the centrifugal forces together and prevents competing languages from chaotic dispersal, or, as Roman Jakobson wrote, 'it rules, determines, and transforms the remaining components [and] guarantees the integrity of the structure'.[8]

In the case of *The Third Policeman* the central ideological dominant is the popular detective mystery, or 'whodunit'. On the surface at least this would seem to contradict Brian McHale when he notes that 'Science-fiction [...] is to post-modernism what detective fiction was to modernism: it is the ontological genre (*par excellence*) as the detective story is the epistemological genre (*par excellence*)'.[9] However, not all post-modern theorists would agree with McHale's rigid demarcation of boundaries. Within the Irish tradition, sci-fi as a genre has never fired the imagination in the same way that it seems to have influenced modern American fiction (with which McHale is primarily concerned). Indeed, two of the best self-consciously post-modernist works to have emerged in Ireland in recent years – John Banville's *The Book of Evidence* (1989) and Patrick McCabe's *The Butcher Boy* (1993) – attest to the Irish fascination with the murder genre.[10] Nonetheless, McHale's analysis is still valuable. According to his conception, the ontological dominant of post-modernism is typified by the grim dystopia or 'death-world' to be found in science-fiction: 'The motif of a world after the holocaust or some apocalyptic breakdown occurs'.[11] Clearly, then, it is science-fiction which influences the construction of the death-world of The Parish: a space–time continuum where sinister forces of science and technology have conspired to create Noman's hell. However, it is the epistemological dominant of the 'whodunit' that explains why Noman has arrived in this hell in the first place. O'Brien's satire of science and philosophy helps construct The Parish, but the 'whodunit' de-constructs it. Consequently, the first part of this current discussion will deal with the construction of the death-world; the second with its deconstruction.

The construction of the death-world

In his thought-provoking essay 'Beyond the Zone of Middle Dimensions: A Relativistic Reading of *The Third Policeman*', Charles Kemnitz argues that the narrative structures of the novel are governed by the theories of Albert Einstein.[12] Certainly, in at least three 'Cruiskeen Lawn' columns, Myles na Gopaleen professed a great fascination with the iconic figure of Einstein, although he seems less impressed with his actual theories: 'I think Einstein was mischievous and futile. [. . .] Einstein's theory is just that – a theory, an explanation of the universe in novel terms; it has no practical application, though it could induce spiritual necrosis in some students of it'.[13] And later, in *The Dalkey Archive*, the reincarnated version of De Selby argues that 'The postulates of the Relativity nonsense of Einstein are mendacious, not to say bogus' (*DA*, p. 14). Nonetheless, Kemnitz contends that the narrative of *The Third*

Policeman is governed by Einstein's theory of relativity and quantum mechanics: 'a literary appropriation of the language and conceptual models of relativity current during the nineteen-thirties'.[14]

Kemnitz demonstrates that the text itself is littered with the buzzwords of the New Physics – 'black-hole', 'flux', 'energy', 'mass', 'atoms', etc. – and 'deftly utilises the comparative language of nuclear physics to enhance the strangeness'.[15] But Kemnitz cannot see (or chooses to ignore) that this is ultimately a formalist strategy of defamiliarisation, and not the key to some subtextual allegory. Often insightful, occasionally absurd, Kemnitz's essay is ultimately damaged by the restrictive limits of his absolutist reading. He is blind to the polyphonic composition of the post-modernist intertext, seemingly oblivious to the playful metalepsis of the metafictional style, and nowhere does he consider that Einstein is being parodied as part of a wider Menippean satire of science.

Using a historical analogy borrowed from nuclear physics, Kemnitz compares the interaction between the primary narrative and the mock footnotes in the novel to a crucial paradox in Quantum Theory, i.e. the dualist paradox that light is both a wave and consists of particles: 'The footnotes in turn act as an electro-magnetic source upon the metal of the narrative: at times the footnotes interfere with the information in the text, at other times they augment the narrative, and at still other times they "kick-out" insights that aid in the experiencing of the text'.[16] As an analogy this is a good generalisation of how that interactive process functions in the text, but it fails to take into account the historical influence of Swift, Sterne, Joyce and others, and their particular contribution to O'Brien's narrative scheme.

Although Flann O'Brien was obviously fascinated by Einstein, Kemnitz overestimates O'Brien's understanding of atomic physics. As Wim Tigges has noted, O'Brien's interest in Einstein is actually 'a side-effect, and surely not the meaning of the book'.[17] In a de-Selbian-length footnote to his essay, Kemnitz cites a discussion with Niall Sheridan – a friend of O'Brien's – who seemed to verify O'Brien's interest in Einstein, albeit with one qualification: 'Mr Sheridan [...] said that yes, O'Nolan had been intensely interested in modern physics as an undergraduate and it was entirely possible that *The Third Policeman* was based on relativity theory. I have no reason to believe that Mr Sheridan was codding me, although that possibility does exist.'[18]

Discussion of O'Brien's work in Ireland has always been a critical minefield, with facts often gleefully abandoned in order to cultishly defend and propagate the roguish Mylesian myth. The inclusion of this footnote suggests that Kemnitz himself may have his tongue firmly embedded in his cheek, and may be 'codding' us all. If this is correct, the Kemnitz essay may be true to the Mylesian spirit; if not, then the essay's thesis is something of a glorious, complicated failure.

Structurally, Kemnitz sees the novel as representing two warring principles in modern physics: the 'Newtonian universe governed by Euclidean geometry' (represented in chapter one of the novel); and the Einsteinian universe 'at the extremes of quantum mechanics and general relativity' (i.e. the world of The Parish).[19] Early on in chapter two, Kemnitz argues, 'the reader is instructed in the most basic concept of relativity: *parallax*', i.e. 'the apparent displacement of an object when viewed from two different points in space'. By way of illustration, Kemnitz cites the apparent distortion experienced by the solipsist narrator when he first enters Old Mathers' house: 'When I reached the floor and jumped noisily down upon it, the open window seemed very far away and much too small to have admitted me' (*3P*, p. 22).[20]

The concept of parallax is not new to science or literature, nor is it unique to Einstein; indeed, it is said to originate with Galileo (1564–1642). The literary representation of parallax has historical antecedents in the metafictional tradition of Laurence Sterne, in the nonsensical tradition of Lewis Carroll, and in Joyce's *Ulysses*. It also seems likely that O'Brien garnered his scientific knowledge of parallax from J.W. Dunne's more populist work *An Experiment with Time* (1927): 'Nothing stays fixed to be looked at. Everything is in a state of flux [. . .]. That you enter houses without passing through walls is, of course, one of the most commonplace of happenings in a four-dimensional world'.[21]

Parallax is a spatial reflection of relativity used by O'Brien as a metaleptic technique to disrupt the plastic representation of objects in realist texts. The temporal equivalent of this principle is the idea of *simultaneity* – itself a classic nonsense procedure in literature.[22] For his scientific knowledge of simultaneity, O'Brien is again most likely indebted to Dunne, although it is also a cornerstone of Einstein's theory of relativity:

> We have to understand that all our judgements in which time plays a part are always judgements of simultaneous events. If, for instance, I say 'That train arrives here at seven o'clock', I mean something like this: 'The pointing of a small hand of my watch to seven and the arrival of the train are simultaneous events'.[23]

This idea that all motion is relative and cannot be detected without reference to an outside point again originates with Galileo. Whatever about the origins of the intertextual source, O'Brien uses this theory of relative time to deconstruct the artificiality of everyday discourse, and to drive a wedge between the real and projected worlds. In the projected world time is relative to the author's design, so that in The Parish 'it was always five o'clock in the afternoon' (*3P*, p. 80).

Kemnitz argues that Noman is transported from the Newtonian, three-dimensional world of chapter one to the relative world of The Parish after the explosion which kills him in chapter two. For Kemnitz, the black box contains an atomic bomb, which 'accelerates the narrator out of the zone of middle dimensions approaching the speed of light, so that normally consecutive events become simultaneous and the universe seems to stand still for an instant'.[24] The actual description of the explosion does in part bear out Kemnitz's idea:

> It was as if the daylight had changed with unnatural suddenness, as if the temperature of the evening had altered greatly in an instant [. . .] just as if it had held the universe standstill for an instant, suspending the planets in their courses, halting the sun and holding in mid-air any falling thing the earth was pulling towards it. (*3P*, p. 23)

In this instant the temperature raises, gravity collapses, and the sun stands still – and Noman is transported to his death-world. The language here is suitably apocalyptic, and it is indeed tempting to read this as an allegory of nuclear annihilation – a powerful leitmotif which hangs spectrally over many post-modernist texts. However, this would be slightly anachronistic: even though the doomsday atomic bomb had been mooted in O'Brien's day, and even if he anticipates it here, the first atomic explosion did not occur until five years after he had first written *The Third Policeman*. Again, it seem as if Noman's travels through the serial universe may owe a greater intertextual debt to Dunne rather than Einstein.

That Noman travels to a relativistic zone or space–time continuum is not in doubt: 'Years or minutes could be swallowed up with equal ease in that indescribable and unaccountable interval' (*3P*, p. 24). At the end of the novel, although only three days have elapsed in The Parish, we discover that Noman has been absent from his 'real' world for over sixteen years. For Kemnitz this scene is a 'literary appropriation of a famous thought experiment [. . .] in relativity physics called the "experience of the prodigal twin'".[25] Kemnitz is alluding here to the hypothetical thought experiment devised by H.A. Lorentz (1853–1928) – one of Einstein's precursors – whereby one twin travels at the speed of light, thus slowing down the passage of time. While the years pass by for the earthbound twin, the time-travelling twin returns in days. Kemnitz sees this experiment reflected in the text when Noman encounters the ghost of Old Mathers: 'In my distress I thought to myself that perhaps it was his twin-brother' (*3P*, p. 25). However, Kemnitz is selective in his quotation; as Joe the Soul informs Noman, this is no twin but a ghost, absurdly bandaged where Noman had smashed him with his spade. Later on, when Noman encounters Policeman Fox, Fox is wearing the face of Old Mathers – a deliberate metaleptic fragmentation of character intended to expose the 'writtenness' of all fictive characters, and not necessarily a parody of a thought experiment.

Again, relative time is not unique to modern physics, and another, more plausible intertextual source for Noman's time-flux is the medieval voyage poetry of the Gaelic tradition with which O'Brien, as a Celtic medievalist, would have been more familiar. The parallels between one such text – *Immram Maíle Dúin* (*The Voyage of Maeldoon*, c. ninth century) – and *The Third Policeman* are many and obvious: both protagonists share the same sins of pride; both journey to Hell and strange lands where they experience visions, hallucinations and dreams; both are haunted by dark murders; and the time-flux that Noman undergoes is shared by Maeldoon.[26]

Other correspondences from *The Voyage of Maeldoon* contradict Kemnitz's relativistic reading. For example, Kemnitz declares that Noman's visit to Eternity is a journey to a 'black hole': 'Eternity, like a black hole, is timeless, suspended between heartbeats, as Sergeant MacCruiskeen [sic] explains: "When you leave here you will be the same age as you were coming in."'[27] Before entering the lift to Eternity, Noman is weighed, which Kemnitz decides 'is necessary in order to establish the amount of energy required for his velocity change: the mass falling into a black hole (eternity) must equal the mass coming back out. Therefore, the narrator cannot take more mass out of eternity than he took in'.[28]

Again, though, this scene has probably more in common with *The Voyage of Maeldoon* than with quantum physics. In the medieval poem, the monk of Tory – like Noman in O'Brien's text – is tantalised by the prospect of inconceivable wealth and power but is forced to abandon his treasures – the *Everyman* moral being 'you cannot take it with you'. This theme is re-cycled in *The Poor Mouth* in the scene where Bonaparte O'Coonassa travels to Hunger-stack Mountain and encounters, under similar circumstances, the decrepit figure of Maeldoon himself. O'Brien thus complicates the allegorical reading of *The Third Policeman* by splicing together different myths and systems of thought in new and sinister contexts, or, as Mary A. O'Toole writes:

> The universe that O'Nolan depicts in *The Third Policeman* is even more horrible than Kemnitz allows because O'Nolan uses a melange of many theories of time, space, matter, and energy, not programatically but eclectically, creating a universe even more incomprehensible and erratic than it would be if only classical and relativistic theories were the basis of the novel.[29]

Consequently, individual intertextual sources can be readily discerned in the novel, but they will not provide the key to absolute meaning. The intermedium is the message here, and the text is the interface of several modes of discourse – a matrix of intertextual fragments – that creates its own meaning or series of meanings.

Inside Eternity, Noman is entertained by various technological wonders. MacCruiskeen lifting a new bicycle from a machine (metafictionally, a typewriter or literary machine) demonstrates for Kemnitz 'the possibility of mass-energy conversion (the basis of atomic and hydrogen bombs)', while the fact that Noman can 'walk ahead to reach the same place here without coming back' (*3P*, p. 134) is for Kemnitz a four-dimensional construction known as a 'tesseract'.[30] Kemnitz also notes the language used by O'Brien to describe the central conversion cabinet: a 'large opening resembling a black hole' (*3P*, p. 135). Other appropriations of relativistic language include Joe's nonsensical mention of 'Signor Bari, the eminent tenor [who] appeared on the balcony of St. Peter's Rome' (*3P*, p. 31), which Kemnitz translates as a passing reference to 'the classic analogue for the size of an atom', and the strange rising and setting of the sun in the East becomes a 'dramatization of particle scattering'.[31]

A simpler explanation for this latter point is that Noman's alternative universe lies on a western plane, an oblique reference perhaps to O'Brien's abiding contempt for the world of the Celtic Twilight, and in particular for Synge's *The Playboy of the Western World*. Noman is in part a reconstructed Christy Mahon – a reincarnated playboy of a post-modernist western world. The road Noman travels 'ran away westwards' (*3P*, p. 37), and de Selby comments that any western path is one of 'unfailing bleakness' (*3P*, p. 38). The sun rises and sets in the east not because (or just because) of particle scattering but because it is an image of a lost world to the east of The Parish, well out of Noman's reach.

On this relativistic scheme, de Selby's quixotic search for the 'second direction', where 'a world of entirely new sensation and experience will be open to humanity' (*3P*, p. 95), is explained in terms of the path of a sub-atomic particle travelling through the space–time continuum: 'The implication of quantum field theory is that it becomes possible to step out of the present world-line into another where time flows differently from our present world-line.'[32]

Kemnitz's explanation here, because of the high-powered language used, seems to have certain potency, but his assertions are often spurious and, permit the pun, rather one-dimensional. The detailed description of de Selby's quest for the 'second direction' is a clear appropriation from J.W. Dunne's theory of Serialism, which will be discussed below. However, this is not to replace relativity theory with Serialism as an absolute model. De Selby's brand of Serialism includes the belief that 'the earth is a sausage' (*3P*, p. 94) – i.e. cylindrical rather than spherical – and this is taken from Anaximander, a philosopher of the Milesian School (c. sixth century BC). Anaximander conceived of (and possibly constructed) a spherical model of the cosmos, at the centre of which he placed a cylindrical earth whose height was one-third its diameter – the de Selbian 'sausage'. Anaximander is thus credited as being the author of the first geometrical model of the universe, a cosmogony 'characterised not by vagueness and mystery but by visual clarity and rational proportion'.[33]

O'Brien makes the point (by implication) that de Selby's theories are not as chaotic as one might first imagine – at one point in western history the 'sausage-shaped' planet was the most coherent and rational cosmogony accepted by philosophers. More important, perhaps, is the fact that the only fragment of Anaximander's work (*On the Nature of Things*) that still exists in its original wording is his famous principle of cosmic justice: 'Out of these things whence is the generation of existing things, into them also does their destruction take place, as is right and due; for they make no retribution and pay the penalty to one another for their offence according to the ordering of time.'[34] Anaximander's theory is the simple natural law which condemns Noman and shapes his destiny (both as a metafictional protagonist and as a Faustian rebel), i.e. a divine retribution or karma governs his existence. When Noman upsets the cosmic order he is punished by that very order.

In a footnote to his essay, Kemnitz tells us that his brief introduction to nuclear physics is indebted to Fritjof Capra's *The Tao of Physics* (1975). However, Kemnitz's rather dogmatic and selective reading ignores the central thrust of Capra's thesis, namely that the scientific crisis precipitated at the turn of the twentieth century necessitated the creation of a new language paradigm to describe such phenomena. Capra finds comparisons to this 'new' language in ancient western and eastern philosophical and mystical traditions, including Anaximander and the Atomists. This is the central paradox at the heart of O'Brien's Menippean satire – namely, that the great cult of modern, technological science, having discovered substance and matter beyond normative epistemological parameters, found it necessary to appropriate the language of ancient metaphysics to begin to talk about their discoveries:

> If physics leads up today to a world view which is essentially mystical, it returns, in a way, to its beginning, 2,500 years ago. [. . .] The roots of physics, as of all Western Science, are to be found in the first period of Greek philosophy in the sixth century BC, in a culture where science, philosophy and religion were not separated.[35]

If anything then, O'Brien seems more indebted to the original Greek Atomists than to Einstein, and certainly Pluck's formulation of his 'Atomic Theory' seems derived from Leucippus and Democritus. As F.C. Copleston writes in *A History of Philosophy*:

> According to Leucippus and Democritus there are an infinite number of indivisible units, which are called atoms. These are imperceptible, since they are too small to be perceived by the senses. The atoms differ in size and shape, but have no quality save that of solidity and impenetrability. Infinite in number, they move in the void.

Copleston also quotes Aristotle's *De Anima*, where Aristotle attributes to Democritus 'a comparison between the atoms of the soul and the motes in a sunbeam, which dart hither and thither in all directions, even when there is not wind'.[36] Compare this to Pluck's description of atoms in *The Third Policeman*:

> 'Everything is composed of small particles of itself and they are flying around in concentric circles and arcs [. . .] too numerous to mention collectively, never standing still or resting but spinning away and darting *hither and thither* [my emphasis] and

back again, all the time on the go. These diminutive gentlemen
are called atoms.' (*3P*, p. 84)

Thus O'Brien's description here suggests Democritus, and
Aristotle, the father of philosophy, rather than Einstein, the father
of the nuclear age. The attempt by the ancients to give a complete
explanation of the world in terms of a mechanical materialism certainly re-emerges with Einstein, but, as Copleston – himself a
Jesuit – reminds us (in the same sceptical spirit as O'Brien): 'The
brilliant hypothesis of Leucippus and Democritus was by no means
the last word [and] subsequent Greek philosophers were to see that
the richness of the world cannot in all its spheres be reduced to the
mechanical interplay of atoms.'[37]

This parallel between modern physics and ancient cosmogony
would have appealed to O'Brien – not just for its ironic historical
cyclicism but because it maps the vast intertextual possibilities of
language. Morally, O'Brien suggests that logic, empiricism and
rationalism *in themselves* become reductive and dehumanising
when separated from the holistic perspective exemplified by
Milesian culture. O'Brien's critique of science and philosophy – personified by Noman and de Selby – has at its core the question of
conscience. This theme is also explored in Aldous Huxley's *Point
Counter Point* (1928), a Menippean satire which exerted considerable influence over O'Brien.[38] As Huxley writes:

> What the scientists are trying to get at is a non-human truth
> [. . .]. By torturing their brains they can get a faint notion of the
> universe as it would seem if looked at through non-human eyes.
> What with their quantum theory, wave mechanics, relativity
> and all the rest of it, they really seem to have got a little way
> outside humanity.[39]

The moral influence of Huxley is overlooked by Kemnitz, to the
detriment of his critique. Incidentally, from Huxley's novel also
comes a theory of despotic authorship – 'a too tyrannical imposition
of the author's will' – as well as a literary representation of the
concept of infinite regress: 'Why draw the line at one novelist inside
your novel? Why not a second inside his [...] and so on to infinity,
like those advertisements of Quaker's Oats where there's a Quaker
holding a box of oats, on which is a picture of another Quaker
holding another box of oats, on which etc., etc.'[40]

Moreover, Huxley shares the same sense of cosmic justice as
O'Brien – 'everything that happens is intrinsically like the man it

happens to' – a concept Huxley derives in turn from Augustine: 'Augustine was right [. . .], we're damned or saved in advance. The things that happen are a providential conspiracy.'[41] The Manichean dualism of Augustine is sublimated deep within the moral fabric of *The Third Policeman*, but is actualised in its re-write *The Dalkey Archive*, when the resurrected ghost of Augustine says:

> Discourse must be in words, and it is possible to give a name to that which is not understood nor cognoscible by human reason. It is our duty to strive towards God by thought and word. But it is our final duty to believe, to have and to nourish faith. (*DA*, p. 41).

This essential dualism is central to our understanding of the mottled nuances of *The Third Policeman*. As O'Brien said of *The Dalkey Archive* (but it equally applies to *The Third Policeman*):

> The book is not meant to be a novel or anything of the kind but a study in derision, various writers with their styles and sundry modes, attitudes and cults being the rats in the cage. There is, for instance, no intention to jeer at God or religion; the idea is to roast the people who seriously do so.[42]

Ultimately, this is the Catholic conscience at the heart of the moral satire. The technological dystopias of the Brave New World and The Parish do not quite fit the Kemnitz paradigm, which infers that O'Brien embraces Einstein's relativistic ethic for positive use in his text. The only relativism that interests O'Brien is a historical and intertextual relativism, with history as a cyclical reminder of the crisis caused when scientific progress divorces itself from spiritual matters. The moral paradox generated by the cult of Einstein echoes the archetypal myth of Faust, or, as Roland Barthes has written:

> Mythologically, Einstein is matter, his power does not spontaneously draw one towards the spiritual, it needs the help of an independent morality, a reminder about the scientist's conscience. [. . .] Through the myth of Einstein, the world blissfully regained the image of knowledge reduced to a formula. Paradoxically the more the genius of the man was materialised under the guise of his brain, the more the product of his inventiveness came to acquire a magical dimension.[43]

This does not prevent Kemnitz from making other, more narrowly programmatic claims. The black box, for example, which contains four ounces of 'omnium' (omniscience), is for Kemnitz a metaphor for nuclear energy – 'atomic in nature, both a bomb for destruction and a means for discovery and creation'.[44] And MacCruiskeen's table of readings (an autocritical graph of narrative progress, as in *Tristram Shandy*) on this relativistic scheme represents the 'four dimensions of the space–time continuum'. Kemnitz, in order to preserve the integrity of his argument, refuses to accept that Noman's death-world is keyed in to de Selby's eccentric philosophy, and prefers to read the novel as 'a dramatization [analogous to the table of reading] on four levels: the physical theorists provide the superstructure for the novel; moral codes and language flesh out the text'.[45]

At this juncture the critic pretty much concedes defeat, and admits that he cannot 'present complete readings of the moral and linguistic aspects of the novel; those subjects require a different type of reading'.[46] This is the first real admission by Kemnitz that his specific allegorical interpretation may ultimately prove too reductive. As a genetic intertextual source the main contribution of relativity theory to the novel is its provision of nuclear buzzwords, which occur with frequency throughout the novel. While the most obvious representation of atomic physics in the novel is Pluck's 'Atomic Theory', Kemnitz fails to grasp its significance to the text in general – a comic denunciation of logic and pedantry, and metafictionally a metaphor for 'transference', i.e. intertextuality. In his discussion of atomic theory, O'Brien shows a rather primitive understanding of nuclear physics (unsurprisingly, perhaps, since it is largely appropriated from the Greek Atomists) but a deep knowledge of fictional structure. Kemnitz's essay presumes a far more sophisticated knowledge of physics on O'Brien's part, and fails to recognise that O'Brien's technique depends on dialogical freedom rather than monological control, i.e. relativism as a problematic ontological condition rather than relativity as a subtextual allegory.

As biographer Anthony Cronin has remarked, O'Brien 'nowhere says anything about relativity that could not have been gleaned from an adequate popularisation'.[47] One key popularisation for O'Brien was a trilogy of books by J.W. Dunne (1875–1949): *An Experiment with Time* (1927), *The Serial Universe* (1934) and *Nothing Dies* (1940). This series was an eccentric melange of speculative theory concerning dreams, death, infinity and the travels of the soul in a four-dimensional or 'serial' universe. As Cronin notes: 'Dunne's books read like fairly classy hokum now but perhaps because they gave the illusion of discussing the problems which

Einstein, whom nobody understood, had dealt with, they were popular in O'Nolan's circle.'[48]

Be that as it may, Dunne's 'classy hokum' was quite amenable to modernist and post-modernist literary representation: Joyce, Borges and William Burroughs all admit that Dunne's Serialism was an influence on their work. In Serialism, for instance, Joyce found theoretical confirmation for his thematic use of Vico's *La Scienza Nuova* (*The New Science*, 1725) in *Finnegans Wake*. The simultaneity of past, present and future suggested by Viconian cyclical progression has analogues in the Serialism postulated in *An Experiment with Time*, a book which 'Joyce regarded highly'.[49] Although Myles na Gopaleen professed his disdain of Vico – 'a muddled Neapolitan' – whose 'influence on Irish intellectuals was baneful',[50] O'Brien himself seemed to admire Dunne's serial model. In a letter to Timothy O'Keeffe in 1962 concerning *The Dalkey Archive*, O'Brien wrote:

> You may remember Dunne's two books *An Experiment with Time* and *The Serial Universe*, also the views of Einstein and others. The idea is that time is as a great flat motionless sea. Time does not pass; it is we who pass. With this concept as basic, fantastic but coherent situations can be easily devised, and in effect the whole universe torn up in a monstrous comic debauch. Such obsessions as nuclear energy, space travel and landing men on the moon can be made to look as childish and insignificant as they probably are.[51]

Again, establishing Dunne as an intertextual source in *The Third Policeman* can only really be useful in terms of the overall satirical context. While O'Brien appropriates various aspects of Serialism, and incorporates and conflates them with other related patterns of thought, only certain elements of Serialism are adhered to: Dunne's theory of dreams and their relationship to a death-world; the movement of the soul on a relative plane; and the simultaneity of time that is at the core of the Serialist paradigm. Of equal importance to the satire, perhaps, is the parody of Dunne's rhetorical style, as O'Brien captures the urbane arrogance yet humane honesty of Dunne's Edwardian prose.

An Experiment with Time began initially as an interpretation of dreaming but ended up as a statement on the immortality of the human soul: 'It contains the first scientific argument for human immortality. This, I may say, was entirely unexpected.'[52] This accidental discovery is also parodied in *The Dalkey Archive* through the figure of De Selby: 'Call me a theologian or a physicist as you will, he said at last rather earnestly, but I am serious and truthful. My discoveries concerning the nature of time were in fact quite accidental. The objective of my research was altogether different' (*DA*, p. 18).

Interestingly, Dunne saw no major clash between Serialism and Freudianism, but stresses that his work is in no way psycho-analytical: 'Wish fulfilment theories are concerned with explaining why a dreamer builds a particular dream edifice: I am interested in the quite different question of whence he collects the bricks.'[53] For Dunne, dreams are a matrix of images supplied by an associated network, constructed in an alternative reality. This belief naturally endears him to post-modernist fiction: 'dream images present them-selves as real – though curiously unstable – episodes in a personal adventure story of an only partially reasonable character.'[54]

Dunne recalls his own personal experience of prophetic dreams, and attempts to construct a system which would scientifically scru-tinise these dreams as tangible phenomena rather than quasi-mystical, archetypal symbols. During the course of his research he worries that his dreams of future events may just be a case of 'identifying paramnesia', a kind of déjà vu that corresponds with Noman's flickering knowledge of himself in the novel: 'it reminded me forcibly, strange and foolish as it may seem, of some-thing I did not understand and had never even heard of' (*3P*, p. 72). Realising that most of his dreams referred to rather mundane events, Dunne has a vital epiphany – 'there was nothing unusual in any of these dreams, they were merely displaced in time'[55] – and from this he derives the first premise of Serialism: 'that dreams [...] were composed of images of past experience and images of future experience, blended together in equal proportions'.[56]

Dunne envisages a universe 'stretched-out' in time, and believes that when we dream we enter a 'fourth-dimension' – a space–time continuum similar to that postulated by Einstein. The associational network of dream-time images flashes backwards and forwards in time when we sleep, but the images are filtered by a mentally imposed barrier when we wake up. This has a correspondence in Noman's immediate waking recollection in *The Third Policeman*: '[I] found myself immediately recalling – the recollection was an absurd paradox – that I had been in the next world yesterday' (*3P*, p. 144), and a chapter later: 'When I awoke again [...] it was not the same day at all but a different one and maybe not even the next day' (*3P*, p. 151).

Dunne then tries to devise a scientific experiment that will overcome the twin difficulties of remembering and associating our dreams, and widen the field of dream observation. He is conscious that classical materialist epistemology would be sceptical of his work, and *that*, for Dunne, is part of the problem. In trying to understand our dreams we develop an innate rationalist 'attention' which focuses on the purely conscious aspects of the mind: 'Acute concentration of attention dulls almost to the point of obliteration the contents of the remaining and greater part of your field of observation; not by reducing the area of that field but by rendering those contents unnoticed.'[57]

Rationalism atrophies the sensual delights and explorative possibilities of the dream-world, and seals the boundaries of infinite knowledge. Serialism has escaped universal recognition in the past, Dunne contends, because the rational mind blocks the proper interpretation between prophetic dream and actual reality. There also exists an innate, natural fear attached to wandering in the dream-zone because both death and dreams occupy the same eternal plane, which he calls 'Time 2', as opposed to 'Time 1' (the 'Now'). Subsequently the waking mind is relieved to wake up, and dismiss its travels as a nightmare: 'Perhaps I was dreaming or in the grip of some horrible hallucination. There was so much that I did not understand and possibly could never understand to my dying day' (*3P*, p. 185).

This populist theorising of relative fields of observation makes Dunne an attractive touchstone for the post-modernist author. As Jorges Luis Borges wrote:

> Dunne assures us that in death we shall finally learn how to handle eternity. We shall recover all the moments of our lives and combine them as we please. God and our friends and Shakespeare will collaborate with us. So splendid a thesis, makes any fallacy committed by the author insignificant.[58]

But although O'Brien appropriates many of Dunne's ideas – sometimes stealing quite directly – the moral force of the Menippean satire continues to exert its presence, especially when O'Brien encounters some of Dunne's more grandiose and magisterial statements. Certain intertextual parallels, however – particularly those concerned with the immortality of the soul – would suggest that O'Brien and Dunne share the same belief in transcendence. Dunne's serial observer, who travels outside his own body, may influence, in part, the depiction of Joe the Soul (who leaves the body of Noman). Although anti-materialist, Dunne expresses his meta-physics within a strangely puritanical prose, to avoid appearing mystical: 'Animism holds that the observer is anything but a non-entity. He is no "conscious automaton". He may, indeed, stand right outside the pictured universe, but he is a "soul", with powers of inter-vention which enable him to alter the course of observed events.'[59]

In the serial universe of The Parish, Joe the Soul has limited powers of intervention. Freed from physical bondage when he enters The Parish (a dream/death-world of Eternal time), Joe has an independent voice and the ability to 'stand outside' observed events. Metafictionally, it is significant that Joe's dialogue is itali-cised: a topographical fragmentation of 'otherness' which reflects the way Joe stands outside the primary mimetic narrative as an autocritical, textual commentator. Although Joe advises Noman and acts as his guide in this death-world, he is prescribed by cir-cumstance and cannot alter the fundamental condition of Noman's ontological status. Noman, for his part, realises that Joe 'was friendly, was my senior in years and was solely concerned for my own welfare' (*3P*, p. 25), yet fails to register the deadly implications of Joe's existence. When Joe at one point threatens to abandon Noman, he tries to let him in on the secret – 'I am your soul and all your souls. When I am gone you are dead' (*3P*, p. 119) – but Noman can scarcely grasp the significance of this. When eventually he does leave, Joe is not quite sure where he is destined, but feels that he will somehow be assimilated into the godhead, and become part of the fabric of all things: 'Sometimes I think that perhaps I might become part of . . . the world, if you understand me?' (*3P*, pp. 161–2), and he fantasises about becoming part of the wind, or the scent of a flower, or a lake. O'Brien resists the temptation to be mocking here, and the tone throughout the novel suggests his own intrinsic belief in some form of transcendence.

The split between Noman and Joe personifies the split between the Newtonian universe of chapter one and the relative universe of The Parish. This actualises Dunne's serialist dualism: '[An] observer who actually does possess the mental structural equip-ment adapted to the viewing of presentations in their four-dimensional entirety, but who endeavours, nevertheless, to regard such presentations as merely three-dimensional phe-nomena.'[60] In *An Experiment with Time*, Dunne's case for the immortality of the soul overpowers his initial dream thesis, but in his later works he pulls back from the precipice of mystic theology, and with a typically droll remark stresses that Serialism will not reveal to us the mind of God: 'If you wish to know how "God" comes into the matter, you have to read, I am afraid, the book in question. I do not feel myself competent to attempt "a brief outline of God".'[61]

In all of this, O'Brien seems in general accord with Dunne, and he uses these concepts in a positive manner, contrary to what other critics have suggested. At a certain point though, O'Brien does depart from Dunne, and begins to use him as satirical fodder for the de Selbian composite. O'Brien's narrative trump card – that Noman is dead as he recounts his story – may well have, as Mary A. O'Toole notes, its origins in Dunne's notion of relative fields of observation:

> If the field of an observer A lagged behind that of an observer B, and A were to intervene in B's career at that point in B's sub-stratum which was level with A, then B would find his experiences in *his* field miraculously altered. In fact, he might find himself miraculously dead, having been slain by A, unknown to himself, some little way back.[62]

After this – literature's first 'serial' killing perhaps? – O'Brien begins to play with the more eccentric aspects of Dunne's theories. The novel becomes a process of planned incongruity, whereby scientific ideas are reconfigured in strange contexts in order to map the absurd physical laws of The Parish. For example, as Mary O'Toole has noted, de Selby's 'accumulations of the black air' (*3P*, p. 32) are probably pirated from Dunne's mention of the 'behaviour of black body radiation' in *The Serial Universe*.[63]

Similarly, de Selby's belief that human existence was 'a succession of static experiences each infinitely brief' (*3P*, p. 50) is also garnered from Dunne. De Selby (as one mock footnote tells us) arrived at this belief from his empirical study of strips of film, having 'examined them patiently picture by picture and imagined that they would be screened in the same way, failing at that time to grasp the principle of the cinematograph' (*3P*, p. 50, fn). A similar image is employed in *Nothing Dies*: 'Imagine that all the sensory impressions which you perceive in the course of your life are standing before you in a row – like a long strip of film.'[64] Dunne may very well have inspired the image but he does not hold the intertextual patent. His throwaway comment suits the satirical design of *The Third Policeman*, but it also serves to question the technological illusion of cinema itself, and the idea of framing and verisimilitude.

Other appropriations include de Selby's 'second direction' (previously discussed in terms of the cosmogony of Anaximander). De

Selby, like Dunne, seeks a way of discovering a second direction, 'along the "barrel" of the sausage [where] unimaginable dimensions will supersede the present order and manifold "unnecessaries" of "one directional" existence will disappear' (*3P*, p. 95).

For Dunne, time stretches 'neither north-and-south nor east-and-west, nor up-and-down, but [...] in a fourth direction'.[65] Similarly, for de Selby:

> North-south is therefore one direction and east-west apparently another. Instead of four directions there are only two. It can be safely inferred, de Selby says, that there is a further similar fallacy inherent here and that there is in fact only one direction properly so-called, because if one leaves any point on the globe, moving and continuing to move in any 'direction', one ultimately reaches the point of departure again. (*3P*, p. 94)

In this example, O'Brien follows Dunne closely enough to create reader confidence in the viability of this theory. He then establishes the crucial Serialist intersection between dreams and death, or, as de Selby puts it, 'death is nearly always present when the new direction is discovered' (*3P*, p. 95). This reflects Dunne's belief that 'Death – that is to say the arrival of a travelling field act at a boundary [...] is like sleep gaps'.[66] These same 'sleep gaps' correspond to de Selby's 'fainting fits' (*3P*, p. 116, fn), which are induced by black volcanic air and which eventually lead to death. Because sleep and death exist on the same plane, de Selby declares that 'it ill becomes any man of sense to be concerned at the illusory approach of the supreme hallucination known as death' (*3P*, epigraph, p. v).

In his rather avuncular conclusion to *An Experiment with Time*, Dunne summarises his findings for the 'man-in-the-street' – the Dunne equivalent of Myles na Gopaleen's 'Plain People of Ireland' – and concludes that '[Serialism] provides us with a satisfactory answer to the "why" of evolution, of birth, of pain, of sleep, of death'.[67] As Mary O'Toole has noted, this is directly parodied in de Selby's *Layman's Atlas* (literally a map for the ubiquitous 'man-in-the-street'): 'In the *Layman's Atlas* he deals explicitly with bereavement, old age, love, sin, death and the other saliencies of existence. It is true that he allows them only six lines but this is due to his devastating assertion that they are all "unnecessary"' (*3P*, p. 93).

Given Dunne's eccentric and idiosyncratic prose style – bombastic, jargonistic, yet boyishly enthusiastic – the transition from intertextual appropriation to full-fledged parody is made quite effortlessly on O'Brien's part. Finally it is Dunne himself (rather than his theories) who participates as a model for the composite archetype of the idiot-savant, de Selby – that 'charming fusion of vast erudition with gross misunderstanding'.[68] Many of Dunne's casual autobiographical remarks provide ample raw material for satire, e.g. 'In 1910 I made the first decisive flight in the first aeroplane which possessed complete inherent stability. It was a rather exciting episode'.[69] Dunne also recollects that as a small boy 'I dreamed that I had invented a flying machine, and was travelling through space therein'.[70] De Selby, like Dunne, had also 'examined aviation as a remedy without success' (*3P*, p. 95), to break through the boundaries of reality and discover the 'second direction'.

O'Brien's parody of footnotes may also have had Dunne in mind. In his brief introductory chapter to *An Experiment with Time*, Dunne emphasises that he would hope to avoid 'that worst of all irritations to a reader – a text repeatedly interrupted by references to footnotes or glossary', yet in that same text produces some footnotes of astoundingly parodic proportions:

> I am indebted to Mr Edward Slosson for this piece of information. Professor Fritz Paneth tells me that Fechner, writing under the name of Dr Mises, published in his *Vier Paradoxe* (1846) an account of Time as a fourth dimension which forestalled Hinton's (mentioned hereafter) and contained a diagram more like that on page 138.[71]

In the final analysis, Dunne can only be considered as only one component in the vast intertextual web that makes up the composition of the death-world in particular, and the Menippean satire in general. As Mary O'Toole remarks:

> The hell of *The Third Policeman*, then, is not one temporal and spatial system but many systems, some historically held, others never a part of any known philosophy of time or space. J.W. Dunne's theories of serialism and infinite regression contribute significantly to the construction and atmosphere of the novel, and the fact that the narrator and the reader are unable to grasp any basis for temporal or spatial stability in this queer universe adds to the intellectual, emotional, and even physical disorientation that this novel produces.[72]

The issue of 'infinite regression' mentioned here is one of the key, pivotal structures of the novel's composition, but discussion of this topic has been deferred until now. In *An Experiment with Time*, Dunne imagines how the 'self-conscious observer' in a serial universe might define himself ontologically: 'This is my-self. And that means that he must be aware of a "self" owning the "self" first considered. Recognition of this second "self" involves, for similar reasons, knowledge of a third "self" – and so on, ad infinitum'.[73]

With the inclusion of infinite regress as a recurrent motif in the novel, many disparate intertextual lines find their point of parabolic intersection: the system of Chinese-box rooms in J.K. Huysmans' *Against Nature* (1884); the Quaker Oats box image in Huxley's *Point Counter Point* (1928); and the paradoxes of Zeno (489 BC).[74] However, Dunne's image of a 'self' inside a 'self' lends itself particularly well to the intertextual world of *The Third Policeman*: 'A body with another body inside it in turn, thousands of such bodies within each other like the skins of an onion, receding to some unimaginable ultimatum? Was I in turn merely a link in a vast sequence of imponderable beings?' (*3P*, p. 118).

This scene is an important turning point in the satire. Noman, the arch-rationalist personified, is horrified by the dizzying implications of infinite regress because his mind cannot translate this Promethean mental construct into a physical, stable image. Sickened, Noman is forced to accept that rationalism cannot accommodate these paradoxes, which transcend the purely rational sphere. His mind is incapable of establishing a basic cause–effect relationship, and contemplation of the infinite inevitably conjures up the possibility of a First Cause or Prime Mover – 'Who or what was the core and what monster in what world was the final uncontained colossus? God? Nothing?' (*3P*, p. 118). At the edge of the metaphysical abyss Noman's privileged system of logic and rationalism is ultimately defeated, or as Anne Clissmann describes it: 'Reason is overthrown and a coherent type of unreason takes its place. The narrator has to accept with his senses what his reason tells him is impossible.'[75]

Noman's confrontation with the infinite in this scene is directly (and strategically) linked not just to God or the Devil but to the immortality of the soul, or, as Joe the Soul tells him:

> Before I go I will tell you this. I am your soul and all your souls. When I am gone you are dead. Past humanity is not only implicit in each new man born but is contained within him. [. . .] When I leave I take with me all that has made you what you are – I take all your significance and importance and all the accumulations of human instinct and appetite and wisdom and dignity. You will be left with nothing behind you and nothing to give the waiting ones. (*3P*, pp. 119–20)

Through his contemplation of infinity Noman is cruelly tortured for his wrongdoings (which have ultimately cost him his eternal soul), and O'Brien's dark existential satire thus finds its deepest focus and most tangible expression. As J.W. Dunne commented in *Nothing Dies*, the absurdity of infinite regress is its triumph over soul-destroying logic: 'When the object of your search begins to recede in this mocking, repetitive fashion, you may rest assured that you are battering against a boundary of possible human knowledge.'[76]

This pattern of infinite regress has a structural reflection in the 'strange loop' which turns the novel into an endlessly repeating cycle. At the end of the novel Noman's psychological shock at his vision of infinity coincides with his realisation of his eternal damnation, and this induces paramnesia: 'The eyes in my head were open but they saw nothing because my mind was void' (*3P*, p. 198). As Sue Asbee has written: 'Already our storyteller seems to have lost access to the information he has just been given and is unaware that he has just crossed back from the first to the second world of the text.'[77] Horribly, Noman must suffer the unrelieved terrors of the illogical Parish, forever.

This motif of infinite regress is of vital importance to our present discussion, but it is first necessary to place it within its proper context as a primary device of 'nonsense' literature. In his essay 'Ireland in Wonderland: Flann O'Brien's *The Third Policeman* as a Nonsense Novel', Wim Tigges notes that, despite obvious differences of opinion and problems of generic classification, previous critiques of the novel all seem to agree on the relentless use (and abuse) of logic as a central device in its composition. For Tigges, the novel is best considered as a work of nonsense in the tradition of Lewis Carroll, and he observes with satisfaction that 'the five prime procedures of nonsense [as outlined by Susan Stewart in her work *Nonsense: Aspects of Intertextuality in Folklore and Literature*] are well exemplified in this novel'.[78] My own reading of *The Third Policeman* would confirm this latter opinion. Before discussing infinity as the prime nonsense procedure of the text (and its importance to the text as a whole), it is worth recapitulating these other categories.

Stewart's first category of nonsense – 'Reversals and Inversions' – is the initial 'splitting-off' in the text of the 'real' and projected worlds, where what was previously metaphorical now becomes literal. This occurs in the opening chapter where the dialogic language of Noman's apparently conventional memoirs undermines logic on a simple syntactical level. The ellipsis of the retrospective plot, the delayed decoding of vital information and the use of time-shift all conspire to break the traditional narrative pact between text and reader. Interpretative acts are complicated by the poly-phonic schism between mimetic and textual voices, e.g. 'I broke my left leg', says the mimetic voice, but this is immediately under-mined by the textual parenthesis '(or, if you like, it was broken for me)' (*3P*, p. 9). This procedure of inversion is continued in chapter two with our introduction to de Selbian theory, when the gap between the mimetic and the textual (and between the real and the projected) begins to widen. Our basic principles of common sense are immediately challenged by the description of de Selby's 'habi-tats' – 'roofless "houses" and "houses" without walls' (*3P*, p. 21), which is an idea taken from Swift's *Gulliver's Travels*.

At this point, the second nonsense procedure – 'Play with Boundaries' – comes into operation. This is a progressive movement away from realism, and towards irony and metafiction. This proce-dure operates along the boundaries of intertextual discourse where different modes collide and begin to throw out 'surpluses of signifi-cation'.[79] Here there is an 'increasing consciousness of the origins and nature of interpretation [and] these texts are concerned with instructions for their own reading'.[80] At this stage in the novel, the gap between the mimetic and textual voices is topographically and schematically actualised in the split between primary text and foot-notes. In this second chapter Noman is transported to the four-dimensional death-world of The Parish where 'Years or minutes could be swallowed up with equal ease' (*3P*, p. 24) – a serial universe where the normal physical laws no longer apply. In 'the space of time which followed,' Noman tells us, 'my reason could give me no assistance' (*3P*, p. 25). The fabric of the Newtonian uni-verse is ripped asunder, and in the space of one page physical and bodily dimensions collapse. Noman begins to engage in a dialogue with his soul and confronts the ghost of Old Mathers, who will answer questions only in the negative. Under Joe's guidance, Noman begins to adapt to the logic of the inverted world: '"Will you refuse to answer a straight question?" I asked. "I will not", he replied. This answer pleased me. It meant that my mind had got to grips with his' (*3P*, p. 28).

As the system of old-world logic begins to break down, much of the black comedy arises from the juxtaposition of nonsensical banality and Noman's growing crisis. Noman's loss of identity, for example, prompts Old Mathers' comment that, without a name, 'how could I tell you where the box was if you could not sign a receipt?' (*3P*, p. 31). Autocritically, the metafiction begins to challenge the reader's logical perceptions of what constitutes identity in a fictional world: Noman is not only split from his soul, but he shares a similar physical handicap with Martin Finnucane, whose speech, in turn, echoes that of John Divney and anticipates that of Sergeant Pluck. Similarly, the name 'de Selby' ('the self' or 'the same person') suggests a satirical subtext and Noman imagines – as narrative voice of the tale – that he is author of his own destiny until he meets Policeman Fox, the apparent architect of The Parish. This, in turn, makes the reader conscious of the author-god himself, hovering above the text in transcendental anonymity.

A third nonsense feature, 'Simultaneity', 'flaunts a problem in both rule and practice – the impossibility of time being in more than one place at once'.[81] This procedure is exemplified by Noman's visit to Eternity, where the conventional categories of both time and space are undermined. Temporally, as the Sergeant explains, 'you don't grow old here. When you leave here you will be the same age as you were coming in' (*3P*, p. 133). Spatially as well, Eternity confounds logical expectations: "'It has no size at all", the Sergeant explained, "because there is no difference anywhere in it and we have no conception of the extent of its unchanging coequality"'(*3P*, p. 133).

A fourth procedure of nonsense – 'Arrangement and Rearrangement in a Closed Field' – occurs when the 'boundaries of the event are given by convention while the space within those boundaries becomes a place of infinite substitution'.[82] An example of this in the novel would be Pluck's perversion of the kind of logic that Noman values so highly: 'If you have no name you possess nothing and you do not exist and even your trousers are not on you although they look as if they were from where I am sitting' (*3P*, p. 62). Other logical travesties include Pluck's theory of transference: 'people who spent most of their natural lives riding iron bicycles over the rocky roads of this parish get their personalities mixed up with the personalities of their bicycles as a result of the interchanging of the atoms of each of them' (*3P*, p. 85).

The most important aspect of this type of nonsense is the way that it mimics the construction of conventional logical syllogisms, carefully establishing a major premise, a minor premise, and a conclusion. Pluck's 'Atomic Theory' illustrates this quite cogently, taking the following syllogistic pattern:

If atoms can transfer from one object to another (major premise);
And humans and bicycles are both made up of atoms (minor premise);
Then humans and bicycles can transfer their atoms to each other
(conclusion).

Lewis Carroll, himself a logician, pointed out the irony of pure
logic in his text *The Game of Logic* (1886): 'it isn't of the slightest
consequence to us, as *Logicians*, whether our premises are true or
false; all *we* have to make out is whether they *lead logically to the
conclusion* so that, if *they* were true, *it* would be true also'.[83]
This logical irony is debated in chapter seven of the novel, where
Pluck decides to hang Noman for murder on circumstantial evidence: 'The Inspector required a captured prisoner [...]. It was your
personal misfortune to be present adjacently at the time [...]. There
is no option but to stretch you for the serious offence' (*3P*, p. 98).
Using the same absurd logic, Noman argues back that on account of
his 'congenital anonymity' (*3P*, p. 99), the due processes of law
cannot be applied. Pluck is almost stumped until he turns that logic
back in on itself: '"For that reason alone', said the Sergeant, "we can
take you and hang the life out of you and you are not hanged at all
and there is no entry to be made in the death papers"' (*3P*, p. 102).
After this scene, Noman's mind is thrown into a state of confusion. Faced with impending execution, he begins to sense the real
significance of his soul – an entity his rational mind finds it difficult
to conceptualise. For perhaps the first time in his life Noman
attempts to abandon his governing faculty of reason, and begins to
feel his way intuitively. As he tries to imagine how Joe the Soul
would feel physically, he 'felt, for no reason, that [Joe's] diminutive
body would be horrible to the human touch' (*3P*, p. 117), to which
Joe mockingly replies: 'That's not very logical' (*3P*, p. 117). At this
point, significantly, Noman has 'a strange idea not unworthy of de
Selby' (*3P*, p. 118), and imagines a whole series of bodies moving
towards a field of infinite regress: 'A body with another body inside
it in turn, thousands of such bodies within each other like the skins
of an onion, receding to some unimaginable ultimatum?' (*3P*, p. 118).
This brings us back to our initial discussion and the most important nonsense procedure in the text, 'Play with Infinity', which
Susan Stewart characterises as follows: 'As fictions move away
from realism and the temporality of the everyday lifeworld, the par-
adoxical spectre of infinite time emerges with its problems of origin
and ending.'[84] Aside from the image of the body-within-a-body, and
the integral 'strange loop' of the text's circular structure, there are
at least six more specific images of infinity discussed in the novel.

The first of these appears in chapter two, when Noman speculates on the artificial quality of Old Mathers' eye: 'was [it] real at all or merely another dummy with its pinhole on the same plane as the first one so that the real eye, possibly behind thousands of these absurd disguises, gazed out through a barrel of serried peep-holes' (*3P*, p. 25). O'Brien is consciously playing here on the old adage that the eye is the 'window of the soul', but Noman does not catch the irony. The concept of infinite regress disturbs him deeply, although he is not sure why – 'Such a conception, possibly with no foundation at all in fact, disturbed me agonisingly' (*3P*, p. 24) – and he dismisses the paradox from his mind.

A second image of infinity occurs in chapter four, with de Selby's assertion that 'a journey is an hallucination' (*3P*, p. 50):

> If one is resting at A, he explains, and desires to rest in a distant place B, one can only do so by resting for infinitely brief intervals in innumerable intermediate places. Thus there is no difference essentially between what happens when one is resting at A before the start of the 'journey' and what happens when one is 'en route', i.e. resting in one or other of the intermediate places. (*3P*, p. 50)

This episode is a direct intertextual appropriation from the Greek philosopher Zeno (*c.* 490 BC–430 BC). Zeno, a disciple of Parmenides, believed that the mutable world of the senses had no fixed relationship with the Real, Permanent world. According to Zeno, not only was the concept of change or motion itself impossible but also any attempt to explain such a concept was inherently futile, and would inevitably lead to contradictions. As F.C. Copleston points out, Zeno's paradoxes are not merely ingenious tricks of sophistry but a serious attempt to show the sometimes absurd consequences of pure logic.[85]

Applying this Zenoist paradox to life, de Selby, on a journey to Folkestone, stays in his room in Bath, and 'with a supply of picture postcards of the areas which would be traversed on such a journey [. . .] emerged after a lapse of seven hours convinced that he was in Folkestone' (*3P*, p. 51). This particular scene is appropriated from Des Esseintes' synaesthesia experiment in Huysmans' *Against Nature*, when the decadent hero tries to 'substitute the vision of a reality for the reality itself'.[86] Ironically, and though he mocks such errant eccentricities, Noman's own journey proves to be just such a 'hallucination'.

From his studies of de Selby, Noman should be aware of infinite regress, but he consistently fails to apply its implications to his own situation. In chapter five, for example, he recalled de Selby's time experiment with mirrors, 'the familiar arrangement of parallel mirrors, each reflecting diminishing images of an interposed object indefinitely' (*3P*, p. 65). Once again Noman scoffs at de Selby's eccentricities, still unconscious of the fact that the laws of de Selbian theory actually govern the hell-world of The Parish. This is confirmed several pages later when MacCruiskeen shows Noman his magical spear, the point of which recedes to infinity. Importantly, the policeman emphasises the explicit epistemological message, and, by extension, the implicit moral message: 'you cannot think of it or try to make it the subject of a little idea because you will hurt your box with the excruciation of it' (*3P*, p. 68). Noman frowns in confusion, and in a subsequent attempt to try and impose some system of order on this incomprehensible concept, offers a bizarre and ludicrous corruption of Cartesian causality: 'You cannot have fire without bricks' (*3P*, p. 68). Faced with the irrational mysteries of infinity, Noman's system of logic begins to break down, and this is reflected in his garbled syntax.

Before Noman has time to recover his composure, the policeman reveals his beautifully crafted, ornamental chest. Having created an object of exquisite, infinite beauty, MacCruiskeen decided 'that the only sole correct thing to contain in the chest was another chest of the same make but littler in cubic dimension' (*3P*, p. 71). Noman's reason is again overthrown, and he begins to intuitively grasp the moral significance of the infinite image: 'It was so fault-less and delightful that it reminded me forcibly, strange and foolish as it may seem, of something I did not understand and had never even heard of' (*3P*, p. 72).

What it 'reminds' him of, of course, is his own soul. Noman has spent his life translating the world into rational images at the expense of his spiritual welfare. The paradox of infinite regress transgresses rational boundaries, forcing him to accept the limita-tions of the intellect and to embrace the idea of a living, immortal soul. By the time MacCruiskeen sets to work on the twelfth chest in the series, Noman is 'content to take a swift look at it and then turn away. But I knew in *my soul* [my emphasis] that it was exactly the same as the others' (*3P*, p. 72). After twenty-eight chests Noman's sense of awe gives way to a sense of sickening terror: 'At this point I became afraid. What he was doing was no longer wonderful but terrible. I shut my eyes and prayed that he would stop while still doing things that were at least possible for a man to do' (*3P*, p. 73).

The final motif of infinite regress occurs during Noman's visit to Eternity, where he discovers a magnifying glass that 'magnifies to invisibility' (*3P*, p. 136). After the previous repetitions of this motif its re-incarnation here is mercifully brief (both for Noman and the reader). It also fulfils another related function as a satirical metaphor for the reductive nature of analytical thought, or, as MacCruiskeen notes: 'It makes everything so big that there is room in the glass for only the smallest particle of it – not enough of it to make it different from any other thing that is dissimilar' (*3P*, p. 136–7).

The de-construction of the death-world

What are we to take from this barrage of high-powered imagery, this jazz-like poetry of paradox? Is it purely, as Wim Tigges suggests, a non-aligned, anti-ideological expression of anarchic nonsense, which he characterises as 'an unresolved balance between meaning and simultaneous absence of meaning, an ultimate lack of emotional involvement, and a reality which is created by means of play with language'?[87]

My own reading of this issue is that *The Third Policeman*, as an early post-modernist text, pursues the poetics of nonsense as a means to a satirical end. In *The Third Policeman* we see the historical transition between the modernist 'epistemological dominant' (characterised by its privileging of the 'whodunit' mode), and the post-modernist 'ontological dominant' (which privileges sci-fi), and so the key difference is an intensely philosophical one.

The projected world of this novel is a pastiche of elements composed from a range of intertextual sources, many real, some imaginary (and this is what makes it tempting to read as an intertextual allegory). As a metafictionalist, the self-conscious author appropriates the traditional conventions of literature as metaphors for the ontological crisis he describes: updating, intensifying and complicating the polyphonic satire. But, as a tortured Catholic moralist with a firm belief in sin and hell, O'Brien is not content to be a mere relative categoriser. The shadow structure of the 'whodunit' dominant not only binds together the intertextual disorder, but it also deconstructs the dystopia and offers an alternative vision. As Broder Christiansen writes of this process in general:

> It happens only rarely that the emotive factors of an aesthetic object participate equally in the effect of the whole. On the contrary, normally a single factor or configuration comes to the fore and assumes a leading role. All the others accompany the

> dominant, intensify it through their harmony, heighten it
> through contrast, and surround it with a play of variations. The
> dominant is the same as the structure of bones in an organic
> body: it contains the theme of the whole, supports the whole,
> enters into relation with it.[88]

The Third Policeman lays bare the conventions that historically divergent works and discourses have in common, and fuses them in a new context. Thus, for example, the relative time-flux of The Parish is a fusion of Celtic voyage poetry, quantum physics, Serialism, and pre-Socratic cosmogonies; and the figure of de Selby is a composite archetype who emerges from a broad range of historical and literary idiot-savants. This intertextual fusion of form represents a new aesthetic that is suitable to the needs of a postmodern world, and the intertextual locus of *The Third Policeman* – the dominant genre that underscores and binds its various concerns – is the popular 'whodunit'.

As Patricia Waugh notes – and here she implicitly contradicts Brian McHale's critique – the poetics of the 'whodunit' has, within its own conventions, 'the potential for the expression of a deep human ontological insecurity through its central image of a man or woman threatened and on the run'.[89] An intensely rational yet often 'literary' form, the powerful motifs of the 'whodunit' genre found new expression in the *film noir* tradition of the 1940s, which helped to consolidate its urban, mythic potency. Within the modernist paradigm the detective story was ultimately a celebration of human reason and deduction, where 'mystery is reduced to flaws in logic [and] the world is made comprehensible', but in the emergent postmodernist world it is used 'to express not order but the irrationality of both the surface of the world and its deep structures'.[90]

Some biographical speculation has arisen over the possibility that Brian O'Nolan himself may have pseudonymously contributed to the 'Sexton Blake Library' – a series of short monthly paperbacks that Anthony Cronin refers to as the 'poor man's Sherlock Holmes'.[91] In a letter in 1955 to Stephen Ashe, one of the editors of the series, O'Nolan wrote that 'I have read the Sexton Blake stories in my day [and] I am sure I could do the job', and he later claimed that he had, in fact, written some of these novellas.[92] Cronin, however, remains sceptical, and no proof has ever been conclusively offered. At any rate, O'Brien's interest in the genre is at least vouchsafed, and in a letter to a friend in 1939 he makes it clear that the 'whodunit' genre was foremost in his mind when writing *The Third Policeman*:

I have not yet done anything about another novel beyond turning over some ideas in my head. [. . .] Briefly, the story I have in mind opens as a very orthodox murder mystery in a rural district. The perplexed parties have recourse to the local barrack which, however, contains some very extraordinary policemen who do not confine their investigations or activities to this world or to any known planes or dimensions. Their most casual remarks create a thousand other mysteries [. . .]. The whole point of my plan will be the most brain-staggering imponderables of the policemen.[93]

As an 'orthodox murder mystery', all the conventional elements of the genre do make an appearance in this novel. In his *Dictionary of Literary Terms*, J.A. Cuddon defines the 'detective story' as follows:

A story in which a mystery, often involving a murder, is solved by a detective. The traditional elements are an apparently insoluble crime, uncooperative or dim-witted police, the detective (often an amateur) who may be an eccentric, the detective's confidant who helps to clarify the problems, a variety of suspects and carefully laid red-herrings to put the reader off the scent, a suspect who appears guilty from circumstantial evidence, and a resolution often startling and unexpected, in which the detective reveals how he has found out the culprit. The good detective story displays impeccable logic and reasoning in its unravelling.[94]

Every one of these features can be usefully traced in *The Third Policeman*. The opening line of the novel, however, would seem to cancel out the first premise of the 'whodunit', because Noman straightaway confesses to being a murderer – 'Not everybody knows how I killed old Phillip Mathers' (*3P*, p. 7). O'Brien cleverly inverts the premise in that Noman lacks an identity (the real mystery to be solved here), and is himself a murder victim, although this is still unknown to the reader – and to Noman – at the start of the story. As Viktor Shklovsky comments on the intertextual use of the whodunit pattern in literary fiction, 'inversion is obligatory, and it sometimes takes the form of a complex omission of separate details'.[95]

The apparent stock stupidity of the policemen is reflected and refracted not only in their ideas but more precisely in their bizarre language – the way, for example, that Pluck's malapropisms and solecisms resonate with multiple, textually coherent meaning, e.g. Pluck's use of 'cog' (*3P*, p. 56) is rich in dialogic potential: it variously suggests a clipped form of 'cognomen' (i.e. a nickname, or, in ancient

Rome, the third and usually last name of a citizen), a bicycle 'cog', a 'cog' in the literary machine, and the Cartesian 'cogito'.

Noman, the arch-materialist, personifies the eccentric amateur detective so beloved of the genre, with Joe the Soul as his trusty confidant. Throughout the text, however, we find ourselves identifying more and more with Noman's predicament, so, metafictionally speaking, the reader too assumes the role of detective, trying to resolve the 'thousand other mysteries' of the novel.

At the end of the story it is finally revealed that John Divney had planted the bomb that killed Noman in chapter two, but this seems almost incidental compared to the startling revelation that Noman is dead and trapped in a cyclical, never-ending Hell. This, in effect, is the primary mystery to be solved. We recall Noman's confession from the opening pages of chapter one: 'Perhaps it is important in the story I am going to tell to remember that it was for de Selby I committed my first serious sin. It was for him that I committed my greatest sin' (*3P*, p. 9). If we apply our own powers of deduction, and substitute 'the self' for de Selby, then this mystery begins to unfold – it is for the self that Noman sells his soul and commits his 'greatest sin'. Now *The Third Policeman* becomes a cautionary parable about the dangers of selfhood and Faustian self-absorption in the purely rational sphere. The traditional 'variety of suspects' is the list of intertextual philosophers that can be discerned in the composite character of de Selby: Anaximander, Aristotle, Vico, Wittgenstein, Dunne, Einstein, Des Esseintes, Walter Shandy, Slawkenbergius, and all the other historical and literary figures parodied in the novel.

The traditional 'red-herrings' that throw the reader-detective off the scent are the vast webs of nested representations or 'tangled hierarchies' which divert us from the primary narrative, as well as the metaleptic strategies that foreground the text as text, and disrupt and defer the narrative progression. As Shklovsky again observes of 'mystery novels': 'the device of using several simultaneous actions whose interrelationship is not immediately specified by the author serves as a plot impediment, a special continuation of the mystery technique'.[96]

The suspect who appears guilty from 'circumstantial evidence' is specifically parodied in the scene of tortuous illogic when Pluck decides to hang Noman out of convenience and on account of his lack of identity: 'You mean that because I have no name I cannot die and that you cannot be held answerable for death even if you kill me?' (*3P*, p. 102). On a more general satirical level, Noman is also guilty from 'circumstantial evidence', on account of his devout empiricism and trust in the material evidence of sense-experience.

Finally, and most importantly perhaps, is the traditional 'startling denouement' in which the truth of the Menippean satire, or mystery, is revealed, and the twin strands of death and identity are resolved. As Patricia Waugh writes:

> In metafiction the detective story plot is useful for exploring readerly expectation [. . .], a form in which tension is wholly generated by the presentation of a mystery and heightened by the retardation of the correct solution. Even characters, for the most part, are merely functions of the plot. Like metafiction it foregrounds the questions of identity. The reader is kept in suspense about the identity of the criminal until the end, when the rational operations of the detective triumph.[97]

The inversion of reason, explored in the deconstructed form of the 'whodunit', exposes the conventional, 'logical' structures of the world for what they are. In the inverted world of *The Third Policeman* it is not logic that triumphs in the end but illogic. For Noman and the reader (both playing the role of detective), reason can be both a tool for discovery and a weapon for destruction, and the 'clues' to this mystery are the numerous motifs of infinite regress which challenge the limits of the intellect, and proclaim the need for faith.

The black box that Noman has killed for – in order to write a book on de Selby – has in turn been used to kill him (Divney's bomb). As Policeman Fox autocritically reveals, the box itself contains 'omnium' (omniscience), so that the murder weapon and the motive for murder are the Faustian 'Book of Knowledge'. At this point, the intertextual levels of the relative universe collapse and converge: the ontological truth that Noman is both dead *and* a metafictional construct fuses with the Faustian theme of the Menippean satire. Noman's existential nausea reinforces the Faustian theme: 'Suddenly I felt horribly ill as if the spinning of the world in the firmament had come against my stomach [...] and my head throbbed, swelling out like a bladder at every surge of blood' (*3P*, p. 183). Noman's final despair at his vision of eternal damnation consciously echoes the cry of Marlowe's Doctor Faustus:

> Stand still, you ever-moving spheres of Heaven, [. . .]
> O, I'll leap up to my God! Who pulls me down?
> See, see where Christ's blood streams in the firmament!
> One drop would save my soul – half a drop: ah, my Christ![98]

Like Faust, Noman has sold his soul for the Book of Knowledge, and the devilish policemen claim him for eternal Hell. This post-modernist Menippean satire ends with a final intertextual explosion, as Kit Marlowe meets Philip Marlowe in the fourth dimension. Only one question remains unsolved in the murder mystery – who really killed Noman?

Epilogue

Given the date of its composition (1939–1940), it seems clear to me that *The Third Policeman*, alongside Joyce's more elitist and difficult *Finnegans Wake*, ranks as the first great work of post-modernism. Part of O'Brien's achievement is his reader-friendly accessibility, which makes a decisive break with modernism and with the paralysing associations of Joyce himself. I think it is much more useful, if comparisons of this sort must be made, to link O'Brien's work with that of Samuel Beckett. Indeed, Sighle Kennedy has drawn a thematic comparison between these two authors' debut novels – *Murphy* (1938), and *At Swim-Two-Birds* (1939):

> Both stray, widely and intentionally, from the path of the real-istic novel; both indulge in witty, erudite, and often outrageous digressions; both are concerned in mysterious ways with the problems of madness; both weave uproarious chess games into their narratives. Most striking of all is the fact that both portray, as their central figures, young men who are primarily interested in retiring to the privacy of their own mental spheres.[99]

Developing on from this, I think a more telling comparison might be made between O'Brien and Beckett's second novels: *The Third Policeman* and *Watt* (1944). Although *Watt* was published four years after *The Third Policeman* was composed, there are some striking post-modernist parallels. These include shared concepts of relativity and language; similar metaleptic intrusions (particularly the use of mock footnotes); and even a metafictional appearance by the author-god of *Watt*: 'For when on Sam the sun shone bright, then in a vacuum panted Watt, and when Watt like a leaf was tossed, then stumbled Sam in deepest night'.[100]

Most important, however, are the metaphysical journeyings of the solipsist protagonists, Watt and Noman, which brings them both to the border of the knowable world. Both texts are liberally littered with paradoxes of infinity, which for Rubin Rabinovitz serve to delineate the limits of human knowledge: 'a gentle reminder from God that since He was after all infinite and omniscient Himself, there were naturally certain areas into which man's understanding could not penetrate'.[101] On this philosophical level, Watt and Noman's picaresque travels are, amongst other things, a movement away from the optimistic rationalism of the Enlightenment values which underpin the modernist project towards a more pessimistic and sceptical position, i.e. post-modernism.

In rejecting both modernism and the Irish revival, O'Brien and Beckett found their paraliterary inspiration in the early Counter-Enlightenment models of Swift and Sterne. For post-modernists, the Enlightenment is the root of it all: where the novel first began its dialogic carnival of vulgar respectability, and where the cult of Authorship and the tyranny of Cartesian thought are born. In their respective studies of medieval literature – Beckett on Dante, O'Brien on Irish nature poetry – both novelists had confronted these Enlightenment legacies. In so doing they encountered the spectre of René Descartes, whom they realised had prefigured and shaped modern epistemology – the author-god of western thought, as it were. Anti-Cartesianism, then, becomes the starting point for these two remarkable Menippean satires, and the springboard for an entirely new direction in Irish (and European) literature. Indeed, as Brian McHale has noted, 'post-modernist metafiction is the heir to Menippean satire and its most recent historical avatar'.[102] At the post-modern core of both *Watt* and *The Third Policeman* lies a serious and sustained critique of modern, secular Cartesianism. As Rabinovitz again writes:

> Watt is a modern Cartesian. He retains the scepticism and analytical method of Descartes, but has no *a priori* belief in God. Without such a belief his scepticism becomes transformed into a frightening encounter with nothingness; his chains of causal reasoning go on endlessly; and yet the more he reasons the less he really knows. He strives to understand the meaning of human knowing because he imagines that with those epistemological inquiries he will reach a point where he will be able confidently say to say 'I think' and thereafter, with equal conviction, 'therefore I exist'.[103]

Noman, too, is a godless Cartesian. The irony of his ontological/metafictional condition is that, despite his worship at the altar of Reason – *cogito ergo sum* – he does not, in fact, exist: Noman is not just a character in a fiction but a long-dead murder victim. This philosophical speculation ties up the last loose strand of the murder mystery, the question of who really killed Noman. In good who-dunit fashion, let this be the final revelation that closes this inquiry: Descartes dunit; Descartes murdered Noman.

Notes and references

INTRODUCTION: BEYOND THE CELTIC TWILIGHT ZONE

1. Roland Barthes, *Roland Barthes*, trans. Richard Howard (New York: Hill & Wang, 1977), opening epigraph.
2. My thanks to the late Prof. Pat Sheeran for having originally suggested this opposition.
3. Roman Jakobson, 'On Realism in Art' (1921), repr. *Readings in Russian Poetics: Formalist and Structuralist Views*, ed. Ladislav Matejka and Krystyna Pomorska (Ann Arbor, Michigan: University of Michigan, 1978), pp. 38–9.
4. ibid., p. 39.
5. Boris Tomashevsky, 'Literature and Biography' (1923), repr. Matejka and Pomorska, p. 51.
6. The term 'fractal' was coined by Benoit Mandelbrot from the infinitive 'frangere' (to break), with a resonance that implies both fracture and fraction. It is a particularly apt metaphor for describing 'Chinese box' fictions such as *At Swim-Two-Birds* and *The Third Policeman*, both of which use *mise en abyme* (or infinite regress) as a key structural and thematic device. As James Gleick notes, 'In the mind's eye, a fractal is a way of seeing infinity'. See Gleick, *Chaos: Making a New Science* (London: Abacus, 1993), p. 98.
7. Gleick, p. 98.
8. Serge Kahili King, *Urban Shaman* (New York: Simon & Schuster, 1990), p. 14.
9. Jeremy Hawthorn, 'Metafiction', in *A Concise Glossary of Contemporary Literary Theory* (London: Edward Arnold, 1992), p. 104.
10. Rüdiger Imhof, Introduction, *Alive-Alive O!: Flann O'Brien's* At Swim-Two-Birds, ed. Imhof (Dublin: Wolfhound, 1985), p. 19.
11. Maria Edgeworth, letter to Michael Pakenham Edgeworth (19 February 1834), repr. *The Field Day Anthology of Irish Writing*, vol. I, ed. Seamus Deane (Derry: Field Day, 1991), p. 1051.
12. J.M. Synge, *The Playboy of the Western World* (1907; London: Methuen, 1961), p. 64.
13. James Joyce, *Ulysses* (1922; London: Bodley Head, 1960), p. 6.
14. Declan Kiberd, 'Irish Literature and Irish History', in *The Oxford Illustrated History of Ireland*, ed. R.F. Foster (Oxford and New York: Oxford UP, 1989), p. 316.
15. Martin Gray, 'Anti-novel', *A Dictionary of Literary Terms* (Essex: Longman York, 1984), p. 21.
16. J.A. Cuddon, 'Anti-novel', *A Dictionary of Literary Terms*, rev. edn. (Harmondsworth: Penguin, 1979), p. 47.

17. Cuddon, p. 47.
18. ibid.
19. M.H. Abrams, 'Anti-novel' [see under 'Novel'], *A Glossary of Literary Terms*, 4th edn. (New York and London: Holt, Rinehart and Winston, 1981), p. 122.
20. Cuddon, p. 47.
21. Bertold Brecht, *Brecht on Theatre: The Development of an Aesthetic*, trans. and ed. John Willet (London: Methuen, 1991), p. 192.
22 Robert Alter, quoted in Brian McHale, *Post-Modernist Fiction* (New York: Routledge, 1991), p. 165.
23. Colin Greenland, 'In My View', *The Sunday Times*, 10 September 1989.
24. Miles Orvell, 'Entirely Fictitious: The Fiction of Flann O'Brien', in Imhof, p.102.
25. Greenland, 'In My View'.
26. Barthes, p. 119.
27. Patricia Waugh, *Metafiction: The Theory and Practice of Self-Conscious Fiction* (London and New York: Methuen, 1984), pp. 21–2.
28. ibid., pp. 23–4.
29. Linda Hutcheon, Preface, *A Poetics of Post-modernism: History, Theory, Fiction* (London and New York: Routledge, 1988), p. xi.
30. ibid., p. 3.
31. Ihab Hassan, 'Towards a Concept of Postmodernism', *The Postmodern Turn: Essays in Postmodern Theory and Culture* (Ohio: Ohio State UP, 1987), pp. 85–86.
32. Hutcheon, p. 6.
33. Arthur Kroker and David Cook, *The Postmodern Scene: Excremental Culture and Hyper-Aesthetics* (London: Macmillan, 1991), p. 8.
34. Hassan, Preface, *The Post-modern Turn*, pp. xiii–xiv.
35. For discussions of the modernist/post-modernist debate in relation to *At Swim-Two-Birds*, see Denell Downum, 'Citation and Spectrality in Flann O'Brien's *At Swim-Two-Birds*, *Irish University Review* 36.2, Autumn/Winter 2006, pp. 304–20; Neil Murphy, 'Flann O'Brien', *The Review of Contemporary Fiction* 25.3, Fall 2005, pp. 7–41; Robert Looby, 'Flann O'Brien, A Postmodernist When It Was Neither Profitable Nor Popular', *The Scriptorium: Flann O'Brien*, 24 July <http://www.themodernworld.com/scriptorium/obrien.html> (accessed 21 January 2008); Monique Gallagher, 'Frontier Instability in Flann O'Brien's *At Swim-Two-Birds*', in *A Casebook on Flann O'Brien's* At Swim-Two-Birds (2004), ed. Thomas C. Foster, <http://www.dalkeyarchive.com/casebooks/gallagher> (accessed 2 December 2008); M. Keith Booker, 'Postmodern and/or Postcolonial?: The Politics of *At Swim-Two-Birds*' (2004), in Foster, <http://www.dalkey-archive.com/casebooks/booker> (accessed 2 December 2008); Joshua Esty, 'Flann O'Brien's *At Swim-Two Birds* and the Post-Post Debate', *ARIEL: A Review of International English Literature* 26.4, October 1995, pp. 23–46; James Edwin Mahon, 'Was Flann O'Brien a Post-modernist?' [review of *Flann O'Brien: A Portrait of the Artist as a Young Post-modernist* by Keith Hopper], *ROPES: Review of Postgraduate Studies* 4, Spring 1995, pp. 56–7; Kim McMullen, 'Culture as Colloquy: Flann O'Brien's Postmodern Dialogue with Irish Tradition', *NOVEL: A Forum on Fiction* 27.1, Autumn 1993, pp. 62–84.
36. Hassan, 'The Literature of Silence', in *The Post-modern Turn*, p. 13. See also Ihab Hassan, *The Dismemberment of Orpheus: Towards a Postmodern Literature* (Oxford and New York: Oxford UP, 1971).
37. Ihab Hassan, Seminar Series, *Yeats International Summer School*, Sligo, August, 1993.
38. Waugh, p. 23.

39. James Joyce, *A Portrait of the Artist as a Young Man* (1916; London: Granada, 1983), pp. 194–5.

40. Waugh, p. 25.

41. McHale, pp. 9–10. The 'dominant' is another crucial Russian Formalist concept. As Roman Jakobson notes: 'The dominant may be defined as the focusing component of a work of art: it rules, determines, and transforms the remaining components. It is the dominant which guarantees the integrity of the structure.' See Jakobson, 'The Dominant' (1935), repr. Matejka and Pomorska, p. 82.

42. Samuel Beckett, 'Moody Man of Letters' [interview with Israel Schenker], *New York Times*, 6 May 1956, quoted in J.C.C. Mays, 'Literalist of the Imagination', in *Myles: Portraits of Brian O'Nolan*, ed. Timothy O'Keeffe (London: Martin Brian & O'Keeffe, 1973), p. 80.

43. Hassan, Seminar Series, August 1993.

44. Anthony Cronin, *No Laughing Matter: The Life and Times of Flann O'Brien* (London: Grafton, 1989); Peter Costello and Peter van de Kamp, *Flann O'Brien: An Illustrated Biography* (London: Bloomsbury, 1987); Anne Clissmann, *Flann O'Brien: A Critical Introduction to his Writings* (Dublin: Gill & Macmillan, 1975); Timothy O'Keeffe, ed. *Myles: Portraits of Brian O'Nolan* (London: Martin Brian & O'Keeffe, 1973).

45. In fairness, this anti-theoretical bias in Flann O'Brien studies was not just restricted to Irish critics. As the American critic Thomas F. Shea noted in 1992:

> O'Brien's texts significantly 're-imagine' the novel and confront, under the guise of mere fun, many of the major literary 'issues' generated by the linguistic and fictional theories of the last half century. It would be reductive, however, merely to accommodate O'Brien's novels to convenient tags such as Shklovsky's 'defamiliarization', Bakhtin's 'carnivalization', Derrida's '*différence*', Barthes's 'myth', or Kristeva's 'semiotic activity'. The unique voices and narrative strategies emerging through O'Brien's novels are best appreciated on their own terms. (See Shea, *Flann O'Brien's Exorbitant Novels* (Lewisburg: Bucknell UP; London: Associated University Presses, 1992), p. 11.)

46. Myles na Gopaleen, quoted in Kevin O'Nolan, 'The First Furlongs', in O'Keeffe, pp. 13–14.

47. Roland Barthes, quoted in Jonathan Culler, *Barthes* (London: Fontana, 1987), p. 11.

48. Roland Barthes, 'The Death of the Author', in *Modern Literary Theory: A Reader*, ed. Philip Rice and Patricia Waugh (London: Edward Arnold, 1992), pp. 116–17.

49. I am thinking here of critics such as Rüdiger Imhof, M. Keith Booker, Sue Asbee, Monique Gallagher and José Lanters, amongst others.

50. Imhof, Introduction, *Alive-Alive O!*, p. 7.

51. Viktor Shklovsky, for example, rather mischievously argued that '*Tristram Shandy* is the most typical novel in world literature'. See Shklovsky, 'Sterne's *Tristram Shandy*: Stylistic Commentary' (1921), in *Russian Formalist Criticism: Four Essays*, trans. and ed. Lee T. Lemon and Marion J. Reis (Lincoln: University of Nebraska Press, 1965), p. 57.

52. Pavel Medvedev, *The Formal Method in Literary Scholarship: A Critical Introduction to Sociological Poetics* (1928), quoted in Peter Steiner, *Russian Formalism: A Metapoetics* (London and Ithaca: Cornell UP, 1984), p. 21.

53. Viktor Shklovsky, *The Third Factory* (1926), quoted in Steiner, p. 65.

54. Roman Jakobson, 'Recent Russian Poetry, Sketch 1' (1921), quoted in Boris

Eichenbaum, 'The Theory of the Formal Method' (1926), repr. Matejka and Pomorska, p. 8.

55. Viktor Shklovsky, *The Technique of the Writer's Trade* (1928), quoted in Steiner, p. 46.

56. Victor Erlich, *Russian Formalism: History-Doctrine*, rev. edn. (London, The Hague and Paris: Mouton, 1965), p. 171. The most vociferous opponent of Russian Formalism was Leon Trotsky: 'The Formalist school represents an abortive idealism applied to the question of art. The Formalists show a fast ripening religiousness. They are followers of St John. They believe that "In the beginning was the Word". But we believe that in the beginning was the deed. The word followed, as its phonetic shadow.' See Trotsky, *Literature and Revolution* (1924), trans. Rose Strunsky (Ann Arbor, Michigan: University of Michigan Press, 1960), p. 183.

57. Steiner, p. 253.

58. Susan Sontag, 'Writing Itself: On Roland Barthes', *A Roland Barthes Reader*, ed. Sontag (London: Vintage, 1993), p. xxiii.

59. Steiner, p. 48.

60. Fredric Jameson, *The Prison-House of Language: A Critical Account of Structuralism and Russian Formalism* (New Jersey: Princeton UP, 1972), p. 31.

61. Barthes, *Roland Barthes*, pp. 175–6.

62. Viktor Shklovsky, 'Art as Technique' (1917), repr. Lemon and Reis, pp. 11–12.

63. Jameson, p. 51.

64. Sontag, pp. ix–x.

CHAPTER ONE: THE TWO TOWERS

1. Bernard Benstock, 'The Three Faces of Brian O'Nolan', *Éire-Ireland* 3.3, October 1968, repr. *Alive-Alive O!: Flann O'Brien's* At Swim-Two Birds, ed. Rüdiger Imhof (Dublin: Wolfhound, 1985), p. 61.

2. J.C.C. Mays, 'Literalist of the Imagination', *Myles: Portraits of Brian O'Nolan*, ed. Timothy O'Keeffe (London: Martin Brian & O'Keeffe, 1973), p. 77.

3. Myles na Gopaleen, 'Literature E'cet'ra', *The Hair of the Dogma: A Further Selection from 'Cruiskeen Lawn'*, ed. Kevin O'Nolan (London: Grafton, 1987), p. 166.

4. John Montague, 'The Siege of Mullingar', *Poets from the North of Ireland*, ed. Frank Ormsby (Belfast: Blackstaff, 1987), p. 92.

5. Myles na Gopaleen, 'Speaking Literally', *The Hair of the Dogma*, p. 103.

6. Breandán Ó Conaire, 'Flann O'Brien, *An Béal Bocht* and Other Irish Matters', *Irish University Review* 3.2, Autumn 1973, p. 122. Note: Myles's surname was spelt 'na gCopaleen' until December 1952 when it became 'na Gopaleen'. For the purposes of clarity, I will use the latter form throughout.

7. Imhof, Introduction, *Alive-Alive O!*, p. 8.

8. Myles na Gopaleen, 'De Me', *New Ireland*, March 1964, p. 41.

9. Brian O'Nolan, letter to Longmans Green & Company, Ltd, 10 November 1938, in 'A Sheaf of Letters', ed. Robert Hogan and Gordon Henderson, in *The Journal of Irish Literature* 3.1, January 1974, ed. Anne Clissmann and David Powell, special Flann O'Brien issue (California: Proscenium, 1974), p. 67.

10. See Donnchadh Ó Corráin and Fidelma Maguire, *Gaelic Personal Names* (Dublin: Academy Press, 1981), p. 105.

11. John Garvin, 'Sweetscented Manuscripts', in O'Keeffe, p. 60.

12. Dion Boucicault, *The Colleen Bawn; or, The Brides of Garryowen: A Domestic Drama in Three Acts* (1860; London: Thomas Hailes Lacy [c.1873]), p. 33.

13. John Cronin, Introduction, *The Collegians* by Gerald Griffin (1829; Belfast: Appletree Press, 1992), p. ix.

14. Griffin, p. 54.
15. ibid., p. 13.
16. Boucicault, p. 15.
17. David Krause, ed. *The Dolmen Boucicault: The Theatre of Dion Boucicault* (Dublin: Dolmen, 1964), p. 28.
18. Krause, p. 113.
19. Na Gopaleen, 'Speaking Literally', p. 103.
20. Hubert Butler, 'The Eggman and the Fairies', in *Escape from the Anthill* (Mullingar: Lilliput Press, 1986), pp. 72–4.
21. Na Gopaleen, 'Speaking Literally', p. 102.
22. Anne Clissmann, *Flann O'Brien: A Critical Introduction to his Writings* (Dublin: Gill & Macmillan, 1975), p. 354n.
23. Edward Said, 'Yeats and Decolonization', in *Nationalism, Colonialism and Literature* (Derry: Field Day, 1988), pp. 8–9.
24. J.M. Synge, *The Playboy of the Western World* (1907; London: Methuen, 1961), p. 110.
25. Myles na Gopaleen, quoted in Alan Warner, *A Guide to Anglo-Irish Literature* (Dublin: Gill & Macmillan, 1981), p. 61.
26. Keith Donohue, *The Irish Anatomist: A Study of Flann O'Brien* (Bethesda, Maryland: Academica Press, 2002), p. 183.
27. Brian O'Nolan, letter to Seán O'Casey (13 April 1942), 'A Sheaf of Letters', in Clissmann and Powell, p. 75.
28. 'A West-Briton-Nationalist, Ballyhaunis' [Brian O'Nolan], quoted in Ó Conaire, p. 121.
29. Boris Tomashevsky, 'Literature and Biography' (1923), repr. *Readings in Russian Poetics: Formalist and Structuralist Views*, ed. Ladislav Matejka and Krystyna Pomorska (Ann Arbor, Michigan: University of Michigan Press, 1978), p. 55.
30. Benedict Kiely, Introduction, *The Various Lives of Keats and Chapman and The Brother* by Myles na Gopaleen, ed. Kiely (London: Grafton, 1988), p. 3.
31. Na Gopaleen, *The Various Lives*, p. 5. For a good discussion of O'Brien's obsession with this Keats poem, see Thomas F. Shea, 'Flann O'Brien and John Keats: "John Duffy's Brother" and Train Allusions', *Éire-Ireland* 24.2, Summer 1989, pp. 109–20.
32. Clissmann, p. 199.
33. Na Gopaleen, *The Various Lives*, pp. 15, 24, 32, 104.
34. Michael Worton and Judith Still (eds.), *Intertextuality: Theories and Practice* (Manchester: Manchester UP, 1991), p. 15.
35. John Fekete, 'Vampire Value, Infinitive Art and Literary Theory: A Topographic Meditation', in *Life After Post-Modernism: Essays on Value and Culture*, ed. John Fekete (London: Macmillan, 1988), p. 71.
36. Karl Kraus, quoted in Harry Zohn, *Karl Kraus* (New York: Twayne, 1971), p. 64.
37. Myles na Gopaleen, 'Social and Personal' (December 1951), quoted in Kiely, *The Various Lives*, p. 4.
38. Myles na Gopaleen, 'Cruiskeen Lawn', *The Irish Times*, 13 April 1960.
39. Peter Costello and Peter van de Kamp, *Flann O'Brien: An Illustrated Biography* (London: Bloomsbury, 1987), p. 47.
40. Stanford Lee Cooper, 'Eire's Columnist: An Interview with Brian O'Nolan', *Time*, 23 August 1943, p. 90.
41. Mays, p. 80.
42. Brian Nolan [Flann O'Brien], 'A Bash in the Tunnel: An Editorial Note', *Envoy* 5.17, April 1951, James Joyce special issue, p. 9.

43. Nolan, 'A Bash in the Tunnel', p. 9.
44. Tomashevsky, pp. 49–50.
45. Nolan, 'A Bash in the Tunnel', p.11.
46. Myles na Gopaleen, 'Finnegan', *The Hair of the Dogma*, p. 154.
47. Myles na Gopaleen, quoted in Anthony Cronin, *No Laughing Matter: The Life and Times of Flann O'Brien* (London: Grafton, 1989), p. 59.
48. Na Gopaleen, *The Hair of the Dogma*, p. 164.
49. Niall Sheridan, in O'Keeffe, pp. 41–2.
50. Sheridan, p. 42.
51. Brother Barnabas, 'Scenes in a Novel', *Comhthrom Féinne* 8.2, May 1934, repr. Clissmann and Powell, pp. 15–16.
52. ibid., p. 15.
53. ibid., p. 16.
54. ibid., p. 17.
55. ibid.
56. ibid.
57. Sean McMahon, 'The Realist Novel after WWII', in *The Genius of Irish Prose*, ed. Augustine Martin (Dublin: Mercier, 1985), p. 199.
58. Brother Barnabas, p. 18.
59. ibid.
60. Jim Collins, *Uncommon Cultures: Popular Culture and Post-Modernism* (London: Routledge, 1989), p. 60.
61. Brother Barnabas, p. 18.
62. Graham Greene, reader's report on *At Swim-Two-Birds* for Longmans Green Ltd, later quoted as blurb on the original Longmans jacket of *At Swim-Two-Birds* (1939), repr. Imhof, *Alive-Alive O!*, pp. 41–42.
63. Greene, p. 42.
64. Clissmann, p. 86.
65. Brian O'Nolan, letter to Ethel Mannin (10 July 1939), 'A Sheaf of Letters', in Clissmann and Powell, p. 69.
66. Anon., 'Nest of Novelists', *Times Literary Supplement*, 18 March 1939, repr. Imhof, *Alive-Alive O!*, p. 43.
67. Frank Swinnerton, 'Right Proportions', *Observer*, 19 March 1939, repr. Imhof, *Alive-Alive O!*, pp. 43–4.
68. Anthony West, 'Inspired Nonsense', *New Statesman and Nation*, 17 June 1939, repr. Imhof, *Alive-Alive O!*, p. 44.
69. Seán Ó Faoláin, *John O'London's Weekly*, quoted in Cronin, *No Laughing Matter*, p. 92.
70. James Joyce, quoted in Costello and van de Kamp, p. 63.
71. Samuel Beckett, reported by Aidan Higgins, 'Discords of Good Humour', BBC Radio 3, 12 November 1980, quoted in Cronin, *No Laughing Matter* p. 172. See also Aidan Higgins, Introduction, *Samuel Beckett: Photographs* by John Minihan (London: Secker & Warburg, 1995), pp. 8–9.
72. Brian O'Nolan, letter to Longmans Green Ltd (1 May 1939), quoted in Cronin, *No Laughing Matter* p. 97.
73. Flann O'Brien, *The Third Policeman*, 'Publisher's Note' [excerpt taken from initial draft manuscript] (1967; London: Grafton, 1986), p. 200.
74. Patience Ross of A.M. Heath & Co. (11 March 1940), quoted in *A Flann O'Brien Reader*, ed. Stephen Jones (New York: Viking Press, 1978), p. 31.
75. Thomas Kilroy, 'The Year in Review', *Irish University Review*, 5.1, Spring 1968, p. 112.
76. Ó Conaire, p. 130.

77. Brian O'Nolan, letter to Seán O'Casey (13 April 1942), 'A Sheaf of Letters', in Clissmann and Powell, p. 75.
78. See William K. Wimsatt and Monroe C. Beardsley, 'The Intentional Fallacy' (1946), repr. *The Verbal Icon: Studies in the Meaning of Poetry* (Lexington: University of Kentucky Press, 1954), p. 3.
79. For a discussion of Myles's persistent attacks on Joyce in the 'Cruiskeen Lawn', see David Powell, 'An Annotated Bibliography of Myles na gCopaleen's "Cruiskeen Lawn" Commentaries on James Joyce', *James Joyce Quarterly* 9.1, Fall 1971, pp. 50–62.

CHAPTER TWO: '*IS IT ABOUT A BICYCLE?*'

1. Brian Nolan [Flann O'Brien], 'A Bash in the Tunnel: An Editorial Note', Envoy 5.17 (April 1951), James Joyce special issue, p. 10.
2. J.C.C. Mays, 'Literalist of the Imagination', in *Myles: Portraits of Brian O'Nolan*, ed. Timothy O'Keeffe (London: Martin Brian & O'Keeffe, 1973), p. 79.
3. Rüdiger Imhof, *Alive-Alive O!: Flann O'Brien's At Swim-Two-Birds*, ed. Imhof (Dublin: Wolfhound, 1985), p. 23.
4. Anthony Cronin, *No Laughing Matter: The Life and Times of Flann O'Brien* (London: Grafton, 1989), p. 101.
5. Cronin, pp. 213–14.
6. James Joyce, *Ulysses* (1922; London: Bodley Head, 1960), p. 45.
7. Under the Customs Consolidation Act (1876, section 42), *Ulysses* was prohibited from entering the country. Although this exclusion order was withdrawn in 1932 – and even though *Ulysses* was never officially banned under the Censorship of Publications Act (1929) – libraries and booksellers continued to impose their own form of censorship (see Michael Adams, *Censorship: The Irish Experience* (Dublin: Scepter Books, 1968), pp. 31 and 172; and Julia Carlson, *Banned in Ireland: Censorship and the Irish Writer* (London: Routledge, 1991), pp. 9–12). As Myles na Gopaleen wrote in June 1954 (on the day that he helped to inaugurate the first-ever Bloomsday celebration): '*Ulysses* is "not banned" in Ireland, which means simply that any person asking for it in a bookshop would probably be lynched' ('J-Day', 'Cruiskeen Lawn', *The Irish Times*, 16 June 1954). In 1954, 'the record for books banned in any one year was established at 1,034' (see Terence Brown, *Ireland: A Social and Cultural History 1922–1985* (London: Fontana, 1985), p. 198).
8. Robert Graves, quoted in Adams, p. 250.
9. See Adams, pp. 240–3. According to Terence Brown, between 1930 and 1939 (when *At Swim-Two-Birds* was first published), 'some 1,200 books and some 140 periodicals fell foul of the Censors' displeasure' (see Brown, p. 149). As late as the 1980s, literary critics such as Roland Barthes and Susan Sontag were added to this list (see Carlson, p. 1).
10. The Censorship Act was amended twice: once in 1946 when provision was made for an Appeal Board (in practice this had little effect as few appeals were lodged); and again in 1967 when the period for which a book could be banned was limited to twelve years (this had considerable impact as thousands of books were automatically 'unbanned').
11. 'The Censorship of Publications Act, 1929', quoted in Carlson, pp. 3–4.
12. Frank O'Connor, 'Frank O'Connor on Censorship', *The Dubliner*, March 1962, p. 39. O'Connor first made this point at a debate in 1962, and by way of illustrating his argument he opened with the following anecdote:

> One day during my time as a librarian a young man asked to see me. He wanted to complain of an indecent book. I asked him what was indecent

about it, and he said there was a dirty word in it. I asked where and he replied promptly 'Page 164'. Obviously page 164 had imprinted itself indelibly on his brain. I read the page and asked 'Which word?' He said 'That word' and he pointed to the word 'navel'. I felt sorry for him and wanted to ask him whether he couldn't find some nice girl to walk out with, but I decided it might be dangerous. (O'Connor, p. 39)

13. Leslie Montgomery, quoted in Adams, pp. 72–3.
14. Carlson, pp. 1–2.
15. Carlson, p. 6.
16. John Broderick, interview with Carlson, p. 40.
17. Brian O'Nolan, letter to Browne and Nolan Ltd (16 April 1941), quoted in Cronin, p. 127.
18. Virginia Woolf, quoted in Elaine Showalter, 'Feminist Criticism in the Wilderness', *The New Feminist Criticism*, ed. Showalter (New York: Pantheon, 1985), pp. 255–6.
19. Brian O'Nolan, letter to Timothy O'Keeffe (1 September 1961), quoted in Cronin, p. 214.
20. The Censorship Board was composed, almost entirely, of devout Catholic laymen. The key lobby group for the Board's creation was the Irish Vigilance Association (founded by the Dominicans in 1911), which disseminated its ideas in *The Irish Rosary*. As one typical editorial in February 1913 phrased it: 'The evil publications against which the fight is being waged are not the product of Irish brains, nor the output of Irish hands. They are foreign to every ideal and aspiration of the clean-minded Celt, and mostly inspired by hatred of the Catholic Faith and Christian morality' (see Adams, pp. 15–16).
21. James Joyce, letter to Grant Richards (23 June 1906), *Letters of James Joyce*, vol. I, ed. Stuart Gilbert (London: Faber, 1957), p. 63.
22. Cronin, p. 217.
23. Sean McMahon, 'The Realist Novel after the Second World War', in *The Genius of Irish Prose*, ed. Augustine Martin (Dublin: Mercier, 1985), pp. 151–2.
24. Judith Fetterley, *The Resisting Reader: A Feminist Approach to American Fiction* (Bloomington: Indiana UP, 1978), p. xii.
25. Wayne Koestenbaum, *Double Talk: The Erotics of Male Literary Collaboration* (London: Routledge, 1989), p. 4.
26. John McGahern, interview with Carlson, pp. 63–4.
27. Cronin, p. 61.
28. Edward Said, 'Yeats and Decolonization', in *Nationalism, Colonialism and Literature* (Derry: Field Day, 1988), p. 15.
29. G.B. Shaw, 'The Rejected Statement', quoted in *The Concise Dictionary of Quotations* (London: Collins, 1985), p. 291.
30. Vivian Mercier, *The Irish Comic Tradition* (London: Oxford UP, 1969), pp. 40–1.
31. Brian O'Nolan, interview with the BBC (7 March 1962), quoted in Sue Asbee, *Flann O'Brien* (Boston: Twayne, 1991), p. 107.
32. Margot Norris, 'Not the Girl She Was at All: Women in "The Dead"', in *James Joyce's The Dead: Case Studies in Contemporary Criticism*, ed. Daniel R. Schwarz (Boston and New York: Bedford Books, 1994), p. 192.
33. Mercier, p. 1.
34. ibid., p. 49.
35. Peter Costello and Peter van de Kamp, *Flann O'Brien: An Illustrated Biography* (London: Bloomsbury, 1987), p. 32.
36. Rosalind Coward, 'Are Women's Novels Feminist Novels?', in *The New Feminist Criticism*, ed. Elaine Showalter (New York: Pantheon, 1985), p. 230.

37. Jean Saunders, *The Craft of Writing Romance: A Practical Guide* (London: Allison and Busby, 1986), p. 47.
38. J. Hillis Miller, 'Stevens' Rock and Criticism as Cure', *Georgia Review* 30.2, Summer 1976, p. 341.
39. Elaine Showalter, 'Towards a Feminist Poetics', in *Modern Literary Theory: A Reader*, ed. Philip Rice and Patricia Waugh (London: Edward Arnold, 1992), p. 100.
40. The Marxist-Feminist Collective, 'Women Writing', in Rice and Waugh, p. 106.
41. As W.B. Yeats noted:
    > The Pooka, *recté* [rightly] Púca, seems essentially an animal spirit. Some derive his name from *poc*, a he-goat; and speculative persons consider him the forefather of Shakespeare's 'Puck'. On solitary mountains and among old ruins he lives, 'grown monstrous with much solitude', and is of the race of the nightmare. [. . .] He has many shapes – is now a horse, now an ass, now a bull, now a goat, now an eagle. Like all spirits, he is only half in the world of form. (See Yeats, ed. 'The Pooka', *Fairy and Folk Tales of the Irish Peasantry* (1888; New York: Dover, 1991), p. 95.)
42. Of the 1,700 books banned in Ireland between 1930 and 1945, approximately one-eighth were on the grounds that they 'advocated the unnatural prevention of conception' or the 'procurement of abortion' (see Adams, pp. 242–3). As Samuel Beckett drolly commented: 'France may commit race suicide, Erin will never. And should she be found at any time deficient in Cuchulains, at least it shall never be said they were contraceived' (see Beckett, 'Censorship in the Saorstat', in *Disjecta: Miscellaneous Writings and a Dramatic Fragment by Samuel Beckett*, ed. Ruby Cohn (London: John Calder, 1983), p. 88).
43. As Samuel Anderson notes, in the first draft typescript of *At Swim-Two-Birds*, 'O'Brien had originally called the process not "aestho-autogamy", as he does in the published novel, but "the immaculate conception" [. . .]. This would have been a shocking blasphemy in Virgin-venerating Ireland and O'Brien was wise to omit it, especially in light of the notorious Censorship of Publication Act' (see Anderson, 'Pink Paper and the Composition of Flann O'Brien's *At Swim-Two-Birds*', MA thesis, Louisiana State University, 2002, p. 25 <http://etd.lsu.edu/docs/available/etd-0830102-090058/unrestricted/Anderson_thesis.pdf> (accessed 21 January 2008).
44. Mercier, p. 77.
45. The author in question is actually the Augustan satirist John Dunton (1659–1733), whose journal *The Athenian Gazette* (1691–7) was republished in four volumes as *The Athenian Oracle* (London: Andrew Bell, 1703–10).
46. It seems clear that O'Brien is referring directly to censorship here. In a letter to Timothy O'Keeffe in September 1961 regarding the offensive strategies employed in *The Hard Life* he wrote: 'the mere name of Father Kurt Fahrt S.J., will justify the thunder clap'. See Cronin, p. 214.
47. By 1940, six Aldous Huxley novels were banned in Ireland (see Adams, p. 241). As J.J. Horgan noted in *The Round Table* in 1930:
    > The first result of the new Censorship of Publications Act has been the banning of seventeen books by the Minister of Justice on the advice of the Censorship Board. The only three of importance are Mr Aldous Huxley's *Point Counter Point*, Miss Radcliffe Hall's *Well of Loneliness* (which has already been banned in England), and Mr Bertrand Russell's *Marriage and Morals*. The remainder of the books censored are principally the works of Dr Marie Stopes and writers of her ilk on the subject of birth control. It is interesting to record that one bookseller who had six copies of Mr Huxley's book which he could not

sell, sold them all on the day the censorship of that volume was announced, and also received orders for twelve additional copies. (See J.J. Horgan, *The Round Table* 20.80, September 1930, p. 834, quoted Brown, pp. 75–6.)

48. Koestenbaum, p. 3.

49. ibid., p. 5.

50. As Andrea Bobotis notes, 'The *OED* cites the first use of *queer* to mean homosexuality in 1922; O'Brien presumably would have been well aware of this connotation' (see Bobotis, 'Queering Knowledge in Flann O'Brien's *The Third Policeman*', *Irish University Review* 32.2, Autumn/Winter 2002, p. 255).

51. During the mock trial-by-fiction, the following exchange takes place:

    Let the Good Fairy take the stand, boomed the Pooka. I've been in the stand all the time, said the voice, the grand stand. Where is this woman? asked Mr Justice Lamphall sharply. If she does not appear quickly I shall issue a bench warrant. This man has no body on him at all, explained the Pooka. (*AS2B*, p. 201)

    As Thomas F. Shea notes, in the MS version held at the Harry Ransom Humanities Research Center (University of Texas at Austin), Mr Justice Lamphall refers to the Good Fairy as a man (i.e. the line originally read: 'Where is this *man*?, asked Mr Justice Lamphall sharply' [my emphasis]), as does the Pooka (see Shea, *Flann O'Brien's Exorbitant Novels* (Lewisberg: Bucknell UP; London and Toronto: Associated University Presses, 1992), pp. 66–7). In these minor amendments to the manuscript, O'Brien seems keen to highlight the ambiguities surrounding the Fairy's gender and sexuality.

52. In a letter to A.M. Heath (3 October 1938), Brian O'Nolan noted how – following his publishers' suggestion – he had changed 'Angel' to 'Fairy': 'I think this change is desirable because "Fairy" corresponds more closely to "Pooka", removes any suggestion of the mock-religious and establishes the thing on a mythological plane.' O'Nolan also remarked that 'coarse words and references have been deleted or watered down and made innocuous' (O'Nolan to A.M. Heath, 'A Sheaf of Letters', ed. Robert Hogan and Gordon Henderson, *The Journal of Irish Literature* 3.1, January 1974, ed. Anne Clissmann and David Powell, special Flann O'Brien issue (California: Proscenium, 1974), p. 66).

53. Anon., 'Nest of Novelists', *Times Literary Supplement*, 18 March 1939, repr. Imhof, *Alive-Alive O!*, p. 43.

54. In a celebrated case, Kate O'Brien's novel *The Land of Spices* was banned in May 1941 on the basis of one, rather flowery sentence: 'she saw Etienne and her Father, in the embrace of love' (see Carlson, p. 11). Ironically, the Censorship Board may have been alerted to this sentence by a review in *The Bell* by the poet Austin Clarke – himself a victim of censorship – a month previously: 'It is an outward shock, purely pathological, and mentioned in a single, euphemistic sentence' (Clarke, quoted in Adams, p. 213).

55. Cronin, p. 62. Elsewhere Cronin wrote: 'The thought of sexual promiscuity was abhorrent to [Brian O'Nolan]; indeed, it may be, the very thought of sex itself' (see Anthony Cronin, *Dead as Doornails* (Oxford and New York: Oxford UP, 1986), p. 117).

56. This is a quite common response amongst male critics of O'Brien. Keith Donohue, for example, who largely agrees with my analysis of the misogynistic elements in O'Brien's work, seems to baulk at the question of homosexuality, though without saying why: 'Brian O'Nolan's ambivalent attitude toward women was primarily a cultural phenomenon and not, as Hopper later argues, a sign of latent homosexual urges' (see Donohue, *The Irish Anatomist: A Study of Flann O'Brien* (Bethesda, Maryland: Academica Press, 2002), p. 60).

57. As Eve Kosofsky Sedgwick notes, '"Homosocial" is a word occasionally used in history and the social sciences, where it describes social bonds between persons of the same sex'. For Sedgwick, though, the boundaries between the social and the sexual are always blurred, and so homosociality and homosexuality are intimately connected and can never be fully disentangled. (See Eve Kosofsky Sedgwick, *Between Men: English Literature and Male Homosocial Desire* (New York: Columbia UP, 1985), p. 1.)

58. Brian O'Nolan, letter to William Saroyan (14 February 1940), repr. 'Publisher's Note', *The Third Policeman* (1967; London: Grafton, 1986), p. 200.

59. Koestenbaum, p. 3.

60. See the entries for 'bicycle' (p. 23) and 'ride' (pp. 268–9) in Bernard Share, *Slanguage: A Dictionary of Slang and Colloquial English in Ireland*, new and expanded edn. (Dublin: Gill & Macmillan, 2005).

61. Bobotis, p. 248.

62. There is a fascination with trains throughout the O'Brien/na Gopaleen *oeuvre*, not least in the short story 'John Duffy's Brother' (1941), where the eponymous protagonist imagines that he has been turned into a train. For a good discussion of this see Thomas F. Shea, 'Flann O'Brien and John Keats: "John Duffy's Brother" and Train Allusions', *Éire-Ireland* 24.2, Summer 1989, pp. 109–20.

63. J.K. Huysmans, *Against Nature (À Rebours)*, trans. Robert Baldrick (1884; London: Penguin, 1959), p. 44.

64. ibid.

65. As Richard Ellmann notes, 'Wilde does not name the book but at his trial he conceded that it was, or almost, Huysmans's *À Rebours* [. . .]. To a correspondent he wrote that he had played a "fantastic variation" upon *À Rebours* and some day must write it down' (see Ellmann, *Oscar Wilde* (London: Vintage, 1988), p. 316). See also *The Picture of Dorian Gray and Other Writings* by Oscar Wilde, ed. with an introduction by Richard Ellmann (New York: Bantam Books, 1982).

66. Christopher Marlowe, *The Complete Plays*, ed. J. B. Steane (London: Penguin, 1978), p. 330.

67. Albert Camus, quoted in Jonathan Dollimore, *Radical Tragedy: Religion, Ideology and Power in the Drama of Shakespeare and his Contemporaries* (Sussex: Harvester Press, 1984), p. 109.

68. Brian O'Nolan, letter to Timothy O'Keeffe (27 November 1963), 'A Sheaf of Letters', in Clissmann and Powell, p. 83.

69. Anne Clissmann, *Flann O'Brien: A Critical Introduction to his Writings* (Dublin: Gill & Macmillan, 1975), p. 316.

70. ibid., p. 323.

71. ibid.

72. Penelope Shuttle and Peter Redgrove, *The Wise Wound: Menstruation and Everywoman* (London: Harper Collins, 1986), p. 20.

73. Brian O'Nolan, letter to Cecil Scott of Macmillan publishers (6 January 1964), 'A Sheaf of Letters', in Clissmann and Powell, p. 86.

74. Norris, p. 192.

75. ibid.

CHAPTER THREE: CHARACTER BUILDING

1. Vladimir Nabokov, *The Real Life of Sebastian Knight* (1941; London: Penguin, 1964), p. 150.

2. Brian McHale, *Post-Modernist Fiction* (New York: Routledge, 1991), p. 116.

3. Viktor Shklovsky, 'Art as Technique' (1917), repr. *Russian Formalist Criticism:*

Four Essays, trans. and ed. Lee T. Lemon and Marion J. Reis (Lincoln: University of Nebraska Press, 1965), p. 12.

4. Jonathan Culler, *Framing the Sign* (Oxford: Blackwell, 1988), p. xi.
5. Susan Stewart, *Nonsense: Aspects of Intertextuality in Folklore and Literature* (Baltimore: Johns Hopkins UP, 1979), p. 22.
6. Henri Bergson, 'Laughter', *Comedy*, ed. Wylie Sypher (1956; New York: Anchor, 1980), p. 121.
7. Martin Esslin, *The Theatre of the Absurd* (London: Eyre & Spottiswoode, 1966), p. 26.
8. ibid., p. 25.
9. McHale, p. 121.
10. Patricia Waugh, *Metafiction: The Theory and Practice of Self-Conscious Fiction* (London and New York: Methuen, 1984), p. 16.
11. McHale, p. 30.
12. Waugh, p. 119.
13. McHale, p. 18.
14. Brother Barnabas [Brian O'Nolan], 'Scenes in a Novel', *Comhthrom Féinne* 8.2, May 1934, repr. *The Journal of Irish Literature* 3.1, January 1974, ed. Anne Clissmann and David Powell, special Flann O'Brien issue (California: Proscenium, 1974), p. 18.
15. Roland Barthes, 'The Death of the Author' (1968), in *Modern Literary Theory: A Reader*, ed. Philip Rice and Patricia Waugh (London: Edward Arnold, 1992), p. 117.
16. ibid., p. 118.
17. Brian O'Nolan, letter to William Saroyan (14 February 1940), included in 'Publisher's Note', *The Third Policeman* (London: Grafton, 1986), p. 200.
18. McHale, p. 101.
19. Sigmund Freud, 'The Uncanny' (1919), in *The Standard Edition of the Complete Psychological Works of Sigmund Freud*, vol. 17, trans. and ed. James Strachey, with Anna Freud, Alix Strachey and Alan Tyson (London: Hogarth Press and the Institute of Psycho-analysis, 1960), pp. 220–1.
20. McHale, p. 112.
21. Flann O'Brien, 'Publisher's Note', *The Third Policeman*, p. 200.
22. Wim Tigges, 'Ireland in Wonderland: Flann O'Brien's *The Third Policeman* as a Nonsense Novel', in *The Clash of Ireland: Literary Contrasts and Connections*, ed. C.C. Barfoot and Theo D'haen (Amsterdam: Rodopi, 1989), p. 207.
23. McHale, p. 160.
24. Ferdinand de Saussure, from *Course in General Linguistics*, in Rice and Waugh, p. 8.
25. Sue Asbee, *Flann O'Brien* (Boston: Twayne, 1991), p. 23.
26. Waugh, p. 54.
27. Michel Foucault, *The Order of Things: An Archaeology of the Human Sciences* (New York: Pantheon, 1970), xviii.
28. J.C.C. Mays, 'Literalist of the Imagination', in *Myles: Portraits of Brian O'Nolan* ed. Timothy O'Keeffe (London: Martin Brian & O'Keeffe, 1973), p. 92.
29. Roland Barthes, 'Theory of the Text', in *Untying the Text: A Post-Structuralist Reader*, ed. Robert Young (London: Routledge, 1981), p. 39.
30. ibid.
31. Ninian Mellamphy, 'Aestho-autogamy and the Anarchy of Imagination: Flann O'Brien's Theory of Fiction', in *At Swim-Two-Birds*', in *Alive-Alive O!: Flann O'Brien's* At Swim-Two-Birds, ed. Rüdiger Imhof (Dublin: Wolfhound, 1985), p. 146.
32. See Mays, p. 92.

33. ibid.
34. Luigi Pirandello, *Six Characters in Search of an Author* (1921), trans. Frederick May (London: Heinemann, 1978), p. 53. For further discussion of this, see Michael McLoughlin, 'At Swim Six Characters or Two Birds in Search of an Author: Fiction, Metafiction and Reality in Pirandello and Flann O'Brien', *Yearbook of the Society for Pirandello Studies* 12, 1992, pp. 24–31.
35. Mays, p. 92.
36. J.K. Huysmans, *À Rebours* (*Against Nature*) (1884), trans. Robert Baldrick (1959; London: Penguin, 1959), p. 29.
37. Brendan McWilliams, 'Winds of a Different Hue', *The Irish Times*, 11 December 1992.
38. Laurence Sterne, *The Life and Opinions of Tristram Shandy, Gentleman* (1759–67; London: McDonald, 1975), p. 179.
39. Mays, p. 91.
40. Saussure, p. 9.
41. Edward Sapir, quoted in Terence Hawkes, *Structuralism and Semiotics* (London: Methuen, 1977), pp. 31–2.
42. Victor Fleming (dir.), *The Wizard of Oz* (USA: MGM, 1939), 101 mins. O'Brien may also have been aware of the original novel by L. Frank Baum, although I can find no direct correspondences between it and *The Third Policeman*; cf. L. Frank Baum, *The Wizard of Oz* (1900; London: Puffin, 1994).
43. *The Voyage of Maeldoon* (*Immram Maíle Dúin*) is a key intertext in both *The Third Policeman* and *An Béal Bocht*. For the standard translation of this tale, see T.W. Rolleston, *Myths and Legends of the Celtic Race* (1911; New York: Schocken, 1986), pp. 309–31.
44. James Joyce, *Ulysses* (1922; London: Bodley Head, 1960), p. 45.
45. Stewart, p. 100.
46. McHale, p. 31.
47. Stewart, p. 102.
48. Saussure, p. 8.
49. Michel Foucault, 'What is an Author?', in *Textual Strategies and Perspectives in Post-Structuralist Criticism*, ed. Josue Harari (Ithaca, New York: Cornell UP, 1979), p. 144.
50. Waugh, p. 32.
51. ibid., p. 43.
52. McHale, p. 75.
53. Lewis Carroll, *Through the Looking-Glass* (1871; London: Macmillan & Co., 1919), p. 94.
54. Sterne, p. 179.
55. Viktor Shklovsky, 'A Parodying Novel: Sterne's Tristram Shandy' (1929), in *Laurence Sterne: A Collection of Critical Essays*, ed. John Traugott (New Jersey: Prentice Hall, 1968), p. 88.
56. McHale, p. 123.
57. Stewart, p. 143.

CHAPTER FOUR: THIS IS NOT A PIPE

1. Laurence Sterne, *The Life and Opinions of Tristram Shandy, Gentleman* (1759–67; London: McDonald, 1975), p. 581.
2. Gerard Genette, *Narrative Discourse: An Essay in Method*, trans. Jane E. Lewin (Ithaca, New York: Cornell UP, 1980), p. 234.
3. Ninian Mellamphy, 'Aestho-autogamy and the Anarchy of the Imagination: Flann O'Brien's Theory of Fiction in *At Swim-Two-Birds*', in *Alive-Alive O!:*

Flann O'Brien's At Swim-Two-Birds, ed. Rüdiger Imhof (Dublin: Wolfhound, 1985), p. 148.

4. Brian McHale, *Post-Modernist Fiction* (New York: Routledge, 1991), p. 160.

5. Rüdiger Imhof, 'Two Meta-Novelists: Sternesque Elements in Novels by Flann O'Brien', in Imhof, *Alive-Alive O!*, p. 161.

6. ibid., p. 162.

7. Sterne, p. 521.

8. Susan Stewart, *Nonsense: Aspects of Intertextuality in Folklore and Literature* (Baltimore: Johns Hopkins UP, 1979), p. 190.

9. McHale, p. 156.

10. ibid., p. 157.

11. Stewart, p. 136.

12. Shari Benstock, 'At the Margins of Discourse: Footnotes in the Fictional Text', *PMLA* 98.2, 1983, p. 208.

13. Stewart, p. 193.

14. Bruno Bettelheim, *The Uses of Enchantment: The Meaning and Importance of Fairy Tales* (London: Penguin, 1976), p. 220.

15. Sterne, p. 452.

16. Viktor Shklovsky, 'A Parodying Novel: Sterne's Tristram Shandy' (1929), repr. *Laurence Sterne: A Collection of Critical Essays*, ed. John Traugott (New Jersey: Prentice Hall, 1968), p. 88.

17. Charles Kemnitz, 'Beyond the Zone of Middle Dimensions: A Relativistic Reading of *The Third Policeman*', *Irish University Review* 15.1, Spring 1985, p. 72.

18. Stewart, p. 185.

19. McHale, p. 182.

20. Sterne, p. 68.

21. ibid., p. 201.

22. Kemnitz, p. 72.

23. Stewart, p. 23.

24. McHale, p. 181.

25. Stewart, p. 74.

26. Benstock, p. 205.

27. Stewart, p. 74.

28. McHale, p. 191.

29. Jonathan Swift, *Gulliver's Travels* (1726; London: Munster Classics, 1968), pp. 249–50.

30. ibid., p. 259.

31. The name 'Le Fournier' may be a nod to Pierre Simon Fournier (1712–68), a French typographer, and/or Alain-Fournier, the pseudonym of Henri Alban-Fournier (1886–1914), author of the French novel *Le Grand Meaulnes* (1913).

32. Benstock, p. 102.

33. *Le roi s'amuse* was the title of a play written by Victor Hugo in 1832 which became the subject of a celebrated censorship case in France.

34. *Non-possum* is possibly *non possumus*, meaning 'a statement of inability to act'. *Noli-me-tangere*, meaning 'don't touch me' is the Latin version of the words spoken by Jesus to Mary Magdalene after his resurrection (John 20:17).

35. Stewart, p. 166.

36. Jean-Luc Godard (dir.), *Le Petit Soldat* (France: Les Productions Georges de Beauregard/Société Nouvelle de Cinématographie, 1960), 83 mins.

37. Hugh Kenner, *Flaubert, Joyce and Beckett: The Stoic Comedians* (London: W.H. Allen, 1964), pp. 39–40.

CHAPTER FIVE: PARADISE LOST, PARADISE REGAINED

1. Mikhail Bakhtin, 'Discourse in the Novel', in *The Dialogic Imagination: Four Essays*, ed. and trans. by Michael Holquist and Caryl Emerson (Austin: University of Texas Press, 1981), p. 259.
2. ibid., p. 276.
3. ibid., p. 279.
4. Susan Stewart, *Nonsense: Aspects of Intertextuality in Folklore and Literature* (Baltimore: Johns Hopkins UP, 1979), p. 17.
5. Brian McHale, *Post-Modernist Fiction* (New York: Routledge, 1991), p. 166.
6. ibid., p. 167.
7. Brian O'Nolan, letter to Longmans Green Ltd (1 May 1939), quoted in Anthony Cronin, *No Laughing Matter: The Life and Times of Flann O'Brien* (London: Grafton, 1989), p. 97.
8. Patricia Waugh, *Metafiction: The Theory and Practice of Self-Conscious Fiction* (London and New York: Methuen, 1984), p. 11.
9. Vladimir Nabokov, *The Real Life of Sebastian Knight* (1941; London: Penguin, 1964), p. 79.
10. Waugh, p. 7.
11. Sue Asbee, *Flann O'Brien* (Boston: Twayne, 1991), p. 57.
12. Stewart, p. 94.
13. McHale, p. 101.
14. Ian Watt, *Conrad in the Nineteenth Century* (London: Chatto & Windus, 1980), p. 175.
15. Stewart, p. 20.
16. Viktor Shklovsky, 'A Parodying Novel: Sterne's Tristram Shandy', in *Laurence Sterne: A Collection of Critical Essays*, ed. John Traugott (New Jersey: Prentice Hall, 1968), p. 68.
17. Laurence Sterne, *The Life and Opinions of Tristram Shandy, Gentleman* (1759–67; London: McDonald, 1975), p. 101.
18. J.C.C. Mays, 'Literalist of the Imagination', in *Myles: Portraits of Brian O'Nolan*, ed. Timothy O'Keeffe (London: Martin Brian & O'Keeffe, 1973), p. 91.
19. Rüdiger Imhof, 'Postmodernist Policeman' [review of *Flann O'Brien: A Portrait of the Artist as a Young Post-modernist* by Keith Hopper], *The Irish Times*, 1 July 1995. In more recent correspondence with the present author (8 December 2006), Prof. Imhof elaborated further:

    'Selby' may indeed be derived from the Old High German pronoun 'selb', which seems to have the same root as the English 'self' (the exact etymological determination is unclear). The substantive of the pronoun is 'Selbst', which corresponds to the English 'self'. So, J.C.C. Mays may have been partly right, after all.

    Where Mays was wrong is to suggest that 'de Selby' is a variation of 'der Selbe'. As far as 'der Selbe' is concerned, my critical remark still stands: it can only mean 'the same person'. It would seem that either Mays or Flann, or indeed both of them made a mistake, namely this: that in order to derive 'the self' from a German expression to do with 'selb', 'Selbe' or 'Selbst', this expression would have to be 'das Selbst' and not 'der Selbe'. If Flann meant us to see the connection between 'de Selby' and 'the self', he got his German derivation in a twist.

    I am grateful to Prof. Imhof for his gracious and erudite scholarship (and apologise for co-opting him into such a de Selbian-style commentary).
20. The concept of the *doppelgänger* is central to a number of important nineteenth-century Gothic fictions – e.g. Poe's 'William Wilson' (1839), Dostoevsky's *The*

Double (1846), Stevenson's *Strange Case of Dr Jekyll and Mr Hyde* (1886) – and the genre has inspired a number of key modernist texts as well, e.g. Conrad's novellas *Heart of Darkness* (1902) and *The Secret Sharer* (1909). Within the realm of post-modernist fiction, the *doppelgänger* features in several works by Vladimir Nabokov, including *The Real Life of Sebastian Knight* (1941), *Lolita* (1955) and *Pale Fire* (1962). More recently, and within the Irish post-modernist tradition, it has been a mainstay in the work of John Banville. Flann O'Brien also has a variation of this 'evil double' scenario in his 1954 short story, 'Two in One', later dramatised for television as *The Dead Spit of Kelly* (1962).

21. For a more materialist take on the origin of de Selby's name, see Conan Kennedy's speculative essay *Looking for De Selby* (Killala, Co. Mayo: Morrigan, 1998), 31 pp.

22. See Roman Jakobson, 'Two Aspects of Language and Two Types of Aphasic Disturbances' (1956), *Language and Literature* (Cambridge, Mass.: Harvard UP, 1987), pp. 95–114.

23. Waugh, p. 38.

24. Wim Tigges, 'Ireland in Wonderland: Flann O'Brien's *The Third Policeman* as a Nonsense Novel', in *The Clash of Ireland: Literary Contrasts and Connections*, ed. C.C. Barfoot and Theo D'haen (Amsterdam: Rodopi, 1989), p. 201.

25. Denis Donoghue, *Jonathan Swift: A Critical Introduction* (Cambridge: Cambridge UP, 1969), p. 139.

26. Christopher Marlowe, *The Complete Plays*, ed. J.B. Steane (London: Penguin, 1978), p. 325.

27. Waugh, p. 88.

28. James Joyce, *Ulysses* (1922; London: Bodley Head, 1960), p. 45.

29. Stewart, pp. 27–8.

30. Sterne, p. 363.

31. ibid., p. 206.

32. J.M. Synge, *The Playboy of the Western World* (1907; London: Methuen, 1961), p. 52.

33. Vivian Mercier, *The Irish Comic Tradition* (London: Oxford UP, 1969), p. 2.

34. Waugh, p. 69.

35. Stewart, p. 200.

36. ibid., p. 199.

37. Rüdiger Imhof, 'Two Meta-Novelists: Sternesque Elements in Novels by Flann O'Brien', in *Alive-Alive O!: Flann O'Brien's* At Swim-Two-Birds ed. Imhof (Dublin: Wolfhound, 1985), p. 178.

38. McHale, p. 75.

39. Brian O'Nolan, letter to Longmans Green Ltd (1 May 1939), quoted Cronin, p. 97.

CHAPTER SIX: RELATIVE WORLDS

1. Woody Allen, 'Conversations with Helmholtz', in *Getting Even* (London: W.H. Allen, 1980), p. 121.

2. Barbara Herrnstein Smith, *On the Margins of Discourse: The Relation of Literature to Language* (Chicago and London: University of Chicago Press, 1978), p. 144.

3. Jeremy Hawthorn, *A Concise Glossary of Contemporary Literary Theory* (London: Edward Arnold, 1992), p. 125.

4. Michael Worton and Judith Still (eds.), *Intertextuality: Theories and Practice* (Manchester: Manchester UP, 1991), p. 1.

5. Wim Tigges, 'Ireland in Wonderland: Flann O'Brien's *The Third Policeman* as a Nonsense Novel', in *The Clash of Ireland: Literary Contrasts and*

Connections, ed. C.C. Barfoot and Theo D'haen (Amsterdam, Rodopi, 1989), p. 203.

6. Mary A. O'Toole, 'The Theory of Serialism in *The Third Policeman*', *Irish University Review* 18.2, Autumn 1988, p. 225.

7. Brian McHale, *Post-Modernist Fiction* (New York: Routledge, 1991), p. 172.

8. Roman Jakobson, 'The Dominant' (1935), repr. *Readings in Russian Poetics: Formalist and Structuralist Views*, ed. Ladislav Matejka and Krystyna Pomorska (Ann Arbor, Michigan: University of Michigan Press, 1978), p. 82.

9. McHale, p. 16.

10. See John Banville, *The Book of Evidence* (London: Secker & Warburg, 1989) and Patrick McCabe, *The Butcher Boy* (London: Picador, 1993).

11. McHale, p. 60.

12. Charles Kemnitz, 'Beyond the Zone of Middle Dimensions: A Relativistic Reading of *The Third Policeman*', *Irish University Review* 15.1, Spring 1985, pp. 56–72.

13. Myles na Gopaleen, *The Hair of the Dogma: A Further Selection from 'Cruiskeen Lawn'*, ed. Kevin O'Nolan (London Grafton, 1987), pp. 140–1.

14. Kemnitz, p. 56.

15. ibid., p. 62.

16. ibid., p. 57.

17. Tigges, p. 204.

18. Kemnitz, letter from Darcy O'Brien (20 May 1983), p. 57, fn.

19. ibid., p. 60.

20. ibid.

21. J.W. Dunne, *An Experiment with Time* (1927; London: Faber, 1934), pp. 170–1.

22. See Susan Stewart, *Nonsense: Aspects of Intertextuality in Folklore and Literature* (Baltimore: Johns Hopkins UP, 1979), pp. 147–68.

23. Albert Einstein, quoted in Joseph Schwartz and Michael McGuinness, *Einstein for Beginners* (London: Unwin, 1986), p. 108.

24. Kemnitz, p. 61.

25. ibid.

26. 'The Voyage of Maeldoon', in T.W. Rolleston, *Myths and Legends of the Celtic Race* (1911; New York: Schocken, 1986), pp. 309–31.

27. Kemnitz, p. 69.

28. ibid.

29. O'Toole, p. 216.

30. Kemnitz, p. 69.

31. ibid., p. 62–3.

32. ibid., p. 64.

33. Paul Edwards, ed. *The Encyclopaedia of Philosophy*, vol. I (London: Collier-Macmillan, 1967), p. 117.

34. ibid., p. 118.

35. Fritjof Capra, *The Tao of Physics: An Exploration of the Parallels between Modern Physics and Eastern Mysticism* (1975; London: Fontana, 1983), p. 24.

36. F.C. Copleston, *A History of Philosophy*, vol. I, Greece and Rome (1946; London: Burns and Oates, 1966), p. 73.

37. ibid., p. 74.

38. See John Garvin, 'Sweetscented Manuscripts', *Myles: Portraits of Brian O'Nolan*, ed. Timothy O'Keeffe (London: Martin Brian & O'Keeffe, 1973), p. 55.

39. Aldous Huxley, *Point Counter Point* (1928; London: Granada, 1978), p. 410.

40. Huxley, pp. 302–3.

41. ibid., pp. 295.

42. Brian O'Nolan, letter to Timothy O'Keeffe (15 November 1963), quoted in *A Flann O'Brien Reader*, ed. Stephen Jones (New York: Viking Press, 1978), p. 376.
43. Roland Barthes, 'The Brain of Einstein', in *Mythologies*, trans. Annette Lavers (London: Jonathan Cape, 1972), pp. 68–9.
44. Kemnitz, p. 70.
45. ibid., p. 71.
46. ibid.
47. Anthony Cronin, *No Laughing Matter: The Life and Times of Flann O'Brien* (London: Grafton, 1989), p. 103.
48. ibid.
49. Eugene Jolas, 'My Friend James Joyce', *Partisan Review* 8.2, March-April 1941, p. 91.
50. Myles na Gopaleen, 'Cruiskeen Lawn' (December 1957), quoted Jones, p. 373.
51. Brian O'Nolan, letter to Timothy O'Keeffe (12 September 1962), in 'A Sheaf of Letters', ed. Robert Hogan and Gordon Henderson, in *The Journal of Irish Literature* 3.1, January 1974, ed. Anne Clissmann and David Powell, special Flann O'Brien issue (California: Proscenium, 1974), p. 80.
52. Dunne, *An Experiment with Time*, p. vii.
53. ibid., p. 207.
54. ibid., p. 34.
55. ibid., p. 50.
56. ibid., p. 59.
57. J.W. Dunne, *Nothing Dies* (London: Faber, 1940), p. 70.
58. Jorges Luis Borges, 'Time and J.W. Dunne' (1940), in *The Total Library: Non-Fiction: 1922–1986*, ed. Eliot Weinberger, trans. Esther Allen, Suzanne Jill Levine, and Eliot Weinberger (London: Allen Lane/Penguin Press, 1999), p. 219.
59. Dunne, *An Experiment with Time*, p. 22.
60. ibid., p. 175.
61. Dunne, *Nothing Dies*, p. 65.
62. Dunne, *An Experiment with Time*, quoted in O'Toole, p. 223.
63. O'Toole, p. 223.
64. Dunne, *Nothing Dies*, p. 76.
65. Dunne, *An Experiment with Time*, p. 166.
66. ibid., p. 109.
67. ibid., p. 196.
68. Alf MacLochlainn, 'De Selby Discovered', *Alive-Alive O!: Flann O'Brien's* At Swim-Two-Birds, ed. Rüdiger Imhof (Dublin: Wolfhound, 1985), p. 190.
69. Dunne, *An Experiment with Time*, p. 94.
70. ibid., p. 95.
71. ibid., p. 12.
72. O'Toole, p. 225.
73. Dunne, *An Experiment with Time*, p. 160.
74. J.K. Huysmans, *Against Nature (À Rebours)*, trans. Robert Baldrick (1884; London: Penguin, 1959), p. 33; Huxley, pp. 302–3.
75. Anne Clissmann, *Flann O'Brien: A Critical Introduction to his Writings* (Dublin: Gill & Macmillan, 1975), p. 159.
76. Dunne, *Nothing Dies*, p. 32.
77. Sue Asbee, *Flann O'Brien* (Boston: Twayne, 1991), p. 66.
78. Tigges, p. 200.
79. Stewart, p. 94.
80. ibid., p. 112.

81. ibid., p. 146.
82. ibid., p. 171.
83. Lewis Carroll, quoted ibid., p. 138.
84. ibid., p. 118.
85. Copleston, p. 59.
86. Huysmans, p. 36.
87. Tigges, p. 195.
88. Broder Christiansen, quoted in Peter Steiner, *Russian Poetics: A Metapoetics* (London and Ithaca, New York: Cornell UP, 1984), p. 104.
89. Patricia Waugh, *Metafiction: The Theory and Practice of Self-Conscious Fiction* (London: Methuen, 1984), p. 79.
90. ibid., p. 82–3.
91. Cronin, p. 198.
92. Brian O'Nolan, letter to Stephen Ashe (7 October 1955), quoted in Cronin, p. 199.
93. Brian O'Nolan, letter to Andy Gillett (1 May 1939), quoted in Asbee, p. 51.
94. J.A. Cuddon, *A Dictionary of Literary Terms*, rev. edn. (Harmondsworth: Penguin, 1979), p. 182.
95. Viktor Shklovsky, 'The Mystery Novel: Dickens's *Little Dorrit*' (1925), in Matejka and Pomorska, p. 221.
96. ibid., p. 222.
97. Waugh, p. 82.
98. Christopher Marlowe, *Doctor Faustus,* in *The Complete Plays*, ed. J.B. Steane (London: Penguin, 1978), p. 336.
99. Sighle Kennedy, 'The Devil and Holy Water: Samuel Beckett's *Murphy* and Flann O'Brien's *At Swim-Two-Birds*', in *Modern Irish Literature: Essays in Honor of William York Tindall*, ed. Raymond J. Porter and James D. Brophy (New York: Iona College Press, 1972), p. 252.
100. Samuel Beckett, *Watt* (1944; London: Picador, 1988), p. 151.
101. Rubin Rabinovitz, '*Watt* from Descartes to Schopenhauer', in Porter and Brophy, *Modern Irish Literature*, p. 265.
102. McHale, p. 172.
103. Rabinovitz, p. 266.

Bibliography

Works by Flann O'Brien/Myles na [gCopaleen] Gopaleen/Brian [O']Nolan

O'Brien, Flann. *At Swim-Two-Birds*. 1939. London: Penguin, 1980.

— *An Béal Bocht*. 1941. Trans. Patrick C. Power. *The Poor Mouth* (1973). London: Grafton, 1986.

— *The Dalkey Archive*. 1964. London: Picador, 1976.

— *The Hard Life*. 1961. London: Grafton, 1986.

— *Rhapsody in Stephen's Green: The Insect Play*. Ed. Robert Tracy. Dublin: Lilliput Press, 1994.

— *Stories and Plays*. 1973. Ed. Claud Cockburn. London: Grafton, 1986.

— *The Third Policeman*. 1967. London: Grafton, 1986.

— 'The Dance Halls'. *The Bell* 1.5, February 1941: 44–52.

— 'Going to the Dogs'. *The Bell* 1.1, October 1940: 19–24.

— 'John Duffy's Brother' [short story]. *Story* 19.90, July–August, 1941: 65–8.

— 'The Trade in Dublin'. *The Bell* 1.2, November 1940: 6–15.

na gCopaleen, Myles. *Flann O'Brien at War*. Ed. John Wyse Jackson. London: Duckworth, 1999.

na Gopaleen, Myles. *The Best of Myles*. 1968. Ed. Kevin O'Nolan. London: Grafton, 1989.

— *The Various Lives of Keats and Chapman and The Brother*. 1976. Ed. Benedict Kiely. London: Grafton, 1988.

— *Myles Away from Dublin*. 1985. Ed. Martin Green. London: Grafton, 1987.

— *The Hair of the Dogma: A Further Selection from 'Cruiskeen Lawn'*. 1977. Ed. Kevin O'Nolan. London: Grafton, 1987.

— *Myles Before Myles: A Selection of the Earlier Writings of Brian O'Nolan*. Ed. John Wyse Jackson. London: Grafton, 1983.

— 'Cruiskeen Lawn'. *The Irish Times*. 4 October 1940–1 April 1966.

— 'Baudelaire and Kavanagh'. *Envoy* 3.12, November 1952: 78–81.

— 'De Me'. *New Ireland*, March 1964: 41–42.

— 'Two in One' [short story]. *The Bell* 19.8, July 1954: 30–4.

Nolan, Brian. 'A Bash in the Tunnel: An Editorial Note'. *Envoy* 5.17, April 1951, James Joyce special issue: 5–11.

— 'The Martyr's Crown' [short story]. *Envoy* 1.3, February 1950: 57–62.

Barnabas, Brother [Brian O'Nolan]. 'Scenes in a Novel'. *Comhthrom Féinne* 8.2, May 1934. *The Journal of Irish Literature* 3.1, January 1974. Ed. Anne Clissmann and David Powell. Special Flann O'Brien issue. California: Proscenium, 1974: 14–18.

O'Nolan, Brian. 'A Sheaf of Letters'. Ed. Robert Hogan and Gordon Henderson. Repr. Clissmann and Powell: 65–103.

Works about Flann O'Brien

Anderson, Samuel. 'Pink Paper and the Composition of Flann O'Brien's *At Swim-Two-Birds*'. MA Thesis. Louisiana State University, 2002. Accessed 21 January 2008. <http://etd.lsu.edu/docs/available/etd-0830102-090058/unrestricted/Anderson_thesis.pdf>.

Anon. 'Nest of Novelists'. *Times Literary Supplement*, 18 March 1939: 161. Repr. *Alive-Alive O!: Flann O'Brien's* At Swim-Two-Birds. Ed. Rüdiger Imhof. Dublin: Wolfhound, 1985. 42–43.

Anspaugh, Kelly. 'Agonizing with Joyce: *At Swim-Two-Birds* as Thanatography'. Repr. *A Casebook on Flann O'Brien's* At Swim-Two-Birds (2004). Ed. Thomas C. Foster. Accessed 21 January 2008. <http://www.dalkeyarchive.com/casebooks/anspaugh>.

— 'Flann O'Brien: Postmodern Judas'. *Notes on Modern Irish Literature* 4, 1992: 11–16.

apRoberts, Ruth. '*At Swim-Two-Birds* as Self-evident Sham'. *Éire-Ireland* 6.2, Summer 1971: 76–97.

Asbee, Sue. *Flann O'Brien*. Twayne's English Authors series. Boston: Twayne, 1991.

Benstock, Bernard. 'The Three Faces of Brian O'Nolan'. *Éire-Ireland* 3.3, Autumn 1968: 51–65.

Bobotis, Andrea. 'Queering Knowledge in Flann O'Brien's *The Third Policeman*'. *Irish University Review* 32.2, Autumn/Winter 2002: 242–58.

Bohman-Kalaja, Kimberly. *Reading Games: An Aesthetics of Play in Flann O'Brien, Samuel Beckett, and Georges Perec*. Illinois: Dalkey Archive Press, 2007.

Booker, M. Keith. 'The Bicycle and Descartes: Epistemology in the Fiction of Beckett and O'Brien'. *Éire-Ireland* 26.1, Spring 1991: 76–94.

— *Flann O'Brien: Bakhtin and Menippean Satire*. Syracuse, New York: Syracuse UP, 1995.

— 'Postmodern and/or Postcolonial?: The Politics of *At Swim-Two-Birds*'. Repr. *A Casebook on Flann O'Brien's* At Swim-Two-Birds (2004). Ed. Thomas C. Foster. Accessed 21 January 2008. <http://www.dalkeyarchive.com/casebooks/booker>.

— 'Science, Philosophy, and *The Third Policeman*: Flann O'Brien and the Epistemology of Futility'. *South Atlantic Review* 56. 4, November 1991: 37–56.

Borges, Jorges Luis. 'When Fiction Lives in Fiction' (1939) [review of *At Swim-Two-Birds*]. *The Total Library: Non-Fiction: 1922–1986*. Ed. Eliot Weinberger. Trans. Esther Allen, Suzanne Jill Levine, and Eliot Weinberger. London: Allen Lane/Penguin Press, 1999. 160–62.

Breuer, Rolf. 'Flann O'Brien and Samuel Beckett'. *Irish University Review* 37.2, Autumn/Winter 2007: 340–51.

Brooker, Joseph. *Flann O'Brien*. Writers and their Work series. Tavistock: Northcote House, 2005.

Brown, Terence. 'Two Post-modern Novelists: Samuel Beckett and Flann O'Brien'. *The Cambridge Companion to the Irish Novel*. Ed. John Wilson Foster. Cambridge: Cambridge UP, 2006. 205–22.

Browne, Joseph. 'Flann O'Brien: *Post* Joyce or *Propter* Joyce?'. *Éire-Ireland* 19.4, Winter 1984: 148–57.

Burgess, Anthony. 'Flann O'Brien: A Note'. *Études Irlandaises* 7, December 1982: 83–86.

Chace, William M. 'Joyce and Flann O'Brien'. *Éire-Ireland* 22.4, Winter 1987: 140–52.

Clissmann, Anne, and David Powell. Eds. *The Journal of Irish Literature* 3.1, January 1974. Special Flann O'Brien issue. California: Proscenium, 1974.

Clissmann, Anne. 'Brian alias Myles alias Flann'. *The Word*, September 1977: 11–13.

— *Flann O'Brien: A Critical Introduction to his Writings*. Dublin: Gill & Macmillan, 1975.

Clune (Clissmann), Anne, and Tess Hurson. Eds. *Conjuring Complexities: Essays on Flann O'Brien*. Belfast: Institute of Irish Studies, 1997.

Cohen, David. 'An Atomy of the Novel: Flann O'Brien's *At Swim-Two-Birds*'. *Twentieth Century Literature* 39.2, Summer 1993: 208–29.

— 'James Joyce and the Decline of Flann O'Brien'. *Éire-Ireland* 22.2, Summer 1987: 153–60.

Conte, Joseph M. 'Metaphor and Metonymy in Flann O'Brien's *At Swim-Two-Birds*'. *Review of Contemporary Fiction* 5.1, 1985: 128–34.

Cooper, Stanford Lee. 'Eire's Columnist: An Interview with Brian O'Nolan'. *Time Magazine*, 23 August 1943: 90–92.

Costello, Peter, and Peter van de Kamp. *Flann O'Brien: An Illustrated Biography*. London: Bloomsbury, 1987.

Costello, Peter. 'Mylesian Mysteries'. *Sunday Independent*, 6 December 1987.

Cronin, Anthony. Chapter 6 [on Brian O'Nolan]. *Dead as Doornails*. Oxford and New York: Oxford UP, 1986.

— *No Laughing Matter: The Life and Times of Flann O'Brien*. London: Grafton, 1989.

Curran, Steve. '"No, This is not from *The Bell*": Brian O'Nolan's 1943 *Cruiskeen Lawn* Anthology'. *Éire-Ireland* 32.2–3, Summer–Autumn 1997: 79–92.

Davison, Neil R. '"We are not a doctor for the body": Catholicism, the

Female Grotesque, and Flann O'Brien's *The Hard Life'. Literature and Psychology: A Journal of Psychoanalytic and Cultural Criticism* 45.4, 1999: 31–57.

Devlin, Joseph. 'The Politics of Comedy in *At Swim-Two-Birds'. Éire-Ireland* 27.4, Winter 1992: 91–105.

Dewsnap, Terence. 'Flann O'Brien and the Politics of Buffoonery'. *Canadian Journal of Irish Studies* 19.1, July 1993: 22–36.

Doherty, Francis. 'Flann O'Brien's Existentialist Hell'. *Canadian Journal of Irish Studies* 15.2, December 1989: 51–67.

Donohue, Keith. *The Irish Anatomist: A Study of Flann O'Brien*. Bethesda, Maryland: Academica Press, 2002.

Donovan, Stewart. 'Finn in Shabby Digs: Myth and the Reductionist Process in *At Swim-Two-Birds. Antigonish Review* 89, 1992: 147–53.

Downum, Denell. 'Citation and Spectrality in Flann O'Brien's *At Swim-Two-Birds'. Irish University Review* 36.2, Autumn/Winter 2006: 304–20.

Dotterer, Ronald. L. 'Flann O'Brien, James Joyce, and *The Dalkey Archive'. New Hibernia Review* 8.2, Summer 2004: 54–63.

Dukes, Gerry. 'Myles the Post-modernist' [review of *Flann O'Brien: A Portrait of the Artist as a Young Post-modernist* by Keith Hopper]. *Irish Independent*, 9 September 1995.

Epp, Michael Henry. 'Saving *Cruiskeen Lawn*: Satirical Parody in the Novels and Journalism of Flann O'Brien (Myles na gCopaleen)'. MA Thesis. McGill University, Toronto, 1999. Accessed 21 January 2008. <http://www.collectionscanada.ca/obj/s4/f2/dsk1/tape9/PQDD_0023/MQ50512.pdf>.

Esty, Joshua. 'Flann O'Brien's *At Swim-Two Birds* and the Post-Post Debate'. *ARIEL: A Review of International English Literature* 26.4, October 1995: 23–46.

Evans, Eibhlin. '"A Lacuna in the Palimpsest": A Reading of Flann O'Brien's *At Swim-Two Birds'. Critical Survey* 15.1, January 2003: 91–107.

Fackler, Herbert V. 'Flann O'Brien's *The Third Policeman*: Banjaxing Natural Order'. *The South Central Bulletin* 38.4, Winter, 1978: 142–45.

Foster, Thomas C. Ed. *A Casebook on Flann O'Brien's* At Swim-Two-Birds. Illinois: Dalkey Archive Press, 2004. Accessed 21 January 2008. <http://www.dalkeyarchive.com/casebooks/introduction_swim>.

Gallagher, Monique. 'Flann O'Brien: Myles from Dublin'. *The Princess Grace Library Lectures*, 7. Gerrards Cross: Colin Smythe, 1991. 7–24.

— 'Frontier Instability in Flann O'Brien's *At Swim-Two-Birds'. A Casebook on Flann O'Brien's* At Swim-Two-Birds (2004). Ed. Thomas C. Foster. <http://www.dalkeyarchive.com/casebooks/gallagher>.

— 'Reflecting Mirrors in Flann O'Brien's *At Swim-Two-Birds'. Journal of Narrative Technique* 22.2, Spring 1992: 128–35.

Greene, Graham. 'A Book in a Thousand'. Extract from the original Longmans jacket of *At Swim-Two-Birds.Alive-Alive O!: Flann O'Brien's* At Swim-Two-Birds. Ed. Rüdiger Imhof. Dublin: Wolfhound, 1985. 41–42.

Hassett, Joseph M. 'Flann O'Brien and the Idea of the City'. *The Irish Writer and the City*. Ed. Maurice Harmon. New Jersey: Barnes and Noble; Gerrards Cross: Colin Smythe, 1984. 115–24.

Henry, P. L. 'The Structure of Flann O'Brien's *At Swim-Two-Birds*'. *Irish University Review* 20.1, 1990: 35–40.

Hogan, Thomas. 'Myles na gCopaleen'. *The Bell* 13.2, November 1946: 129–40.

Hopper, Keith. 'The Dismemberment of Orpheus: Flann O'Brien and the Censorship Code'. *Barcelona English Language and Literature Studies* (Proceedings of 1999 IASIL Conference), no. 11, 2000: 119–131. Revised and expanded version in *Literature and Ethics: Questions of Responsibility in Literary Studies*. Eds. Daniel Jernigan, Neil Murphy, Brendan Quigley and Tamara Wagner. New York: Cambria Press, 2009.

Hunt, Roy L. 'Hell Goes Round and Round: Flann O'Brien'. *Canadian Journal of Irish Studies* 14.2, January 1989: 60–73.

Hurson, Tess. 'Criticism as Fiction: Fiction as Criticism: Flann O'Brien's *At Swim-Two-Birds*'. Seminar Paper, International Association for the Study of Anglo-Irish Literature, Triennial Conference. Belfast, 1985. 1–14.

Imhof, Rüdiger. Ed. *Alive-Alive O!: Flann O'Brien's* At Swim-Two-Birds. Dublin: Wolfhound, 1985.

— 'Chinese Box: Flann O'Brien in the Metafiction of Alasdair Gray, John Fowles and Robert Coover'. *Éire-Ireland* 25.1, Spring 1990: 64–79.

— 'Cronin's Miles Inglorious' [review of *No Laughing Matter: The Life and Times of Flann O'Brien* by Anthony Cronin]. *The Irish Times*, 11 November 1989.

— 'Flann O'Brien: A Checklist'. *Etudes Irlandaises* 4, 1979: 125–48.

— 'Postmodernist Policeman' [review of *Flann O'Brien: A Portrait of the Artist as a Young Post-modernist* by Keith Hopper]. *The Irish Times*, 1 July 1995.

— 'Two Meta-Novelists: Sternesque Elements in the Novels of Flann O'Brien'. *Alive-Alive O!: Flann O'Brien's* At Swim-Two-Birds. Ed. Rüdiger Imhof. Dublin: Wolfhound, 1985. 160–90.

Ingersoll, Earl G. 'Irish Jokes: A Lacanian Reading of Short Stories by James Joyce, Flann O'Brien, and Bryan MacMahon'. *Studies in Short Fiction* 27.2, Spring 1990: 237–45.

Jacek, Eva. 'The Conundrum of Clichés: Flann O'Brien's "The Catechism of Cliché" and Jonathan Swift's *A Complete Collection of Genteel and Ingenious Conversation (Polite Conversation)*'. *Canadian Journal of Irish Studies* 25.1–2, July–December 1999: 497–509.

Jacquin, Danielle. 'Never Apply Your Front Breaks First, or Flann O'Brien and the Theme of the Fall'. *The Irish Novel in Our Time*. Ed. Patrick Rafroidi and Maurice Harmon. Lille: Publications de l'Université de Lille III, 1976. 187–97.

Janik, Del Ivan. 'Flann O'Brien: The Novelist as Critic'. *Éire-Ireland* 4.4, Winter 1969: 64–72.

Jones, Stephen. Ed. *A Flann O'Brien Reader*. New York: Viking Press, 1978.

Johnston, Denis. 'Myles na Gopaleen'. *Myth and Reality in Irish Literature*. Ed. Joseph Ronsley. Ontario: Wilfred Laurier UP, 1977. 297–304.

Kemnitz, Charles. 'Beyond the Zone of Middle Dimensions: A Relativistic Reading of *The Third Policeman*'. *Irish University Review* 15.1, Spring 1985: 56–72.

Kennedy, Conan. *Looking for De Selby*. Killala, Mayo: Morrigan, 1998. 31 pp.

Kennedy, Maurice. '*At Swim-Two-Birds*'. *The Irish Times*, 5 November 1962.

Kennedy, Sighle. 'The Devil and Holy Water: Samuel Beckett's *Murphy* and Flann O'Brien's *At Swim-Two-Birds*'. *Modern Irish Literature*. Eds. Raymond A. Porter and James D. Brophy. New York: Iona College Press, 1972. 251–60.

Kenner, Hugh. 'The Mocker'. *A Colder Eye: The Modern Irish Writers*. New York: Alfred A. Knopf, 1983. 253–61.

Kiberd, Declan. 'Flann O'Brien, Myles, and The Poor Mouth'. *Inventing Ireland: The Literature of the Modern Nation*. London: Vintage, 1996. 497–512.

Kiely, Benedict. 'Bells are Ringing for a Work of High Genius'. *Irish Press*, 11 November 1961.

— 'Fun After Death'. *New York Times Book Review*, 12 November 1967.

— 'Rare Roads to Hell'. *The Irish Times*, 2 September 1967.

Kilroy, Thomas. 'Tellers of Tales'. *Times Literary Supplement*, 17 March 1972: 301–02.

— 'The Year in Review'. *Irish University Review* 5.1, Spring 1968: 112–17.

Lanters, José. 'Fiction within Fiction: The Role of the Author in Flann O'Brien's *At Swim-Two-Birds* and *The Third Policeman*'. *Dutch Quarterly Review of Anglo-American Letters* 13, 1983: 267–81.

— 'Flann O'Brien (1911–1966)'. *Unauthorised Versions: Irish Menippean Satire, 1919–1952*. Washington D.C.: Catholic University of America Press, 2000. 173–234.

— '"Still Life" Versus Real Life: The English Writings of Brian O'Nolan'. *Explorations in the Field of Nonsense*. Ed. Wim Tigges. Amsterdam: Rodopi, 1987. 161–81.

Lee, L.L. 'The Dublin Cowboys of Flann O'Brien'. *Western American Literature* 4.3, Fall 1969: 219–25.

Looby, Robert. 'Flann O'Brien: A Postmodernist When It Was Neither Profitable Nor Popular'. *The Scriptorium: Flann O'Brien*, 24 July 2004). Accessed 21 January 2008. <http://www.themodernword.com/scriptorium/obrien.html>.

Mahon, James Edwin. 'Was Flann O'Brien a Post-modernist?' [review of *Flann O'Brien: A Portrait of the Artist as a Young Post-modernist* by Keith Hopper]. *ROPES: Review of Postgraduate Studies* 4, Spring 1995: 56–57.

Martin, Augustine. 'Worlds Within Worlds'. *Irish Press*, 23 September 1967.

Mathewes, Jeffrey. 'The Manichaean Body in The Third Policeman: or Why Joe's Skin *Is* Scaly'. *The Scriptorium: Flann O'Brien*. Accessed 21 January 2008. <http://www.themodernword.com/scriptorium/obrien_mathewes.pdf>.

Mays, J.C.C. 'Brian O'Nolan and Joyce on Art and Life'. *James Joyce Quarterly* 11.3, Spring 1974: 238–56.

— 'Literalist of the Imagination'. *Myles: Portraits of Brian O'Nolan*. Ed. Timothy O'Keeffe. London: Martin Brian & O'Keeffe, 1973. 77–119.

Mazullo, Concetta. 'Flann O'Brien's Hellish Otherworld: From *Buile Suibhne* to *The Third Policeman*. *Irish University Review* 25.2, Autumn/Winter 1995: 318–27.

MacMahon, Barbara. 'The Effects of Word Substitution in Slips of the Tongue: *Finnegans Wake* and *The Third Policeman*'. *English Studies* 82.3, 2001: 231–46.

McGuire, Jerry L. 'Teasing after Death: Metatextuality in *The Third Policeman*'. *Éire-Ireland* 16.2, Summer 1981: 107–21.

McKibben, Sarah E. '*An Béal Bocht*: Mouthing Off at National Identity'. *Éire-Ireland* 38.1–2, Spring-summer 2003: 37–53.

— 'The Poor Mouth: A Parody of (Post)Colonial Irish Manhood'. *Research in African Literatures* 34.4, Winter 2003: 96–114.

McLoughlin, Michael. 'At Swim Six Characters or Two Birds in Search of an Author: Fiction, Metafiction and Reality in Pirandello and Flann O'Brien'. *Yearbook of the Society for Pirandello Studies* 12, 1992: 24–31.

McMinn, Joseph. 'Theorising the Provincial' [review of *Flann O'Brien: A Portrait of the Artist as a Young Post-modernist* by Keith Hopper]. *The Irish Review* 17–18, Winter 1995: 185–87.

McMullen, Kim. 'Culture as Colloquy: Flann O'Brien's Postmodern Dialogue with Irish Tradition'. *NOVEL: A Forum on Fiction* 27.1, Autumn 1993: 62–84.

McWilliams, Brendan. 'Winds of a Different Hue'. *The Irish Times*, 11 December 1992.

Mellamphy, Ninian. 'Aestho-autogamy and the Anarchy of Imagination: Flann O'Brien's Theory of Fiction in *At Swim-Two-Birds*. *Canadian Journal of Irish Studies* 4.1, June 1978: 8–25. Repr. *Alive-Alive O!: Flann O'Brien's* At Swim-Two-Birds. Ed. Rüdiger Imhof. Dublin: Wolfhound, 1985. 140–60.

Mercier, Vivian. '*At Swim-Two-Birds*'. *Commonweal* 54.3, 27 April 1951: 68–69.

Merritt, Henry. 'Games, Ending and Dying in Flann O'Brien's *At Swim-Two-Birds*'. *Irish University Review* 25, Autumn/Winter 1995: 308–17.

Montgomery, Niall. 'An Aristrophanic Sorcerer'.*The Irish Times*, 2 April 1966.

Montresor, Jaye Berman. 'Gilbert Sorrentino: At Swim in the Wake of His Gene Pool'. *Modern Language Studies* 23.2, Spring 1993: 4–12.

Murfi, Mikel. Dir. *John Duffy's Brother*. Ireland: Park Films, 2006. 14 mins.

Murphy, Neil. 'Flann O'Brien'. *The Review of Contemporary Fiction* 25.3, Fall 2005: 7–41.

O'Brien, Kate. 'Fiction' [includes review of *At Swim-Two-Birds*]. *Spectator*, 14 April 1939: 646.

Ó Conaire, Breandán. 'Flann O'Brien, *An Béal Bocht* and Other Irish Matters'. *Irish University Review* 3.2, Autumn, 1973: 121–40.

O'Donoghue, Bernard. 'Humour and Verbal Logic'. *Critical Quarterly* 24.1, Spring 1982: 33–40.

O'Grady, Thomas B. '*At Swim-Two-Birds* and the Bardic Schools'. *Éire-Ireland* 24.3, Autumn 1989: 65–77.

Ó Háinle, Cathal G. 'Fionn and Suibhne in *At Swim-Two-Birds*'. *Hermathena* 142, 1987: 13–49.

O'Hara, Patricia. 'Finn MacCool and the Bard's Lament in Flann O'Brien's *At Swim-Two-Birds*'. *Journal of Irish Literature* 15.1, January 1986: 55–61.

O'Hehir, Brendan P. 'Flann O'Brien and the Big World'. *Literary Interrelations: Ireland, England and the World*. Studies in English and Comparative Literature, vol. 3: National Images and Stereotypes. Ed. Wolfgang Zach and Heinz Kosok, Tübingen: Gunter Narr Verlag, 1987. 207–16.

O'Keeffe, Timothy. Ed. Myles: *Portraits of Brian O'Nolan*. London: Martin Brian & O'Keeffe, 1973.

Ó Nualláin, Ciarán. *The Early Years of Brian O'Nolan / Flann O'Brien / Myles na gCopaleen*. Trans. from the Irish by Róisín Ní Nualláin. Ed. Niall O'Nolan. Dublin: Lilliput Press, 1998.

Orvell, Miles. 'Entirely Fictitious: The Fiction of Flann O'Brien'. *Alive-Alive O!: Flann O'Brien's* At Swim-Two-Birds. Ed. Rüdiger Imhof. Dublin: Wolfhound, 1985. 101–06.

Orvell, Miles, and David Powell. 'Myles na Gopaleen: Mystic, Horse-Doctor, Hackney Journalist and Ideological Catalyst'. *Éire-Ireland* 10.2, Summer 1975: 44–72.

O'Toole, Mary A. 'The Theory of Serialism in *The Third Policeman*'. *Irish University Review* 18.2, Autumn 1988: 215–25.

Palm, Kurt. Dir. *In Schwimmen-Zwei-Vögel* [*At Swim-Two-Birds*]. Austria: Fischer Film, 1997. 93 mins.

Pinsker, Sanford. 'Flann O'Brien's Uncles and Orphans'. *Éire-Ireland* 20.2, Summer 1985: 133–38.

Powell, David. 'An Annotated Bibliography of Myles na gCopaleen's "Cruiskeen Lawn" Commentaries on James Joyce'. *James Joyce Quarterly* 9.1, Fall 1971: 50–62.

Power, Mary. 'Flann O'Brien and Classical Satire: An Exegesis of *The Hard Life*'. *Éire-Ireland* 13.1, Spring 1978: 87–102.

Quintelli-Neary, Marguerite. 'Flann O'Brien: *At Swim-Two-Birds, The Third Policeman* – Temporal and Spatial Incongruities'. *Folklore and the Fantastic in Twelve Modern Irish Novels*. Westport, Connecticut: Greenwood, 1997. 83–97.

Riggs, Pádraigín, and Norman Vance. 'Irish Prose Fiction' [includes section on Flann O'Brien]. *The Cambridge Companion to Modern Irish Culture*. Ed. Joe Cleary and Claire Connolly. Cambridge: Cambridge UP, 2005. 245–66.

Sage, Lorna. 'Flann O'Brien'. *Two Decades of Irish Writing: A Critical Survey*. Ed. Douglas Dunn. Pennsylvania: Dufour, 1975. 197–206.

Shea, Thomas F. *Flann O'Brien's Exorbitant Novels*. Lewisburg: Bucknell UP; London: Associated University Presses, 1992.

— 'Flann O'Brien and John Keats: "John Duffy's Brother" and Train Allusions'. *Éire-Ireland* 24.2, Summer 1989: 109–20.

— 'Patrick McGinley's Impressions of Flann O'Brien: *The Devil's Diary* and *At Swim-Two-Birds*'. *Twentieth Century Literature* 40.2, Summer 1994: 272–81.

Sheridan, Niall. 'Brian, Flann and Myles'. *The Irish Times*, 2 April 1966.

Silverthorne J. M. 'Time, Literature, and Failure: Flann O'Brien's *At Swim Two Birds* and *The Third Policeman*'. *Éire-Ireland* 11.4, Winter 1976: 66–83.

Sorrentino, Gilbert. 'Reading Flann Brian O'Brien O'Nolan'. *Context* 1, April 2005. Accessed 21 January 2008. <http://www.dalkeyarchive.com/articlc/show/2>.

Spenser, Andrew. 'Many Worlds: The New Physics in Flann O'Brien's *The Third Policeman*'. *Éire-Ireland* 30.1, Spring 1995: 145–58.

Sweeney, Maurice. Dir. *Flann O'Brien: The Lives of Brian* [documentary]. Ireland: RTÉ / Mint Productions, 2006. 53 mins.

Swinnerton, Frank. 'Right Proportions'. *Observer*, 19 March 1939. Repr. *Alive-Alive O!: Flann O'Brien's* At Swim-Two-Birds. Ed. Rüdiger Imhof. Dublin: Wolfhound, 1985. 43–44.

Taaffe, Carol. *Ireland Through the Looking Glass: Flann O'Brien, Myles na gCopaleen and the Irish Cultural Debate*. Cork: Cork UP, 2008.

Thibodeau, Clay. 'Treating the Literary Literally: The Reflexive Structure of Flann O'Brien's *At Swim-Two-Birds*'. MA Thesis. University of Saskatchewan, 2003. Accessed 21 January 2008. <http://library2.usask.ca/theses/available/etd-09082003-31223/unrestricted/Thibodeau.pdf>.

Throne, Marilyn. 'The Provocative Bicycle of Flann O'Brien's *The Third Policeman*'. *Éire-Ireland* 21.4, Winter 1986: 36–44.

Tigges, Wim. 'Ireland in Wonderland: Flann O'Brien's *The Third Policeman* as a Nonsense Novel'. *The Clash of Ireland: Literary Contrasts and Connections*. Ed. C.C. Barfoot and Theo D'haen. Amsterdam: Rodopi, 1989. 195–208.

Toynbee, Phillip. 'A Comic Heir of James Joyce'. *Observer*, 24 July 1960. Repr. *Alive-Alive O!: Flann O'Brien's* At Swim-Two-Birds. Ed. Rüdiger Imhof. Dublin: Wolfhound, 1985. 47–50.

Updike, John. 'Back Chat, Funny Cracks: The Novels of Flann O'Brien'. *New Yorker*, 11 and 18 February 2008: 148–52.

Voelker, Joseph C. '"Doublends Jined": The Fiction of Flann O'Brien'. *Journal of Irish Literature* 12.1, January 1983: 87–95.

Wain, John. 'To Write for My Own Race: The Fiction of Flann O'Brien'. *Encounter* 29, July 1967: 71–85. Revised and expanded version in John Wain, *A House for the Truth: Critical Essays*. London: Macmillan, 1988. 67–104.

Wall, Mervyn. 'A Nightmare of Horror and Humour'. *Hibernia* 31.9, September 1967: 22.

— 'The Man Who Hated Only Cods'. *The Irish Times*, 2 April 1966.

Wäppling, Eva. 'Four Irish Legendary Figures in *At Swim-Two-Birds*: Flann O'Brien's Use of Finn, Suibhne, the Pooka and the Good Fairy'. PhD Diss. Uppsala University, 1984.

Warner, Alan. 'Flann O'Brien'. *A Guide to Anglo-Irish Literature*. Dublin: Gill & Macmillan, 1981. 153–65.

West, Anthony. 'Inspired Nonsense'. *New Statesman and Nation*, 17 June 1939. Repr. *Alive-Alive O!: Flann O'Brien's* At Swim-Two-Birds. Ed. Rüdiger Imhof. Dublin: Wolfhound, 1985. 44–45.

Yurkoski, Chris. 'Self-evident Shams: Metafiction and Comedy in Three of Flann O'Brien's Novels'. MA Thesis. University of Western Ontario, 1998. Accessed 21 January 2008. <http://www.collectionscanada.ca/obj/s4/f2/dsk2/tape15/PQDD_0010/MQ33473.pdf>.

Other works cited

Abrams, M.H. *A Glossary of Literary Terms*. 4th edn. New York and London: Holt, Rinehart & Winston, 1981.

Adams, Michael. *Censorship: The Irish Experience*. Dublin: Scepter Books, 1968.

Allen, Woody. *Getting Even*. London: W.H. Allen, 1980.

Alter, Robert. *Partial Magic: The Novel as a Self-Conscious Genre*. Berkeley, Los Angeles and London: University of California Press, 1975.

Anon. Ed. *The Concise Dictionary of Quotations*. London: Collins, 1985.

Ashcroft, Bill, Gareth Griffiths and Helen Tiffin. *The Empire Writes Back: Theory and Practice in Post-Colonial Literatures*. London: Routledge, 1987.

Augustine. *Confessions*. London: Penguin, 1967.

Bakhtin, Mikhail. *The Dialogic Imagination: Four Essays*. Trans. and ed. Michael Holquist and Caryl Emerson. Austin: University of Texas Press, 1981.

Bakhtin, Mikhail, and P.N Medvedev. *The Formal Method in Literary Scholarship: A Critical Introduction to Sociological Poetics*. Harvard: Johns Hopkins UP, 1985.

Banville, John. *The Book of Evidence*. London: Secker & Warburg, 1979.

Barthes, Roland. *Camera Lucida*. Trans. Richard Howard. London: Fontana, 1980.

— The Death of the Author' (1968). Repr. *Modern Literary Theory: A Reader*. 2nd edn. Ed. Philip Rice and Patricia Waugh. London: Edward Arnold, 1992. 114–18.

— *Mythologies*. Trans. Annette Lavers. London: Jonathan Cape, 1972.

— *Roland Barthes*. Trans. Richard Howard. New York: Hill & Wang, 1977.

— 'Theory of the Text'. *Untying the Text: A Post-Structuralist Reader*. Ed. Robert Young. London: Routledge, 1981. 31–47.

Baudrillard, Jean. *Revenge of the Crystal: Selected Writings on the Modern Object and its Destiny, 1968–1983*. Trans. and ed. Paul Foss and Julian Pefanis. London: Pluto Press, 1990.

— *Seduction*. Trans. Brian Singer. London: Macmillan, 1990.

— *Selected Writings*. Ed. Mark Poster. Cambridge: Polity Press, 1988.

Baum, L. Frank. *The Wizard of Oz*. 1900. London: Puffin, 1994.

Beckett, Samuel. 'Censorship in the Saorstat'. *Disjecta: Miscellaneous Writings and a Dramatic Fragment by Samuel Beckett*. Ed. Ruby Cohn. London: John Calder, 1983. 84–88.

— *Watt*. 1944. London: Picador, 1988.

Benedict, Julius. *The Lily of Killarney: Opera in Three Acts, Being a Musical Version of the Drama of 'The Colleen Bawn'*. 1862. Hull: White & Farrell, [c.1900].

Benstock, Shari. 'At the Margins of Discourse: Footnotes in the Fictional Text'. *PMLA* 98.2, 1983: 204–25.

Bergson, Henri. 'Laughter'. *Comedy*. Ed. Wylie Sypher. 1956. New York: Anchor, 1980. 61–145.

Bettelheim, Bruno. *The Uses of Enchantment: The Meaning and Importance of Fairy Tales*. London: Penguin, 1976.

Borges, Jorges Luis. 'Time and J.W. Dunne' (1940). *The Total Library: Non-Fiction: 1922–1986*. Ed. Eliot Weinberger. Trans. Esther Allen, Suzanne Jill Levine, and Eliot Weinberger. London: Allen Lane/Penguin Press, 1999. 214–19.

Boucicault, Dion. *The Colleen Bawn; or, The Brides of Garryowen: A Domestic Drama in Three Acts*. 1860. London: Thomas Hailes Lacy, [c.1873].

Bradbury, Malcolm, and James McFarlane. Eds. *Modernism: 1890–1930*. Harmondsworth: Penguin, 1976.

Brecht, Bertold. *Brecht on Theatre: The Development of an Aesthetic*. Trans. and ed. John Willet. London: Methuen, 1991.

Brontë, Charlotte. *Jane Eyre*. 1847. Harmondsworth: Penguin, 1966.

Brown, Stephen. *Ireland in Fiction: A Guide to Irish Novels, Tales, Romances*. Shannon: Irish University Press, 1969.

Brown, Terence. *Ireland: A Social and Cultural History 1922–1985*. London: Fontana, 1985.

Bullitt, J.M. *Jonathan Swift and the Anatomy of Satire: A Study of Satiric Technique*. Cambridge, Mass.: Harvard UP, 1956.

Butler, Hubert. *Escape from the Anthill*. Mullingar: Lilliput, 1986.

Cabell, James Branch. *The Cream of the Jest*. 1917. New York: The Modern Library, 1927.

Callinicos, Alex. *Against Postmodernism: A Marxist Critique*. Cambridge: Polity Press, 1989.

Capra, Fritjof. *The Tao of Physics: An Exploration of the Parallels Between*

Modern Physics and Eastern Mysticism. 1975. London: Fontana, 1983.

Carlson, Julia. *Banned in Ireland: Censorship and the Irish Writer.* London: Routledge, 1991.

Carroll, Lewis. *Through the Looking-Glass.* 1871. London: Macmillan, 1919.

Collins, Jim. *Uncommon Cultures: Popular Culture and Post-Modernism.* London: Routledge, 1989.

Connor, Stephen. *Postmodernist Culture: An Introduction to Theories of the Contemporary.* Oxford: Basil Blackwell, 1989.

Copleston, F.C. *A History of Philosophy*, vol. I, Greece and Rome. 1946. London: Burns and Oates, 1966.

Coward, Rosalind. 'Are Women's Novels Feminist Novels?' *The New Feminist Criticism.* Ed. Elaine Showalter. New York: Pantheon, 1985. 225–39.

Cronin, Anthony. *Heiritage Now: Irish Literature in the English Language.* Kerry: Brandon Books, 1982.

Cuddon, J.A. *A Dictionary of Literary Terms.* Rev. edn. Harmondsworth: Penguin, 1979.

Culler, Jonathan. *Barthes.* London: Fontana, 1987.

— *Framing the Sign.* Oxford: Blackwell, 1988.

de Saussure, Ferdinand. 'Course in General Linguistics'. Extract repr. *Modern Literary Theory: A Reader.* 2nd edn. Ed. Philip Rice and Patricia Waugh. London: Edward Arnold, 1992. 8–15.

Deane, Seamus. *A Short History of Irish Literature.* London: Hutchinson, 1986.

— Ed. *The Field Day Anthology of Irish Writing.* Derry: Field Day, 1991.

Dollimore, Jonathan. *Radical Tragedy: Religion, Ideology and Power in the Drama of Shakespeare and his Contemporaries.* Sussex: Harvester Press, 1984.

Donoghue, Denis. *Jonathan Swift: A Critical Introduction.* Cambridge: Cambridge UP, 1969.

Dunne, J.W. *An Experiment with Time.* 1928. London: Faber, 1934.

— *Nothing Dies.* London: Faber, 1940.

Dunton, John. *The Athenian Oracle.* London: Andrew Bell, 1703–10.

Edwards, Paul. Ed. *The Encyclopaedia of Philosophy*, vol. I. London: Collier-Macmillan, 1967.

Edgeworth, Maria. Letter to Michael Pakenham Edgeworth, 19 February 1834. Repr. *The Field Day Anthology of Irish Writing*, vol. I. Ed. Seamus Deane. Derry: Field Day, 1991. 1051.

Eichenbaum, Boris. 'The Theory of the Formal Method' (1926). Repr. *Readings in Russian Poetics: Formalist and Structuralist Views.* Ed. Ladislav Matejka and Krystyna Pomorska. Ann Arbor, Michigan: University of Michigan, 1978. 3–37.

Ellmann, Richard. *Oscar Wilde.* London: Vintage, 1988.

Esslin, Martin. *The Theatre of the Absurd.* London: Eyre and Spottiswoode, 1966.

Erlich, Victor. *Russian Formalism: History-Doctrine*. 2nd edn. London, The Hague and Paris: Mouton, 1965.

Fekete, John. 'Vampire Value, Infinitive Art and Literary Theory: A Topographic Meditation'. *Life After Post-Modernism: Essays on Value and Culture*. Ed. John Fekete. London: Macmillan, 1988. 64–85.

Fetterley, Judith. *The Resisting Reader: A Feminist Approach to American Fiction*. Bloomington: Indiana UP, 1978.

Fleming, Victor. Dir. *The Wizard of Oz*. USA: MGM, 1939. 101 mins.

Foucault, Michel. 'What is an Author?'. *Textual Strategies and Perspectives in Post-Structuralist Criticism*. Ed. Josue Harari. Ithaca, New York: Cornell UP, 1979. 141–60.

— *The Order of Things: An Archaeology of the Human Sciences*. New York: Pantheon, 1970.

Freud, Sigmund. 'The Uncanny' (1919). *The Standard Edition of the Complete Psychological Works of Sigmund Freud*, vol. 17. Trans. and ed. James Strachey, with Anna Freud, Alix Strachey and Alan Tyson. London: Hogarth Press and the Institute of Psycho-analysis, 1960. 217–252.

Genette, Gerard. *Narrative Discourse: An Essay in Method*. Trans. Jane E. Lewin. Ithaca, New York: Cornell UP, 1980.

Gilbert, Stuart. Ed. *Letters of James Joyce*, vol. I. London: Faber, 1957.

Gleick, James. *Chaos: Making a New Science*. London: Abacus, 1993.

Godard, Jean-Luc. Dir. *Le Petit Soldat*. France: Société Nouvelle de Cinématographie, 1960. 88 mins.

Gray, Martin. *A Dictionary of Literary Terms*. Essex: Longman York, 1984.

Griffin, Gerald. *The Collegians*. 1829. Belfast: Appletree Press, 1992.

Greenland, Colin. 'In My View'. *Sunday Times*, 10 September 1989.

Harvey, David. *The Condition of Postmodernity: An Enquiry into the Origins of Cultural Change*. Oxford: Basil Blackwell, 1989.

Hassan, Ihab. *The Postmodern Turn: Essays in Postmodern Theory and Culture*. Ohio: Ohio State UP, 1987.

— *The Dismemberment of Orpheus: Towards a Postmodern Literature*. New York and Oxford: Oxford UP, 1971.

Hawkes, Terence. *Structuralism and Semiotics*. London: Methuen, 1977.

Hawthorn, Jeremy. *A Concise Glossary of Contemporary Literary Theory*. London: Edward Arnold, 1992.

Higgins, Aidan. Introduction. *Samuel Beckett: Photographs* by John Minihan. London: Secker & Warburg, 1995. 1–25.

Hirschkop, Ken, and David Shepherd. *Bakhtin and Cultural Theory*. Manchester: Manchester UP, 1989.

Hutcheon, Linda. *A Poetics of Postmodernism: History, Theory, Fiction*. London and New York: Routledge, 1988.

— *The Politics of Postmodernism*. London and New York: Routledge, 1989.

Huxley, Aldous. *Point Counter Point*. 1928. London: Granada, 1978.

Huysmans, J.K. *Against Nature* [*À Rebours*]. 1884. Trans. from the French by Robert Baldrick. London: Penguin, 1959.

Jakobson, Roman. 'The Dominant' (1935). Repr. *Readings in Russian Poetics: Formalist and Structuralist Views*. Ed. Ladislav Matejka and Krystyna Pomorska. Ann Arbor, Michigan: University of Michigan, 1978. 82–87.

— 'On Realism in Art' (1921). Repr. *Readings in Russian Poetics: Formalistand Structuralist Views*. Ed. Ladislav Matejka and Krystyna Pomorska. Ann Arbor, Michigan: University of Michigan, 1978. 38–46.

— 'Two Aspects of Language and Two Types of Aphasic Disturbances' (1956). *Language and Literature*. Cambridge, Mass.: Harvard UP, 1987). 95–114.

Jackson, K.H. *A Celtic Miscellany*. Harmondsworth: Penguin, 1971.

Jameson, Fredric. *The Prison House of Language: A Critical Account of Structuralism and Russian Formalism*. New Jersey: Princeton UP, 1972.

Jeffares, A. Norman. *Anglo-Irish Literature*. Dublin: Macmillan Press, 1982.

Jolas, Eugene. 'My Friend James Joyce'. *Partisan Review* 8.2, March–April 1941. 82–93.

Joyce, James. *A Portrait of the Artist as a Young Man*. 1916. London: Granada, 1983.

— *Finnegans Wake*. 1939. London: Faber & Faber, 1986.

— *Dubliners*. 1914. London: Grafton, 1985.

— *Stephen Hero*. 1944. Ed. Theodore Spencer. London: Granada, 1977.

— *Ulysses*. 1922. London: Bodley Head, 1960.

Kaplan, E. Ann. Ed. *Postmodernism and its Discontents: Theories, Practices*. London: Verso, 1988.

Kearney, Richard. *Transitions: Narratives in Modern Irish Culture*. Manchester: Manchester UP, 1988.

Kenner, Hugh. *Flaubert, Joyce and Beckett: The Stoic Comedians*. London: W.H. Allen, 1964.

— *Samuel Beckett: A Critical Study*. Berkley: University of California Press, 1968.

Kiberd, Declan. 'Irish Literature and Irish History'. *The Oxford Illustrated History of Ireland*. Ed. R.F. Foster. Oxford and New York: Oxford UP, 1989. 275–337.

King, Serge Kahili. *Urban Shaman*. New York: Simon & Schuster, 1990.

Koestenbaum, Wayne. *Double Talk: The Erotics of Male Literary Collaboration*. London: Routledge, 1989.

Krause, David. Ed. *The Dolmen Boucicault: The Theatre of Dion Boucicault*. Dublin: Dolmen, 1964.

Kristeva, Julia. 'The Ruins of a Poetics'. *Russian Formalism: A Collection of Articles and Texts in Translation*. Ed. Stephen Bann and John E. Bowlt. Edinburgh: Scottish Academic Press, 1973. 102–119.

Kroker, Arthur, and David Cook. *The Postmodern Scene: Excremental Culture and Hyper-Aesthetics*. London: Macmillan, 1991.

Kroker, Arthur, Marilouise Kroker, and David Cook. Eds. *Panic*

Encyclopedia: The Definitive Guide to the Postmodern Scene. London: Macmillan, 1989.

Lodge, David. *After Bakhtin: Essays on Fiction and Criticism*. London: Routledge, 1990.

MacNamara, Brinsley. *Margaret Gillan*. London: Allen & Unwin, 1934. [This play, first performed at the Abbey Theatre in 1933, was later translated into Irish by Brian Ó Nualláin [Brian O'Nolan] under the title of *Mairéad Gillan*. Baile Átha Cliath: Ofig an tSoláthair, 1953.]

Marlowe, Christopher. *The Complete Plays*. Ed. J.B. Steane. London: Penguin, 1978.

Marxist-Feminist Collective, The. 'Women Writing'. *Modern Literary Theory: A Reader*. 2nd edn. Ed. Philip Rice and Patricia Waugh. London: Edward Arnold, 1992. 102–07.

Matejka, Ladislav, and Krystyna Pomorska. Eds. *Readings in Russian Poetics: Formalist and Structuralist Views*. Ann Abor, Michigan: University of Michigan, 1978.

Miller, J. Hillis. 'Stevens' Rock and Criticism as Cure'. *Georgia Review* 30.2, Summer 1976: 330–348.

McCabe, Patrick. *The Butcher Boy*. London: Picador, 1993.

McHale, Brian. *Post-Modernist Fiction*. New York: Routledge, 1991.

McHugh, Roger, and Maurice Harmon. *A Short History of Anglo-Irish Literature*. Dublin: Wolfhound, 1982.

McMahon, Sean. 'The Realist Novel After WWII'. *The Genius of Irish Prose*. Ed. Augustine Martin. Dublin: Mercier, 1985.

Mercier, Vivian. *The Irish Comic Tradition*. London: Oxford UP, 1969.

Montague, John. 'The Siege of Mullingar'. *Poets from the North of Ireland*. Ed. Frank Ormsby. Belfast: Blackstaff, 1987.

Morson, Gary Saul. *Bakhtin: Essays and Dialogues on his Work*. Chicago: University of Chicago Press, 1986.

Nabokov, Vladimir. *The Real Life of Sebastian Knight*. 1941. London: Penguin, 1964.

Norris, Christopher. *Deconstruction: Theory and Practice*. London: Methuen, 1982.

Norris, Margot. 'Not the Girl She Was at All: Women in "The Dead"'. *James Joyce's The Dead: Case Studies in Contemporary Criticism*. Ed. Daniel R. Schwarz. Boston and New York: Bedford Books, 1994. 190–205.

O'Connor, Frank. 'Frank O'Connor on Censorship'. *The Dubliner*, March 1962: 39–44.

Ó Corráin, Donnchadh, and Fidelma Maguire. *Gaelic Personal Names*. Dublin: Academy Press, 1981.

O'Crohan, Tomás. *The Islandman [An tOileánach]*. 1937. Trans. from the Irish by Robin Flower. Oxford: Oxford UP, 1990.

Ó Muirthe, Diarmaid. 'Pooka'. *Irish Words and Phrases*. Dublin: Gill & Macmillan, 2002. 42–43.

Partridge, A.C. *Language and Society in Anglo-Irish Literature*. New Jersey: Barnes and Noble, 1984.

Pears, David. *Wittgenstein*. London: Fontana, 1988.

Pirandello, Luigi. *Six Characters in Search of an Author*. 1921. Trans. Frederick May. London: Heinemann, 1978.

Rabinovitz, Rubin. '*Watt* from Descartes to Schopenhauer'. *Modern Irish Literature: Essays in Honor of William York Tindall*. Ed. Raymond A. Porter and James D. Brophy. New Rochelle, New York: Iona College Press, 1972. 261–87.

Rolleston, T.W. *Myths and Legends of the Celtic Race*. 1911. New York: Schocken, 1986.

Ryan, John. *Remembering How We Stood*. Dublin: Lilliput, 1975.

Said, Edward. 'Yeats and Decolonization'. *Nationalism, Colonialism and Literature*. A Field Day Pamphlet, 15. Derry: Field Day, 1988.

Saunders, Jean. *The Craft of Writing Romance: A Practical Guide*. London: Allison & Busby, 1986.

Sedgwick, Eve Kosofsky. *Between Men: English Literature and Male Homosocial Desire*. New York: Columbia UP, 1985.

Schwartz, Joseph, and Michael McGuinness. *Einstein for Beginners*. London: Unwin, 1986.

Share, Bernard. *Slanguage: A Dictionary of Slang and Colloquial English in Ireland*. New and expanded edn. Dublin: Gill & Macmillan, 2005.

Shklovsky, Viktor. 'Art as Technique' (1917). Repr. *Russian Formalist Criticism: Four Essays*. Trans. and ed. Lee T. Lemon and Marion J. Reis. Lincoln: University of Nebraska Press, 1965. 3–24.

— 'Sterne's *Tristram Shandy*: Stylistic Commentary' (1921). Repr. *Russian Formalist Criticism: Four Essays*. Trans. and ed. Lee T. Lemon and Marion J. Reis. Lincoln: University of Nebraska Press, 1965. 25–57.

— 'The Mystery Novel: Dickens's *Little Dorrit*' (1925). Repr. *Readings in Russian Poetics: Formalist and Structuralist Views*. Ed. Ladislav Matejka and Krystyna Pomorska. Ann Arbor, Michigan: University of Michigan, 1978. 220–26.

— *A Sentimental Journey: Memoirs, 1917–22* (1923). Trans. Richard Sheldon. Ithaca, New York: Cornell UP, 1984.

Showalter, Elaine. 'Feminist Criticism in the Wilderness'. *The New Feminist Criticism*. Ed. Elaine Showalter. New York: Pantheon, 1985. 243–70.

— Towards a Feminist Poetics'. *Modern Literary Theory: A Reader*. 2nd edn. Ed. Philip Rice and Patricia Waugh. London: Edward Arnold, 1992. 92–102.

Shuttle, Penelope, and Peter Redgrove. *The Wise Wound*. London: Harper Collins, 1986.

Smith, Barbara Herrnstein. *On the Margins of Discourse: The Relation of Literature to Language*. Chicago and London: University of Chicago Press, 1978.

Sontag, Susan. *A Roland Barthes Reader*. London: Vintage, 1993.

Stacy, R.H. 'The Formalists'. *Russian Literary Criticism: A Short History*. Syracuse, New York: Syracuse UP, 1974. 163–84.

Stephens, James. *The Crock of Gold.* 1912. London: Macmillan, 1980.

Steiner, Peter. *Russian Formalism: A Metapoetics.* London and Ithaca, New York: Cornell UP, 1984.

Sterne, Laurence. *The Life and Opinions of Tristram Shandy, Gentleman.* 1759–67; London: McDonald, 1975.

Stewart, Susan. *Nonsense: Aspects of Intertextuality in Folklore and Literature.* Baltimore: Johns Hopkins UP, 1979.

Swift, Jonathan. *Gulliver's Travels.* 1726. London: Munster Classics, 1968.

Synge, J.M. *The Playboy of the Western World.* 1907. London: Methuen, 1961.

Tomashevsky, Boris. 'Literature and Biography' (1923). Repr. *Readings in Russian Poetics: Formalist and Structuralist Views.* Ed. Ladislav Matejka and Krystyna Pomorska. Ann Arbor, Michigan: University of Michigan, 1978. 47–55.

— 'Thematics' (1925). Repr. *Russian Formalist Criticism: Four Essays.* Trans. and ed. Lee T. Lemon and Marion J. Reis. Lincoln: University of Nebraska Press, 1965. 61–95.

Trotsky, Leon. *Literature and Revolution* (1924). Trans. Rose Strunsky. Ann Arbor, Michigan: University of Michigan Press, 1960.

Wakefield, Neville. *Post-Modernism: The Twilight of the Real.* London: Pluto, 1990.

Watt, Ian. *Conrad in the Nineteenth Century.* London: Chatto & Windus, 1980.

Waugh, Patricia. *Metafiction: The Theory and Practice of Self-Conscious Fiction.* London and New York: Methuen, 1984.

Wilde, Oscar. *The Picture of Dorian Gray and Other Writings.* Ed. with an introduction by Richard Ellmann. New York: Bantam Books, 1982.

Wimsatt, William K. and Monroe C. Beardsley. 'The Intentional Fallacy' (1946). Repr. *The Verbal Icon: Studies in the Meaning of Poetry.* Lexington: University of Kentucky Press, 1954. 3–18.

Wittgenstein, Ludwig. *Trachtatus Logico-Philosophicus.* 1921. London: Routledge & Kegan Paul, 1972.

Woolf, Virginia. *A Room of One's Own.* 1929. London: Grafton, 1989.

Worton, Michael, and Judith Still. Eds. *Intertextuality: Theories and Practice.* Manchester: Manchester UP, 1991.

Yeats, W.B. 'The Pooka'. *Fairy and Folk Tales of the Irish Peasantry.* Ed. W.B. Yeats. 1888. New York: Dover, 1991. 95.

— Remorse for Intemperate Speech' (1931). *Collected Poems.* Dublin: Gill & Macmillan, 1989. 287–88.

Zohn, Harry. *Karl Kraus.* New York: Twayne, 1971.

Index